PENGUIN MODERN CLASSICS

Ecology of Wisdom

ARNE NAESS was born in Slemdal, Norway, in 1912. After completing his master's degree at the University of Oslo in 1933, he spent two years studying in Paris and Vienna. While at the University of Vienna, he was invited to participate in the discussions of the famous Schlick Circle, alongside philosophers like Karl Popper, Rudolf Carnap and Otto Neurath. After earning his PhD at age 27, he became the University of Oslo's youngest professor, and Norway's only Professor of Philosophy.

Naess was also a keen mountaineer, environmentalist and social activist. In 1938, he finished building an isolated wooden hut high in the Hallingskarvet mountains, where he would spend a quarter of his life. It was here that he developed his concept of 'ecosophy', and his lifelong commitment to the environmental movement. His activity within the movement ranged from grassroots protest, to candidacy for political office with the Green Party, to a post as the first chairman of Greenpeace Norway in 1988.

From 1965, Naess's work focused increasingly on serious environmental problems and non-violent campaigns for social justice. He co-founded the deep ecology movement, building on the 'ecosophy' he developed in more than thirty books, four hundred academic articles, and countless lectures delivered in countries throughout the world. Belated reading of Rachel Carson's *Silent Spring* (1962) led Naess to resign from his professorship and devote the rest of his life to environmental work. He continued to lecture and write, and in 2000 published *Livsfilosofi*, a bestseller in Norway.

His achievements as a philosopher, ecologist, and activist were widely recognized during his lifetime. In 2005 he was knighted and made a Commander with Star of the Royal Norwegian order of St Olav First Class. He died in Oslo in 2009.

ARNE NAESS

Ecology of Wisdom

Edited by Alan Drengson and Bill Devall

PENGUIN BOOKS

PENGUIN CLASSICS

UK | USA | Canada | Ireland | Australia
India | New Zealand | South Africa

Penguin Books is part of the Penguin Random House group of companies
whose addresses can be found at global.penguinrandomhouse.com.

First published in the United States of America by Counterpoint 2008
First published in Great Britain in Penguin Classics 2016

010

Printed and bound in Great Britain by Clays Ltd, Elcograf S.p.A.

A CIP catalogue record for this book is available from the British Library

ISBN: 978-0-241-25719-7

Contents

Preface

Arne Naess is a mountaineer, a Gandhian boxer, a professor, an activist, and a student of life's philosophy. You may never have heard of Arne Naess, or you may be his devoted student. You may never have heard the phrase *long-range deep ecology movement*, but you might be a supporter of the movement and are awakening to your intuition of deep ecology.

Wherever you are coming from, as a reader, you will discover mountains of inspiration in the *Ecology of Wisdom*.

Arne Naess does not see himself as an academic philosopher. He considers himself a teacher who attempts to inspire his students to articulate their own *ecosophy*. Ecosophy is derived from the word *ecology*, "the study of interrelationships," and *sophia*, "wisdom." Literally, this collection of some of Arne's essays is intended to inspire diverse ecosophies among readers with the intent of actualizing self-realization and cross-cultural understanding.

The essays included in this book engage readers in some of the most important aspects of Arne's approach to life's philosophy. These aspects are especially relevant during the early decades of the twenty-first century, an era of globalization of economy and accelerating cultural transformation.

The reader can begin reading this anthology at any essay or any section in the book. The essays are not presented in chronological order but in thematic gestalts. The editors have grouped essays in sections that seem appropriate to explore various aspects of Arne's whole approach to life's philosophy. Readers who want more in-depth access to Arne's lifework are referred to the ten-volume series, *The Selected Works of Arne Naess (SWAN)*.

This anthology begins with an exploration of Arne's life and work by Alan Drengson. This essay explores how Arne developed and articulated his own life philosophy grounded in a place. Arne's life is used as one possible model, among many, that readers can use to develop their own ecosophies. Pluralism and diversity are key words to understanding Naess's approach to living in an ecologically responsible way in harmony with nature.

The essays in Section 1, "Places in the Real World," convey Arne's views on the importance of *place* in grounding the expression of our ecosophies. Arne's special place was Tvergastein. In this place in the mountains of Norway, he explored his own life's philosophy. At Tvergastein, he learned lessons of modesty, the real interrelationships of humans in nature, and articulated self-realization as a general principle for life's philosophy. But this leads us to ask, "What is this self to be realized?" When we explore the nature of the self, we find that what we are is interdependent with our relationships and places. To know ourselves deeply is something only each of us can achieve through our own personal inquiry. Since we and everything we know are always changing, our inquiries become part of daily life. We never stop learning and creatively adapting to our changing life circumstances. Thus we become lifelong learners.

Section 2, "The Long-Range Deep Ecology Movement," includes some of Arne's thoughts on the relationships of the three great movements—peace, social justice, and ecological sustainability. These essays emphasize the importance of diversity, cooperation, and beautiful actions, with the high quality of a joyful life based on nonviolence and low consumption.

Section 3, "Methodology and Systems," focuses on Arne's approach to total views, methodology, pluralism, intensity, and creativity in articulating our own ecosophies in the cultural contexts within which we dwell. This section explores Naess's gestalt ontology and the role of creativity in the way we act and live from moment to moment.

Section 4, "Nonviolence and Gandhi, Spinoza and Wholeness," includes essays on Gandhi's approach to group conflict. From the 1930s onward, Arne has been a student of Gandhi's methods, and the essays in this section reflect the enduring relevance of nonviolent direct action as a way to cultural transformation. The American leader of the civil rights movement, the Reverend Martin Luther King, Jr., visited India during the 1950s to study Gandhi's methods before he began his civil rights campaign in America. King returned to the United States convinced that he could transform American society using Gandhi's methods. In the essays in this section, Arne demonstrates why Gandhi's methods are vital to those seeking cultural transformation during the twenty-first century.

The article on Spinoza and wholeness includes essays that explore the continued relevance of Spinoza's approach to a total life philosophy. Arne encourages creative reinterpretation of Spinoza to explore the richness and diversity that the study of his writings provides for people seeking to realize their own ecosophies under their present life challenges. Spinoza's philosophy exemplifies a unified approach to life as a whole, from our feelings and thoughts to our actions and relationships. He emphasizes equanimity and positive feelings and ever deeper insight into the rich unities of our whole spontaneous experience.

Section 5, "Problems and Ways Forward," begins with the supposition that during the early decades of the twenty-first century, cultures and societies are faced with massive problems, environmental, social, and personal. Arne offers suggestions on how to approach these problems, conceptually frame them, communicate about them in appropriate language, and advance positive cultural transformations in our actions. He stresses that our effectiveness depends on our being nonviolent, even in our language. We need to build cooperative relationships at every level of our lives and society to solve the wide range of problems and hazards we now face. Naess believes that each of us is capable of far more than we believe and that we usually greatly underestimate our own abilities.

As you read these essays, enjoy yourself and be in peace.

Alan Drengson and Bill Devall

Acknowledgments

Professor Naess is grateful to the Research School of Social Sciences, the Australian National University, for giving him the opportunity to be a Visiting Fellow and to discuss and rewrite (in September 1984) what he has thought about the relationship of our *Lebenswelt* to objective reality, discussed in the essay "The World of Concrete Contents" in this book.

Alan Drengson and Bill Devall are grateful for the support and help of Arne and Kit-Fai Naess, the Foundation for Deep Ecology, and the people at Counterpoint Press for making this book possible.

ECOLOGY OF WISDOM

Introduction

The Life and Work of Arne Naess:
An Appreciative Overview by Alan Drengson

Part 1 of this introduction concentrates on Arne Naess's life and accomplishments. It describes his spirit of free inquiry, love of nature, and commitment to nonviolence, as these matured from his Norwegian origins. Part 2 looks in depth at his comprehensive approach to the international deep ecology movement, worldviews, and philosophies of life, especially if the latter are ecosophies. (*Ecosophy* is Naess's term for personal life philosophies aiming for ecological harmony.) This article describes Naess's approach to *total views* and how this engagement opens abundant depth, diversity, and unity to wisdom, which improves life quality. Global views should include and respect linguistic and cultural diversity and the plurality of religions and treasure the vast number of personal philosophies on earth. Naess feels that major interdisciplinary efforts are needed to study the ecology and evolution of human and other communication systems of cultures in their home places.

Deep ecology supporters appreciate the inherent value of all beings and of diversity. Therefore, research and communication should be inclusive and nonviolent. The ecological crisis, as driven by the modern model of industrial progress and human population growth, threatens the integrity of planetary ecosystems with their accumulated wealth of diverse forms of life, cultures, and worldviews. No single philosophy can solve all of these problems. Global progress requires broad cooperation at the level of collective action and common principles, with innovation and unique solutions at policy and local personal levels. Naess sees the deep ecology movement as one of many international grassroots liberation movements of the twentieth century for social justice, peace, and ecological responsibility (i.e., freedom from tyranny and inequity, from war and violence, from pollution of our bodies, and from the destruction of our home place).

For Naess, free nature is critical to cultural flourishing, community health, and personal self-realization. Personal, cultural, ecological, and evolutionary diversity are great treasures of the earth, probably even of cosmic significance. There is room for a wide range of initiatives and actions to better care for and restore our shared home planet. The essays assembled in this book are devoted to Naess's work and his approach to complex global problems. As readers will see from this varied collection of his writings, Naess's interests range over wide areas of scholarship and personal explorations, especially in the wild areas of the planet, intellect, and spirit. In his later years, he concentrated more and more on integrating his various interests and writings by means of a comprehensive, global approach using analytic, empirical, comparative, and other methods. All these and more are represented here and are organized by ecological issues and themes.

Finally, as the reader will see, much of Naess's focus in his professional life has been on language and communication. His approach to communication is holistic and grounded in a field naturalist's way of researching and organizing knowledge. As a philosopher, Naess has looked beyond knowledge to the depth of wisdom needed to live well in our world of change. He has always been primarily concerned with gaining knowledge that will improve the quality of life but will lower the demands and impacts on others. This is for him the essence of the way of nonviolence. He applies this to communication as a way to resolve conflicts and problems rather than generate abstract theories. Naess also loves theoretical work, but his priorities limit the time spent on such pursuits.

PART 1: LIFE, EXPLORATION, AND INQUIRY IN NORWAY AND BEYOND

In a Norwegian survey of young people (preteen to twenty years old), an overwhelming majority said that the person they would most like to talk with was Arne Naess. In Norway, Naess is a hero and national treasure. He is well-known for his social activism, writings, talks, textbooks, climbing, practical jokes, and other exploits. He is admired for his sense of humor and positive attitude toward life. A book of his published in Norway in 2000 had the title *Livsfilosofi* (Life's philosophy). It was a best seller for months and at last count had sold over 120,000 copies in Norwegian. It has since been translated and published in English.[1]

Naess's contributions have been honored by many awards. Some of the more noteworthy are the Star of St. Olav's Order, presented by the king of Norway in 2005; the Peer Gynt Award in 2004 for his contributions to making Norway better known internationally; the Nordic Council Award for Nature and Environment in 2002; the Uggla Prize for Humanistic Studies from Stockholm University in 2002; a diploma and medal in 1998 from King Harald V of Norway for Naess's contribution to the Intelligence Agency XU during the German occupation; the Medal of the Presidency of the Italian Republic in 1998; the Nordic Prize from the Swedish Academy in 1996; the Mountain Tradition Award by the Red Cross in 1996; the Mahatma Gandhi Prize for Non-violent Peace in 1994; the Fridtjof Nansen Award for the promotion of science in 1983; and the Sonning Prize in Denmark for contributions to European culture in 1977. He has received two honorary doctorates, one from Stockholm University in 1972 and the other from the Norwegian National University of Sports and Physical Education in 1995. He also holds honorary memberships in the Norwegian Alpine Club and the Norwegian Tourist Association (both awarded in 2002). He has taken his message of peace and harmony with the natural world to audiences in Bali, Beijing, Berkeley, Bucharest, Canton, Chendu, Devon, Dubrovnik, Hangzhou, Helsinki, Hong Kong, Japan, Jerusalem, London, Melbourne, Reykjavik, Santa Cruz, Taiwan, Tartu (Estonia), Tromso, Vancouver and Victoria in Canada, and Warsaw. The Foundation for Deep Ecology was inspired by his work, as was the Institute for Deep Ecology. The online journal *The Trumpeter: Journal of Ecosophy* was also founded on inspiration from Naess's work. There have been many Festschrifts in his honor as well as anthologies and special issues of journals (see references at the end of this book). Naess has been an active supporter of many charitable causes and has given much of his prize money to organizations such as Amnesty International.

In scholarly circles, Naess is known for his work in logic, communication studies, empirical semantics, foundational studies of science, research on international conflict and peace studies (which included cross-cultural discussions of freedom and democracy), and his in-depth studies of major philosophers such as Spinoza, Gandhi, and Wittgenstein. His published scholarly writings number well over thirty books and four hundred articles, and he has written about three hundred unpublished articles. He has worked in several disciplines and established *Inquiry*, a widely respected interdisciplinary journal for the humanities and social sciences. Many of Naess's works have never appeared in English, and many of those written in English have long been unavailable. Because of the importance of his life's work and his original contributions to human society, it is the aim of the Selected Works of Arne Naess (SWAN) project to make a substantial and representative portion of his work available to English-reading scholars and others interested in his life and work. The ten volumes of his writings offered in SWAN represent central works.[2] They are organized to conclude with his most recent work detailing the way in which the analysis of deep ecology represents the integration of all elements of his life and work as they are relevant to the three great grassroots movements of the twentieth century: the peace, social justice, and ecology movements.[3]

Naess is fluent in several languages and knows a great deal about many classical languages, including Sanskrit, ancient Greek, and Latin. He writes in Norwegian, English, German, and French. One of his major works, a two-volume historical study of Eastern and Western philosophies, is published only in Norwegian. Naess's scholarly work is impressive for its depth, breadth, and originality, and this alone has made him a recognized figure in international scholarly circles.

His work since 1965 has increasingly focused on serious environmental problems, including the destruction of cultural and biological diversity. These ecological writings are collected in SWAN, volume 10, *The Deep Ecology of Wisdom*. It was he who first characterized the short-term shallow ecology movement and compared it to the long-range deep ecology movement. When Naess began his study and activism in the ecology movement, he had already been active in the peace and social justice movements for years. He has for a long time seen himself as a wandering seeker of truth, knowledge, understanding, and wisdom. Using classical Greek, he says that he is a *zetetic*, one who seeks truth and knowledge but does not claim it.[4]

When in high school, he was given a copy of Spinoza's *Ethics* in the original Latin. He began reading it with great care and attention and continued to read and study it throughout his life. By the time he was ready to graduate from secondary education and move on to higher learning, he already felt a strong identification with Spinoza's *Ethics*.[5] Also by this time, he had already decided he wanted to be a philosopher. He deeply trusted Spinoza and felt that Spinoza's account of his worldview and life's philosophy had shown the way to deep inquiry and practical action that leads to community, friendship, and joy. Naess has never stopped learning from Spinoza's texts. In the course of his studies, he realized that Spinoza's work, even though made as precise as possible in the timeless language of Medieval Latin, cannot be given one single, definitive interpretation. As is true for many such philosophical and other texts, they are rich in interpretive possibilities. This is also true of Naess's own writings.

Early in his intellectual development, he began to reflect on the relationships between persons and nations and wondered how serious conflicts could be defused or even avoided. His concerns for peaceful accord and shared inquiry eventually came together in his first major work, published in SWAN, volume 1, *Interpretation and Preciseness*. He had earlier read Gandhi's works and studied his nonviolent campaigns for social justice in South Africa and India. Naess was committed to nonviolent communication and research.

Naess also traveled to other places in Europe while working on his graduate studies. He spent time in Vienna, where he was invited to join the discussions of the famous Vienna Circle. This group included such leading figures as Moritz Schlick, Rudolf Carnap, Otto Neurath, and Frederick Waismann. Ludwig Wittgenstein's *Tractatus Logico-Philosophicus* had influenced their discussions.[6] What impressed Naess most about the members of the discussion circle was their open attitude to exploring any question. They engaged in philosophical activity as a collegial undertaking of joint investigation, working together to deepen their understanding and knowledge, helping each other to more carefully formulate their insights and feelings.

His study and acceptance of the principles of nonviolence and his embrace of the open-inquiry methods of the Vienna Circle led him away from pure mathematics, logic, and formal studies in spite of his intense love for these subjects. His work has always had applied connections based on his practical and passionate concerns. He felt that academic philosophy in the West had become too abstract and esoteric and that it was characterized by obscure terminology and was only remotely connected to daily life. There was high specialization among academic philosophers and an attitude that only experts are qualified to speak on such subjects as the nature of truth and justice. Naess believed otherwise. He noted that the debating techniques used in philosophy classes, conferences, and journals often shed little light, even though they can produce a lot of heat. From the Vienna Circle, he learned the importance of doing empirical research, but he did not accept the positivistic conclusions that many in the circle drew from this. He rejected the attempt to reduce all experience to the contents of the five senses. From his early years, his own spontaneous experiences in the natural world as an amateur naturalist and mountain climber had impressed on him the wholeness of other beings and the natural world; he was impressed by the diversity and community found in the world, and by its complexity and uniqueness.

Born on January 27, 1912, Arne Dekke Naess was the fourth and last child of the Ragnar and Christine Naess family, which was originally from Bergen, Norway. Arne was born in a house in Slemdal, on the outskirts of Oslo, with a wild garden that blended into woods. At his birth, his three siblings were Ragnar, 11; Erling, 10; and his sister, Kiki, 5. Because of their age differences, Arne spent many happy hours playing alone in natural settings. Before he was a year old, his father died of cancer. Christine had her hands full with many social engagements and his older siblings, but he had a nanny named Mina, for whom he felt a great affection. She doted on him and was the unconditionally loving mother that we all want. When he was still quite young, his mother believed that he was being spoiled by the governess and so let Mina go. This created a deep sorrow within him. He says he never felt the same close connection with his own mother.

His mother had a cabin near Ustaoset, a small community high in the mountains on the train route between Oslo and Bergen. The community is on the slopes of a broad mountain plateau that is part of the Hardangervidda, the largest alpine plateau in Europe (10,000 square kilometers, or 3,860 square miles). It goes from the southern cliffs of Mt. Hallingskarvet west to the fjords on the coast and south to the mountain plateau above the Otra River in Setesdal. This enormous mountain area is crisscrossed by trails and some roads and is dotted by cabins. It is home to thousands of wild caribou, or reindeer, as they are called in Norway. Mt. Hallingskarvet, a major landmark in the north of this area, can be seen from great distances. It has about 40 kilometers of cliffs that form its south side. From a distance, its top looks flat. But when standing on its summit in the summer, when the snow is gone, you find that it is covered with large boulders. In the winter, the boulders lie under snow. To the north of Mt. Hallingskarvet are the peaks of the Jotunheimen, literally, "the home of the giants." These are the highest mountains in Norway. Arne's mother would take her family to the Ustaoset cabin, going by train, a four-hour trip from Oslo.

By the time he was ten, Naess had developed a strong sense of connection with the mountains and especially Mt. Hallingskarvet. He begin to feel a mythopoetic connection with the mountain, which became like a father to him. Eventually, in 1938, he built his own hut high on the mountain at the foot of its massive cliffs, a three-hour hike uphill from the train station at Ustaoset. He called his hut and its immediate area Tvergastein, which, roughly translated, means "crossed stones." Over his lifetime, he has spent years at this hut. It is the place where he has done much of his most original creative writing and other work. There are endless cliffs to climb and a view with few equals for its extent and impressiveness. A book on the mountain and the hut was published in 1995 in Norwegian. A rough English translation of the title is "Hallingskarvet: How to have a long life with an old father."

Arne has early memories of being in nature and becoming aware of its responsiveness when he would wade and play in the water of the fjords near Oslo. He felt an intense sense of belonging and connection with the natural world around him. Through this spontaneous experience of the inner-responsive nature of the world and its many inhabitants, he realized that even the tiniest of beings can respond to us, depending on how we act and feel about them. He felt it was wonderful to have these creatures in the water exploring his body when he remained very still, and moving away when he became active. Throughout his life, this exploratory wonder and experimental attitude have characterized his approach to the world and our many dimensional relationships.

When others in philosophy focused on what experts thought and consulted texts, Naess developed empirical methods to find out how language is actually used and what experts and nonexperts think about important and deep subjects. These studies begin with his earliest work on truth in the 1930s and continue to the 1990s in his research on intrinsic values in nature.[7] Early in life, he realized that language and everything about human life are constantly changing and that no subject is ever definitively finished. He sees his own creative work and teachings as works in progress. They are part of a lifelong commitment to be always learning, just as he continued through the years to find new routes to the top of Mt. Hallingskarvet and other mountains in Norway and around the world.

After completing his secondary education, Naess studied at the University of Oslo, where he graduated in 1933. He completed a master's degree in math and science and received his Ph.D. from the University of Oslo in 1936. While still doing graduate studies in 1934 and 1935, he spent time in Paris and Vienna. He took part in discussions of the Vienna Circle and climbed in the Alps. During this time, the Nazis were coming to power in Germany. While in Vienna, Naess met and went into psychoanalysis with Dr. Edvard Hitschmann, one of Freud's associates. Naess plunged into his own psychic depths, undergoing analysis for fourteen months, six days a week. Dr. Hitschmann was keen for him to become a psychotherapist and arranged for him to spend time working in a psychiatric ward, where Naess developed great empathy for the patients.

Naess had decided to study in Vienna because of the mountains there and because it was a center of philosophical and cultural activity. He went there also to study concert piano with one of the leading teachers of the day. But after some time, his teacher informed him that although Naess was excellent musically, he could not keep up with others in the classes because he would not practice more than six hours a day. Realizing that his deeper interests intellectually lay elsewhere, Naess put most of his energy into philosophy and mountain climbing.

After he finished his dissertation, *Knowledge Acquisition and the Behavior of Scientists* (1936), Naess decided to go to the University of California in Berkeley, where Edward Chace Tolman was doing experimental work in learning theory by studying rats in a laboratory setting. Tolman invited Naess to join in these experimental studies and arranged for him to have his own lab with rats as subjects. After just a few months of work, Naess learned that rats have a higher tolerance than humans do for multiple options. He felt empathy for the rats in cages and began to consider other empirical studies worth doing that did not involve caged animals. It is known among rat experimenters that even though the rats used in the experiments have been bred for generations to be easily handled in the lab, they will still do creative things and will revert to wild behavior if they escape from their cages.

He began to study the behavior of the psychologists who were studying the rats. As in mountain climbing, he was happy to be moving on to another route or another peak, to seek different perspectives and different ways of looking at things. During his studies of the scientists, he continued to think of the possibility of developing a science of science. All these efforts were later connected to his examination of the role of different paradigms and the significant changes in orientation that can result from paradigm shifts in science, and how these in turn are embedded in larger historical and cross-cultural perspectives. From a global perspective, we live on a planet with enormous cultural, linguistic, and biological diversity. Just as he applied empirical methods and observation to the study of animals and plants in nature, Naess applied similar methods to the study of philosophies of life and worldviews.[8]

Naess enjoyed being in California. There were inviting seashores, deserts, and mountains to explore and a stimulating intellectual and artistic culture in which to engage. He was asked if he would be willing to stay as an associate professor, but simultaneously was invited to apply for a full professor-ship opening at the University of Oslo. For many reasons having to do with his family, he decided to return to Norway. He was offered and accepted the professorship, and he served there with distinction from 1939 to 1969. In 1969, he took early retirement so that he could "live and not just function," and to devote his remaining years and energies to the active support of the long-range deep ecology movement. Since 1991, he has been working with the Senter for utvikling og miljø (SUM, translated as the Center for Devel-opment and the Environment, Web address www.sum.uio.no), a research institute associated with the University of Oslo.

During his years as a professor, he had many adventures and pioneered many fields of study that were always related to issues of practical and moral importance. By the time he returned to Norway, Germany had gone to war. Soon after he took his position at the University of Oslo, Norway was invaded by almost half a million German soldiers and administrators. Dur-ing the five years of occupation, Naess was active in nonviolent resistance to the Nazi occupation. He sees his most active work in the peace movement as the period from 1940 to 1955. After the war was over and the Germans left Norway, the Norwegians thought they might be invaded by the Soviet Union. For this reason, people active in the resistance did not divulge the many ways they resisted the Nazis until years later.

When World War II ended, large areas of Europe were under Soviet control with the presence of its large army. There were increasing tensions between East and West and the beginning of the Cold War. The founding of the United Nations and UNESCO were major efforts aimed at preventing other world wars. At the end of World War II, atomic weapons were used against the Japanese by the United States. Later, the Soviets also developed atomic weapons. The Cold War was a long period of conflicts and end-less wars of national liberation, characterized by suspicion and fear and the building of absurd atomic arsenals by the Soviets and the West. These even-tually threatened the survival of the ecosphere and all nations. During this period, much of Naess's work was motivated by his desire to defuse violent conflicts and to increase and improve contacts and communication between those who were in deep disagreement. This desire motivated his work on a UNESCO project that studied what experts and others thought about free-dom and democracy in the Eastern and Western blocs.[9]

From his studies of what experts and ordinary people mean by truth to his studies of democracy and freedom in different cultural contexts, Naess was guided by his insights into the nature of language, interpretation, and communication—insights that were rooted in Spinozan and similar texts. Because he was multilingual and grew up in Norway, a country with highly diverse landscapes and dialects, Naess appreciated that we cannot prescriptively determine what basic terms stand for. How words get their meaning is always bound up with a context that includes a place, culture, and customs. Even today, Norway does not have one central authority that defines the correct and proper use and meaning of Norwegian words. There are three ways to write in Norwegian and many alternative spellings and pronunciations of ordinary words. Despite this diversity, Norwegians manage to communicate and learn from one another.

Many of the scholars with whom Naess rubbed shoulders emphasized analysis and took a somewhat prescriptive attitude toward the role of the scholar. Naess felt that what was needed most were empirical studies of the way that words are used in their natural setting and cultural context. This was at the heart of the Oslo School of Empirical Semantics, which developed during the war years and after. Those studies led Naess and others to realize that even when specialists carefully define their terms, one cannot be certain that these experts stick to their own definitions. One must therefore analyze their text in a painstaking way, as shown in SWAN, volume. 1, *Interpretation and Preciseness*. From his long-term studies of Spinoza's texts, he had already realized the degree to which texts are artifacts having rich possibilities for interpretation.[10] One can see the direct relevance of language interpretation to religious conflicts. Often, these conflicts turn on the way different individuals or groups interpret what they read in the Bible or other holy writings. The original Jesus or Buddha taught in person, using the direct and open spoken language of everyday life. When their sayings were written down, there was already an act of interpretation involved. And then, as the texts were copied and recopied, they diverged further from the original words. None of these texts comes with a guide on how they should be interpreted. Moreover, as Naess observes, living, spoken languages are not fixed but flowing and changing like a river.

In our ordinary discourse, we usually get along fine without attempting to be very precise. The conclusion is easily reached that our disagreements and misunderstandings might be capable of being resolved if we make an effort to be more clear with respect to specific concepts or words. We can find ourselves in such conflict situations when discussing subjects such as politics and religion because we often have strong feelings about them. Those we live and work with have different feelings and thoughts about many of the same phrases, and so we should try to make our language more precise by explaining in the context what we mean by key terms and phrases. Naess did not follow the direction taken by Wittgenstein in his early work represented by the *Tractatus Logico-Philosophicus,* in which Wittgenstein seeks to have a perfect language with complete precision.[11] Precision is a relative matter dependent on the context and purposes of those involved, as the later Wittgenstein and Naess both realized. Naess has always had a deep respect for the abilities and talents of ordinary people. He has always thought that we are each far more capable and have more knowledge than we give ourselves credit for. Thus, it was only natural for him to develop a means for improving discussion through clarification, a method he calls *precisization.* This approach can be applied wherever language is in use and we are dealing with meanings and values that we feel strongly about.[12]

By the time Naess became a full professor at the University of Oslo, he was already married to his first wife, Else (who was also a mountaineer). They had two sons, Ragnar and Arild. While he was still a professor, Arne and Else divorced and Naess married Siri, with whom he had a daughter named Charlotte (Lotte). They, too, divorced after many years, and Naess married Kit-Fai, whom he had met in Hong Kong when he lived there as a visiting professor. She has worked with him for over thirty years and is one of the most knowledgeable people on the organization of his collected works.

Naess's professorial duties at the University of Oslo were enormous. He did administrative work, taught classes, worked with graduate students, did research, and wrote for publication. It was his responsibility to design the tests in logic and philosophy that all university students in Norway are required to take. In connection with this, he developed a logic and communication course designed to help students learn to reason and argue more effectively and to recognize the common pitfalls in discussion and debate. SWAN, volume 7, *Communication and Argument,* is based on the text used for this purpose. His two-volume *History of Eastern and Western Philosophy* (in Norwegian) was read by students at the beginning university level. Some of his texts were read by high school students. Eventually, the courses based on *Communication and Argument* enrolled over one hundred thousand students. Naess's approach to teaching the course came under some criticism because he was helping his students learn how to think for themselves and how to criticize poor argumentation in popular debates by using examples from all walks of life. He encouraged even first-year students in other courses to develop and spell out their own philosophy of life and worldview.[13]

When he began his early empirical and philosophical studies, Naess thought it was possible to do value-free inquiries. After a great deal of effort, however, he began to despair because he realized that this could not be done. Even pure logic, he saw, must recognize certain norms such as consistency. After further reflection, he realized that values are inextricably bound up with everything we are, feel, and do. We cannot evade responsibility for clarifying and stating what our values are and what we think about the nature of reality. This led him to study normative systems in more depth.[14] He appreciated more fully how well his encounters with the mature philosophy of Spinoza had taught him how to have a sense for the whole of the world and life. This sense for a total view, which can only be spelled out in a fragmentary way, enabled him to enter into high-level discussions with members of the Vienna Circle when he was a mere youth. They treated him as an equal, because, he believes, he had the confidence of a person with a high degree of integration in his personal philosophy.[15] This also was in part a result of his longtime participation in Norwegian *friluftsliv* (literally, "free-air-life") and mountaineering, both of which deepened his whole sense of connection with the natural world and other beings.

Naess's sense of wonder was awakened at an early age and was continually fed by the adventures and discoveries he enjoyed in the world of wild nature and in his excursions into the wild world of unexplored ideas and worldviews. His philosophical development is characterized by continuous growth and evolution. From studies of minute topics and problems that involve distilling complex topics to simple formulas, to an ever-expanding, inclusive movement toward greater wholeness and completeness of his total view, his studies reach global and cosmic levels. He compares and contrasts different cultural and scientific approaches to the world and to reality. Because of the diversity of languages, cultures, and personal experiences, it is not only possible but necessary to have great *pluralism*; reality admits to many characterizations and levels of description. Each of us and our cultures are part of a larger context that itself has many complex and rich facets and is part of a larger whole. This led him to develop what he calls a gestalt ontology that recognizes and honors individual nuances of feeling, thought, and experience.[16]

Always respecting the dignity, worth, and freedom of the individual, he has championed, encouraged, and empowered people to be their own teachers and experts. Whether in discussion or in heated debate, he always remains calm and open to considering other points of view. I remember many times when he presented material to seminars for discussion and his statements were vigorously attacked. His response was always to listen with

the greatest sympathy and care, to take notes of what the critics were saying, and even to agree with them and thank them. In most of these circumstances, the other person started softening his or her criticism and began
trying to help Naess articulate his approach to avoid the difficulty the critic
thought was there. Even after World War II, when those who were considered traitors were brought to judgment in Norway, Naess spoke for treating
them with the utmost consideration. As a follower of Gandhi, he emphasizes
the importance of respecting the humanity of others, even when we disagree
with them intensely.[17] He has by example taught others in the peace, social
justice, and environmental movements the importance of nonviolence in
word and deed.

Naess is not an elitist or a member of the cult of the expert and specialist.
He is always willing to take a humble role. One time when he was visiting
our campus, I invited him to observe an Aikido class I was teaching. He got
there before me, and my assistant, who did not know that he was the distinguished, seventy-five-year-old Professor Naess, asked him if he was there for
the Aikido class. Naess said yes. My assistant handed him a broom and told
him to sweep the mats. When I arrived at class, I was surprised to see Naess
diligently sweeping the floor with the greatest of care and enthusiasm. I
thanked him for his effort, and he then sat down to observe the class. During
the class, my students and I gave some demonstrations and I explained the
basic philosophy of Aikido, which is to harmonize with a would-be opponent. In our practice, we call our attacker our partner. After class, Naess told
me that Aikido philosophy and practice were similar to what he practiced as
Gandhian boxing and tennis. These sports are not competitive in the usual
sense. In Gandhian tennis, for example, if the ball is returned in a way that is
impossible to play, then the point is in favor of the would-be receiver. After
a moment's reflection, I could see the possibilities for enriching other games
using this approach.

His playfulness and curiosity are legendary. He is given to becoming
transfixed in observing some tiny thing. On the way to a lecture, he became
engrossed in observing an insect he had not seen before. He had to be
reminded that he was to be at a lecture soon. On one of his visits to Victoria, Canada, we had a party at our house in his honor. We invited a number of environmental activists and university faculty to meet him. When
we could not find him in the house, I searched the yard. I found him in a
plum tree with our then nine-year-old daughter, Anna. They were climbing around, and she was asking him if he could do different things that she
could do in the tree. I invited them to come inside, but they were reluctant.

On another occasion, we were at a weeklong conference at the Naropa Institute in Boulder, Colorado. Having been in meetings all day, several of us, including Naess, decided to walk in the nearby hills. After we had gone up the trail a short distance, Naess spied some cliffs nearby. He said he needed some time alone and wanted to climb on the rocks. When we got higher on the hill, we encountered some climbers who were looking for him. They had heard that Arne Naess was going to be in the area. We told them where we last saw him. They gathered up their gear and went in search for him. They wanted to climb with him and to talk with him about his climbs and passion for climbing.

Naess has climbed in mountains all over the world. He has done first ascents from small peaks to large Himalayan mountains.[18] One time when he was visiting California, some friends suggested they go car camping to see the Grand Canyon. He had already been to the Sierras and Death Valley. They pulled up at a beautiful spot and asked Naess if he thought this was a good place to camp. "No," he said. They continued on and looked for something more beautiful and having even more richness. Each time they stopped, he said no. Finally, they asked him why these were not suitable. He said that they were "too spectacular!" So they asked him to choose a spot. He had them pull over in a not very impressive place. He took his pack and walked away from the road for some distance, and that was where they camped. When asked about this, he explained that we should try to avoid overusing the spectacular and that we can find something wonderful in places that seem to be not so amazing.

His years of experience as a researcher doing interdisciplinary work made it natural for him to study grassroots movements. His approach to studying these is to try to clarify and distill the main principles and values of the movement according to empirical and other studies. When he characterized the deep ecology movement, it was originally to try to state an outline of its main points. These eventually were distilled to what he calls the eight points or the platform principles of the deep ecology movement. He is not in favor of trying to develop one culture for the world as a whole. This is akin to the biological simplification brought about by industrial agriculture, but applied to culture and language. He has long been a spokesperson for cultural diversity and its preservation. He sees biodiversity and cultural diversity as inextricably interconnected. To develop cooperation and communication at the international level does not require that we all become members of one culture. He appreciates the creative genius of local people to solve local problems.

Given the preceding discussion, it is easy to see why he does not support a certain kind of globalization, when this involves forcing other cultures to adhere to modern Western methodologies and practices. Cultural richness and personal diversity are intertwined. He sees the great range of personal diversity of worldviews and life philosophies as enriching our lives in much the same way that the biological diversity of tropical and temperate rain forests leaves us with deep feelings of wonder and joy. As a result of technological and scientific developments in the West and their spread globally, we are witnessing an increasing threat to diversity of all kinds. This is why he supports the principle that richness and diversity are good in themselves, just as each being has intrinsic worth. He has strong feelings for the uniqueness of each individual, whether a rock, an insect, or a person, and at the same time he is able to appreciate their unities and common biological and ecological grounds.

He talks of looking into a microscope and seeing a flea die in agony in the acid solution on the slide. He felt distress at the insect's plight. He sets an example of careful treatment of others and the natural world. He celebrates the possibilities for each of us to realize our potentials and to act beautifully to benefit ourselves and our neighbors. He says that most of us eventually realize that some of our basic ways of knowing rest on intuitions such as "everything hangs together" and "live and let live." All philosophies of life consist of basic value norms and basic hypotheses about the nature of the world. When these philosophies take careful account of ecological responsibilities, they become *ecosophies*, a word he coined for ecological wisdom.

When I reflect on the distilled norms, formulas, principles, slogans, mottoes, and outlines he has written and repeated, I have a growing list of favorites, which include the following:

Everything hangs together.
Act beautifully.
Anything can happen.
Reality is all possibilities.
Live and let live.
The front of the deep ecology movement is very long and deep.
From the mountains, we learn modesty; their size makes us feel small
      and humble, and so we participate in their greatness.
Seek truth but do not claim it.
We all act as if we have a total view.
Seek a total view, but always be open to new views and perspectives.

Seek the center of a conflict, and treat opponents with the
   utmost respect.

Be nonviolent in language, judgment, and action.

Seek whole and complete communication.

Be open to making yourselves more precise and clear.

Emphasize positive, active feelings.

Negative, passive emotions decrease us and make us smaller.

Question yourself deeply.

None of us mean what we say with great precision.

Realize yourself, and help others to realize themselves.

The more diversity the better.

High quality of life does not depend on high material consumption.

Find joy in simple things.

Complexity, not complication.

Simple in means, rich in ends.

There is no value-free inquiry.

Inquire into your values, feelings, and judgments.

All things are open to inquiry.

Not positivist reduction, but whole, unified experience.

Our spontaneous experience is far richer than any abstractions about it.

Every event has many descriptions and aspects.

The quality of our experience depends on our choice of norms.

Trust, don't doubt; trust and inquire.

Open inquiry is not a specialization; it is open to anyone and cuts
   across all disciplines.

We seriously underestimate ourselves.

Philosophy begins and ends in wonder.

From the observations made so far, we can summarize Naess's main interests in philosophy, science, and social science. They include behaviorist epistemology, empirical semantics and communication theory, skepticism, scientific and cultural pluralism, Gandhi and Spinoza scholarship, normative systems theory, gestalt ontology, and the focus on total views. These interests and others are reflected in the titles and subtitles of SWAN. The ten volumes show a progressive move toward greater inclusiveness, culminating in volume 10, *Deep Ecology of Wisdom*, which connects all of Naess's research and writing projects in one volume.

In volume 10, Naess uses the deep ecology movement and his own Ecosophy T to integrate the wide range of diverse elements that go into any total view. All his active participation in various projects and protests comes together in this volume, including his papers looking to the years ahead, even to the twenty-second century, and his papers on modernism and sustainability. He has been personally active in the peace, social justice, and environmental movements and has participated in nonviolent activities to protest dam building and in antiglobalization efforts. He has contributed to conservation biology, wildlands philanthropy, green economics, ecological design, restoration ecology, sustainable forestry, wildlife and fisheries management, green business and building design, and voluntary simplicity. During his life, he has given much to charitable organizations. He has also anticipated the rising slow-food movement, which is becoming a global movement to slow life down and retake control of our lives. (See www. slowfood.com.) Years before the slow movement surfaced publicly, he was advocating doing things more slowly and taking the time to enjoy each activity. At ninety-two, he still cut wood for his stove with a handsaw and carried it home in his backpack.

Always Inquiring

Whether reflecting on modesty in mountain climbing, on how to interpret the call for sustainable development, or on the ecology of self, Naess followed an approach of continuous open inquiry, of always going deeper to get to the roots of a problem or an issue.[19] Why are we using this policy? Why is this form of education not working? What are our ultimate values? What is the best forestry for this watershed? What values take priority in this development? Naess embodies the spirit of philosophy in its original sense as a loving pursuit of wisdom. It is a deep exploration of our whole lives and context in pursuit of living wisely. This is the essence of the Socratic inquiry to know ourselves. From his work on Pyrrhonian skepticism to his discussion of total views, culminating in his positive statements on pluralism and possibilism, Naess says that he is a "philosophical vagabond" or "wandering seeker," what the ancient Greeks called a *zetetic*.[20] His deep inquiry into science as an enterprise reflects on the actual day-to-day work of scientists.[21] He tentatively concludes that the future is not determined. Our possibilities for the future are creatively abundant. Every relationship, event, and individual can be described in a multitude of ways and has rich possibilities. Even if we combined all that we can think or survey, we could not fully characterize the subject in question. No single perspective takes precedence over these many possibilities, whether they are in science or in other fields of study. Our spontaneous experience in the world is far richer than we can ever say.

According to Naess, there is never one definitive interpretation of philosophical texts; there is never one single description of an event or a single theory of things that is the whole and only truth. Every event and all processes are complex interactions involving many changing forces and relations, internal and external. Experience and the processes around us form changing patterns or gestalts. The nature of reality is multidimensional and creative. This is also true for our language systems. Whether printed or spoken statements, utterances have many possible interpretations. Even scientific theories are open to interpretation. There is no single scientific worldview; there are many. Naess favors using gestalt ontology to describe our basic ways of organizing the world of our experience. He also says that every whole has within it gestalts that reflect the character of the whole piece. For example, the parts of a sonata have their sense and resolution in the whole piece. Our spontaneous experience is so rich and deep that we can never give a complete account of it in any language, be it mathematics, science, music, or art. Art and music can come closer to our feelings, but even they cannot capture it all. As a deep questioner and seeker, Naess remains free of dogmatic and monolithic doctrines about the world. This is what partly explains why he celebrates a movement supported by diverse people with many worldviews. It creates richness when we are all different and have different experiences. This is also related to his commitment to nonviolence, insofar as we must respect the integrity of each person and recognize that everyone has greater capacities for self-realization than he or she might be aware of. As a philosopher and person, Naess has been influenced by his cultural experience and native place.

Naess in Norway

When I went to Norway the first time, my purpose was to visit Naess to learn how he and this very old nation live in their places. I had known him for many years and had heard him say many times that a nation can have a small population and a very diverse and rich culture. This is certainly true of Norway, which has a population of close to five million, and is blessed by a rich, ancient heritage and much free wilderness. Quality of life and complexity as richness do not depend on sheer numbers of people or quantities of things. I was amazed by the tremendous diversity of Norway—cultural, topographical, and local.

When I was in Oslo, Naess suggested that I go to Bigdøy Island to see the Folk Art Museum that honors the diverse local practices, arts, and traditions of Norway. The country's complex, mountainous terrain; deep valleys; wide range of latitudes, the northernmost of which goes above the Arctic Circle; and fjord-punctuated coastline have led to a great diversity of local conditions and habitats. When Norway was controlled by Denmark and then Sweden for about 350 years, its own dialects and cultural traditions were kept alive in the local areas away from such urban centers as Oslo. The result is a great diversity in local patterns of speech, spelling, folk music, folk dance, building styles, ceremonial costumes, local legends, folktales, arts and crafts, sweater styles, jewelry design, and so on. Despite this diversity, Norway has a cultural identity and sense of national unity that are unmistakable as you travel the country, talk with its people, and visit its cities, villages, museums, and farms.

Norway has a large expanse of land called *free nature*. Very old farms and villages blend into this open country. Many farms are blessed with several summer farms (called setters) with buildings on the mountain plateaus. In villages with the traditional way of life, people take the sheep and cattle to the mountain meadows in the summer. The men do farmwork on the cultivated crops, while the women and children take the cattle to the high country. Some farms have as many as three summer setters, each further away and coming to pasture conditions later in the season. In the old tradition, after the main farmwork was done, the men joined the others in the high country for the rest of the summer. In the fall, the people would take the herds back to the valley for the winter. In many areas, this pattern continues today. Naess has lived this seasonal mountain plateau life by going regularly to his hut, Tvergastein.

This old pattern of living in two seasonal places, in the valley in winter and in the high country in the summer, contributes to rich cultural practices and traditions. It adds to the complexity and diversity of Norwegian life and culture. Because of Norway's northern location, summers bring very long days; on some summer days in the far north, the sun does not set. And on some days in the winter, the sun does not rise. The long winter nights can be blessed with fantastic displays of Northern Lights, and in summer, the sun casts glorious light on the dramatic landscapes. Norway is a land of incredible beauty, but it also has extreme conditions. It has a tremendous number of lakes, rivers, and streams and a very long sea shoreline with countless islands, harbors, and fjords. It has abundant small hydroelectric plants, many placed deep inside the rocky mountains.

The pattern of seasonal migration led to the cabin tradition in Norway. Almost every person there has access to a mountain, forest, or waterfront hut or cabin where he or she can go for weekends or longer. These huts are usually simple shelters, with minimum technological complications. Associated with the huts and the outdoors is a tradition called *friluftsliv*. It is said that anytime during a weekend, over half the people will be outdoors doing something in nature such as running, walking, bicycling, skiing, ice skating, sailing, mountain climbing, swimming, or sunbathing. Norwegians strongly identify with their land and free nature. Though an advanced and sophisticated country in education and technical skills, it keeps older traditions alive. Over 90 percent of the land is privately owned (mostly in the old farms and their setters), but everyone has the right to hike and camp anywhere except within a certain distance of a home. The land is owned, but the air is free and everyone is free to use these large areas of open land in the mountains and lowlands.

To go to a cabin for a weekend is to return to a less complicated way of life more in touch with nature. Many cabins I stayed in had no plumbing or electricity. They were snug and comfortable and usually had simple bunk beds with a mattress upon which to throw a sleeping bag. For cooking, the cabins had a simple wood or gas camp stove. You often have to carry water from a spring or get it from a well with a hand pump. Such cabins are all over Norway, and many are available for public use. Many cabins along the roads and highways are privately owned but available for rent. Norway has extensive trail systems and many ski areas for cross-country and downhill skiing. Most cities have ski jumps and other facilities to encourage outdoor activities. The *friluftsliv* tradition has grown in recent years. There is much reflection on what it is, what it ought to be, and its significance. Naess has contributed to these discussions.

At the beginning of the twentieth century, Norway was one of the poorest countries in Europe. Today, it is one of the richest and has a very high quality of life. It has high levels of education, and most Norwegians speak three languages. Naess was deeply involved in the reform of Norwegian education and in reinvigorating Norwegian philosophy in the twentieth century. Norway has outstanding social services and excellent public transport. There is not so great a gap between the people at the top wealth level and those at the bottom. As I traveled in Norway, I did not see people living on the street. In my extensive travels, I saw no derelict buildings or slums.

Norway has an amazing number of very old buildings, boats, and ships that are in use and in fine shape. It has some of the oldest wood buildings in the world, such as the Viking stave churches that are over a thousand years old. Many of the farms have barns and log houses that are four to five hundred or more years old. I traveled in Norway during the hay season one year, and in some valleys, I saw every form of hay harvest method being practiced, from hand cutting and hanging on lines to dry to several types of baling systems, and even the recent large, round rolls of hay wrapped in plastic. The traditional arts and crafts are practiced in the villages. The farms are run by families who take the name of the farm and keep up its traditions. In these rural village traditions, many of the arts and crafts are passed on from person to person and are not taught from texts. Norway does not have one official dialect or only one official spelling or pronunciation of Norwegian words. There are three forms representing the spoken words, and a large number of dialects. The unrelated Saami language is one of the official languages of the country, spoken mostly in the north by the Saami (or Lapp) people.

Summing Up Before Going On

The preceding sketch offers a mere glimpse of the rich context in which Naess was born and raised. He reflects this heritage and its traditions that respect local ways and free nature. In his empirical studies of language (called empirical semantics), he found that individuals with no special training are able to reflect deeply on the meaning of such words as *freedom* and *truth*. This challenges the bias of academic scholars, who thought only they could provide exact definitions of important concepts. Naess found that languages as spoken and written by ordinary people are very rich and complex, with considerable diversity and depth in meanings. Academic philosophers thought that they themselves had some special insight into these matters and that they knew what so-called ordinary people thought about the world and the meaning of key words. In his empirical studies, Naess found that the cultural world is far richer and more open-ended than was generally thought. He thinks that we all are capable of far grander things than we usually realize. He believes that we have much more freedom and greater possibilities than we think. He sees the natural world as creative and the future as open. There is no scientific basis for denying our freedom. We are limited mainly by our own attitudes, feelings, and ideas. The more open and exploratory we become, the more we discover our own native capacity to be wandering, insightful seekers.

This willingness to study how people actually communicate on a daily basis in different places was part of the background for Naess's study of the development of grassroots political movements. From the time he was a young man, he has practiced nonviolence. He saw how nonviolence should embrace both our actions and our forms of communication. Attempts to centrally dictate how people should speak and think are not only futile but wrong. When we welcome the diversity naturally present in local places, we realize not only that this is very enriching, but that it also reflects the way the natural and cultural world evolves in different places with their wonderful variety of habitats, traditions, and other conditions. We gain deep respect for the abilities and integrity of individual persons and local communities. This background and Naess's travels influenced his descriptions of international grassroots movements.

There are some common misunderstandings of Naess's work in relation to the deep ecology movement. These could be avoided if people knew about the background just described. When he first characterized the deep ecology movement, he already had extensive knowledge of international grassroots movements and of cross-cultural comparative studies in worldviews and other aspects of culture, including studies in empirical semantics. He was deeply sympathetic to the rising global ecology movement that is a response of ordinary people to environmental degradation and other forms of violence against the natural world. He saw that these people did not all have the same cultural conditioning or share the same worldview, but that as with other international movements, there were also common grounds. It was these matters that he described, based on empirical and conceptual studies, when he talked about the shallow and deep ecology movements. In part 2 of this introduction, I focus in greater depth on Naess's way of approaching and characterizing a total view. I will concentrate on his account of the deep ecology movement and of ecosophies, especially on his own personal philosophy of life called Ecosophy T.

PART 2: DEEP ECOLOGY, ECOSOPHY T, AND TOTAL VIEWS: THE SHALLOW AND DEEP ECOLOGY MOVEMENTS IN DETAIL

As we have seen so far, philosopher, mountaineer, and activist Arne Naess is a pioneer in cross-cultural, interdisciplinary research and especially the study of nonviolent, grassroots, sociopolitical movements and worldviews. International studies helped him describe the long-range deep ecology movement as one of the three important global movements of the twentieth century: for social justice, world peace, and ecological responsibility.

The phrase *deep ecology movement* was first used by Naess at the Third World Future Research Conference, held in Bucharest in 1972. He discussed the historical background of the ecology movement and its connection to values respecting nature and the inherent worth of other beings. As a mountaineer, activist, teacher, and researcher, he has climbed and traveled worldwide. He observed political and social activism in many cultures and was an activist in the peace and social justice movements. He has been a follower of Gandhi's way of nonviolence since a young man. He has lived through wars and depressions. During the five years that Norway was occupied by German armies in World War II, he was a nonviolent underground leader of resistance to this occupation. He was a leader in interdisciplinary cross-cultural research. When he traveled, he participated in local forums and international workshops. He spoke with numerous people who had extensive cross-cultural experience. He carried on scholarly research in several languages and corresponded with many scholars in other parts of the world. He studied and had firsthand activist experience in the emerging grassroots ecology movement, which is supported by social activists from all parts of the political spectrum and from different cultures around the world. He says he was also inspired by Rachel Carson's *Silent Spring* (1962) and the controversy surrounding its publication.[22]

Naess's Bucharest talk, and the seminal paper published from it, explained the differences between the shallow and the deep ecology movements in broad terms.[23] He noted that the distinctive aspects of the deep ecology movement are its general platform principles that recognize the inherent value of ecological and cultural diversity and of all living beings. Supporters use these principles to shape national and local environmental policies and actions. Those who work for social changes are motivated by caring for humans, other living beings, and nature. They recognize that we cannot go on with business as usual, or we will destroy the diversity and beauty of the world. Naess articulated central elements of deep human concern being expressed around the world. Whatever their spiritual orientation, supporters of the deep ecology movement *feel* sorrow for the widespread suffering caused by destructive practices. They feel strongly that these practices are wrong.

A deep response to the environmental crisis involves getting a "total view," to use Naess's words, which goes beyond the forms of knowledge in specialized conventional Western disciplines. A person who wants to live wisely realizes that many environmental problems are not merely technical, but also personal and local; they have community *and* global dimensions. Their global extent poses the question: How can our diverse human family, living in so many different cultures and places, work together to end violence, improve social justice, and promote world peace *and* harmony with nature? All these are *possible*, according to Naess. As a possibilist, he says, "Anything can happen." The choices we make do matter. The future is open. He invites us to engage in deep questioning and to reflect on our own motives and ultimate values. What *is* most important to us?

From his studies and travels, Naess was aware of the many ways people can abide by principles cutting across cultural boundaries, such as Gandhi's principles of nonviolence and the principles of human rights and social justice. By analyzing texts, through conversations, and by empirical methods (some of which he developed), he identified two main responses to the awareness that we are disrupting the natural world.[24] The short-term shallow ecology movement relies on quick, technical fixes and pursues business as usual without any deep value questioning or long-range changes in practices and the system. Supporters of the long-range deep ecology movement take a broader view. They look for long-term solutions, engage in deep questioning, and pursue alternative patterns of action. They strive to build sustainability. We cannot go on with business as usual in the developed industrial societies. We should change our lifestyles toward higher *quality* of life and pursue lower levels of production and consumption of natural resources. Naess says that even Norway, with all its open land of free nature, is overdeveloped in some ways but not in others. He says repeatedly that for many people in the world whose lives are in jeopardy and dire straits, there must be a great effort to improve their conditions so as to meet their vital needs. But no single solution will work everywhere; many solutions, each appropriate to the place and people concerned, must be applied.

Supporters of the shallow ecology movement do not question deeply but focus on short-term, narrow, human interests. They only tinker with the built systems, but do not question their own *fundamental* methods, values, and purposes. They do not look deeply into the nature of our relationships with each other and other beings. They assume that we can do fine without making basic changes. This is the approach of our mainstream institutions. Their development models are deeply influenced by control-oriented mechanistic systems that are applied to the human and natural world. The planning and development models are based on an outmoded economic philosophy that fails to include the ecological context. These models are being replaced in leading-edge work in science and philosophy, but there is a cultural lag related to vested interests and institutional inertia. The deep, long-range approach is to create institutional practices that are evolving, self-organizing, and creative. Many people in leading-edge businesses are trying to do this by putting ecological and social responsibility into the values that guide their practices.

The deep questioning approach of the long-range deep ecology movement examines our basic values and lifestyles and reflects on our fundamental relationships with nature and who we are. Followers of the deep ecology movement seek ways to live less violently in *all* their relations. They realize that quality of life depends on the quality of their relationships. Supporters ask how to change their activities to bring them into harmony with local ecological and human communities. They realize we humans do not know how to manage the incredibly complex natural world, but must learn from the integrity and diversity that are there. When we use violent methods such as toxic sprays to control other plants and organisms, we not only harm other beings, but also set off long-range problems that are worse than the ones we are trying to solve. Trying to control the whole of nature is futile and wrong. Our challenge is to manage ourselves as responsible members of an ecosphere that includes diverse species, communities, and unique individuals who deserve our respect.

The shallow ecology movement is *anthropocentric*, that is, it has a humans-first value system. The deep ecology movement principles specifically emphasize respect for the intrinsic worth of all beings (from microbes to elephants and humans) and treasure all forms of biological and cultural diversity. The shallow ecology movement is more evident in the policies of developed nations, where there is support for a mix of shallow policies with some lip service to deeper values such as biodiversity.

Cross-cultural studies and experience have helped us, as Naess says, to appreciate the diversity of worldviews on earth. At the level of international cooperation, we have created institutions such as the United Nations to enable us to work together globally despite cultural differences. The broadly accepted principles of social justice and the principles of nonviolent conflict resolution are part of international agreements that most of us can affirm from our diverse ultimate philosophies and religions. Nations should and do develop policies that honor broad principles agreed to in international bodies and multilateral treaties. National policies encourage certain courses of action to improve conditions in specific relationships and places. Many transition strategies are in use in different places. As Naess says, the front of the movement for ecological responsibility is very long and deep.

Just as we have made progress in human rights and the nonviolent resolution of conflicts, so too have we made progress nationally and internationally in recognizing the serious depth of the environmental crisis. Common themes and principles have emerged in many agreements, declarations, and treaties put forth in different local, regional, national, and international forums. These affirm some of the original deep ecology movement principles that Naess and George Sessions first articulated in 1984 (which isare very close to the version below) as a basis for collective and collaborative actions in our different cultural settings.[25] Most recently, Naess articulated the platform principles as the following eight points:

1. All living beings have intrinsic value.
2. The richness and diversity of life has intrinsic value.
3. Except to satisfy *vital* needs, humans do not have the right to reduce this diversity and richness.
4. It would be better for humans if there were fewer of them, and much better for other living creatures.
5. Today the extent and nature of human interference in the various ecosystems is not sustainable, and the lack of sustainability is rising.
6. Decisive improvement requires considerable changes: social, economic, technological, and ideological.
7. An ideological change would essentially entail seeking a better quality of life rather than a raised standard of living.
8. Those who accept the aforementioned points are responsible for trying to contribute directly or indirectly to the necessary changes.[26]

Let us first compare these eight points to similar documents that have been offered as a platform for action to move to sustainable and responsible lifestyles and cultural changes. The United Nations issued an Earth Charter for Nature several years ago, and an independent grassroots organization has followed this initiative by developing an Earth Charter of greater depth. (For more on this initiative, see www.earthcharter.org.) Here is a quote from the official pamphlet of the Earth Charter Organization:

> *Preamble:* We stand at a critical moment in Earth's history, a time when humanity must choose its future. As the world becomes increasingly interdependent and fragile, the future at once holds great peril and great promise. To move forward we must recognize that in the midst of a magnificent diversity of cultures and life forms we are one human family and one Earth community with

a common destiny. We must join together to bring forth a sustainable global society founded on respect for nature, universal human rights, economic justice, and a culture of peace. Towards this end, it is imperative that we, the peoples of the Earth, declare our responsibility to one another, to the greater community of life, and to future generations.

Earth Our Home: Humanity is part of a vast evolving universe. Earth, our home, is alive with a unique community of life. The forces of nature make existence a demanding and uncertain adventure, but Earth has provided the conditions essential to life's evolution. The resilience of the community of life and the well-being of humanity depend upon preserving a healthy biosphere with all its ecological systems, a rich variety of plants and animals, fertile soils, pure waters, and clean air. The global environment with its finite resources is a common concern of all peoples. The protection of the Earth's vitality, diversity, and beauty is a sacred trust.

The Global Situation: The dominant patterns of production and consumption are causing environmental devastation, the depletion of resources, and a massive extinction of species. Communities are being undermined. The benefits of development are not shared equitably and the gap between rich and poor is widening. Injustice, poverty, ignorance, and violent conflict are widespread and the cause of great suffering. An unprecedented rise in human population has overburdened ecological and social systems. The foundations of global security are threatened. These trends are perilous—but not inevitable.

The Challenges Ahead: The choice is ours: form a global partnership to care for the Earth and one another or risk the destruction of ourselves and the diversity of life. Fundamental changes are needed in our values, institutions, and ways of living. We must realize that when basic needs have been met, human development is about being more, not having more. We have the knowledge and technology to provide for all and to reduce our impacts on the environment. The emergence of a global civil society is creating new opportunities to build a democratic and humane world. Our environmental, economic, political, social and spiritual challenges are interconnected, and together we can forge inclusive solutions.[27]

The values and observations in these passages are mostly consistent with the platform principles of the deep ecology movement. These statements are typical of the many mission statements of countless organizations around the world. One can see many points of common agreement between the platform principles above and these statements. It should be stressed that Naess and other movement supporters do not regard the present version of the platform as final. He invites people to suggest modifications if they see fit. It must be *underscored* that this description of the deep ecology movement and its platform is *not* an account of Naess's personal philosophy, called Ecosophy T. The platform principles are supported by people from diverse backgrounds who are, for example, Buddhists, Shintoists, Taoists, Shamanists, Christians, and ecofeminists. They each could also have their own personal ecosophy. Naess feels that mature persons should be able to say what their values and priorities are; they should have the ability to express their own philosophy of life through actions and other means. We are more effective when we are well integrated and open to further learning.

Buddhist followers, for example, can support the platform, given their spiritual teachings. They can formulate and support policies that will help mitigate and prevent environmental degradation in their own area and place. We are empowered to take practical actions when we know others actively support these principles in their own home places. This sense of global solidarity helps us persist in our efforts. Exactly what policies and actions we undertake depends on our personal situation, cultural context, and individual place. *No single solution can be applied to every place.* One size does not fit all. As Naess likes to say, "The more diversity, the better." For example, the vernacular practices of people doing ecoagriculture or ecoforestry are not mechanized standardized monocultures, but they are low-impact and tailored to specific places.[28] The common ground is in principles that support a diversity of practices attuned to local places, conditions, cultures, and ecological communities. The spirit of the deep ecology movement is to fit ourselves into the values and qualities of our watersheds and specific places (localization) in long-range, sustainable ways. We need broad, long-range, deep vision to include many diverse stories and individual voices. We each should go deep into ourselves, our places, and nature, where we will find these fertile connections. Naess encourages each of us to realize our own potential so that we can contribute local and global support to the three international movements of social justice, world peace, and ecological responsibility.

For Naess and others, the platform principles of the long-range deep ecology movement do not make up an ultimate philosophy any more than do the principles of social justice. It is a platform for multilevel cooperation to engender practical policies and positive actions by individuals and groups in diverse places and cultures. Naess calls those who endorse these platform principles supporters of the long-range deep ecology movement, *not* deep ecologists—the latter term he regards as immodest. He also does not call people who support mainstream approaches shallow ecologists, for he feels this is demeaning. The platform principles provide a way to foster international agreement to further multicultural cooperation on behalf of the earth and its ecological communities. Reflecting on the platform locally helps us see how to get to the roots of the environmental crisis in our own context. We can work with others to make ecologically responsible changes in education, international institutions, trade agreements, resource use, work practices, development models, and our personal daily lives. Policies and actions guided by these principles (as embodied, for example, in the Earth Charter) will further a local and global consensus for cooperative solutions to social and environmental problems.

In his description of the deep ecology movement, Naess is careful to explain that he is describing an international grassroots movement characterized by a diversity of worldviews including people from cultures all around the world. They are people who agree that the earth is being damaged and that we need to act. Naess emphasizes that the principles of an international movement should not imperil individual and cultural diversity.

For Naess, these eight principles are a *working* platform for the deep ecology movement. He believes these can be acknowledged as the most general principles of wide agreement in the international ecology movement. They are more refined than slogans, but have a similar use. They are meant to be inclusive and flexible in interpretation so as to lend themselves to support from diverse ecosophies, religions, and worldviews. Thus, interpretation of the principles will vary from place to place and person to person, depending on his or her culture and personal worldviews or ecosophies.

Ecosophy in More Depth

Many supporters of the deep ecology movement have articulated personal ecosophies very similar to Naess's. His original account of *ecosophy* characterizes it as follows:

By an ecosophy I mean a philosophy of ecological harmony or equilibrium. A philosophy as a kind of sofia (or) wisdom, is openly normative, it contains both norms, rules, postulates, value priority announcements *and* hypotheses concerning the states of affairs in our universe. Wisdom is policy wisdom, prescription, not only scientific description and prediction. The details of an ecosophy will show many variations due to significant differences concerning not only the "facts" of pollution, resources, population, etc., but also value priorities.[29]

He elaborates on this account in a later work:

We study ecophilosophy, but to approach practical situations involving ourselves, we aim to develop our own ecosophies. In this book I introduce one ecosophy, arbitrarily called Ecosophy T. You are not expected to agree with all of its values and paths of derivation, but to learn the means for developing your own systems or guides, say, Ecosophies X, Y, or Z. Saying "your own" does not imply that the ecosophy is in any way an original creation by yourself. It is enough that it is a kind of total view which you feel at home with, "where you philosophically belong." Along with one's own life, it is always changing.

Etymologically, the word "ecosophy" combines *oikos* and *sophia*, "household" and "wisdom." As in "ecology," "eco-" has an appreciably broader meaning than the immediate family, household, and community. "Earth household" is closer to the mark. So an ecosophy becomes *a philosophical world-view or system inspired by the conditions of life in the ecosphere*. It should then be able to serve as an individual's philosophical grounding for an acceptance of the principles or platform of deep ecology as outlined.[30]

Putting these observations together, then, we can say, as we noted earlier, that Naess distinguishes among ultimate philosophies or worldviews, platform principles that unite people with different ultimate views, policy formulations applied in specific national or jurisdictional contexts, and statements about practical actions taken by specific individuals in local places. He offers a three-dimensional apron diagram to explain these levels, which I simplify in this two-dimensional chart.[31]

FOUR LEVELS OF ORGANIZATION
FOR THE QUESTIONING AND ARTICULATION OF TOTAL VIEWS

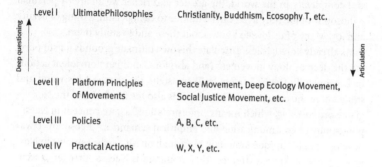

Level I   UltimatePhilosophies   Christianity, Buddhism, Ecosophy T, etc.

Level II   Platform Principles   Peace Movement, Deep Ecology Movement,
            of Movements   Social Justice Movement, etc.

Level III   Policies   A, B, C, etc.

Level IV   Practical Actions   W, X, Y, etc.

Naess notes that in our global discussions, we engage in all four of these general levels of articulation and derivation. He says that we recognize these four basic levels of discourse when we talk about values and actions in relation to the environmental crisis and global grassroots movements. He and others have articulated principles that unite the international movements for social justice, peace, and environmental responsibility. According to him, these four levels of discourse are found in international, national, and local discussions: Level 1 is ultimate philosophies with ultimate value norms; level 2 includes systems of broad principles, such as platform principles of a movement; level 3 involves policy and other guiding formulations; and level 4 includes statements about practical actions.[32]

As already mentioned, Naess calls his own personal (level 1) ultimate philosophy Ecosophy T.[33] Ecosophies are not platforms for a political movement or policies, but are personal philosophies of life in a worldview. The international deep ecology movement is characterized in terms of platform principles (level 2). The platform of this international movement does not constitute a religion or an ultimate philosophy. It invites support from people with diverse ultimate philosophies and religions (level 1) to seek global solutions.[34]

The eight platform principles listed above exemplify level 2 articulation. These principles can be derived from a wide variety of worldviews and religions, just as the globally agreed-upon principles of social justice and peace are supported from a wide variety of level 1 ultimate philosophies. There is great diversity in the ecology movement at levels 1, 3, and 4, but common agreement at level 2. Naess is glad that supporters of the deep ecology movement have different ultimate philosophies; he does not urge others to accept his ultimate ecological philosophy.[35] In his view, the more diversity and complexity in the world, the greater and richer we all are. A personal philosophy of life fully lived can be unique to each person, a thing of beauty and joy. Many of us love to know about them and to study them.

As already noted, Naess articulates his own ultimate grounds for supporting the deep ecology movement (and also for Gandhian nonviolent action) in Ecosophy T. The "T" refers to Tvergastein, the name of his wood and stone hut in the mountains of Norway. T is also the first letter of the Norwegian word *tolkning*, which means "interpretation," a core concept in Naess's philosophy of communication and empirical semantics.[36] Ecosophy T was developed in his unique mountain place high on Mt. Hallingskarvet in Norway, a place of Arctic extremes. This mountain is Naess's surrogate parent for the father he lost before he was a year old. It has some of the oldest rocks in Europe. Hallingskarvet is his spiritual home, where he worked out the details of his ecosophy based on the norm Self-realization! which he interprets in Gandhian and Spinozan ways, thereby bringing together East and West. It includes *practices of extending our care*. Naess's way of sytematizing his philosophy is to state it in terms of ultimate value norms and hypotheses about the world. He then organizes these in chains of derivation. Here is how he presents these in *Ecology, Community and Lifestyle*:

FORMULATION OF THE MOST BASIC NORMS (N)
AND HYPOTHESES (H)
N1: Self-realisation!
H1: The higher the Self-realisation attained by anyone, the broader and deeper the identification with others.
H2: The higher the level of Self-realisation attained by anyone, the more its further increase depends upon the Self-realisation of others.
H3: Complete Self-realisation of anyone depends on that of all.
N2: Self-realisation for all living beings![37]

Later in the same chapter, he offers the following:

NORMS AND HYPOTHESES ORIGINATING IN ECOLOGY
H4: Diversity of life increases Self-realisation potentials.
N3: Diversity of Life!
H5: Complexity of life increases Self-realisation potentials.

N4: Complexity!
H6: Life resources of the Earth are limited.
H7: Symbiosis maximises Self-realisation potentials under conditions of limited resources.
N5: Symbiosis!

Naess uses the exclamation point to emphasize and mark that a statement is a value norm. As a norm, it entails that we ought to do something. In the case of the norm Self-realisation! we should strive to realize ourselves and help others to realize themselves. In the case of Diversity! we should honor and support diversity on every level in any way we can, and so on. Using norms and hypotheses, he articulates in systematic outline form the basic elements of his personal ecosophy.

Naess's ecosophy as a life philosophy and worldview is influenced by Gandhi's teachings on self-realization and nonviolence. It is also related to the Mahayana Buddhist distinction between the small ego-self and the expansive Self of Buddha nature. In the Mahayana teachings, one vows to work for the enlightenment of all beings. It is recognized that we are all interdependent.[38] Naess is also influenced by many aspects of Spinoza's philosophy, including the Dutch philosopher's nonhierarchical view of all beings and his account of active and passive emotions.[39] Active emotions such as love and compassion expand our sense of self and awareness, whereas passive emotions such as hatred and jealousy diminish us. Spinoza says we are as large as our active love. For him, emotions are more like actions we can undertake, and active positive emotions increase our power and enjoyment for life. Naess says that our sense of identification can, through care, extend to include our ecological self. This is facilitated by our giving full attention to the things and beings in our surroundings. His ecosophy is deeply influenced by the Norwegian love of the natural world as exemplified in the *friluftsliv* movement involving outdoor activities in free nature, which he has practiced for his whole life. His life at Tvergastein is *friluftsliv*.

At Home in the Mountains

To be with Naess at Tvergastein is to share in details of his personal ecosophy—details that you would miss when you visit him in Oslo.[40] He talks of different things in the two places. When I was with him, I could sense profound differences in mood and vitality. Being on the mountain at Tvergastein gives him power and energy. I felt that he spoke for the mountain in a perfectly natural way, reflecting what he has learned from it over the years. Some of the many things noticed: the way he sparingly uses water and fuel; the Spartan diet and uncluttered, simple surroundings; the stories that emerge as we walk in different places away from the hut; the tales about the plant life around the hut, as we walk near it; the story of the attempt to build the first higher smaller hut (the Eagle's Nest) that ended in disaster—told in sight of that place; the story of the dream that led to building the Eagle's Nest, which is a smaller cabin now perched high above Tvergastein on the edge of the escarpment cliffs of Mt. Hallingskarvet; from Naess's desk in the library, the fantastic view of the hut looking south over the Hardangervidda, the largest mountain plateau in Norway, which still has large herds of wild reindeer; the tiny and beautiful wildflowers that grow around the hut and in which he takes such delight; the joy he gets from appreciating how each rock he picks up is a unique individual with its own story to tell. These and so many other things are part of Naess's living Ecosophy T, with Tvergastein as their home place. Perhaps because of his interest in and study of the rocks of the area, Naess is sometimes referred to as the Stones' Philosopher, the title of a documentary made about him by Bullfrog Films.

Over the long years, Naess has developed a very deep and extensive identification with this whole place and knows its geology, its history, and its relationships to the Jotunheimen, Norway's highest mountains immediately to the north. All of this is interwoven with his love of the mountains and his extensive climbing experience in Norway and around the world. This is his home place with which he has a deep identification. We discussed this process of wider and deeper identification while I was visiting him at his hut. He mentioned that he did not mean anything technical by this use of *identification*. He has seen this same process at work among people living in different cultures and places. In his writings, he refers to this process as developing from a healthy, well-integrated ego to a social self and then beyond that to what he calls the metaphysical self. In his ecology writings, he uses the words "ecological self" to refer to the metaphysical self.[41]

Having an extended sense of identification leads us to say that we defend our home place as part of ourselves. We identify with the ecological community that the place is part of, and we feel that the beings in our community are our companions and friends, with whom we have symbiotic relationships. To develop this sense of extended self is a natural process of maturing, and it does not destroy our ego but helps moderate earlier tendencies to be self-centered in the narrow sense. When we care for our place and others, we come to identify with their needs and well-being, and we have a greatly enhanced and larger sense of community and interdependence. Our well-being and that of our community are closely aligned. Thus, Naess says, we naturally and spontaneously care for our place and seek to protect it. For this we do not need a moral axiology, a set of rules or enforcements held over us to force us to act. We are able to act beautifully with expansive grace, gratitude, and generosity. This brings us deep knowledge of others and a great sense of joy that can expand indefinitely. We also enjoy a higher quality of life, which does not depend on material consumption. It enables us to have a fine and joyful life by living in a very simple and appreciative way, in harmony with others and nature.

Warwick Fox suggests that those, including Naess, whose ultimate premises call for an extended sense of identification with an ecological self be called *transpersonal ecologists*, but Naess would say that they have transpersonal ecosophies.[42] Fox says that the emphasis on *self*-realization leads to exploring all levels of awareness, from the pre-personal (sentient and reactive) to the personal (cognitive and deliberative) to the transpersonal (wise and reciprocally responsive). In extending our sense of identification and care, and in opening our capacity to love, we flourish and realize ourselves in harmony with others. We come to understand, as Naess says, that our own self-realization is interconnected with the self-realization of others, including other beings. We cannot flourish and realize ourselves if we destroy others' homes and otherwise interfere with their possibilities for self-realization.

Naess's way of thinking, experiencing, and acting in the world with an extended sense of self-identification and expansion of care to the small details of daily life, transcending small ego self, is a deepening, transformative process that he humbly calls becoming more mature. Some other supporters of the deep ecology movement use this same type of extension of identification in approaching their own ecosophy. When they translate this into their own practices, there are some subtle differences from Naess's version, and that is good. You can get a sense for this practice by asking yourself, "What is the most expansive sense of self-identification that I care for?" Some people readily feel that they identify with their place and land. This is true for many people in tribal cultures. In contrast, the self in modernism is confined to the individualistic lone ego. It does not identify with the land, tribe, or wild beings, but with a small, conditioned sense of historical self. Naess invites us to also explore our greater, deeper ecological self and shows us how to do it.

Deep ecology movement supporters, as noted earlier, have articulated ultimate philosophies based on such religious worldviews as Buddhism,

Confucianism, Shinto, Hinduism, Islam, Neo-paganism, and Shamanism. Many have said their interpretation of these spiritual traditions emphasizes humility, love for others, and respectful treatment of *all beings*. Mahayana Buddhism, Shinto, and Taoism *explicitly* stress respect for other beings and emphasize that we should live in harmony with, and in gratitude to, them and nature. All beings have Buddha nature, *Kami* occur throughout all of nature, and so on. We are dependent on all our relations, not just our human ones, for who we are and for our long-term survival.

If you have no religious or tribal background, then, as Naess suggests, you can create your own ultimate philosophy based on ecocentric principles, values, and norms. You can call your own personal philosophy Ecosophy X, where for the X, you can use whatever name feels best to you. It could be a descriptive name or a name from your place. A person could work in his or her own place where an ecosophy is learned, practiced, and shared. It then becomes a place with increasing ecological harmony and wisdom, and it can be given a special name. For example, we could call it our "ecostery." We work in a particular place to live our unique ecosophy, and as we do, our homes become harmonious dwelling places. We never stop learning or adapting in this process, as Naess shows in his experimental approach to Ecosophy T and the way he lives at Tvergastein under the extreme conditions found there. When in the city, he uses many of the same gentle, conserving methods that he uses in Tvergastein.

The old Norwegian farms all have a name that is retained for generations, giving the farm a meaningful identity. The people who look after these farms identify with them, and as mentioned earlier, they take the name of the farm: When adults move to these farms, they often take the name of the farm as their surname, even today. These farms have a character, a transgenerational life with meaning. They are in many ways multigenerational places with their own identity and life. In a similar way, we can imbue our own home place with such meaning through a variety of daily practices. Naess seriously considered changing his surname so that he would be called Arne Tvergastein.

A person can fail to identify with an ecological community, when he or she identifies too narrowly with an insecure, small ego-self. Sometimes, expanding one's awareness beyond ego requires painful self-examination and self-criticism, therapy, and extended healing and support. A principal norm for a transpersonal ecosophy could be Naess's N2 (norm 2): "Self-realisation for all living beings!" Used as an ultimate norm, it leads to nonviolence, humility, and gratitude. We encourage others to flourish and realize themselves.

As self-reflective ecosophers, we make choices for a better *quality* of life, instead of merely going for a higher standard of living, as measured by money, fame, power, and other things. How can we realize the higher quality of values while using less material and energy? An inquiry into our ultimate values and beliefs about the nature of our wild energies leads us to seek the sacred, spiritual dimensions of daily life, with many options for expanding our understanding, compassion, and range of positive actions and active feelings. This shift leads to a different *quality of experience*. Ecophilosophy explores the rich complexity of qualitative appreciation found not only in human communities in concert with others, but also in places of wild free nature.

Many Diverse Ecosophies

Naess invites us to create our own ecosophies inspired by commitment to the deep ecology platform principles. We do not have to wait for the experts and mainstream organizations in order to act on our own. We each can do something of long-term importance on a regular basis, starting today. Many people and groups are developing their personal ecosophy as their way to live richly in harmony with others and the natural world. There is a diversity of ecosophies that reflects the individual and ecological diversity of the self-organizing creative powers found in people and other beings everywhere. We are more effective when we have a sense of wholeness through an integrated total view.

Many people have coincidentally developed ecosophies very similar to Naess's. Their ecosophies are based on the practice of *extended identification, increased awareness, and care for their ecological self*. For example, Matthew Fox's version of *creation spirituality* (which has a long history as a minority tradition in Christianity and should not be confused with Creationism) can be seen as a transpersonal ecosophy using Christian practices of love and humility to find the spirit of Christ revealed in the ongoing creation of the world.[43] *Christ* is interpreted as this creative power that we can feel, participate in, and should revere. This interpretation gives us an expansive communal sense of self overflowing with the spirit of compassion. It gives us joy and light. It is closely related to an early Gnostic Christian spiritual tradition called the Way of Light. Divinity is found everywhere, within and without.

We can learn from the wisdom of our home places (as Naess shows in his life at Tvergastein) and from the many beings who inhabit them. The comprehensive and inclusive value systems compatible with the platform can help us see that all cultures have a mutual interest in caring for the earth with all its diversity. We want it to continue for its own sake and because we love it. Most people want to flourish and realize themselves in harmony with other beings and cultures, not at the expense and suffering of others. It is possible to develop common understandings that enable us to work together with civility to achieve harmony with other creatures and beings. The deep ecology platform principles can help us move in this direction. *Respect for diversity* (the second principle) can lead us in time to recognize how ecological wisdom grows out of specific actions in unique places and contexts. Thus, in developing their ecosophies, supporters of the deep ecology movement stress place-specific ecological wisdom and vernacular technology practices.[44] *No one philosophy or technology is applicable to the whole planet.* Our diversity is a celebration of the unique creativity of life and its many beings.

As Naess makes clear, ecological wisdom is not just knowledge and information. It involves intuition and insight that energizes our spirits, minds, feelings, and senses with unified understanding. It gives us an embodied *sense* for our ecos and place. Since we are always learning more about ourselves, other beings, relationships, places, and contexts, our sensibilities are constantly modified by new discoveries; our actions are thus guided by awareness of our ignorance and limitations. Precautionary principles are wisely applied. Abstract knowledge is not sufficient for a full life. Aspects of nature and the cosmos will always be a mystery to us. Living our ecosophy is a deep, long-term commitment to our home place; our narrative traditions and practical activities are within our place and include its ecological communities. We do not try to control the world. We do not abstract ourselves from the living world around us.

One way to realize ecosophy is to live day by day with *increasing mindfulness* so as to harmonize all our relationships with other humans, the animals, plants, rivers, and rocks. How we do this will vary from person to person and place to place. We should "live and let live," as Naess likes to say. Modifying our lifestyles a little at a time, day by day, can make for major changes over the long term. Many meditations, ceremonies, celebrations, rituals, and other practices can help us deepen our respect for, and commune with, the wild energies of nature and the spirits of our places. We can become inspired to act beautifully, doing more than our share and giving back more to the earth than we take. Our own quality of life deepens when we give and share. We each receive from the earth gifts that enable us to live, and we each can give gifts back to the earth so that others can thrive.

Through these and many other practices, our sense of self matures from ego-centered to a more inclusive sense of ecological self as we identify with our ecological community. This more mature self-identification generates deeper respect for other beings and nature as we open more of the dimensions of valuing awareness. Mindful practice brings our ecosophy alive from moment to moment. Love and care live only in the present. This opens our awareness to the deep past and our concern for the distant future for many generations. Ecosophies have earth-based values of their home places that are a common ground for people to meet and learn from each other. Diverse ecosophies add to ecological complexity, create greater richness, and result in a higher quality of life. Through them we can enjoy friendship with each other, companionship with other beings, community, and the joy of living deeply and well. That is Naess's sense of unity and diversity in his total view.

Section 1:

PLACES IN THE REAL WORLD

An Example of a Place: Tvergastein

THE GLOBAL PLACE-CORROSIVE PROCESS

When the majority of people were living off the land, with little mobility, it was natural to feel at home at certain places. One stayed at home, left home, or went home. But home was not a building. The advertising of homes to be bought is not an offer of a home in the connotation relevant in our analysis. Home was where one belonged. Being "part of myself," the idea of home delimited an ecological self, rich in *internal* relations to what is now called environment. But humanity today suffers from a place-corrosive process.

Urbanization, centralization, increased mobility (although nomads have proven that not all sorts of moving around destroy the relation of belonging somewhere), the dependence on goods and technologies from where one does not belong, the increase of structural complication of life—all these factors weaken or disrupt the steady belongingness to a place, or even hinder its formation. There seems to be no place for PLACE anymore.

But the loss of place is felt, the longing persists, and so we feel the need to articulate what it means to belong to a place. The movement toward the development of a sense of place is strengthened through a tightening of the interrelation between the self and the environment. This movement is of prime importance in the deep ecology movement. Most supporters of the deep ecology movement are intimately acquainted with urbanization, which actually facilitates the capacity to think globally. People who are completely absorbed in the land have no need for high levels of abstraction and articulation, nor the training to make their *implicit* global attitudes a basis for action.

The implicit global attitude does, sometimes, show itself in action. In the

1950s, when people were asked to contribute money to help fisheries in the south of India, the nonurbanized, relatively poor people in the extreme Arctic of Norway contributed the most. But, of course, what is of most importance to these nonurban people is their homestead. It is clear that only the destruction of fisheries through overkill, and the consequent destruction of local and provincial markets, would make them consider leaving their homestead, their *hjemsted* (home-place).

It is important that those who have experienced the place-corrosive process but who somehow have saved their belongingness to a place (at least in somewhat modified form) should tell others about how their sense of place survived. This may help others to strengthen their motivations. And it may also strengthen and purify the way those who feel they still belong somewhere act out their chosen way of life and priorities.

This introduction may seem somewhat bombastic in relation to my discussion of Tvergastein. Not many people are in the position, or would have the inclination, to identify with a place like Tvergastein. But the development of a place in which a person feels at home and feels a sense of belonging shows exceptionally clearly some of the forces at work in the establishment of a place (or perhaps I should say, "establishment of a place as a Place"). Unfortunately, the reader will have to consider some autobiographical details about how I came to look toward Tvergastein as my future place.

GEOGRAPHY

About 200 kilometers east of Bergen there are two great landmarks, the Hardangerjøkul (a dome-shaped glacier about 80 square kilometers, a remnant of when Norway, like Greenland, was covered with ice) and Hallingskarvet (a 40-kilometer long, broad mountain running from east to west). Hallingskarvet is composed of hard, eruptive rocks that were laid bare millions of years ago through the erosion of softer mountains. From its southeastern slopes, one may survey an enormous part of southern Norway (tens of thousands of square kilometers). On these slopes, we find a place called Tvergastein, 1,500 meters above sea level, with a lake named Tvergasteintjernet. Softer rocks have been protected by the overlaying hard, 200-meter, near-vertical part of Hallingskarvet.

The stupendous, majestic Hallingskarvet captured my imagination from the time I was about five years old. For Easter and the summers of my early years, I stayed in a cottage at Ustaoset, a tiny village about 8 kilometers from the mythogenic mountain where I developed my place.

In documents, *Tvergastein* is the name of the cottage at Tvergastein, the place. In terms of geography, the place is the name of the cottage *and* its immediate surroundings, that is, about 50 feet in all directions from the walls of the cottage. But a wider usage, referring to a greater gestalt, treats the place as comprising the lake, Tvergasteintjernet, and a whole shelf on the slopes of Hallingskarvet as seen from the cottage (which is situated straight under the precipices of Hallingskarvet). Geographically, this is an area a couple of kilometers long and rich in contrasts. Compared to the region of *seter*, "mountain pastures," it is a world apart, reflecting the Arctic conditions at 1,500 meters altitude and 60.5 degrees north, and very different from the 1,000-meter level below (Arctic, yes, but influenced by the Gulf Stream from the west). From Tvergastein, the mountains and glaciers around the great Hardangerfjord are clearly seen—and appreciated.

Even from a distance, Hallingskarvet looks greenish, but is clearly not the result of grass. The place asked to be studied, and the greenish cliffs asked to be recognized as such. But when observed closely, it revealed innumerable patches of beautiful green lichen. The Tvergastein Naturalist Library revealed that a particular species, *Geographicus,* was responsible for the green color. There were lots of other lichens, but they were not identified, because their identification required the use of a microscope. Nevertheless, the surface of the most "barren" parts of the visible surface of Hallingskarvet was alive, even in the narrow sense of consisting of organisms—myriads of lichens on every square foot. The lichens are strangely connected beings: algae intimately interrelated with fungi. A still stranger connection: algae, fungi, humans.

In the summer mornings (at three or four o'clock), the huge shadow of Hallingskarvet keeps the southern and western landscape sleeping in semi-darkness. But already by five o'clock, the sunshine brightens hundreds of small lakes and tiny patches of water on the plains below Tvergastein, and by about seven, the sun appears over the mountain and penetrates the east window of the library, hitting a wooden plate painted stark black, thus contributing to the heating up of the small room.

The early morning sun also lightens up a faraway (thirty miles long) string of metallic electric masts and thick wires—hydroelectric power destined for Oslo, two hundred miles away. Each mast is an elegant structure revealing much love and ingenuity on the part of the engineers, but such a string of masts transforms the landscape. If only a few mountainous landscapes were changed in this way—why complain and feel sorrow? But the number of landscapes without these strange beings diminishes rapidly. There are now more than two million gigantic masts around. The masts would have a less disturbing character if the power was used to increase the quality of life. But to a large extent, the power is wasted, which contributes to making people unaware of their fantastic material richness. What does a gallon of boiling water mean in the cities? Nothing. At Tvergastein, it is a formidable luxury, enough to satisfy a host of essential services, a gift of nature of the most astonishing character.

FLOWERS

When one arrives at Tvergastein from below, all flowers may seem so small, inconspicuous, unspectacular, poor, insignificant. Let us say we point to green patches of *Salix herbacea* (mouse ears). If we say, "Look!" some people would answer, "What? What do you see?" They see tiny, unspectacular leaves like ears of mice (*musøre*). These plants ("huddling together") rarely grow one inch from the rock—you see no soil. In front of the cottage, they grow half an inch tall. Of course, they are not huddling together; they are probably having a very good life together. Their flowers—hardly detectable without an observer's squatting down near the plant—are well formed, their reddish nuts very conspicuous after a while.

This plant seems to delight in tiny cracks in the stony ground—cracks sometimes much less than an inch wide. It joins the lichens and "dominates" where no organic life is capable of having a good time. *Salix herbacea* seems to be everywhere at Tvergastein. We walk on the plants without the slightest regret. We make soup of them without thinking about extinction or interference with their habitat.

Whereas we humans only gradually come to appreciate the "mouse-ears," some tiny creatures, a kind of wasp, make red, applelike "houses" on the mouse-ears. If we open the walls of the "house," we see a tiny, white "worm" (larva), which will probably die from exposure. But, as the larvae are so tiny, we don't care very much. Why can't we inspect one of the million interesting red dots on the leaves? Note our ineradicable inconsistency! When interested, I would still (after writing about this "cruelty") disturb such worms.

There are fraction-of-an-inch flowering plants of unsurpassed beauty—the *Gentiana nivalis,* with a typically ethnocentric Nordic name: "Jesus blue eyes." In the most authoritative botanical reference work, that of Johannes Lid, the height of the flower is given as seven centimeters, nearly three inches! Most of the specimens in front of the cottage are less than one centimeter. But the dark blue color is so intense that, if you happen by the small groups of *Gentiana nivalis* on a windless, sunny day in late July, the flowers look incredible and clamor for your attention. Unfortunately (or perhaps fortunately, for the sake of the plant), there are few such days, and in most days of late July, the flowers are closed. The plant is then difficult to find. And the rest of the year—where is it? The plant lives only one year. In order not to become extinct at Tvergastein, the plant must somehow start a new generation from its seeds in July of the next year (or the following July after that, if the next July is cold). Obviously, the existence of the plant at Tvergastein is precarious.

Other flowers are typical Arctic plants, like *Dryas octopetala* ("reindeer rose"). The species has big, beautiful, white flowers—often bigger than the rest of the plant. The plants thrive even where there is no soil to be seen, keeping together so that several hundred might occupy a single square meter. Still richer with white flowers is a square meter of well-shaped, downy-haired *Cerastium alpinum*. More than six hundred specimens of *Cerastium* (between three and four inches tall) filled one square meter at a spot near the famous windy northeast corner of the cottage, a sight of overwhelming richness!

Before leaving the "tiny" flowers, I must mention a particularly delicate, beautiful, and modest plant, *Cassiope hypnoides*. Thousands of these tiny plants create a carpet of green with white spots. The flower's shape is misleading, bending as if unworthy of looking at us. The plant has fragility but no weakness, flowering even in dry summers in spite of its shallow roots and when there is no soil to be seen. It does not creep, but turns its stem straight out into the air—even as high as an inch.

Compared with some of the small flowers, a kind of dandelion (*Taraxacum alpinum* and similar Arctic species) looks at first glance not only crude, but squarely indecent. It need not be higher than an inch, but produces a flower two inches in circumference. But to be just, the "flower" is really a basket of flowers, about a hundred of them. From its seeds, each dangling from a parachute, we should all understand that the "flower" is a luxurious basket.

Upon arriving at Tvergastein, you find that not only a few easily changeable attitudes have to be more or less unconsciously modified. Everything is different from Ustaoset (eight kilometers away) and vastly different from the coast (fifty kilometers to the west). Conversely, the adjustment again to the sea coast (not to mention much farther south to the tropical rain forests) is immense, if not terrifying. The flora scream at you. A rose is seen as a caricature of beauty. A tree is unnecessarily tall, grossly overdone, obstructing your alpine freedom of movement. At Tvergastein, attitudes and personality change, at least temporarily. After one week, there is a noticeable difference;

three weeks—that is a very good stay. The last two weeks, the effects of mere contrast are largely gone. You are genuinely *there*. You are not seeing things through glasses from somewhere else. After a month or two, getting back down, and to town, is exciting but painful, harassing.

The distribution of snow is peculiar in windy Arctic mountainous landscapes. If asked, "What is the snow depth at Tvergastein now?" there is no answer. There is no definite thickness, no small area with even distribution. The wind shapes the snow. After a strong wind from the west, there may be two meters of snow east of the east wall. But if "the same wind" reaches hurricane force, all the snow is carried away. There is no snow anywhere near the cottage. There is practically no snow *anywhere* at Tvergastein, even in January. But not far away, five to ten meters of snow might fill a wind-protected valley or gully. This makes skiing in August possible!

There is a highly romantic consequence of the uneven distribution of snow. On some normally snowless protruding cliffs with tiny cracks, a "tiny" flower, which tolerates freezing coldness, uses the light and occasional twenty-hour sunshine to bloom in the middle of May. It is the famous *Saxifraga oppositifolia*, so well-known and so cherished in the Arctic. It is the very first flower in spring, and its red color stands out vividly in a world of snow and rock at Tvergastein. And so, you go skiing and at the same time enjoy the flowery season. Further down (1,200–1,000 meters down), there are no flowers; they appear much later in the season (one reason is that the soil is deeper and frost keeps it rock-hard).

In the precipices of Hallingskarvet, above Tvergastein, the *Saxifraga* also occur in May. The rays of the sun heat up the rocks. When the sun stands at twenty degrees above the horizon, the plants on seventy-degree cliffs (with a minimum of soil) are enjoying rays coming in at a ninety-degree angle—again, a story of the special quality of the Arctic mountain climate. There are beautiful flowers combined with below-freezing temperatures, a hot sun warming the cliffs, and deep, crystalline, new snow in protected areas. With this story about *Saxifraga oppositifolia*, a hero that may even have survived the ice age in Norway, we close our discussion of flowering plants.

ANIMALS

Many animals live at Tvergastein and belong there. The mountain mice deserve to be mentioned first. Soon after the cottage was built, some mouse families established themselves under the cottage. Later, when the cottage was enlarged, they were welcome to the big western room. Sometimes a family makes a nest there, but mostly they just like to investigate everything in peace and at their leisure. The mice have access to other rooms only upon special invitation. They are never invited to the kitchen.

When a human being enters their room, the mice hide for a couple of minutes, disturbed by the excessive noise, but then go on with their business. Sometimes the human occupiers of the place do not like them to nibble or eat certain things. It is a joy to find out how to limit the mice's access to these things.

When caught, the Tvergastein mice reveal an astonishing diversity of character. Some are very shy, others more easily pacified. One likes to rest on the downy slippers of the human occupier—something that made the person's moving around very awkward. Another mouse is mainly interested in climbing and other sports; another is a great eater but shows few other interests. Still another is far more inquisitive and alert. Most Tvergastein mice tend to bite when handled, making small, neat holes in the fingers. Better not "caress" them!

The mice are at home all the way to the top plateau of Hallingskarvet, that is, as high as there are shelves with vegetation. In wintertime, their nests under the snow keep them warm, at least above freezing temperatures.

After the mice, the reindeer should be mentioned. From time to time, as long as there is snow around Tvergastein, herds of reindeer, one hundred to five hundred individual reindeer, appear near the cottage. One evening, the leaders decided they had been traveling enough and lay down between the cottage and the precipices. Most of the others leisurely lay down behind the leaders. But some restless youngsters kept on moving and lay down in front of the leaders, who had to get up and place themselves ahead of their insubordinates. This happened again, but then the leaders did not bother. One should not take the youngsters too seriously.

Among the carnivores, the *Mustela erminea* (ermine) is exceedingly popular, but rarely seen. If seen, it tends to jump around from rock to rock with unbelievable elegance, speed, and tenacity. Exhibitionism? The tiny *Mustela nivalis* (least weasel) is just as unpopular as its relative, *M. erminea*, is popular: It is capable of getting through the established official mice entrances into the cottage and can track the rodents down under the cottage. The result: indiscriminate slaughter. Now there have been no mice for about three years. The place is not as it should be without mice children carefully inspecting the world outside the cottage every morning for some seconds and then running with lightning speed back to safety.

The sight of the strong, sinister *Gulo gulo* (wolverine) is very rare, and bears have not been seen around Hallingskarvet since the twentieth century. What's more, it is too high for them to live here. Neither *Gulo gulo* nor bears belong here. But several big birds do—the *Haliaeetus albicilla* (ocean eagle) being the biggest and most regal. If the nest is above, or near, the mountain-climbing routes behind the cottage, the male may treat the climber to an exquisite dive, keeping wings close to its body, and aiming at the intruder's head. It turns away just above the head at the first dive, then gets less interested and impressive, turning away much too soon. Once, the human occupier of Tvergastein felt the bird had shouted, "Abominable!" after a really bad dive. Anyhow, we do not approach their nests.

All in all, compared with the richness and diversity of big animals—animals bigger than mice—in mountains in milder climates, the diversity and numbers of big animals around Tvergastein are poor. This is scarcely because of human interference, I suppose. Lots of ptarmigan are shot, but it is said, apparently with some supporting evidence, that this is not a main reason for the bird's scarcity.

GENESIS OF A PLACE-PERSON

How did we, who belong to a place, get to belong there in spite of not being raised there and not having always lived there? Here is one example of the genesis of a place-person, reconstructed from sometimes inevitably speculative evidence.

My father, who died a year after I was born, had a small cottage above the timberline (one thousand meters above sea level) at Ustaoset, a station on the railway between Oslo and Bergen. From the time I was a small boy, my mother, sister, and two brothers (five, ten, and eleven years older than I) lived in the cottage in summertime and at Easter.

Largely rejecting my mother and sister as persons to imitate, I was happiest when my brothers played with me, sometimes in a rough way. When I was still only five or six years old, for instance, they had great fun on a cold, windy day at Easter seeing whether the wind could physically push me up a small hill on skis. Their love was particularly manifest, or so I thought, when I was on the verge of crying because of their wild ways of playing. Perhaps I felt loved mainly through such play.

The steam engine of the train carrying us from below to above the timberline barely managed to do the job. The grade was steep. The vast world above the trees, and the process of getting through the timberline, made an impression so profound and so deeply gratifying that it left an intense longing to get back to that vast world just as soon as I was again in my usual surroundings—a big house on a fairly large, partly forested property in the hilly suburbs of Oslo.

The dense landscape I could see from my window in Oslo was completely dominated by big, dark spruce trees with branches that sorrowfully pointed slightly downward. On windy days, these sinister trees rocked slowly back and forth, murmuring what I would much later articulate as "Damned, damned, you are damned, damned." The feeling of being imprisoned and damned was vivid. It reflected a not entirely happy life situation I need not discuss here. But I mention the fateful trees blocking the view because the contrast with the free view above the timberline is obvious.

Whatever the influences, the experience of elevation (of moving from darkness to light, from being hemmed in to a life in a seemingly unlimited and friendly world) was so strong that I attached myself too much to this free-floating longing for the land beyond and above the forests. It promised to be a land of freedom beyond anything imaginable lower down. This is what I felt living at my parents' mountain cottage.

Along the distant horizon toward the north lived the massive Hallings-karvet. It looked different every day while still retaining its supreme poise. When a visitor greeted it some August morning, it might suddenly have turned white from autumn snow, sometimes from the summit plateau down to 1,500 meters, sometimes all the way down to its foot, at 1,200 meters. This is one of the grand characteristics of great mountains: to turn brilliant white in the summer.

This faraway, supreme, powerful, serene, distant, beautiful mountain gradually gained in status, revealing itself to me as the benevolent, protect-ing father or even divine being. I made Hallingskarvet into the symbol of everything good that was lacking in the world and in myself. When still a boy, I was able to reach its knees; later, I roamed around on its shoulders and on the vast summit plateau with its surface of big, greenish rocks rounded through erosion.

It became a great dream to stay *on* the mountain—not compelled to get down before darkness or because of rain and thunderstorms. And in 1937, when I was twenty-five years old, I chose the best possible place to build a cottage: not too high or difficult to reach for transporting materials over snow, but high enough on the flank of Hallingskarvet for me to feel that I was living on the mountain and to have a superb view of a large part of Norway through the window.

A friend at Ustaoset who had a horse promised to transport enough material for a very sturdy wooden cottage eight by five meters big. He told me that he needed fifteen trips to get the material up to the site of the cottage. Because of the difficult terrain and uneven snow, it actually took sixty-two trips. "Madness!" was the judgment of people at Ustaoset: the highest private cottage in Northern Europe and in a climate unsuitable for "normal" cottage life.

HUMAN LIFE AT TVERGASTEIN

After staying a while, one realizes that Tvergastein is teeming with life. In summer and early autumn, even the snow slopes become alive, turning reddish from the great populations of the green alga *Chlamydomonas nivalis* (the red pigment is the same one found in salmon). And, after a while, we get a much more realistic view of the excellent living conditions at such Arctic places. Even ecologists sometimes talk about "extreme," "destitute," "difficult," "marginal," "poor," "stressful," "disadvantaged," "harsh," and even "hostile" conditions of life in this place. This is improper, shameful language! Some species of flowers don't become as tall as lower down, but what has tallness got to do with well-being? Where the living beings use the excellent microclimate close to soil, and behind rocks, why bother to climb high into the atmosphere? Most flowers at Tvergastein simply dislike rich soil. Some flourish where no soil is seen. The lichens and mosses grow big and dominate, even where snow covers the ground nine to ten months of the year. *Ranunculus glacialis* (glacier buttercup) grows large and fat at such places, and nowhere else. The snow does not hurt things; it makes life sleep and wait. Admittedly, in winter, there is not much life to be seen, but mammals, like the fox, know where to push away snow and find mice and lemmings. In short, there is generally nothing wrong with life at Tvergastein. But what about humans?

The choice of geographical place was based on a more or less set of requirements, but now the question was, What would the place require of me? What kind of lifestyle, activities, and ceremonies would be appropriate for this place? What would be a life worthy of Hallingskarvet and in solidarity with, and respect for, the other life-forms?

The difficulty and cost of transporting things by horse, together with the obvious peculiarities of the place, clearly suggested a simple lifestyle with maximum self-reliance. Clumsy attempts on my part to produce some vegetables were complete failures. Of the plants, only the mouse-ear was both edible and sufficient in quantity to serve the human occupier of the cottage.

Hunting was possible further down, but distasteful. In short, I had to rely on "importing" things, mostly by rucksack.

The question of heating the cottage was central. But the few junipers at 1,400 to 1,500 meters were small and rarely more than two to five inches high. Obviously, they should be protected, living precariously at the upper limits of their reach. Again, the obvious solution was to import. So there were two major unpleasant conclusions. There was no question of living on the land by the land.

But what about wind power? Inquiries suggested that because of the terrific downslope winds from the precipices of Hallingskarvet, the windmills would have to be specially built and of great bulk. I reluctantly gave up this idea. Solar power was a possibility, but here also, there are complications to overcome.

In 1937, a little firewood was transported by horse, and during the war, by rucksack. Then storms more or less regularly carried away major parts of the roof, despite increasing conservation measures, including cables to hold the roof down. This roof loss, however, resulted in a splendid by-product: enough wood for austere use of firewood through the end of the century!

In an attempt to trace the psychological and social determiners of my professional philosophy, some key terms stand out—*unruffledness, equanimity, austerity, distance, aloofness, nonviolence, diversity, egalitarianism*. Most of them seemed to help in forming a lifestyle appropriate to the place.

Several lifestyle issues had to be addressed as I set up my home in Tvergastein:

Temperature: obviously very low inside the cottage. But below nine degrees Celsius, everything gets wet, including paper, and the interesting fungi thrive *too well*. A marvelous effect of low indoor temperature for weeks or months is the increased blood circulation near the surface of the skin. A person enjoys a feeling of physical activeness and fitness as if after a hike outside. But during short stays, it is not possible to adapt completely. And so in 1960, I succumbed to a revolution: the acceptance of a rule not to let the temperature drop below fourteen degrees Celsius. The temperature is much lower only in the morning, but on the increase.

Rooms heated: normally only one room, 2.5 by 2.5 meters. In this room, there is space enough for two, but it is a little strenuous for a family life of three or four.

Food: simple, nourishing. My appetite is inevitably strong.

Keeping warm: If one slowly gets uncomfortable, engage in some strenuous exercise. Five minutes of very vigorous muscular movement is
enough to heat the human body. A person occupies less than 1 percent of the volume of the room. Why heat more than 99 percent just
to heat that little volume?

Indoor occupations: research, reading, writing. The usual housework is
kept to a minimum. Another occupation: listening to the wind and
other kinds of music.

Given that the transporting of food and other essentials is fairly complicated, the reuse concept is central. It is amusing to make extended and
surprising use of everything brought in. An important result regarding the
quality of life is that everything brought in is looked upon as having more
value than before. Hence, one experiences an increasing feeling of quality
and richness.

Water carried by hand from sources two hundred to three hundred meters
away becomes more valuable. It is important to remember that many calo-
ries are needed to melt snow (i.e., a temperature increase from minus one to
plus one degree Celsius). For the last twenty years, I have found water under
the deep snow but *above* the thick ice along the shore of Lake Tvergastein.
Consequently, we carry water from there instead of melting snow. I am surprised that other cottage people don't know about the presence of such water
under deep snow along the shores of lakes.

When a person who has *grown up* in a city *grows into* a nonurbanized personal place, how does this affect his friends and relatives? Obviously, there
are sources of tension and personal tragedies—or the extension of influence
so that one's nearest friends and family also establish a relationship with the
same place. For thirty years, there was no serious problem of this kind associated with living at Tvergastein. My closest family and friends approved of
the area and its lifestyle. With increasing mobility and other factors, steady
life in good company at Tvergastein was getting less frequent. Evidently, the
more peculiar and isolated a place, the fewer are the chances to establish
satisfactory social relationships. It is impossible to deny that the climate of
Tvergastein challenges the main outdoor activities of hiking, skiing, and
climbing. More than the low temperatures, the high winds demand tough-
ness and hardiness. With increasing age, fewer people are able or willing to
adapt. Big storm number eleven is not as romantic as the first ten.

What is remarkable about Tvergastein and similar places is their capacity to furnish the basis of a life of simplicity of means and richness of ends.

The richness of ends depends on a place's evolution from just a location to a very special personal place. With increasing intensity of commitment, the place will satisfy an increasing variety of needs and will allow for an increasing variety of cherished goals to be reached. The little time and effort spent on the simple means frees up time for dwelling in situations characterized by intrinsic values.

But, for most of us, the personal place cannot permanently satisfy every need. Perhaps the time spent there decreases over the years or is never more than a minor part of the year. This holds true for Tvergastein.

However, it is remarkable how a place, even when it is uninhabited most of the year, largely determines one's attitudes, one's likes and dislikes, and one's general outlook. One is caught up in the place, hopefully with good consequences, but inevitably causing some maladjustments in locality very different from the place.

A personal place occasionally tyrannizes, imposes itself, gives orders. To disobey these orders creates a feeling of guilt or weakness of character. This is unavoidable. Phenomenologically speaking, the orders given by the place and the orders given by oneself are inseparable. Only philosophies that impose a sharp subject-object dualism try to trace a border between the self and "its" geographical surroundings.

In psychology, the concept of superego is common, and using this terminology, one may say that the orders given by the place are parts of the orders given by the superego. This conceptualization is not incompatible with the concept of person-place.

One example is the disposal of trash. In the 1930s, given the geographical remoteness of Tvergastein from human habitation and the mild norms among people enjoying cottage life, solid trash was placed beyond a moderately large rock 150 meters from the cottage. For twenty years, the trash was the object of joyful study because of the enormous number of interesting changes of the flora within a meter of the trash. One plant, *Cerastium alpinum*, benefited tremendously and multiplied and grew to inordinate size, at least five inches. Further, the delicate alpine and Arctic grasses were largely suppressed by coarser, darker species. There were at least one hundred clearly discernible changes within the radius of one meter. Outside this area, no change was seen.

Liquid trash was placed nearer the cottage in a crack between two smaller stones. The effect was the same, but on a grander scale. There was a new world of excessive growth, luxurious, but clearly foreign to the general character of the landscape.

But there were problems. Big, solid things fell to pieces—often smashed when carried away by the wind—which necessitated some kind of burying ground. This was found in deep black holes between enormous boulders in a region without any life-forms except lichens.

Then came the 1960s with the environmental conflicts. Evidently, those engaged in the battle to clean up trash *everywhere* had to be very careful with what they did themselves. So a disagreeable situation arose. More and more trash was carried down the mountain in rucksacks and sometimes transported all the way to Oslo.

The trash example illustrates many relations of importance:

1. "With increasing quantity, quantity changes into quality." This Hegelian slogan is admirably illustrated. With an increasing quantity of trash, it sooner or later degrades a wild place, a mountain, a landscape. But before this happens, when quantities are microscopic, the quality of a place is not disturbed. In environmental conflicts, we must conserve our sense of proportion.
2. The defenders of wild nature against further encroachments by humans tend to view any kind of trash (however diminutive in size or "innocent" in kind) as an evil. Of course, a piece of an orange peel has a color and coarse fabric that cries out as a foreign element in the Tvergastein landscape. But there are limits beyond which it begins to be ridiculous to demand a "cleaning up of the trash." In short: Beware of fanaticism; beware of allowing admirable feelings to run amok. Personal relations with antagonists in environmental conflicts should not be threatened by fanatical demands.
3. "Absolute consistency is impossible." Suppose we wholeheartedly accept the following: P_1: Remove trash from wild places! P_2: Tvergastein is a wild place. P_3: x is a piece of trash. P_4: x is at Tvergastein. C: Remove x!

What holds concerning the "remove-the-trash" norm holds as well for hundreds of other norms that are important in environmental conflicts. The formulations are short and, of course, vague and ambiguous to some extent. They have an indispensable function as slogans. To use logic before the formulations are made more precise is to ignore important aspects of slogans. But even after the formulations are reformulated, the formal logic of consistency, in any strict sense, is only moderately applicable, because of the nature of normative systems we cannot avoid. "All things hang together"—even in thinking! It is not here a question of the validity of the formal logic of consistency, but rather of the limitations of application in concrete situations.

CLIMBING

Classical European music consists of pieces of various degrees of difficulty to perform. In concerts, you are supposed to follow the notes of the compositions. But some nontraditional performers and improvisation by individuals or small bands are very popular today. There are professional musicians and amateur musicians, and the latter form the great majority of music lovers who do more than just listen. Similarly in dancing, there are highly structured, definite sequences of steps, but free improvisations are more popular than ever.

Climbing also offers definite routes of various degrees of difficulty on the one hand and the freedom to improvise on the other. Children climb stairs, chairs, and tables and advance to trees and boulders if any are available. No special equipment is used. Climbing on Hallingskarvet is more closely related to informal dancing, music improvisation, and childish play than to the climbing of established routes described in climbing guides. But let me be more specific about the Tvergastein variety, a fifty-year tradition of climbing.

Hallingskarvet has more than thirty kilometers of precipices, most of them between fifty and two hundred meters high and very steep. The rock itself is hard (eruptive), but there are often loose stones and moss. The rock's moss and loose stone covering and isolation from roads make it rarely visited by climbers. But the climbing, a fifteen- to twenty-minute walk from Tvergastein cottage, is excellent. Many routes are described, *but never published*. Some climbs were the most difficult done in Norway at the time they were first climbed. But improvisation is the rule.

Full security when climbing is axiomatic. There is no question of taking chances, not even the temptation to do so. But "full security from serious injury" is not the same as "absolute security" (the absence of the *possibility* of serious injury). It is as with skiing: Neither Tvergastein climbing nor skiing is "dangerous."

In Norway, climbing, but not skiing, is supposed to be dangerous. Why? Skiing, especially cross-country skiing, is part of the general culture, and the vast majority of skiers are not tempted to risk life or limbs (although sometimes limbs!). Though one always risks the *possibility* of getting seriously hurt, the joy of skiing does not derive from seeking extremes of physical challenge. Climbing, done by a small minority, *looks* very dangerous to most people. Whereas concern for safety when learning to ski is a subordinate theme, safety is rather central in climbing. But at Tvergastein, the result is the same as with skiing: full security.

It should be unnecessary to discuss the metaphysical background of mountain climbing.[1] It plays a role at Tvergastein, but so does the simple joy of rhythm and movement, of exciting challenges, and the appreciation of lichens, rocks and stones, flowers, animals, the sky.

The high precipice, a fifteen-minute walk from the cottage, has fairly broad shelves in its lower part. The exuberance of the vegetation is astonishing. Flowers are much taller than at the cottage and even farther down. Growing on the shelves are flowers that ordinarily grow only much further down (below one thousand meters above sea level). The reason is largely unknown to the public, but is very clear: The climate in the precipices of Hallingskarvet is generally much milder than below, because there is much less wind. Also, the effect of steepness is favorable to this growth. If the shelf is thirty degrees steep, the rays of the sun strike the vegetation at about a ninety-degree angle at this high latitude.

The nearness of the climbs, the informality, the fabulous view, the beautiful vegetation in between the sheer rock formations, and the milder climate all make it natural to go climbing rather often. In summertime, one *may* go climbing several times during the day, being away each time for a couple of hours or less. (Daylight is from three o'clock in the morning to ten at night.)

In short, climbing is normally integrated into life at Tvergastein, but it is a sort of climbing that differs from the risk- and competition-colored images of climbing propagated by the mass media.

TVERGASTEIN AMATEUR RESEARCH

It is difficult to separate unimportant biographical details from an adequate biographical description. The main thing is that a favored place relentlessly and remorselessly determines the details of one's life. It may enrich life, but may also lead to a manifold of habits and ways of thinking that are peculiar and a source of irritation to anybody not adapted to that special life. I find that attachment to places should not be praised uncritically.

Unlike some of my ecosophically inclined friends, I do not consider science and, above all, research incompatible with profound positive feelings toward nature. Tvergastein as "object" of botanical, zoological, mineralogical, meteorological, and other scientific research did not detract in the least from the immediate experience of togetherness, of identification and appreciation. On the contrary. In the great naturalist tradition, exemplified by the systematics (taxonomy) of butterflies, the motivation is not mainly cognitive, but conative. Feelings are just as much directing the search as is abstract thinking.

In Einstein's scientific thinking, which is very different from that of a typical naturalist, the external world as a field of lifelong research is essentially impersonal. The very impersonal character in part determined his strong motivation as a scientist:

> It is quite clear to me that the religious paradise of youth, which was thus lost, was a first attempt to free myself from the chains of the "merely-personal," from an existence which is dominated by wishes, hopes and primitive feelings. Out yonder there was this huge world, which exists independently of us human beings and which stands before us like a great, eternal riddle, at least partially accessible to our inspection and thinking. The contemplation of this world beckoned like a liberation, and I soon noticed that many a man whom I had learned to esteem and to admire had found inner freedom and security in devoted occupation with it.[2]

This way of liberation leads to abstract thinking and imagination of a special kind: "All our thinking is of this nature of a free play with concepts; the justification for this play lies in the measure of survey over the experience of the senses which we are able to achieve with its aid."

The way of liberation through "natural history" is different: very little abstract thinking, very much seeing, listening, hearing, touching. The secondary and especially the tertiary qualities are in focus—the worlds of concrete contents—not the primary qualities studied in physics.[3] There are worlds of minerals, rocks, rivers and tiny rivulets, plants, hardly visible animals or big ones (larger than a centimeter), plant and animal societies, tiny and great ecosystems—all more or less easily available for enjoyment, study, and contemplation. The meaningfulness inherent in even the tiniest living beings makes the amateur naturalist quiver with emotion. There is communication: The "things" express, talk, proclaim—without words. Within a few yards from the gnarled wooden walls of the Tvergastein cottage, there are rich and diverse changing worlds big enough to be entirely unsurveyable.

When I was only fifteen years old, I met the paleontologist Johan Kiær. We were in the Jotunheimen, a range that is home to the highest mountains in Norway. He was eager to tell about his exciting search for fossils in Svalbard (Spitsbergen). Clearly, he was engaged emotionally, telling how groups of animals trapped in ash from volcanic eruptions clung together in death. He was yearning for a closer understanding of evolution. Two years later, being permitted to use Norway's biggest library, I found thick volumes with beautiful drawings of one-celled organisms. Evidently, scientists were the only persons who really loved nature and life, attending to even the smallest forms of life with unbelievable accuracy! Poets did appreciate only a small fraction of living beings. It took me decades to get rid of this illusion about scientists and to understand that what I admired was only found among a small minority of them.

At Tvergastein, I could wholeheartedly engage in amateur research. Collections of stones were seen as the Tvergastein petrographical institute, a few quartz crystals and the like formed its mineralogical institute. Thanks to low indoor temperatures and poor ventilation, the institute of fungiology (mycology) had several branches. Temperatures in the kitchen in winter were below freezing, which resulted in interesting glacial formations down the walls. Glaciological institute! Hundreds of questions were formed, few were answered. This intensified wonder. This state of mind plus an appreciation of the richness and diversity of phenomena within reach seemed to be an essential trait of free research—however amateurish.

"To develop the taste and appreciation of what there is enough of"—this has always been a pillar of ecosophical education. With growing insight into the *limits of growth*, that is, growth of material production and interference, the educational motto is getting more important every year. With this introductory note, I shall describe more closely the new branch of amateur research—Tvergastein chemistry.

With a kerosene lamp at the work table close to my head, it was practicable to heat chemical solutions above the lamp and in clear view. The smooth waves of different colors in never-repeated variety cannot but make a profound impression on anybody who is willing to dwell on them. In short: The most elementary chemical processes reveal a fascinating world. Tvergastein chemistry requires very little raw material, very little heating. Boiling more than a few seconds is prohibited, because the room has little ventilation. Gases must be kept under strict control. In short, "the game" has rules that conform to strict ecosophical norms. There is one, and only one, *main* Tvergastein method of making exciting new chemical substances: mixing two substances that are soluble in water, with the more or less well-founded hope that a certain new, insoluble substance will appear. It is, however, somewhat difficult to get hold of fairly pure substances straight from nature. The valuable self-reliance of the Tvergastein institute of chemistry was severely undercut after a talk with the president of Oslo University, who happened to be a chemist. When expressing my concern about self-made, very impure chemicals at Tvergastein, he naturally was delighted to help create the new branch of (amateur) chemistry by offering me free access to the pure chemicals of his own institute. A helping hand from one institute to another!

Compromise and inconsistency! Consider for instance the 25 grams of bismuth trichloride I acquired—enough for twenty-five experiments at the level of Tvergastein ecological resource utilization. But the compound was presumably made by one of the worst polluting, gigantic chemical factories along the Rhine. I supported the poisoning of this magnificent river and added a little to the North Sea! Worse still, from an amateur point of view, the stuff had a ridiculously high level of purity. The level of arsenic contamination was *guaranteed* to be less than one part per million, for example. This implies that a great deal of energy from coal or gas had been used in a series of wasteful operations to clean the substance of any kind of impurities whatsoever. Such chemicals are far removed from nature: from cliffs to stones, from stones to minerals, from minerals to chemical separations, some of which are not found in free nature at all. There is nothing wrong with such new substances, but we may note the distance of their study from those of a consistent naturalist.

Whatever the inconsistencies, the Tvergastein chemistry is an example of something of central importance in the rich industrial society: to assist youth in the warm *appreciation* and understanding of basic natural processes such as beautiful solutions, miraculous transformation of some substance into others, and the re-creation of thousands of beautiful colors and dyes. Those who are offered the opportunity for such experiences are changed, their life quality enhanced. They can live with less dependence on what there is *not* enough of for all.

Unfortunately, the large-scale realization of ecoeducation requires a new politics, green politics, a politics that does not systematically favor people who concentrate mainly on getting more of what there is not enough of.

Taking naturalist science and research, professional or amateur, as the paradigm of science and research, ecosophies may without inconsistency hail these human undertakings. It is counterproductive, I think, to make *science* and *research* negative terms, dyslogisms. From the naturalist amateur researcher's point of view, there are immense opportunities at Tvergastein, as at other places. *Researcher* fits in with the concept of a personal place.

What can we learn from each other? Can tragic developments be avoided? The classic case of belonging to a place is that of being born and raised somewhere, just somewhere in a geographical sense, and then the place develops into the Place. But when the place is physically destroyed or unfit for living because of other factors, can a different place develop into the Place? Certainly it can, and this happened with the Tvergastein area. The same will happen to many people in the future—they experience a longing and a satisfaction that elicit such utterances as "Here is where I belong!" We may even be drawn to two places, and a conscious choice is possible. In such cases, certainly one thing can be inferred on the basis of experience at Tvergastein: Choose a place that is not so specific that it discourages your intimates. Furthermore, choose a place that you will be likely to be able to master when you are older. Then, this is a place where you can live and die.

Tvergastein is extreme in many ways and unfit for many purposes. The development could only be more or less tragic. But even so, it is difficult for us who have a place where we feel we belong not to be glad and grateful to have one. Why is this so? That is difficult to say.

Modesty and the Conquest of Mountains[4]

There are many ways of experiencing mountains. I would rather assert, how-ever, that mountains have innumerable aspects or, even better, that the term *mountain* may be used to designate vastly different entities. What I describe in the following pages are mountains. They are connected with what other people call mountains through some sort of interpersonal, social structure, a marvelous common frame of reference. Thus, I may locate the mountains I speak about, may give details about the minerals of which they are said to consist, may even discuss their age—all this without getting into trouble with identification. The common frame of reference, however, is not the mountains themselves—not the mountains I know. The motive here for try-ing to describe mountains as I know them is not the rather indifferent detail that I know them, but that many others know them the same way but do not always or consistently act upon their knowledge.

Now, what are they?

The words I use must come as an anticlimax, perhaps. They are very com-mon words, they are crude, and only the reader's intense willingness to go along with me can help me convey what I know.

Mountains are big, very big, but they are also great. Very great. They have dignity and other aspects of greatness.

They are solid, stable, unmoving. A Sanskrit word for them is *a-ga*, that which does not go. Curiously enough, though, there is a lot of movement in them. Thus, a ridge is sometimes ascending; there is a strong upward move-ment, perhaps broken with spires and towers but resuming the upward trend, toward the sky or even toward heaven. The ridge or contour not only has movement up and up, but also may point upward, may invite elevation.

When we are climbing a mountain, it may witness our behavior with a somewhat remote or mild benevolence. The mountain never fights against us, and it will hold back avalanches as long as it can, but sometimes human stupidity and hubris and a lack of intimate feeling for the environment result in human catastrophes—that is, catastrophes for mothers, fathers, wives, children, and friends. (The climbers themselves die in a way that I cannot class as catastrophic.)

So much for mountain appreciation and worship, or the cult of mountains. Many people may have similar sentiments but perhaps will not feel the same way about mountain people. On the other hand, many people feel the same way about mountain people but have no tendency toward mountain worship. This may perhaps be most simply explained through a short account of my own first encounter with mountain people.

When I was fifteen years old, I managed through sheer persistence of appeals to travel alone in early June to the highest mountain region of Norway—Jotunheimen. At the foot of the mountain, I was stopped by deep, rotten snow and could find nowhere to sleep. Eventually, I came across a very old man who was digging away the snow surrounding and partly covering a closed cottage belonging to an association for mountaineering and tourism. We stayed together for a week in a tiny nearby hut. As far as I can remember, we ate only one dish: oatmeal porridge with dry bread. The porridge had been stored in the snow from the previous autumn—that is what I thought the old man said. Later, I came to doubt it, to believe that I had misunderstood him. The porridge was served cold, and if any tiny bit was left over on my plate, he would eat it. In the evenings, he talked incidentally about mountains, about reindeer, about hunting and other occupations in the highest regions. Mostly, though, he played the violin. It was part of the local culture to mark the rhythm with the feet, and he would not give up trying to make me capable of joining him in this. How difficult it was! The old man's rhythms seemed more complex than anything I had ever heard.

The effect of this week, along with similar experiences later, established my conviction of an inner relation between mountains and mountain people: a certain greatness, a cleanness, a concentration on what is essential, a self-sufficiency, and consequently a disregard of luxury, of complicated means of all kinds. From the outside, the mountain way of life seemed Spartan, rough, and rigid, but the playing of the violin and the obvious fondness for all things above the timberline, living or "dead," bore witness to a rich, sensual attachment to life, a deep pleasure in what can be experienced with wide-open eyes and mind.

It is unnecessary to add that local mountain cultures are incompatible with cosmopolitan and urban ones. The intrusion of new values and life-styles rapidly undermines the alpine culture. In the Himalayas, individual Sherpas and their families have enhanced their wealth and status through expeditions, but their communities and culture have suffered unduly. Their great festivals and religious life are fading. There is, however, some cult of mountains remaining. Thus, Tseringma (Gauri Sankar) is still worshipped. When we suggested to the Sherpas of Beding, beneath Tseringma, that they might like to have its fabulous peaks protected from "conquests" and big expeditions, they responded with enthusiasm. A special meeting was announced, and the families voted unanimously to ask the central authorities in Kathmandu to refuse permission for climbing expeditions to Tseringma. Gönden, the leader of Beding, walked all the way to Kathmandu to contact the administration.

In Nepal, though, as in so many other countries far away, local communities have little chance of being heard. The Sherpas would not mind "losing" the money they could earn from expeditions to Tseringma, but central administrations do not think the same way. As expected, the great alpine clubs the world over have largely ignored Gönden's initiative. Perhaps the organizers of expeditions think that mountains, being great stone heaps, need no "protection" and that the "enlightened" Sherpas certainly would tolerate their climbing friends' going anywhere. The mountain climbers are in part right, but I do not think we should in this case make unrestricted use of the Sherpas' tolerance.

These reflections are supposed to serve the idea of modesty—modesty in human relationships with mountains and with mountain people. As I see it, modesty is of little value if it is not a natural consequence of much deeper feelings and, even more important in our special context, a consequence of a way of understanding ourselves as part of nature in a wide sense of the term. This way is such that the smaller we come to feel ourselves compared with the mountain, the nearer we come to participating in its greatness. I do not know why this is so.

Avalanches as Social Constructions[5]

Having been taken at least twice by avalanches, I have never felt them to be social constructions. But every word I utter about them may have social origins, and the same applies to the meanings of these words. The meanings also have individual components in the sense that the conceptions of people who study or have experienced avalanches show marked individual differences. I say I have been taken at least twice, because a third avalanche was so tiny that most people would reject using that term. But had I been carried twenty feet further, I might have perished because my skis had got into an awkward and painful position under very deep snow.

Every word in this narrative, including the word *avalanche*, has, of course, social and individual shades of connotations, but they do not affect the corresponding denotation. I have not used the word *nature* here, but the preceding observation holds for that word as well. In the last hundred years, the great diversity of usages of the word *nature* has been discussed, especially in the context of the history of ideas. Some people prefer to talk about nature as "social constructions," but the more traditional way, the talk about various conceptions and ideas of nature, is not inferior. The use of the term *deconstruction* has elicited much discussion, including the debate on the positive value of deconstruction of construction.

Curiously enough, many people criticize the deep ecology movement's assertion that every living being has intrinsic or inherent value. Critics argue that the statement rejects the wholly social (and individual) nature of living beings in nature, and ignores the vast sufferings of fellow humans. But the view that we have particular duties toward suffering fellow humans does not conflict with the view that it is meaningful to do things for nonhumans strictly for their own sake. Extended care for life on earth, deepened care for humans!

Mick Smith has the following to say about nature:

> While all would agree that "nature" is a prerequisite for social life, to speak of "nature" as being valuable in itself is still symptomatic for many on the left of a moral failure to prioritize the compelling immediacy of human suffering over our maltreatment of the environment.[6]

Smith puts quotation marks around "nature," as if he were writing about the *word*, but perhaps he is not. If not, does he speak about nature? Anyhow, supporters of the deep ecology movement need not consider nature to have inherent value. Especially when we use the word *nature* as a near synonym for the cosmos, I certainly do not apply the term *inherent value* to it. It is not empirically correct, I think, to suspect that certain supporters downplay the efforts to relieve human suffering. It is not uncommon to criticize people who work, for instance, for less painful transport of pigs, while the same people neglect problems of human suffering, but I think we agree that there are limits to what we can tolerate when it comes to such transport. Analogously, we may think that it is morally justifiable to use some fraction of a percent of what is spent on diminishing vast human suffering to defend the richness and diversity of life on this planet. In strange contrast to the usual view among researchers that there are immense differences of conceptions of nature and of ways of relating to nature, Mick Smith concludes: "Almost inevitably, the conclusion of such studies is 'that there is no singular "nature" as such, only a diversity of contested natures; and that each such nature is constructed through a variety of sociocultural processes.'"

Basically, it is philosophically rather trivial whether there is only one conception of what is called "nature" or a thousand. Most conceptions have been heavily determined by important magical views or by manifestations of the activity of gods. Fossils are sometimes considered the play of the devil. None of these views is *disproved* by modern natural science. Proofs belong in mathematics.

The World of Concrete Contents[7]

THE NEITHER-NOR AND THE BOTH-AND ANSWERS

In environmental debates, there is a persistent criticism that those who fight to "save" a natural entity (a river, a wood, a sea, a kind of animal or plant, a landscape) mainly express feelings and subjective likes and dislikes. The objects of this criticism are said to lack a sense of objectivity and ultimately to lack adequate reference to *reality as it is in fact* and not only reality as they feel it.[8]

Effective counterarguments need not be of a philosophical kind. But those who feel at home with epistemology and related more or less abstruse subjects might use this to their advantage.

Suppose we put our right hand, which has been exposed to cold air, into a pot of water, and we exclaim, "Warm!" We then put our left hand, which has not been exposed, into the same pot, and we exclaim, "Cold!"

Question: Is the water warm or cold?

Galileo's kind of answer: *Neither* warm *nor* cold. The water as such, or in itself, is neither warm nor cold. These are *secondary* qualities. The water has only *primary* qualities.[9]

Protagoras' answer, according to Sextus Empiricus: *Both* warm *and* cold. The water has both qualities, but the condition of the hands has the effect that one of them only *registers* the warmth, the other only coldness:

> Now, this man says that matter is a state of flux . . . and the senses undergo transformation and alternation in accordance with one's age and with other conditions of the body . . . And men apprehend

different things at different times because the conditions they are in are different.[10]

Suppose we put our right foot, which has been exposed to cold air, into the calm sea. We might exclaim, "Delicious!" or "Encouraging!" or "Cheering!" When we then put our left foot, which has not been exposed, into the sea at the same spot, we now might exclaim, "Detestable!" or "Discouraging!" or "Abominable!"

According to Sextus' interpretation, Protagoras' opinion might also be that the sea is *both* encouraging and discouraging, and both delicious and detestable. Consequently, according to Protagoras, as interpreted by Sextus, and as interpreted by me, water has all kinds of qualities, but a sensitive being is only able to experience a limited number of them. What a being will experience depends on its state.

The most interesting interpretation of "matter" is that it comprises all that human beings can ever experience in any state. And the possibility is not excluded that other sensitive beings can experience additional "things" that humans cannot.

The most plausible interpretation of the preceding passage by Sextus is, unfortunately, not consistent with the above addition. This conclusion seems unavoidable if we consider Sextus' next statement:

Therefore man becomes, according to him, the criterion of the existence of things. For all things, in so far as they appear to men, also exist, while those things that appear to no man do not exist at all.

Strangely enough, "matter" seems to be dependent upon the states of humans: It cannot comprise anything that cannot be apprehended by human beings. The set of states of human equals the set of states of matter.

Protagoras' "matter" I take to be an *ens rationis*, a tentative abstract structure invented to somehow support "the appearances," like the elephant or tortoise invented to support the earth.

In what follows, I shall maintain that Galileo's neither-nor position leads to absurdities. The position of Protagoras is deeply problematic, but can be saved from absurdity if somewhat freely interpreted. Furthermore, I shall maintain that it is philosophically tenable to maintain that the world we live in (the *Lebenswelt*) has secondary and tertiary qualities. What we feel about something belongs to the qualities of the world as we know it. What does not have such qualities is abstract structure.

Environmentalists talk about reality as it is in fact when they talk in terms of feelings.

REJECTION OF ABSOLUTIST *DING AN SICH* CONCEPTIONS

The Galileo type of answer uses a distinction that is useful within limits, but breaks down if absolutized. It is the famous distinction between things in themselves and things in relation to other things. (The term *thing* is taken in a very broad sense.)

Essential to ecological thinking, and to thinking in quantum physics, is the insistence that things cannot be separated from what surrounds them without smaller or greater arbitrariness. Thing A cannot be thought of in and of itself, because of internal relation to thing B. But neither is thing B separable, except superficially, from C, and so on.

As we know them, things have properties referring to sensing, action, and comprehension. Such primary qualities as the shape of a thing vary with the perspective. There is no absolute shape of the thing in itself. No quality of a thing is such that it is separable from others. General relativity excludes even movement or rest. There are no primary *qualities*. A triangle is either without extension, as in axiomatic, formal geometry, or has a color, for instance, black.

In thought and communication, we need to separate and make distinctions; otherwise, orientation gets to be impossible. The utterance "warm" relates to a whole set or constellation, but nominally and grammatically, the utterance refers in our example just to water. More precisely and specifically, it refers to *water in relation to* a complex set or constellation of relata, of which the *most obvious* are the hand, the water, the medium, and the subject's uttering "Warm!"

These relata, individually or collectively, are not things or entities in themselves, in spite of the existence of words and phrases suggesting the possibility of isolating each of them. The relations between the relata are internal.

There is similarity between this view and those expressed by the Buddhist formula *sarvam dharmam nihsvsbhavam*. Every element is without "self-existence." But the views I defend need no support from Buddhist philosophy. Western traditions suffice.

In short, the both-and answer may be thus formulated: There are no completely separable objects and, therefore, no separable water or medium or organism. A concrete content can only be one-to-one related to an indivisible structure, a *constellation* of factors. Concrete *contents* and abstract structures make up reality as it is in fact. It is misleading to call it *real* only *as felt by a subject*.

The notion of irreducible constellations eliminates both objectivist and subjectivist views as characterized, for instance, by J. J. C. Smart in relation to color.[11] On the other hand, Protagoras' view as interpreted by Sextus is an objectivist view. Water as a piece of matter *is* cold. Both answers can be saved, however, by expanding the basis of the question: It should be related, not to water as a separable object, but to constellations corresponding to concrete contents.

SECONDARY AND TERTIARY QUALITIES
AND THE THEORY OF PROJECTION

As late as in the last part of the nineteenth century, mechanical conceptions of warmth and coldness were thought to imply the neither-nor answer. The experienced warmness or coldness is not a property of the water *itself*. Different temperatures of the water correspond to certain levels of intensity of the motion of its molecules. In its capacity as a primary quality, *motion* is a property of the water in itself. Primary qualities, intrinsic or in the objects themselves, were conceived to be part of *reality itself*. The felt warmth was considered to have only a strange kind of subjective existence: not *in* the brain, not *in* space. General relativity and quantum physics undermined the *thing-in-itself* conception, but did not cause any widespread major change of opinion.

Concrete contents have a one-to-one correlation with constellations; there is an isomorphy between the concrete and the abstract. When we say that the sea is now gray, the water of the sea is only one part of the constellation. Nevertheless, it is somehow the dominant part. We would not say that the air between the sea and us is gray, or that we are gray. The sea has thousands of individual color hues as inherent properties, but not as an isolated thing. One must take the color of the heavens, the color of the plankton, the waves, the senses of the observers, into consideration. The colors of the sea are parts of innumerable gestalts.

According to the traditional doctrine of primary, secondary, and tertiary qualities or properties, color is the *projection* upon the surfaces of things of color-sensations generated by the senses. Only as a consequence of this projection do things *look* green, white, black, and so forth. The perception of greenness in the mind is projected into the external world.

The identification of primary properties with those of objects themselves leads to a conception of *nature without any of the qualities we experience spontaneously*. There is no good reason why we should not look upon such a bleak nature as just a resource. Every appeal to save parts of nature based on reference to sense qualities of any kind becomes meaningless. Every passionate appeal revealing deep feelings, empathy, and even identification with natural phenomena must then be ruled out as irrelevant. The sphere of real facts is narrowed down to those of mechanically interpreted mathematical physics.

Worse still: The question of how secondary and tertiary qualities come to be unreal is often answered by pointing to a (truly miraculous) capacity of the human senses and the human mind to *create* the colors and the beauty. A poet, says A. N. Whitehead ironically, should not praise the roses but himself who makes the roses red and beautiful. (Whitehead is, incidentally, one of the few Western philosophers who clearly opposed the doctrine of primary qualities.)

With these aberrations in mind, I think it might be of value in deep ecology theorizing to suggest ontologies in which secondary and tertiary qualities are at least on a par with the primary ones. The ontology I wish to defend is such that the primary properties (in a narrow sense) are *entia rationis* characteristics of abstract structures, but not contents of reality. Structures may be both, namely, structures of gestalts, but not the ones I now refer to. The geometry *of* the world is not a geometry *in* the world.

The both-and answer as elaborated here emphatically rejects the theory of projection. *There is no such process as projection of sense-qualities.* The theory is a clever invention that makes it possible to retain the notion that things in themselves retain their separate identity in spite of the bewildering diversity of secondary and tertiary qualities. But the price of this conservation of the Galilean ontology is high: There is no evidence whatsoever of a process of projection.

THE SUBJECT-OBJECT DISTINCTION AND THE THEORY OF DUPLICATION

Suppose three people are said to point to *the same* tree but to attribute to the tree three completely different sets of secondary and tertiary qualities. How should we deal with the contradiction?

At a superficial level, contradictions are avoided by certain ways of talking: "The tree *looks* such and such *to me*." "I *feel* the tree to be such and such." A mere diversity of conscious experience is acknowledged; therefore, no contradiction arises on this level.

Here is how it works: Inside the consciousness of person, P_1, there is an experience or image, E_1, of a tree with the following characteristics: . . . In P_2, there is E_2; in P_3, E_3; and so on. The experiences E_1, E_2, and E_3, and so forth, are all different. The tree in the external world confronting P_1, P_2, and P_3 may be *the same*, and its properties are the primary ones, most adequately described by contemporary physics. Consequently, in the example, we get as many as four trees, one external, and three internal. When nobody looks at the tree, the three internal ones disappear and the external one remains.

This way of avoiding contradictions between two or more observers results in the famous *duplication:* There is a tree outside in the external world and a tree inside in the mind of the observer. The tree outside is today conceived in extremely abstract form because of the development of physics, as a structure with no similarity to the internal trees. In the 1890s, the external tree still had some perceptual (*anschauliche*) properties. Since the days of Einstein and Heisenberg, these are *all* gone. But Bohr has shown how this disappearance brings us back to the reality of laboratory constellations with secondary qualities.

The tree in the mind no longer has the character of an image or a copy, because the external tree of physics has no similarity to the internal one. Furthermore, the internal is *in* the mind in a *nonspatial sense*. It is not *in* the brain, because then it would have been seen long ago by scientists. It is not even *near* the brain. If the external tree and the body of the observer are in Rome, this does not imply that the tree in the observer's mind is in or near Rome. The internal tree is no nearer to Rome than it is to the Andromeda nebula. It is not in physical space at all. Where is it?

The tree in the mind is private in principle, belonging to a specific person or animal; it is *subjective*. The tree outside is *objective*, supposedly completely independent of any perceivers and a thing in itself.

All this is rather confusing. The duplication theory does not seem understandable to anybody. Nevertheless, if we take the neither-nor answer as a basic assumption, it is difficult to avoid accepting a kind of duplication theory and a sharp, pervasive subject-object dualism.

The both-and answer is also far from intuitively obvious, at least in *our* culture. But I think it can be effectively defended.

SPONTANEOUS EXPERIENCE WITHOUT SUBJECT-OBJECT CLEAVAGE: ABSTRACT STRUCTURES

When absorbed in the contemplation of a concrete, natural thing, a person does not experience a subject-object relation. Nor does a person have this experience when absorbed in vivid action, whether in movement or not. There is no epistemological ego reaching out to see and understand a tree or an opponent in a fight, or a problem of decision. A tree is always part of a total, a gestalt. Analysis may discover many structural ingredients, sometimes an ego-relation, sometimes not. The gestalt is a whole, self-contained and self-sufficient. If we call it "experience of the gestalt," we are easily misled in a subjectivist direction.

When describing a constellation of gestalt relations, we must not let the usual stress on the epistemological subject-object distinction dominate the expression. In a spontaneous experience, there may or may not be any ingredient corresponding to the distinction.

"Tiny me looking into the eye of a big whale" may be a concrete content with an ego-relation as a genuine part. It is different from previous examples because the qualities are not all sense-qualities. The unity of this concrete contact is best understood by stressing its gestalt character. The example refers to a gestalt of a fairly high order, that is, having lower-order gestalts as "parts."

If "cheerful tree" and "dark and threatening tree" are two spontaneous expressions, analysis in terms of relations may conclude that they refer to "the same" tree. But this sameness is definable only in terms of an *abstract structure*, whereas utterances refer to two *concrete contents*.

The structure referred to is abstract and not to be confused with gestalt structures within the concrete content. The tree may have branches and the color may contrast with a dark background. This reveals a structure within the total gestalt. This structure is given *phenomenologically,* as structure within the concrete content. The sameness of the tree defined through abstract structures presupposes location in space of a kind that cannot be conceived as structure of a gestalt. It is an abstract structure, an *ens rationis*, insofar as every theory, including that of gravitation, is human-made.

My analysis at this point presumably implies a rather radical form of nominalism, but I shall not try to make it explicit. I only mention that it is closely related to the view that relations between things, or more specifically concrete contents, are not *part* of the world. Primary qualities, for instance, shape, do not occur in our life space except as contrasts between colors, for instance, a black circle on white background. The concept "circle" as abstracted from this concrete content is an *ens rationis* according to the above. The nominalism implied here is a nominalism of abstract relations. Problematic is the place of *entia rationis* "themselves" within gestalts of high order. A discussion of this is important, as is the more general question of intentional entities and intentionality, but lies outside the scope of this essay.[12]

FROM ETHICS TO ONTOLOGY AND FROM ONTOLOGY TO ETHICS

Confrontations between developers and conservationists reveal differences in estimating what is *real*. What a conservationist *sees* and experiences as *reality* the developer does not see—and vice versa. A conservationist *sees* and experiences a forest as a unity, a gestalt, and when speaking of the heart of the forest, he or she is not referring to the geometrical center. A developer sees square kilometers of trees and argues that a road through the forest covers very few square kilometers, so why make so much fuss? And if the conservationists insist, the developer will assert that the road does not touch the *center* of the forest. The *heart* is then saved, he or she thinks. The difference between the antagonists is one of ontology rather than one of ethics.[13] The gestalts "the heart of the forest," "the life of the river," and "the quietness of the lake" are parts of reality for the conservationist. To the conservationist, the developer seems to suffer from a kind of deeply based blindness. But the developer's ethics on environmental questions are based largely on how he or she sees reality. There is no way of making the developer eager to save a forest as long as he or she retains the conception of it as a set of trees. The charge that the conservationist is motivated by subjective feelings is firmly based on the developer's view of reality. The strong positive feelings toward development he or she considers are based on objective reality, and as long as the society is dominated by developers, the developer need not be passionate. It is the struggling minorities who are passionate, rather than those who follow the mainstream.

It is important in the philosophy of environmentalism to move from ethics to ontology and back. Clarification of differences in ontology may contribute significantly to the clarification of different policies and their ethical basis. And one of the first things to do might be to get rid of the belief that humankind is something *placed in* an environment!

Starting from concrete contents in our analysis, the is-ought and fact-value dichotomies look a little different than from where Hume started, namely, from factual and value *affirmations*. Expressions of concrete contents are designations, not declarative sentences.

Expressions of the kind "object *x* has value *y*" immediately lead to the question, Given an object *x*, how do I assess its value *y*? If we start with designations of concrete contents, for instance, "delicious, red tomato to be eaten at once!" or "repugnant, rotten tomato," the evaluative terms are there from the very beginning of our analysis. And there is no separable tomato to value!

In "Is/Ought Dichotomy and Environmental Ethics," David Bennett says that John Passmore and Aldo Leopold "agree on the basic ecological fact, but differ on how to value this fact. Passmore imports a restricted sense of obligation and maintains the fact-value dichotomy. Leopold accepts the community as both a descriptive and prescriptive statement."

Perhaps Leopold's point of view could be explicated by starting with designations of concrete contents of various sorts expressing what Leopold sees and experiences as community. The terms of the designations will inevitably include valuations. There would then be, strictly speaking, no fact that they agree about or any value that they disagree about. Bennett seems to take an ontological point of view, close to that of Callicott, who says: "Ecology changes our values by changing our *concepts* of the world of ourselves in relation to the world. It reveals new relations among objects which, once revealed, stir our ancient centers of moral feeling."[14] The stirring is part of a gestalt and, as such, is not to be isolated from the "objects." I have tried to explicate what kind of change in concept of the world and status of the subject is at issue.

I propose to *identify the world with the set of contents, not with structures*. This means that the two contents referred to above are two parts of the world. The world has structures, but does not *reveal* them. We make conceptual constructs to cope with them, but they are all human-made. Gravity does not pull planets!

Between the parts of the world conceived as *contents* in the form of gestalts, there are internal structural relations. But these are distinguished from the *abstract* structure found or invented by science. The physicist's "world of science" is entirely one of abstract structure. Even the hues of colors are defined structurally through places in color atlases. The ecosystem concept is used to describe abstract structures, and the movement of deep ecology is to a large extent concerned with abstract structures. The importance of abstract structural considerations cannot be overestimated.

But the factors introduced in abstract analysis should not, as is usually done, be identified with objects in the world. They do not belong to the content of the world we are genuinely part of. Abstract structures are structures *of* the world, not *in* the world.

APPEARANCE AND REALITY: PERSPECTIVISM

If we permit ourselves to use the terms *realness* and *reality*, I shall maintain that there is no reality "behind" the contents. The abstract structures may be called real, but any definite structure in the form of a theoretical construct is an *ens rationis* and is not "behind" or "underneath" the contents.

What, then, can one say about the distinction between appearance and reality? Does the stress on contents favor appearance? No. If it did, something in the above argumentation has gone wrong.

We have useful kinds of expressions, such as "It appears to be such and such, but it is not really such and such." If I express a content through the words "cheerful tree" and we add, "Let us place it in our window!" then my friend may say, "The tree is in reality very big and cannot be placed in our window. You are deceived by the great distance!" Or, when somebody stands on the southern rim of the Grand Canyon, pointing north toward the northern side, the person may utter, "How is it that there is only moss on the northern rim?" But a friend may not agree: "You are mistaken. The 'moss' is really some woods. The distance deceives you." The appearance-reality distinction in these examples relates to statements that are true or false, not to designations of concrete contents.

If by "appearance" we mean something that by definition or intrinsically is appearance to a person, we have presumed a subject-object distinction that cannot be generalized and adapted to a description of the world as concrete contents.

The rhetoric of environmentalism favors positive evaluation of natural phenomena. But, of course, concrete contents may include the negative. A prisoner in 1977 on Antarctic Dawson Island uttered, "sun, cold and unfriendly," and similar expressions are common in any climate. The ontological emancipation of tertiary qualities does not imply uniformly positive evaluation of natural phenomena. In the terminology of gestalts, one may say that religion has tried to conceive the most comprehensive gestalt to be (intrinsically, of course) good, and Spinoza uses the term *perfect* characterizing *Deus sive Natura*. But the problem of evil is still open. Nietzsche and others have used the term *perspective* in a way similar to that of the above term *content*: The world is the total set of perspectives. But usually we find the subject-object distinction implied in perspective. The world is seen *by subjects* in different perspectives. The tree *looks* different according to the perspective of the observer. By walking around, we see the tree from different angles. Thus, "perspectivism" may mislead.

Similar reflections hold concerning Dewey's and others' use of the term *experience*. It is too natural to say "experience by whom?" "my experience," "your experience," and so forth. The term *content* does not so easily lend itself to the introduction of a subject-object division. But if used carefully, the term *experience* may not mislead.

GESTALT ONTOLOGY AND THE DEEP ECOLOGY MOVEMENT

Our starting point has been the "neither-nor" and "both-and" answers to questions about whether a thing has one quality or another. As already mentioned, elaboration of the answers may lead to different directions, and my elaboration is not the only consistent one. The situation in epistemology and ontology is rather problematic. I maintain that the framework of gestalt ontology is adequate, but scarcely the only adequate one, in any attempt to give the principles of the deep ecology movement a philosophical foundation. *The world of concrete contents has gestalt character, not atomic character.* I know of no better frame of reference than that of gestalts.

This account does not, as mentioned, minimize the importance of abstract structures such as ecosystems (with the stress on *system*). But clearly the theoretical debate centering on such concepts as mature ecosystem shows the human-made character of the conceptual world. When some ecologists negate the existence of mature systems, this does not imply the negation of any content of the world we live in (the *Lebenswelt*).

Self-Realization: An Ecological Approach to Being in the World[15]

Humanity has struggled, for about 2,500 years, with basic questions about who we are, where we are headed, and the nature of the reality in which we are included. This is a short period in the lifetime of a species, and an even shorter time in the history of the earth, to which we belong as mobile beings. I am not capable of saying very new things in answer to these questions, but I can look at them from a *somewhat* different angle, using somewhat different conceptual tools and images.

What I am going to say, more or less in my own way and in that of my friends, can be condensed roughly into the following points:

1. We underestimate ourselves. And I emphasize *selves*. We tend to confuse our "self" with the narrow ego.
2. Human nature is such that, with sufficient comprehensive maturity, we cannot help but identify ourselves with all living beings, beautiful or ugly, big or small, sentient or not. The adjective *comprehensive*, meaning "all-sided," as in "comprehensive maturity," deserves a note: Descartes seemed to be rather immature in his relationship with animals; Schopenhauer was not very advanced in his relationship to his family (kicking his mother down a staircase?); Heidegger was amateurish—to say the least—in his political behavior. Weak identification with nonhumans is compatible with maturity in some major sets of relationships, such as those toward one's family or friends. And so I use the qualification *comprehensive* to mean "being mature in *all* major relationships."

3. Traditionally, the *maturity of the self* has been considered to develop through three stages: from ego to social self (comprising the ego), and from social self to a metaphysical self (comprising the social self). But in this conception of the maturity of the self, nature is largely left out. Our immediate environment, our home (where we belong as children), and the identification with nonhuman living beings are largely ignored. Therefore, I tentatively introduce, perhaps for the very first time, the concept of *ecological self.* We may be said to be in, and of, nature from the very beginning of ourselves. Society and human relationships are important, but our own self is much richer in its constitutive relationships. These relationships are not only those we have with other humans and the human community (I have elsewhere introduced the term *mixed community* to mean those communities in which we consciously and deliberately live close together with certain animals), but also those we have with other living beings.

4. The meaning of life, and the joy we experience in living, is enhanced through increased self-realization, that is, through the fulfillment of potentials that each of us has, but that are never the same for any two living beings. Whatever the differences between beings, increased self-realization implies a broadening and deepening of the self.

5. Because of an inescapable process of identification with others, with increasing maturity, the self is widened and deepened. We "see ourselves in others." Our self-realization is hindered if the self-realization of others, with whom we identify, is hindered. Our self-love will fight this hindrance by assisting in the self-realization of others according to the formula "Live and let live!" Thus, everything that can be achieved by altruism—the *dutiful, moral* consideration for others—can be achieved, and much more, by the process of widening and deepening ourselves. Following Kant, we then act *beautifully*, but neither morally nor immorally (in the sense of from duty).

6. One of the great challenges today is to save the planet from further ecological devastation, which violates both the enlightened self-interest of humans and the self-interest of nonhumans and decreases the potential of joyful existence for all.

Now, proceeding to elaborate these points, I shall start with the peculiar and fascinating terms *ego* and *self*.

The simplest answer to who or what I am is to point to my body. But clearly I cannot identify myself, or even my ego, with my body. For example, compare the following sentences:

I know Mr. Smith.	My body knows Mr. Smith.
I like poetry.	My body likes poetry.
The only difference between us is that you are a Presbyterian and I am a Baptist.	The only difference between our bodies is that you are a Presbyterian and I am a Baptist.

In the preceding sentences, we cannot substitute "my body" for "I." Nor can we substitute "my mind" or "my mind and my body" for "I." More adequately, we may substitute "I as a person" for "I," but this does not, of course, tell us what the ego or the self is.

Several thousand years of philosophical, psychological, and social-psychological thinking has not brought us any adequate conception of the *I*, the *ego*, or the *self*. In modern psychotherapy, these notions play an indispensable role, but, of course, the practical goal of therapy does not necessitate philosophical clarification of these terms. It is important to remind ourselves about the strange and marvelous phenomena with which we are dealing. Perhaps the extreme closeness and nearness of these objects of thought and reflection add to our difficulties. I shall offer only one simple sentence that resembles a definition of the ecological self: The *ecological self* of a person is that with which this person identifies.

The key sentence (rather than a definition) about the self shifts the burden of clarification from the term *self* to that of *identification*, or rather, the process of identification.

I shall continue to concentrate on the ecology of the self, but shall first say some things about identification. What would be a paradigm situation involving identification? It would be a situation that elicits intense empathy. My standard example involves a nonhuman being I met in the 1940s. I was looking through an old-fashioned microscope at the dramatic meeting of two drops of different chemicals. At that moment, a flea jumped from a lemming that was strolling along the table. The insect landed in the middle of the acid chemicals. To save it was impossible. It took minutes for the flea to die. The tiny being's movements were dreadfully expressive. Naturally, I felt a painful sense of compassion and empathy. But the empathy was *not* basic. Rather, it was a process of identification: I saw myself in the flea. If I had been *alienated* from the flea, not seeing intuitively anything even resembling myself, the death struggle would have left me feeling indifferent. So there must be identification for there to be compassion and, among humans, solidarity.

One of the authors contributing admirably to a clarification of the study of the self is Eric Fromm:

> The doctrine that love for oneself is identical with "selfishness" and an alternative to love for others has pervaded theology, philosophy, and popular thought; the same doctrine has been rationalized in scientific language in Freud's theory of narcissism. Freud's concept presupposes a fixed amount of libido. In the infant, all of the libido has the child's own person as its objective, the stage of "primary narcissism," as Freud calls it. During the individual's development, the libido is shifted from one's own person toward other objects. If a person is blocked in his "object-relationships," the libido is withdrawn from the objects and returned to his or her own person; this is called "secondary narcissism." According to Freud, the more love I turn toward the outside world the less love is left for myself, and vice versa. He thus describes the phenomenon of love as an impoverishment of one's self-love because all libido is turned to an object outside oneself.[16]

What Fromm attributes here to Freud we can now attribute to the shrinkage of self-perception implied in the fascination for ego trips. Fromm opposes such a shrinkage of self. The following quotation from Fromm concerns love of persons but, as "ecosophers," we find the notions of care, respect, responsibility, and knowledge applicable to living beings in the wide sense.

> Love of others and love of ourselves are not alternatives. On the contrary, an attitude of love toward themselves will be found in all those who are capable of loving others. Love, in principle, is indivisible as far as the connection between "objects" and one's own self is concerned. Genuine love is an expression of productiveness and implies care, respect, responsibility, and knowledge. It is not an "effect" in the sense of being affected by somebody, but an active striving for the growth and happiness of the loved person, rooted in one's own capacity to love.[17]

Fromm is very instructive about unselfishness—it is diametrically opposed to selfishness, but is still based on alienation and a narrow perception of self. We might add that what he says also applies to persons sacrificing of themselves:

> The nature of unselfishness becomes particularly apparent in its effect on others and most frequently, in our culture, in the effect the "unselfish" mother has on her children. She believes that by her unselfishness her children will experience what it means to be loved and to learn, in turn, what it means to love. The effect of her unselfishness, however, does not at all correspond to her expectations. The children do not show the happiness of persons who are convinced that they are loved; they are anxious, tense, afraid of the mother's disapproval, and anxious to live up to her expectations. Usually, they are affected by their mother's hidden hostility against life, which they sense rather than recognize, and eventually become imbued with it themselves . . .
>
> If one has a chance to study the effect of a mother with genuine self-love, one can see that there is nothing more conducive to giving a child the experience of what love, joy, and happiness are than being loved by a mother who loves herself.[18]

We need environmental ethics, but when people feel that they unselfishly give up, or even sacrifice, their self-interests to show love for nature, this is probably, in the long run, a treacherous basis for conservation. Through identification, they may come to see that their own interests are served by conservation, through genuine self-love, the love of a widened and deepened self.

At this point, the notion of a being's interests furnishes a bridge from self-love to self-realization. It should not surprise us that Fromm, influenced as he is by Spinoza and William James, makes use of that bridge. "What is considered self-interest?" Fromm asks. His answer:

> There are two fundamentally different approaches to this problem. One is the objectivistic approach most clearly formulated by Spinoza. To him self-interest or the interest "to seek one's profit" is identical with virtue.
>
> "The more," he says, "each person strives and is able to seek his profit, that is to say, to preserve his being, the more virtue does he

possess; on the other hand, in so far as each person neglects his own profit he is impotent." According to this view, the interest of humans is to preserve their existence, which is the same as realizing their inherent potentialities. This concept of self-interest is objectivistic inasmuch as "interest" is not conceived in terms of the subjective feeling of what one's interest is but in terms of what the nature of a human is, "objectively."[19]

"Realizing inherent potentialities" is one of the good, less-than-ten-word clarifications of "self-realization." The questions "What are the inherent potentialities of the beings of species x?" and "What are the inherent potentialities of this specimen of the species y?" obviously lead to reflections about, and studies of, x and y.

As humans we cannot just follow the impulses of the moment when asking what our inherent potentialities are. Fromm means something like this when he calls an approach "objectivistic" as opposed to an approach "in terms of subjective feeling." Because of the high estimation of feeling and a correspondingly low estimate of so-called objectification (verdinglichung, reification) within deep ecology, Fromm's terminology is inadequate today, but what he means to say is appropriate. And it is obviously relevant when we deal with species other than humans: Animals and plants have interests in the sense of ways of realizing inherent potentialities, which we can study only by interacting with these beings. We cannot rely on our momentary impulses, however important they are in general.

The expression "preserve his being," in the quotation from Spinoza, is better than "preserve his existence," since the latter is often associated with physical survival and a struggle for survival. An even better translation is perhaps "persevere in his being" (perseverare in suo esse). This has to do with acting from one's own nature. Survival is only a necessary condition, not a sufficient condition of continued self-realization. (An act of self-realization may discontinue self-realization because it leads to immediate death. This opinion goes probably against what Spinoza would say.)

The concept of self-realization, as dependent upon insight into our own potentialities, makes it easy to see the possibilities of ignorance and misunderstanding in terms of what these potentialities are. The ego-trip interpretation of the potentialities of humans presupposes a major underestimation of the richness and broadness of our potentialities. As Fromm puts it, "man can deceive himself about his real self-interest if he is ignorant of his self and its real needs."[20]

The "everything hangs together" maxim of ecology applies to the self and its relation to other living beings, ecosystems, the ecosphere, and the earth, with its long history.

The existence and importance of the ecological self are easy to illustrate with some examples of what has happened in my own country, Norway.

The scattered human habitation along the Arctic coast of Norway is uneconomic and unprofitable, from the point of view of the current economic policy of our welfare state. The welfare norms require that every family should have a connection by telephone (in case of illness). This costs a considerable amount of money. The same holds for mail and other services. Local fisheries are largely uneconomic perhaps because a foreign armada of big trawlers of immense capacity is fishing just outside the fjords. The availability of jobs was decreasing in the mid-1980s.

The government, therefore, heavily subsidized the resettlement of people from the Arctic wilderness, concentrating them in so-called centers of development, that is, small areas with a town at the center. But the people are clearly not the same when their bodies have been thus transported. The social, economic, *and natural setting* is now vastly different. The objects with which people work and live are completely different. There is a consequent loss of personal identity. "Who am I?" they ask. Their self-respect, self-esteem, is impaired. What is adequate in the so-called periphery of the country is different from what counts at the so-called centers.

If people are relocated or, rather, transplanted from a steep, mountainous place to a plain, they also realize, but too late, that their home-place has been part of themselves—that they have identified with features of the place. And the way of life in the tiny locality, the density of social relations, has formed their persons. Again, they are not the same as they were.

Tragic cases can be seen in other parts of the Arctic. We all regret the fate of the Inuit, their difficulties in finding *a new identity,* a new social self, and a new, more comprehensive ecological self. The Lapps of Arctic Norway have been hurt by the diversion of a river for hydroelectricity. In court, accused of an illegal demonstration at the river, one Lapp said that the part of the river in question was "part of himself." This kind of spontaneous answer is not uncommon among people. They have not heard about the philosophy of the wider and deeper self, but they talk spontaneously as if they had.

We may try to make the sentence "This place is part of myself" more intellectually understandable by reformulations. For example, we might say, "My relation to this place is part of myself," or "If this place is destroyed, something in me is destroyed," or "My relation to this place is such that if the place is changed, I am changed."

One drawback with these reformulations is that they make it easy to continue thinking of two completely separable, real entities, a self and the place, joined by an external relation. The original sentence, rather, conveys the impression that there is an internal relation of sorts. I say "of sorts," because we must take into account that it may not be reciprocal. If I am changed, even destroyed, the place would be destroyed according to one usual interpretation of *internal relation*. From the point of phenomenology and the concrete-content view, the reciprocity holds, but that is a special interpretation. We may use an interpretation such that if we are changed, the river need not be changed.

The reformulation "If this place is destroyed, something in me is killed" perhaps articulates some of the feelings usually felt when people see the destruction of places they deeply love or to which they have the intense feeling of belonging. Today, more space per human being is violently transformed than ever, at the same time as the number of human beings increases. The kind of "killing" referred to occurs all over the globe, but very rarely does it lead to strong counteraction. Resignation prevails: "You cannot stop progress."

The newborn lacks, of course, any conceptions, however rudimentary, corresponding to the tripartition: subject, object, medium. The conception (not the concept) of one's own ego probably comes rather late, say, after the first year. A vague network of relations comes first. This network of perceived and conceived relations is neutral, fitting what in British philosophy was called *neutral monism*. In a sense, it is this basic sort of crude monism we are working out anew, not by trying to be babies again, but by better understanding our ecological self. It has not had favorable conditions of development since before the time that the Renaissance glorified our ego by putting it in some kind of opposition to the rest of reality.

What is now the practical importance of this conception of a wide and deep ecological self?

Opponents often argue that we defend nature in our rich, industrial society in order to secure beauty, recreation, sport, and other nonvital interests for ourselves. It makes us strong if, after honest reflection, we find that we feel threatened in our innermost self. If so, we more convincingly defend a *vital* interest, not only something out there. We are engaged in self-defense. And to defend fundamental *human* rights is vital self-defense.

The best introduction to the psychology of the self is still to be found in the excellent and superbly readable book *Principles of Psychology,* published in 1890 by the American psychologist and philosopher William James. His hundred-page chapter on the consciousness of self stresses the plurality of components of the wide and deep self as a complex entity. (Unfortunately, he prefers to talk about the plurality of selves. I think it may be better to talk about the plurality of the components of the wide self.)

The plurality of components can be easily illustrated by reference to the dramatic phenomenon of alternating personality. "Any man becomes, as we say, *inconsistent* with himself if he forgets his engagements, pledges, knowledge, and habits . . . In the hypnotic trance we can easily produce an alternation of personality . . . by telling him he is an altogether imaginary personage."[21]

If we say that somebody is not himself or herself today, we may refer to a great many different *relations* to other people, to material things, and, certainly, to what we call his or her environment, the home, the garden, the neighborhood.

When James says that these relata *belong* to the self, it is, of course, not in the sense that the self has eaten the home, the environment, and so forth. Such an interpretation testifies that the self is still identified with the body. Nor does it mean that an *image* of the house *inside* the consciousness of the person belongs to the self. When somebody says that a part of a river landscape is part of himself or herself, we intuitively grasp roughly what the person means. But it is of course difficult to elucidate the meaning in philosophical or psychological terminology.

A last example from William James: We understand what is meant when somebody says, "As a man I pity you, but as an official I must show you no mercy." Obviously, the self of an official cannot empirically be defined except as a relation in a complex social setting. Thus, the self cannot possibly be inside the body or inside a consciousness.

Enough! The main point is that we do not hesitate *today*, being inspired by ecology and a revived intimate relation to nature, to recognize and accept wholeheartedly our ecological self.

The next section is rather metaphysical. I do not *defend* all the views presented in this part of my discussion. I wish primarily to inform you about them. As a student and admirer since 1930 of Gandhi's nonviolent, direct actions in bloody conflicts, I am inevitably influenced by his metaphysics, which to him personally furnished tremendously powerful motivation and which contributed to keeping him going until his death. His supreme aim was not India's *political* liberation. He led a crusade against extreme poverty, caste suppression, and terror in the name of religion. This crusade was necessary, but the liberation of the individual human being was his supreme aim. It is strange for many to listen to what he himself said about his ultimate goal: "What I want to achieve—what I have been striving and pining to achieve these thirty years—is self-realization, to see God face to face, to attain *Moksha* (Liberation). I live and move and have my being in pursuit of that goal. All that I do by way of speaking and writing, and all my ventures in the political field, are directed to this same end."[22]

This sounds individualistic to the Western mind—a common misunderstanding. If the self Gandhi is speaking about were the ego or the "narrow" self (*jiva*) of egocentric interest, the "ego trips," why then work for the poor? It is for him the supreme or universal Self—the *Atman*—that is to be realized. Paradoxically, it seems, he tries to reach self-realization through *selfless action*, that is, through the reduction of the dominance of the narrow self or the ego. Through the wider Self, every living being is connected intimately, and from this intimacy follows the capacity of *identification* and, as its natural consequences, practice of nonviolence. No moralizing is needed, just as we do not need morals to breathe. We need to cultivate our insight: The rock-bottom foundation of the technique for achieving the power of nonviolence is belief in the essential oneness of all life.

Historically, we have seen how nature conservation is nonviolent at its very core. Gandhi says: "I believe in *advaita* (nonduality), I believe in the essential unity of man and, for that matter, of all that lives. Therefore I believe that if one man gains spirituality, the whole world gains with him and, if one man fails, the whole world fails to that extent."

Surprisingly enough, Gandhi was extreme in his personal consideration for the self-realization of living beings other than humans. When traveling, he brought a goat with him to satisfy his need for milk. This was part of a nonviolent demonstration against certain cruel features in Hindu ways of milking cows. Furthermore, some European companions who lived with Gandhi in his ashrams were taken aback that he let snakes, scorpions, and spiders move unhindered into their bedrooms—animals fulfilling their lives. He even prohibited people from having a stock of medicines against poisonous bites. He believed in the possibility of satisfactory coexistence, and he proved right. There were no accidents. Ashram people would naturally look into their shoes for scorpions before using them. Even when moving over the floor in darkness, one could easily avoid trampling on one's fellow beings. Thus, Gandhi recognized a basic, common right to live and blossom, to self-realization in a wide sense applicable to any being that can be said to have interests or needs.

Gandhi made manifest the internal relation between self-realization, non-violence, and what sometimes has been called biospherical egalitarianism.

In the environment in which I grew up, I heard that what is serious in life is to get *to be* somebody—to outdo others in something, being victorious in a comparison of abilities. What makes this conception of the meaning and goal of life especially dangerous today is the vast, international economic competition. Free market, perhaps, yes, but the law of supply and demand of separate, isolatable "goods and services," independent of needs, must not be made to reign over increasing other areas of our life.

The ability to cooperate, to work with people, to make them feel good, *pays*, of course, in a fiercely individualist society, and high positions may require this, but only as long as, ultimately, it is subordinated to the career, to the basic norms of the ego trip, not to a self-realization beyond the ego.

To identify self-realization with the ego trip manifests a vast underestimation of the human self.

According to a common translation of Pali or Sanskrit texts, Buddha taught his disciples that the human mind should embrace all living things as a mother cares for her son, her only son. Some of you who never would feel it meaningful or possible that a human *self* could embrace all living things might stick to the usual translation. We shall then only ask that your *mind* embraces all living beings and that your good intention is to care and feel and act with compassion.

If the Sanskrit word translated into English is *Atman,* it is instructive to note that this term has the basic meaning of "self," rather than "mind" or "spirit," as you see in translations. The superiority of the translation using the word "self" stems from the consideration that if your *self* in the wide sense embraces another being, you need no moral exhortation to show care. Surely, you care for yourself without feeling any moral pressure to do it—provided you have not succumbed to a neurosis of some kind, developing self-destructive tendencies or hating yourself.

Incidentally, the Australian ecological feminist Patsy Hallen uses a formula close to that of Buddha: We are here to embrace rather than conquer the world. It is of interest to notice that the term "world" is used here, rather than "living beings." I suspect that our thinking need not proceed from the notion of living being to that of the world, but we will conceive reality or the world we live in as alive in a wide, not easily defined sense. There will then be no nonliving beings to care for.

If self-realization or self-fulfillment is today habitually associated with lifelong ego trips, isn't it stupid to use this term for self-realization in the widely different sense of Gandhi or, less religiously loaded, as a term for widening and deepening your self so that it embraces all life-forms? Perhaps it is. But I think the very popularity of the term makes people listen for a moment, feeling safe. In that moment, the notion of a greater self should be introduced to show that if people equate self-realization with ego trips, they seriously *underestimate* themselves. "You are much greater, deeper, generous, and capable of more dignity and joy than you think! A wealth of noncompetitive joy is open to you!"

But I have another important reason for inviting people to think in terms of deepening and widening their *self*, starting with the ego trip as a crudest, but inescapable, point zero. It has to do with a notion usually placed as the opposite of the egoism of the ego trip, namely, the notion of *altruism*. The Latin term *ego* has as its opposite the *alter*. Altruism implies that *ego* sacrifices its interest in favor of the other, the *alter*. The motivation is primarily that of duty: It is said that we *ought* to love others as strongly as we love ourselves.

Unfortunately, humankind is very limited in what it can love from mere duty or, more generally, from moral exhortation. From the Renaissance to World War II, about four hundred cruel wars were fought by Christian nations for the flimsiest of reasons. It seems to me that in the future, more emphasis has to be given to the conditions under which we most naturally widen and deepen our self. With a sufficiently wide and deep self, *ego* and *alter* as opposites are eliminated stage by stage. The distinction is in a way transcended.

Early in life, the social self is sufficiently developed so that we do not prefer to eat a big cake alone. We share the cake with our friends and our nearest. We identify with these people sufficiently to see our joy in their joy and to see our disappointment in theirs.

Now is the time *to share* with all life on our maltreated earth through the deepening identification with life-forms and the greater units, the ecosystems, and Gaia, the fabulous, old planet of ours.

Immanuel Kant introduced a pair of contrasting concepts that deserve to be extensively used in our effort to live harmoniously in, for, and of nature: the concepts of the *moral act* and the *beautiful act*.

Moral acts are those motivated by the intention to follow the moral laws, at whatever cost, that is, to do our moral duty solely out of respect for that duty. Therefore, the supreme *test* of our success in performing a pure, moral act is that we do it completely against our inclination, that we, so to say, hate to do it, but are compelled by our respect for the moral law. Kant was deeply awed by two phenomena, "the heaven with its stars above me and the moral law within me."

But if we do something we should do according to a moral law, but do it out of inclination and with pleasure—what then? Should we then abstain or try to work up some displeasure? Not at all, according to Kant. If we do what morals say is right because of positive inclination, then we perform a *beautiful* act. Now, my point is that in environmental affairs, perhaps we should try primarily to influence people toward beautiful acts. Work on their inclinations rather than morals. Unhappily, the extensive moralizing within environmentalism has given the public the false impression that we primarily ask them to sacrifice, to show more responsibility, more concern, better morals. As I see it, we need the immense variety of sources of joy opened through increased sensitivity toward the richness and diversity of life and the landscapes of free nature. We all can contribute to this individually, but it is also a question of politics, local and global. Part of the joy stems from the consciousness of our intimate relation to something bigger than our ego, something that has endured through millions of years and is worthy of continued life for millions of years. The requisite care flows naturally if the self is widened and deepened so that protection of free nature is felt and conceived as protection of ourselves.

Academically speaking, what I suggest is the supremacy of environmental ontology and realism over environmental ethics as a means of invigorating the environmental movement in the years to come. If reality is experienced by the ecological self, our behavior *naturally* and beautifully follows norms of strict environmental ethics. We certainly need to hear about our ethical shortcomings from time to time, but we more easily change through encouragement and through a deepened perception of reality and our own self. That is, deepened realism. How is this to be brought about? The question lies outside the scope of this essay! It is more a question of community therapy than community science: healing our relations to the widest community, that of all living beings.

The subtitle of this essay is "An Ecological Approach to Being in the World." I am now going to discuss a little about "nature," with all the qualities we spontaneously experience, as identical with the reality we live in. That means a movement from being in the world to being in nature. Then, finally, I shall ask for the goal or purpose of being in the world.

Is joy in the subject? I would say no. Joy is just as much or as little *in the* object. The joy of a joyful tree is primarily *in* the tree, we should say—if we are pressed to make a choice between the two possibilities. But we should not be pressed. There is a third position. The joy is a feature of the *indivisible*, concrete unit of subject, object, and medium. In a sense, self-realization involves experiences of the infinitely rich, joyful aspect of reality. It is misleading, according to my intuition, to locate joy inside my consciousness. What is joyful is something that is not subjective; joy is an attribute of a reality wider than a conscious ego. This is philosophically how I contribute to the explanation of the internal relation between joy, happiness, and human self-realization. But this conceptual exercise is mainly of interest to an academic philosopher. What I am driving at is probably something that may be suggested with less conceptual gymnastics: It is unwarranted to believe that how we feel nature to be is not like how nature really is. It is rather that reality is so rich that we cannot see everything at once, but separate parts or aspects in separate moods. The joyful tree I see in the morning light is not the sorrowful one I see in the night, even if, in their abstract structure, they (physically) are the same.

It is very human to ask for the ultimate goal or purpose of being in the world. This may be a misleading way of framing a question. It may seem to suggest that the goal or purpose must somehow lie outside or beyond the world. Perhaps this can be avoided by living out "in the world." It is characteristic of our time that we subjectivize and individualize the question asked of each of us: What do you consider the ultimate goal or purpose for *your* life? Or, we leave out the question of priorities and simply ask for goals and purposes.

The main title of this essay is partly motivated by the conviction that *self-realization* is an adequate key-term expression one uses to answer the question of ultimate goal. It is of course only a key term. An answer by a philosopher can scarcely be shorter than the little book *Ethics* by Spinoza.

To understand the function of the term *self-realization* in this capacity, it is useful to compare it with two others, *pleasure* and *happiness*. The first suggests hedonism, the second eudaemonism in a professional philosophical, but just as vague and ambiguous, jargon. Both terms broadly connote states of feeling. Having pleasure or being happy is to *feel* well. One may, of course, use the term *happiness* to connote something different, but in the way I use the term, one standard set of replies to the question "How do you feel?" is "I feel happy" or "I feel unhappy." The following set of answers would be rather awkward: "I feel self-realized" or "I do not feel self-realized."

The most important feature of self-realization as compared with pleasure and happiness is its dependence upon a view of human capacities or, better, potentialities. This again implies a view of what human nature is. In practice, it does not imply a general doctrine of human nature. That is work for philosophical fields of research.

An individual whose attitudes are such that I would say that he or she takes self-realization as the ultimate or fundamental goal has to have a view of his or her nature and potentialities. The more they are realized, the more there is self-realization. The question "How do you feel?" may be honestly answered in the positive or negative, whatever the level of self-realization. The question may, in principle, be answered in the negative, but like Spinoza, I think the valid answer is positive. The realization of fulfillment—using a somewhat less philosophical jargon—of the potentialities of oneself is *internally* related to happiness, but not in such a way that by *looking* for happiness, you will realize yourself. This is a clear point, incidentally, in John Stuart Mill's philosophy. You should not look hard for happiness. That is a bad way, even if you take, as Mill does, happiness as the ultimate or fundamental goal in life. I think that to look for self-realization is a better way. That is, to develop your capacities—using a rather dangerous word because the term *capacities* is easily interpreted in the direction of interpersonal, not intrapersonal, competition. But even the striving implied in the latter term may mislead. Dwelling in situations of intrinsic value, spontaneous nondirected awareness, relaxing from striving, is conducive to self-realization as I understand it. But there are, of course, infinite variations among humans according to cultural, social, and individual differences. This makes the key term *self-realization* abstract in its generality. But nothing more can be expected when the question is posed as it is: "What might deserve to be called an ultimate or a fundamental goal?" We may reject the meaningfulness of such a question—I don't—but for us for whom it has meaning, the answer using few words is bound to be abstract and general.

Going back to the three key terms of pleasure, happiness, and self-realization, the third has the merit of being clearly and forcefully applicable to any being with a specific range of potentialities. I limit the range to living beings, using the word *living* in a rather broad sense. The terms *pleasure* and *happiness* are not so easily generalized. With the rather general concept of ecological self already introduced, the concept of self-realization naturally follows.

Let us consider the praying mantis, a formidable, voracious insect. These creatures have a nature fascinating to many people. Mating is part of their self-realization, but some males are eaten when performing the act of copulation. Is he happy; is he having pleasure? We don't know. Well done if he does! Actually, he feeds his partner so that she gets strong offspring. But it does not make sense to me to attribute happiness to these males. Self-realization, yes; happiness, no. I maintain the internal relationship between self-realization and happiness among people and among some animal groups. As a professional philosopher, I am tempted to add a point inspired by Zen Buddhism and Spinoza: Happiness is a feeling, yes, but the act of realizing a potential is always an interaction involving one single concrete unit, one gestalt, I would say, and three abstract aspects, subject, object, medium. What I said about joyfulness in nature holds for happiness in nature. We should not conceive them as merely subjective feelings.

The rich reality of the world is getting even richer through our specific human endowments; we are the first kind of living beings we know of who have the potential to live in community with all other living beings. It is our hope that all those potentialities will be realized—if not in the near future, then at least in the somewhat more remote future.

Section 2:

THE LONG-RANGE DEEP ECOLOGY MOVEMENT

The Three Great Movements[1]

At the end of the twentieth century, we saw a convergence of three areas of self-destructiveness: the self-destructiveness of war, the self-destructiveness of exploitation and suppression among humans, and the self-destructiveness of suppression of nonhuman beings and of the degradation of life conditions in general. The movement to eradicate wars has a long history as a global movement. The movement against abject poverty and cruel exploitation and domination is younger. The third movement is quite young. These are the great movements that require intense participation on the grassroots level far into this new century.

The supporters of the peace movement have always asked for policies that have often been clearly "politically impossible" to accept by governments. The same applies to the second and third movements. But today, the first two can at least point to people in power who declare strong sympathy for their radical points of view. Halvard Lange, a prominent supporter of stronger NATO forces, declared that at heart he was a pacifist (which made his wife whisper irreverently, "Then I am a virgin"). Such sincere, *publicly declared* sympathy is not yet probably at the government level, say, in support of the deep ecology movement.

The urgency of preserving nature for "the future generations," meaning "future generations of humans" and not "future generations of living beings," has won acclaim among power elites. What I, perhaps misleadingly, have called the "shallow," "reform," or "nondeep" ecological movement has started to have an impact on the government level. Environmental organizations are listened to, and their advice has occasionally been used in practice. But future generations of nonhumans seem to be valued publicly only for the sake of future humans.

It is the task of dictionary editors to offer definitions of the *deep ecology movement*. I have difficulty doing more than to propose a tentative formulation of views that most supporters have in common. These are the so-called eight points that are discussed in the introduction and the next chapter ("The Basics of the Deep Ecology Movement") and that I shall not repeat here.

The realization of the points requires significant changes in both the rich and the poor countries and affects social, economic, technical, and lifestyle factors. Goals *include* the protection of the planet and its richness and diversity of life *for its own sake*.[2] The specific urgency accorded to this third movement is due to the time factor: It is obvious that delays rapidly make the ecological crisis more difficult to overcome. Wait five years, and the process may take fifty years more. Such nonlinear function of time does not restrict the other two movements.

What can be more urgent than the elimination of extreme poverty and suppression? We may answer that nothing can be more urgent. But whereas the general costs are roughly constant year after year, or increase linearly, the specific character of the ecological crisis makes the cost to reach ecological sustainability increase exponentially.

Whether in civil war or international war, the mentality created is that of almost complete indifference toward the destruction of nature. Destruction is even used as a weapon. To ask for mercy toward nonhumans would, in war, tend to be considered frivolous. The same also holds to some extent when the destruction caused by the gigantic military-industrial complex is placed increasingly under ecological scrutiny and is being made known in wide circles.

Evidently, the goals of the deep ecology movement cannot be reached without decisive victories of the peace movement. This should add to the motivation of people using much of their time and energy within the peace movement. Some peace people have changed focus and are now active in the ecology movement, finding the change comparable to a change of focus within a wider peace movement: work for peace with nature, ending brutal invasions. The change of focus undertaken by prominent peace activists such as E. F. Schumacher has not resulted in noticeable polemics about the relative importance of the two movements.

The many branches of the social justice movement have a more complex relation to the deep ecology movement. In the West, since the industrial revolution and at least through the twentieth century, labor was treated worse than cattle. For several hundred years, pollution at the workplace and in urban slums has damaged the health of the underprivileged, not the privileged.

A worker in the logging industry might have this to say about proposals to cease operations because of environmental problems: "*You* speak of environmental degradation. *We* have suffered that for hundreds of years. *You* close down a factory because of poisons. But what are the consequences for *you* and what for *us*? The managers lose their jobs, but they take a long vacation in superb nature, and get new jobs. *We* increase the legions of the unemployed, we cannot move around easily with our families, we remain in an unhealthy environment, many of us lose our way of life, and our problems persist. You say the deep ecology movement asks for widening care so that nonhuman beings get more chance. But you should also support the increased care for the underprivileged humans." It is quite right that deep ecology theorists like the peace and social justice theorists and activists in public talk about the concerns they have focused on. Their writings, if they write, also reflect their specialties. But it is difficult to assess what they do privately without knowing them well. General conclusions about the various concerns of the supporters of the three movements are rather shaky.

It is an embarrassing scandal that the rich industrial nations do not use the urgency of work to be done to overcome the global ecological crisis as a basis for the significant reduction of unemployment. The jobs in this area are clearly more labor-intensive than jobs in industry.

Looking at philosophical "schools" of the 1960s and later, we see that anarchists, Marxists, neo-Marxists, the Frankfurt school, and hermeneutics have not felt at home with the tenets of the deep ecology movement—and not only because of the special terminology of its theoreticians. This is not the place to go into professional philosophical debates, but in spite of different philosophical and terminological leanings, the three groups—the supporters of social ecology, the ecofeminists, and the deep ecology movements—cooperate well in praxis, learning from each other's special activities. The frontier of work is long, and we need to express our appreciation of work done in different sectors from our own. The convergence of problems within the three great movements may be expected to increase, and their impact on policies correspondingly strengthened.

It is of historical interest to trace the various kinds of physical, social, and other changes that have triggered the convergence of the three movements. Here I shall not try anything like that, but make some general reflections about these movements, starting with conceptual considerations.

It is not by chance that I have used the term *self* in the short characterizations of the lines of thinking, feeling, and acting. The terminology suggests itself when I was trying out a conceptual unification of a normative system with Self-realization! as the basic norm—expressed, inadequately of course, through one single word. For those who habitually look at the three global movements with the conceptualizations of the third movement in mind, the concepts of ecosystems, not human-environment, are central. The human self is then basically an ecological self, that is, a kind of part of ecosystems, and the doings of humans in war and peace and as masters or slaves are processes going on with accelerating speed and causal weight all over the globe. The self-destructiveness of present policies seems clear to a great many and has been adequately formulated, but to turn the tide seems politically overwhelmingly difficult. The self-destructiveness of wars has been announced clearly since the atomic bomb changed "everything." By now, many people realize that the long-range self-destructiveness of large-scale exploitation and suppression based on race, sex, or dominant economy gradually undermines the exploiters or suppressors themselves. (False masculinity has crippled the male sex.) At least this is clear if we take into account concepts of self on a scale nearer to the great Self than to the concepts of hard egos. The development of human maturity may perhaps be impaired when restricted by the counterintuitive perceptions of other human beings with whom one interacts. In this case, according to my terminology, there is a limit of Self-realization not being transcended. But it seems that most humans have either been exploited or suppressed most of their lives. The high levels of self-realization have been difficult but not impossible to reach under such circumstances.

In most cultures, some animals have been taken better care of and treated more respectfully than some humans have been treated. During the early days of the industrial revolution in England, this presumably was the case with pets and even pigs. In the same country, however, a brand of utilitarianism arose that strengthened the third line of thinking and feeling—that of Jeremy Bentham (1748–1832): "The question is not, can they reason? Nor, can they talk? But, can they suffer?"

So far as I can understand, all-around maturity of humans facilitates acts of identification with every kind of living being. This again facilitates negative attitudes toward the wanton limitation of the fulfillment of life potentialities of such beings. When manifest exploitation and suppression are performed, a reason is demanded: Are they necessary for the satisfaction of the vital needs of humans? The deepening and widening of the human ecological self increasingly limit its own realization when exploitation and suppression are applied. Potentialities of self-realization are destroyed. In this sense, the third movement seeks to reduce the self-destructiveness of present globally relevant human behavior.

Within the three great movements, there are several organizations. One problem they all have is that of eager members who wish to change or, more often, to expand the basic mandates of the organization. In some countries, the successful movement against nuclear weapons had to use much time to restrain members who wished to expand the movement as a more general peace organization. That would have reduced its thrust.

Amnesty International is a tremendously successful organization within the human rights movement—part of the general, loosely connected social justice movement (in my terminology). The organization's success is in part due to careful limitation of a core problem: to get political prisoners out of devastating prisons through nonviolent action. Its main procedure: letters to people in power. Because of its success, some eager members and outsiders are, of course, pressing the organization to extend its mandate, for instance, into being a general human rights organization.

As a general goal, the deep ecology movement aims to participate in overcoming the ecological crisis. But supporters share, for instance, a strong sense of the intrinsic value of every living being and its right to live and blossom—values that are independent of usefulness. Like other movements, especially as long as it seems to be successful, it will always be under pressure to extend its mandate. Such efforts tend to confuse more than strengthen a movement. But cooperation with other movements is obviously an important task. The contemporary complex social situation makes isolation rather unnatural.

Again, the very special situation today must be kept in mind: An increasing portion of the populace in the industrial countries is aware of the colossal changes taking place on land, in the oceans, and in the atmosphere, threatening everybody everywhere. The interconnectedness of everything is manifested in a more dramatic and convincing way than in 1970 or 1980. Many of those who were young in 1970 and got some ecological education are now firmly established and influential. But it is not my job to trace the ecological, social, and political factors determining the historically important convergence of the three movements and the ascendancy of the ecological issues on par with the traditionally most crucial social and political ones.

POSTSCRIPT 1993

I still smile, thinking about the fate of a certain criminal called "Yellow Cheese" (*Gulosten*) among his fellow burglars. He was also a great patriot, and on April 9, 1940, the very day the Nazis invaded Oslo, the capital of Norway, Yellow Cheese ran around collecting dynamite. His personal plan was immediately to bomb the places where the Nazis congregated in Oslo. Fortunately for him and for the five-year-long resistance movement, a wiser fighter stopped him: Direct actions must be carefully planned, and priorities established. Risk your life, yes, but the movement needs people who are not sent to German concentration camps within a week of drastic activity. Think in terms of years! Yellow Cheese understood and survived five years of fight. Honored to see the king, he became a personal friend of His Majesty.

"The key is thinking BIG, both in space and in time," says Michael Soulé.[3] Properly explained, this is not the same as being moderate. Yellow Cheese was never moderate, but his later direct actions were planned carefully and rarely dramatic. Tactical and strategic considerations went hand in hand.

In the ecological movement, there is the need to think not only in terms of days and years, but also in terms of generations. A response to the article by Soulé says a lot of things compatible with his appropriate-time-scale principle: "Any remaining old growth forest . . . should be afforded the highest levels of protection"; it is "unconscionable to suggest that it is not important to preserve the remaining patches on the national forests." From a point of view of appropriate time scale, a slogan like "Stop logging old growth immediately!" is justifiable, but we know that we have to select a small number of places, perhaps only one at a time, where we can try to stop logging or at least convince people that we seriously mean that no more logging should be undertaken. So we have to ask, Are there spots that have a lower priority than other spots? This is not compromising in essentials, but admitting that we have neither the manpower nor the funds available to offer visible resistance everywhere. Tactical considerations? Sure, but they are caused by the limitation of resources. It is like in any protracted warlike situation, only that we are trying to remain strictly nonviolent. In short, let us join short-range and long-range considerations, and remember that the long-range considerations in no way should diminish our concern for the local in time and space.

The Basics of the Deep Ecology Movement[4]

The deep ecology movement will thrive despite whatever professional philosophers like myself publish about their conception of it. Perhaps what I say about it is expressed in a way that is not natural for many of its warm supporters. But we cannot expect, or even wish, to have a single way of expressing ourselves. I have mine.

Supporters of the deep ecology movement refer approvingly to a diversity of philosophers, cultural traditions, and religious trends. Some authors ask for clarification: Where is the essence or core? Is there a definite general philosophy of deep ecology, or at least a kind of philosophy? Or is it essentially a movement with exasperatingly vague outlines?

I do not think it is desirable to do more than tentatively suggest what might be the essential ingredients of a deep ecology theoretical point of view. In what follows, I formulate some remarks that might be considered dogmatic. They are, however, only meant as proposals for people with a background similar to my own.

In order to facilitate discussion about the deep ecology movement among philosophers, it may be helpful to distinguish a *common platform* of deep ecology from the fundamental features of philosophies and religions from which that platform is derived, provided it is tentatively formulated as a set of norms and hypotheses (factual assumptions). The term *platform* is preferred to *principle*, because the latter may be misunderstood to refer to ultimate premises. Furthermore, the formulations of a platform should be short and concise (as a synopsis), whereas the fundamental premises are Buddhist, Taoist, Christian, or of other religious kinds, or they are philosophical with affinities to the basic views of Spinoza, Whitehead, Heidegger, or others. Different sets of fundamentals are normally more or less incompatible, or at least difficult to compare in terms of cognitive contents. Supporters of deep ecology may have great difficulties in understanding each other's ultimate view, but not sets of penultimate views as formulated as a kind of platform they have largely in common.

The platform of the deep ecology movement can be grounded in religion or philosophy, including ethics. It can also be said to be *derived* from these fundaments. As used here, the term *derived* is open to a variety of interpretations. If the validity of a norm or a hypothesis is justified by reference to one definite set of assumptions of a philosophical or religious kind, the norm or hypothesis is in a sense derived from those assumptions. The set acquires a character of premises for particular conclusions. But closely similar or even identical conclusions may be drawn from divergent or even incompatible premises. This explains in a natural way that diversity of views at the deepest level can be felt by some to be bewildering and makes deep ecology too vague to deserve analytical scrutiny.

One must avoid looking for one definite philosophy or religious view among the supporters of the deep ecology movement. There is a rich manifold of fundamental views compatible with the deep ecology platform. And without this, the movement would lose its transcultural character. The transcultural character of the movement makes it natural that the wording of a version of the platform cannot be the same everywhere. A term like *our planet*, for instance, is unsuitable where people have no clear notion corresponding to the Western concept of a planet.

The discussion has four levels: (1) verbalized fundamental philosophical and religious views, (2) the deep ecology platform, (3) the more or less general consequences derived from the platform—guidelines for lifestyles and for policies of every kind, and (4) prescriptions related to concrete situations and dateable decisions made in them. The term *dateable* refers to the trivial circumstance that a decision is made at a definite time, even if it has taken a year to arrive at.

From the point of view of derivation, one may use the accompanying Apron diagram. The direction of derivation proceeds down the page, as is usual and convenient. But some may prefer the opposite: having the roots on the deepest level at the bottom of the page and letting the other levels develop like the branches of a tree. Still others would prefer a more holistic or artistic illustration avoiding straight lines and preferring circles. The root may be conceived in terms of the premise-conclusion relation, psychological or social motivation, or some other relations. The Apron is a premise-conclusion diagram.

The Apron diagram is rather abstract, so I shall give an example of a justification of a concrete action formulated in terms of the apron. Let NN be a mythical person, a supporter of the deep ecology movement, living somewhere near the unique old-growth forests of the northwestern United States. He happens to have fundamental beliefs of a Spinozistic kind, but has no knowledge of Spinoza. One early Monday, he spikes some trees and puts up some posters clearly announcing that trees in the neighborhood are spiked. I use NN as an example of how he in principle, not in practice, makes use of the Apron diagram. The concrete action of spiking is chosen because of its controversial character. Some supporters do not find the spiking procedure justifiable. Exactly where is the disagreement to be located?

ILLUSTRATION 1: THE APRON DIAGRAM

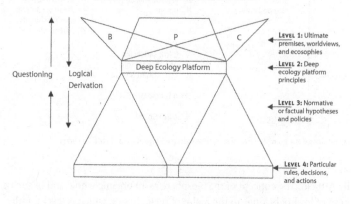

B = Buddhist   C = Christian   P = Philosophical (e.g., Spinozist or Whiteheadian)

In assessing constructive criticism of deep ecology as a form of activism, we find it useful to try to determine which level is involved. For example, in the introduction to *Ethics of Environmental Concern*, Robin Attfield says: "I do not accept, with the so-called 'deep, long-range ecology movement,' the view that our principal loyalty should be focussed not on fellow-humans or fellow creatures but on the biosphere as an organic whole."[5]

I suppose that some supporters of the deep ecology movement propose focusing loyalty on the biosphere as an organic whole in the sense suggested

ILLUSTRATION 2: EXAMPLE OF THE JUSTIFICATION OF
A CONCRETE ACTION FORMULATED IN TERMS OF THE APRON DIAGRAM

Example

LEVEL 1			A SET OF ULTIMATE SPINOZIST PRINCIPLES			
LEVEL 2	N & H		The 8 point platform principles of DEM			
LEVEL 3	H1 The logging at P decreases richness & diversity & is not necessary to satisfy vital needs		H Logging at P is illegal		N Direct actions should be nonviolent	
			N Tree spiking, & properly done, H is nonviolent and may contribute to stop logging		H All normal means to stop it have been tried but have failed	
	H Logging at P should be stopped now		N Tree spiking at P & is justifiable and H urgent		N Supporters of DEM living near P and considering spiking should participate	
LEVEL 4			N I, NN, satisfy the & above conditions H I could start Monday			
			H It is now Monday			
			N (NN:) Spike!			

Abbreviations: N = norm; H = hypothesis; DEM = deep ecology movement; NN = a person

by Attfield. The concept of the biosphere as an organic whole and of such a kind of loyalty belongs to the realm of metaphysics, which is level 1, rather than to the other levels. Therefore, the fact that Attfield does not accept the view he describes is not relevant in argumentation for or against the deep ecology movement. You may or may not have your principal loyalty focused on the biosphere as an organic whole; you cannot even be sure what is meant by the terms. One main point in deep ecology is the *deep* argumentation, that is, argumentation from ultimate (philosophical, religious) premises, but there is room for very different sets of such premises.

If the view outlined by Attfield seems to be implicit in deep ecology views on level 2 platform principles, his nonacceptance would amount to a non-acceptance of something basic in the deep ecology movement (insofar as it is verbally articulated). If the view seems to be implicit in views belonging to level 3, this would also be relevant to acceptance of deep ecology, and the same applies to level 4. Attfield could mean that, on the whole, decisions made or advocated by supporters of the deep ecology platform seem to imply the view he does not accept. Perhaps, perhaps not. Therefore, the distinction of levels is useful when one is trying to pin down exactly what a criticism is focusing on.

The Apron diagram furnishes only a static model. A supporter of the deep ecology movement will normally modify the sentences at the different levels from time to time. New information may change any hypotheses and therefore also change norms that have partly been justified on the basis of the hypotheses being changed.

New ethical or other intuitions may make the supporter change any norm. If a norm is changed, new sets of hypotheses are normally involved, and old ones are discarded. This again will cause reverberations in a smaller or greater part of the field.

For example, Diprinzio, supporter of the deep ecology movement, reads something like this in the *Canberra Times:*

> MELBOURNE. Victoria's mountain people brought their own legend to Melbourne's streets today to show their anger about the State Government's plan to extend the Alpine National Parks.
>
> The Alpine families arrived with their dogs, their drays and their stockwhips.
>
> They rode in wagons or horseback wearing moleskins, bush hats and oilskins.
>
> They provided one of the most colourful protests Melbourne has seen and were cheered by hordes of people lining the route to Parliament House.
>
> The people of the high country say the Government's plan threatens to destroy their heritage and the future of the 120 families who have been grazing cattle in the Alps for the past 150 years.

The article and a most touching picture make this staunch supporter of deep ecology exclaim, "Yes, we cannot do this to the 120 families. The plan must be fought today! I am joining the demonstration!" His decision belongs to level 4. But he soon realizes that it may go against a lot of his own norms and hypotheses of level 2 and level 3. The deep ecology platform clearly implies a no! if Diprinzio does not start to make changes at level 3. He feels that his tentative yes might not touch the platform formulations if he makes proper changes of level 3 hypotheses. So he sees what can be done at level 3. There he finds hypotheses about compensation to people in awkward situations similar to those of the mountain people. He also tries to clarify and assess his position in general. After some reflection, he reverses his conclusion: The plan should be upheld, but he decides to study it more carefully.

From a point of view of normative systematizations, what goes on when changes are made at one or more levels is rather complicated. But part of it is processes of derivation. The Apron diagram pretends only to illustrate important differences of the levels of derivation and the specific character of level 2. It represents a condensed formulation of the deepest-level norms and hypotheses that most supporters of the deep ecology movement can agree upon. This level is illustrated as the penultimate level of argumentation characteristic of those supporters of deep ecology who try to articulate their very basic views. At levels 3 and 4, disagreements may arise. At level 1, supporters with entirely different backgrounds disagree or find each other's views more or less incomprehensible.

A direction of derivation is not a measure of value priorities or of ethical priorities. And it does not imply that what is derived is a *means* in relation to what it is derived from. A simple example is enough to clarify this. From "Do not kill humans!" follows, if you concede "*All* mothers are humans," the conclusion "Do not kill your mother!" This rather concrete norm is here *derived* from the more general and abstract one. But this does not imply that humans in general have a higher value or priority in relation to mothers. It does not say that in a norm conflict, you should be more careful not to kill humans than not to kill your mother. An absurd position! And finally, it is rather strange to refrain from killing your mother as a means to a goal, namely, not to kill humans.

The formulations of level 2 have the character of proposals. The proposals may differ substantially or show a natural diversity of terminological and conceptual idiosyncrasies. Unhappily, it is quite common, in a broad sense, to mix the logical relation of derivation with other relations. These are at least as important, but nevertheless are different.

Rather often, the relation of justification, ethical or otherwise, coincides with the relation of derivation. Thus, many people adhere to a general, rather intuitive norm of "the right to live and flourish" without considering exactly what the norm, taken so-called literally, has as consequences. Confronted with questions like "What about poisonous snakes?" "What about beetles eating our vegetables?" some will hesitate, but eventually take up a firm, positive stand, justifying this by reference to the general norm. In such cases, the derivation relation coincides with the justification relation (for these people). Schematically, the general premise can be stated as this: "There is a right that every living being x has, in principle, to live and flourish." The special premise: "y is a living being." Conclusion: "There is a right that y has . . ." The conclusion is ethically as well as syllogistically derived from the general premise. In spite of the many cases of such coincidences, the relations should be kept apart by people interested in philosophical articulation of deep ecology principles.

There is no point in trying to formulate a short (or long) version of level 2 that all supporters of deep ecology would like. The most remarkable similarities of positions and attitudes belong to levels 3 and 4. There are typical shallow and typical deep argumentation patterns, and there are environmental policies and decisions in relation to which supporters of deep ecology show an astonishingly high level of agreement.

Here is, slightly modified, an eight-point proposal for level 2:

1. The flourishing of human and nonhuman life on earth has inherent value. The value of nonhuman life-forms is independent of the usefulness of the nonhuman world for human purposes.
2. Richness and diversity of life-forms are also values in themselves and contribute to the flourishing of human and nonhuman life on earth.
3. Humans have no right to reduce this richness and diversity except to satisfy *vital* needs.
4. The flourishing of human life and cultures is compatible with a substantial decrease of the human population. The flourishing of nonhuman life requires such a decrease.
5. Present human interference with the nonhuman world is excessive, and the situation is rapidly worsening.
6. In view of the foregoing points, policies must be changed. The changes in policies affect basic economic, technological, and ideological structures. The resulting state of affairs will be deeply different from the present and make possible a more joyful experience of the connectedness of all things.
7. The ideological change is mainly that of appreciating life quality

(dwelling in situations of inherent value) rather than adhering to an increasingly higher standard of living. There will be a profound awareness of the difference between big and great.

8. Those who subscribe to the foregoing points have an obligation directly or indirectly to participate in the attempt to implement the necessary changes.

The eight formulations, of course, need clarification, elaboration, and comments. Here they are, slightly modified:

Point 1: Instead of *biosphere*, we might use the term *ecosphere* to stress that we, of course, do not limit our concern to the life-forms in a narrow sense. The term *life* is used here in a comprehensive, nontechnical way to refer also to what biologists classify as nonliving: rivers (watersheds), landscapes, cultures, ecosystems, the living earth. Slogans such as "Let the river live" illustrate the broader usage so common in many different cultures. Only in our Western schools is the term *living* firmly associated with the science of biology.

Point 2: So-called simple, lower, or primitive species of plants and animals contribute essentially to the richness and diversity of life. They have value in themselves and are not merely steps toward the so-called higher or rational life-forms.

Complexity, as referred to here, is different from complication. Urban life may be more complicated than life in a natural setting without being more complex in the sense of being multifaceted.

Why talk about diversity *and* richness? Suppose humans interfere with an ecosystem to such a degree that one thousand vertebrate species are each reduced to a survival minimum. This is clearly an unacceptable state of affairs. We demand abundance of interconnected habitats through "bridges." The main point is that life on earth may be excessively interfered with, even if diversity is upheld.

Point 3: This formulation is perhaps too strong. But considering the mass of proclamations about what humans have the right to, it may be sobering to announce a norm about what they have no right to. That is, we must take into account situations in which we humans cannot evoke and appeal to a right. The formulation is not intended to automatically condemn as *wrong* all the actions to which we cannot invoke a right.

The term *vital need* is left deliberately vague to allow for considerable latitude in judgment. Differences in climate and related factors, together with differences in the structures of societies as they now exist, need to be considered. Also, the difference between a *means* to the satisfaction of the need and the need itself must be considered. If a whaler quits whaling, he may risk unemployment under the present economic conditions. Whaling is for him an important means. But he and his boat are urgently needed in the control of overfishing and the use of barbarous methods. And the whaling nations are rich enough to finance such inspection, especially along the coasts of developing countries. So there is not a question of vital need to kill whales.

Point 4: The stabilization and reduction of the human population will take time. Interim strategies need to be developed. But this in no way excuses the present complacency; the extreme seriousness of our current situation must first be realized. But the longer we wait, the more drastic will be the measures needed. Until deep changes are made, substantial decreases in richness and diversity are liable to occur: The rate of extinction of species will be ten to one hundred times greater than in any other period of earth's history.

It may validly be objected that if the present billions of humans deeply changed their behavior in the direction of ecological responsibility, nonhuman life could flourish.

Point 5: People in the materially richest countries cannot be expected to reduce their excessive interference with the nonhuman world to a moderate level overnight. Less interference does not imply that humans should not modify some ecosystems as do other species. Humans have modified the earth and will probably continue to do so. At issue are the nature and extent of such interference.

The fight to preserve and extend areas of wilderness or near wilderness should continue and should focus on the general ecological functions of these areas. Very large wilderness areas are required in the biosphere for the continued evolutionary speciation of animals and plants. Present designated wilderness areas are too small and too few.

Point 6: Economic growth as conceived and implemented today by the industrial states is incompatible with points 1 through 6. "Green" economists have to be consulted.

Whereas *self-determination; decentralization; local community;* and *think globally, act locally,* will remain key terms in the ecology of human societies, the implementation of deep changes nevertheless requires increasingly global action in the sense of action across every border. And often, local communities or areas with scattered population are uncritically in favor of so-called development and must be forced to a more ecological responsible policy by central authorities. There are important limits to decentralization of ecologically relevant decisions.

Support for global action through nongovernmental organizations becomes increasingly important. Many of these organizations are able to act globally "from grassroots to grassroots," thus avoiding negative government interference.

Cultural diversity today requires advanced technology, that is, techniques that advance the basic goals of each culture. So-called soft, intermediate, and alternative technologies are steps in this direction. What is called advanced technology rarely fits the name.

Point 7: Some economists criticize the term *quality of life* because it is supposed to be vague. But on closer inspection, what they consider vague is actually the nonquantitative nature of the term. One cannot quantify adequately what is important for the quality of life, as discussed here, and there is no need to do so.

Point 8: There is ample room for different opinions about priorities: What should be done first, and what next? What is more urgent? What is necessary as opposed to what is highly desirable? Differences of opinion do not exclude vigorous cooperation. "The frontier is long."

What is gained from tentatively formulating basic views shared today by most or all supporters of the deep ecology movement? Hopefully, it makes it a little easier to localize the movement among the many alternative movements. And hopefully, this does not lead to isolation but rather to even better cooperation with many other alternative movements. It might also make some of us more clear about where we stand and which disagreements might profitably be reduced and which ones might profitably be sharpened.

A GLOBAL APRON DIAGRAM EXPLAINED

I see the deep ecology movement and its supporters as part of a total view that comprises many levels and many ultimate philosophies and diverse practices in close contact with each other. To illustrate this, I use a diagram. The Apron diagram illustrates logical, as distinct from genetic, relations between views. By "logical relations," I mean verbally articulated relations between the premises and conclusions. The premises and conclusions move down the diagram in stages: Some conclusions become premises for new conclusions. By "genetic relations," I refer to influences, motivations, inspirations, and cause-and-effect relations. They are not indicated anywhere in the Apron diagram. They may move up and down or anywhere, and they involve time.

The platform principles of the deep ecology movement can be grounded for individual supporters in a religion or an ultimate philosophy. There is a great diversity of religions and philosophies from which people can support these principles. In a loose sense, the deep ecology movement can be said to be derived from these kinds of fundamentals. The situation reminds us that a set of very similar or even identical conclusions may be drawn from divergent premises. The platform can be the same, even though the fundamental premises differ. One must avoid looking for one definite philosophy or religion among all the supporters of the deep ecology movement. Fortunately, there is a rich manifold of fundamental views compatible with the platform of the deep ecology movement. Supporters live in different cultures and have different religions. Furthermore, there is a plethora of consequences derived from the platform because of these and other differences.

We must take four levels into account: (1) verbalized fundamental philosophical and religious ideas and intuitions, (2) the platform of the deep ecology movement, (3) more or less general consequences derived from the platform—lifestyles and general policies of every kind, and (4) concrete situations and practical decisions made in them.

The possibility that the platform principles may be derived from a plurality of mutually inconsistent premises—the B-set and the C-set—is illustrated in the upper part of the diagram. B can be Buddhism, C can be Christianity, P may be Spinoza's philosophy, or it could be Ecosophy T. Similarly, the lower part of the diagram illustrates how, with one or more of the eight principles as part of a set of premises, mutually inconsistent conclusions may logically be derived, leading to the C-set or B-set of concrete decisions. C might be inspired by a sort of Christianity, and B by a sort of Buddhism. Or, again, P may be Spinoza-inspired while P2 follows a certain ecological philosophy. (Unfortunately, the relation of deepness in the Apron diagram leads upward. To avoid mixing metaphors, the apron could be turned upside down.)

The distinctions among the four levels are important. Supporters of the deep ecology movement have ultimate views from which they derive their acceptance of the platform, but those views may be very different from person to person, and from group to group. Likewise, supporters may disagree about what follows from the eight points, partly because they interpret the points differently and partly because what follows does not follow from those eight points alone, but from a wider set of premises, and these might be in conflict.

The deep ecology movement thus can be seen to manifest both plurality and unity: unity at level 2, as is true for many global grassroots movements, and plurality at other levels. The Apron diagram can be used to illustrate the same general aspects of other international movements, such as the social justice and peace movements.

FURTHER ELABORATION AND EXAMPLES

First, let us start with the question, Which beliefs of the supporters of the deep ecology movement might separate these people from the rest of the supporters of the environmental movement? What might separate them on a general and abstract level? No single answer is supposed to be *the* correct one, and the question itself may be interpreted in somewhat different ways.

Suppose one proposal contains eight points, each expressed in one, two, or three sentences. We are now going to study such a proposal from one and only one point of view, the premise-conclusion point of view.

Second, we can ask, How do supporters of the deep ecology movement justify their stated beliefs? Are some beliefs based on other beliefs they have? Their beliefs cannot be based on other beliefs, because then you would have to have infinitely many. You must stop somewhere. Some are ultimate, at least temporarily ultimate, beliefs. (Note that speaking of *beliefs*, we do not intend to say that they are "*only* beliefs," that is, *not* being certain or true or right or expressing facts.)

According to my experience, supporters of the deep ecology movement usually state beliefs on which they base some or all of their "eight-point beliefs." These normally, but not always, have the character of ultimate beliefs, making out premises for their eight-point beliefs. That is, from the former beliefs, the eight-point beliefs follow as conclusions and are therefore accepted as premises.

For example, Peter, a supporter of the deep ecology movement, says that all living beings have value in themselves. We ask him to justify that, if he does not think it is self-evident. Peter answers with two sentences: "All the creatures that God has created have value in themselves. God created and creates every living kind of being." We will say that Peter infers "All living beings have a value in themselves" as a conclusion from the two premises. He may use the conclusion as a premise for new conclusions, for instance, "Bacteria have value in themselves." He only needs one more premise, namely, "Bacteria are living beings." The new conclusion may again be used as one of the premises for reaching new conclusions. We get *a chain of* premise-conclusion relations.

We now introduce a distinction between level 1 and level 2 beliefs. Premises of the beliefs stated in the list of eight points are level 1 beliefs, and the eight points themselves are level 2 beliefs. Or, speaking more generally, a set of beliefs that presents a proposal of what supporters of the deep ecology movement have *in common* on a general and abstract level is a set of level 2 beliefs. The premises suggested by supporters of the deep ecology movement of such a set we call level 1 beliefs.

In the example, the supporter of the deep ecology movement clearly has the existence of God as a creator as a premise. If he happens to have premises for his beliefs in this, we say that they also belong to level 1. That is, *any* premise Peter uses for his level 2 beliefs we class as belonging to his level 1 beliefs. Here we are not interested in *what* they are, but that they are premises of the level 2 beliefs.

Third, it turns out that different supporters of the deep ecology movement announce different level 1 beliefs. Often, these are incompatible sets. Or, different supporters do not understand each other's level 1 beliefs or at least some of these beliefs. To me, a couple of Gary Snyder's Buddhist level 1 beliefs, or, rather, some of his sentences expressing these beliefs, are not understandable. I might understand them if I studied Buddhism carefully enough, but such a study has no high priority: We agree on level 2.

The diversity of level 1 beliefs is a strength, not a weakness. No deep cultural differences can exist without diversity at level 1! There is unity in diversity: unity at level 2, diversity at level 1!

Finally, we jump to level 4: practical decisions in concrete (dateable) situations. "Ah, a moose is in our garden. What do we do? Call the police!" Fifty years ago, some people in Oslo ran for their guns. Now (decent) people call the police, who are in charge of the practical decisions: shoot in earnest, shoot to tranquilize and transport them far out of Oslo, and so forth. A supporter of the deep ecology movement may decide to call the police, because he or she knows the rules and finds it is the best solution for the *moose*.

The level 4 decision cannot be based solely on level 2 beliefs. Critical, complex thinking involving a variety of beliefs—so-called level 3 beliefs—intervenes. Only under rare and special conditions do we try to articulate as fully as we can the additional premises leading from level 2 to level 4, that is, "leading" in terms of a premise-conclusion chain. Difficult? In theory, yes, but we all sometimes use the aspects of premise and conclusion.

More or less inevitably, level 1 contains philosophical or religious beliefs (or both). I propose to characterize, or even define, a supporter of the deep ecology movement as a person whose environmentally relevant beliefs are based on philosophical or religious beliefs in the sense of having level 1 beliefs that are at least in a broad, *nonprofessional* sense philosophical or religious.

The overall argumentation pattern of a supporter of the deep ecology movement reveals references to *ultimate premises*. This relates to the preferred sense of the term *deep*: The argumentation, if the supporter of the deep ecology movement tries to tell what he or she ultimately stands for (in questions related to the environment and the ecological crisis) is, touch rock-bottom questions. But sheer deepness is not enough, since the argumentation goes through level 2! James Watt—the U.S. administrator of environmental policy under President Reagan—based his decisions on rock-bottom beliefs within his form of Christianity. ("Why so much preservation when the end of the world is near?") He certainly did not accept any of the eight points of the platform or similar proposals.

A small technicality: Some supporters of the deep ecology movement find that the intrinsic value of living beings is obvious, self-evident. Do we then say that these people have no level 1 beliefs at this point? We may, but we may also say that the point does belong to *both* level 1 and level 2 for this particular supporter of the deep ecology movement. Logically it is OK, they tell us, that from premise *P*, the conclusion *P* follows. Anyhow, to hold that every living being has a value in itself is to enter the sphere of philosophical considerations. Naturally, a host of questions related to the four-level concept leads us into difficulties, but these lie outside the scope of this discussion.

What, then, is the four-level concept good for? It is useful for sorting out agreements and disagreements. For example, if by *ecofeminism* you mean that the ecological crisis is essentially due to the domination of sorts of masculine-value priorities, this can be articulated on level 3. The strategy of overcoming the crisis, the level 4 decision, will be colored by a point of view belonging in deep ecology movement argumentation patterns. It shows up in the argumentation pattern of well-known deep ecology ecofeminists like Patsy Hallen.[6] Some supporters of the deep ecology movement will not entirely agree, and you get disagreement between supporters of the deep ecology movement on levels 3 and 4.

The Apron diagram illustrates the kinds of room for agreement and disagreement. It is, however, not meant to suggest that only one definite set of level 2 beliefs should be available. Change one or more of the eight points of the platform, and changes will follow on the other levels. A movement is dynamic and manifests changes of emphasis.

Two things are often forgotten: The Apron is made to clarify the specific character of a subspecies of the environmental movement. In a subspecies characterization, one does not include characters of the species as a whole. The shallow or reform movement tends to argue only on level 3 and level 4. That is, their argumentation pattern when described in terms of the Apron is wholly contained at those levels.

Against the term *shallow*, the reformists argue that going into philosophy, questions about intrinsic value, meaning of life, and so forth, is sidetracking the issue, getting lost in a blind alley. And it undermines realistic cost-benefit analysis. It is therefore a plus, not a minus, to limit oneself to levels 3 and 4.

The second thing easily forgotten is that the Apron consistently limits itself to premise-conclusion relations. This arrangement is only one among many others, the "genetic" arrangements.

Cultural Diversity and the Deep Ecology Movement[7]

THE NEW CULTURAL ANTHROPOLOGY

Cultural anthropology and the general history of the main families of cultures on earth reveal vast differences of attitudes, beliefs, assumptions, and premises of individual, social, political, and metaphysical patterns.[8] How deep or basic are these differences? That is an open question. Inevitably, tentative answers require that we also answer questions about what is precisely meant by *deepness* in this context.

Since the 1940s, there have been theories about the future of humankind emphasizing the need for continued richness and diversity of human cultures in order to avoid stagnation of human development. Development in terms of biological evolution may take thousands or even millions of years, but the extreme flexibility of humans may ensure development through deep cultural changes rather than manifest biological divergence. But such changes may partly depend upon the sheer plurality of cultural differences, whatever their deepness.[9]

Plurality requires moderation of the contemporary rapid cultural invasion of other cultures, a process we have seen accelerating since the twentieth century. I look upon moderation efforts as part of the general effort to maintain richness and diversity of life on earth. At least in some easily observable ways, there is a convergence of cultures rather than diversification. Here we must, however, take into account the present diversification of subcultures—rapidly changing groups of people trying out "new" ways of life in conscious opposition to the "normal" within a particular culture.

From the very start of the deep ecology movement in the industrial societies, the obvious question was raised: Are there or have there been cultures with a more ecologically responsible relationship between humans and the nonhuman world than that of the present materially rich national cultures? In the United States, various North American Indian cultures were studied with special care and furnished a clear answer: yes. At the same time, Europeans with a critical attitude toward industrial societies started to study African cultures with renewed interest. Did they really work harder, and had they really less time and opportunity for cultural achievements independent of those serving mere survival? Marshall Sahlins answered no. His main work appeared in English under the title *Stone Age Economics.* In his opinion, the most affluent stone age societies supported their rich cultures.[10]

A new generation of cultural anthropologists grew up in the 1960s with rather ambivalent feelings toward the basic politics of industrial societies. New versions favored new concepts such as those of the postindustrial society, the green society, and a new conception about development: the distinction between underdeveloped and developed nations was largely given up as a near synonym for poor nonindustrial versus rich industrial nations. The basic question was raised: How can the poor nations eliminate the kind of poverty that has hurt their quality of life (though this is not necessarily the kind of poverty seen from a rich consumerist society's point of view)? How can they develop *without* following the tracks of the rich Western nations?

From the point of view of the deep ecology movement, these new vistas were of prime importance. If the majority of humans tried to live the same way as the average person in the rich industrial societies, the doomsday prophecies might come true. When we appreciate a manifest cultural difference, do we react in the same way as when we appreciate a difference between plants and animals? We do not look upon humans as animals in a zoological garden.

People active in the various life sciences may easily go too far in finding similarities between phenomena in human societies and those in the animal and vegetable world. One has to be clear about the many pitfalls. In the history of ideas, the important line of ideas from Protestantism through Hegel, Marx to the Frankfurt School, has contributed to the acute awareness of this tendency. On the other hand, there is also a spiritual arrogance that may hide important analogies and counteract the identification with living beings other than fellow humans. In the worst concentration camps of the twentieth century, the conscious efforts of tyrants to educate guards in brutality have mainly consisted in teaching them to look upon inmates as animals: "They are only animals!" Brutes should be handled with brutality—they don't understand decency. One must expect that equating human cultural diversity with nonhuman diversity will sometimes elicit deep-seated repugnance. The recent, rather confusing debate over E. O. Wilson's sociobiology illustrates both tendencies, exaggerating similarities or letting repugnance take over.

Julian Huxley, the biologist and leader of UNESCO in the late 1940s, and many others at that time hypothesized that in the very long run, cultural diversity and cultural "evolution" will play an *analogous* role for the species of *Homo sapiens*, as do mutations and species variation among nonhumans. It has been thought to result in a development much faster than real speciation among nonhumans. This is made possible through the extremely loose programming of humans: Their options in life are more varied, and "instinctive" determinants are less dominating even if very strong. The term *analogous* is used rather than *similar* because some differences are deep and important.

DEPTH OF CULTURAL DIFFERENCES

If we subsume human cultural diversity under the concept of intrinsic valuable diversity of life-forms, the adjective *deep* is appropriate. Differences in details are not often important. If people in culture A must put something on their heads when entering a church, whereas people in culture B must take care not to wear any head coverings in church, the difference in behavior is not deep. The attitudes toward a church may be very much alike. Today, we are mostly concerned about the continued existence of deep cultural differences, not only small variations of mores and habits.

From the point of view of cultural anthropology, the criterion of deep versus shallow cannot be precise, but the literature of that science clearly shows the important presence of a distinction, such as deep-shallow (or, rather, deep–less deep), big-small, and essential-nonessential. Classifications of cultures into groups attest to such discriminations.

The Place of Joy in a World of Fact

The solution of environmental problems is presupposed in all utopias. For example, every family is to enjoy free nature under Marxian communism. "In a communist society," Marx says in a famous passage in *The German Ideology*, "nobody has one exclusive sphere of activity but each can be accomplished in any branch he wishes. Society regulates the general production and thus makes it possible for me to do one thing today and another tomorrow: to hunt in the morning, fish in the afternoon, tend cattle in the evening, engage in literary criticism after dinner, just as I have in mind, without ever becoming a hunter, fisherman, shepherd, or critic."[11]

The complete individual is not a specialist; he or she is a generalist and an amateur. This does not mean that the person has no special interests, never works hard, or does not partake in the life of the community. The complete individual does so, however, from personal inclination, with joy, and within the framework of his or her value priorities.

In the future ideal society, whether outlined by Marx or by more bourgeois prophets, there will be people who might use most of their energy doing highly specialized, difficult things, but as amateurs—that is, from inclination and from a mature philosophy of life. There will be no fragmentary men and women, and certainly no fragmentary ecologists.

We all, I suppose, admire the pioneers who, through endless meetings held in contaminated city air, have succeeded in establishing wilderness areas in the United States. Unfortunately, their constant work in offices and corridors has largely ruined their capacity to enjoy these wilderness areas. They have lost the capacity to show, *in action*, what they care for; otherwise, they would spend much more time (and even live) in the wilderness. Many people verbally admire wilderness areas, but have not stepped down from their exalted positions, as chairs of this or that, to enjoy these areas at least part of the year.

What I say here about advocates of wilderness seems, unhappily, to be valid for advocates of a better environment in general. Ordinary people show a good deal of skepticism toward verbally declared values that are not expressed in the lifestyle of the propagandist. Environmentalists sometimes succumb to a joyless life that belies their concern for a better environment. This cult of dissatisfaction is apt to add to the already fairly advanced joylessness we find among socially responsible, successful people and to undermine one of the chief presuppositions of the ecological movement: that joy is related to the environment and to nature.

In short, the best way to promote a good cause is to provide a good example. One ought not to be afraid that the example will go unnoticed. For example, Albert Schweitzer hid himself in Africa, but his public relations prospered and so did the sale of his books.

So much for utopias. My next concern is with how to get nearer to our utopias. I shall take up only one aspect: the relation between personal lifestyle and teaching.

THE LIFESTYLE OF ENVIRONMENTALISTS

Joy is contagious. If we only talk about the joys of a good environment, though, it is of little avail.

I know that many *have* turned their backs on more lucrative careers and a life of security, cultivating well-established sciences. This is not enough, however. Life should manifest the peaks of our value priorities. Working for a better environment is, after all, only of instrumental value. We remain on the level of techniques. What criterion shall we use to follow the lead of our personal priorities? We do have one that is underrated among conscientious, responsible people: joy.

JOY ACCORDING TO "PESSIMISTIC" PHILOSOPHERS

Suppose someone openly adhered to the doctrine that there cannot be too much cheerfulness under any circumstances—even at a funeral. The sad truth is, I think, that he or she would be classified as shallow, cynical, disrespectful, irreligious, or mocking.

Søren Kierkegaard is an important figure here. He *seems* to take anguish, desperation, a sense of guilt, and suffering as the necessary, and sometimes even sufficient, condition of authentic living, but he also insists upon continuous joy as a condition of living. Whatever is done without joy is of no avail. "At seventy thousand fathoms' depth," you should be glad. At seventy thousand fathoms, one should retain "a joyful mind." He sometimes calls himself Hilarius, the one permeated with *hilaritas* (Latin for "cheerfulness").

Dread is the technical existentialist word for the kind of anxiety that opens the way to a deeper understanding of life. According to Heidegger (another hero of modern pessimism), dread is not an isolated, negative sensation. The mind is in a complex state in which dread cannot exist without joy; that is, one who thinks he or she has the dread experience but lacks joy suffers from an illusion. Dread has an internal relation to joy.

Our problem is not that we lack high levels of integration (that is, that we are immature and therefore joyless), but rather that we glorify immaturity. Do the most influential philosophers of our time and culture represent high degrees of maturity and integration? I have in mind not only Heidegger, Sartre, Kierkegaard, and Wittgenstein, but also Marx and Nietzsche. Tentatively, I must answer no. There are lesser-known but perhaps more mature philosophers, like Jaspers and Whitehead.

Should the world's misery and the approaching ecocatastrophe make one sad? My point is that there is no good reason to feel sad about all this. According to the philosophies I am defending, such regret is a sign of immaturity, the immaturity of unconquered passiveness and lack of integration.

The remedy (or psychotherapy) against sadness caused by the world's misery is to do something about it. I shall refrain from mentioning Florence Nightingale, but let me note that Gandhi loved to care for, wash, and massage lepers; he simply enjoyed it. It is very common to find those who constantly deal with extreme misery to be more than usually cheerful. According to Spinoza, the power of an individual is infinitely small compared with that of the entire universe, so we must not expect to save the whole world. The main point—which is built into the basic conceptual framework of Spinoza's philosophy—is that of activeness. By interacting with extreme misery, one gains cheerfulness. This interaction need not be direct. Most of us can do more in indirect ways by using our privileged positions in rich societies.

There are clear reasons for us not to concentrate all our efforts directly on extreme miseries, but rather to attack the causes, conditions, and other factors indirectly contributing to this misery. And, just as important, we need to encourage the factors that directly cause or facilitate the emergence of active (and therefore cheerful) work to alleviate misery.

Behind the prevailing widespread passivity found throughout the world is a lot of despair and pessimism concerning our capacity to have a good time. We tend to enjoy ourselves (except during vacations) in a private world of thoughtlessness, well insulated from the great issues of the day.

One of the strangest and next-to-paradoxical theses of Spinoza (and of Thomas Aquinas and others) is that knowledge of evil, or of misery, is inadequate knowledge. In short, there is no such object, whereas there is something good to know. Evil is always an absence of something, a lack of something positive. Their theory of knowledge holds that objects of knowledge are always something. When you say that you see that the glass is transparent, what you see, for example, is a red rose behind the glass. You do not see the transparency, which is not an object of perception.

In any event, while I do not think that the positive nonexistence of evil things can be shown without a great deal of redefinition of words, I nevertheless do not consider this view totally ridiculous. Like so many other strange points of view in major philosophies, it has an appeal and points in the right direction without perhaps stating anything clearly in the "scientific" sense.

SPINOZA ON JOY

Spinoza operates with three main concepts of joy and three of sorrow. *Laetitia*, *hilaritas*, and *titillatio* are the three Latin terms for the positive emotions of joy. Translations of these terms are, to a surprising degree, arbitrary, because their function in Spinoza's system can be discovered only by studying the complex total structure of his system. Isolating one concept from the others is not possible. Moreover, the system is more than the sum of its parts. From a strict, professional point of view, you must take it or leave it as a whole.

I translate *laetitia* as "joy"—a generic term comprising several important subkinds of joy. The main classification of joy is *hilaritas* (cheerfulness) and *titillatio* (pleasurable excitement). *Hilaritas* is the serene thing, coloring the whole personality, or better, the whole world.

Spinoza defines *hilaritas* as a joy to which every part of the body contributes. It does not affect just a subgroup of functions of the organism, but every one, and therefore the totality of the organism. Spinoza contends that there cannot be too much *hilaritas*.

The other main kind of joy, *titillatio*, affects a subgroup of the parts of the body. If very narrowly based and strong, it dominates and thereby inhibits the other kinds of joy. Accordingly, there can be too much of it. Here Spinoza mentions love of money, sexual infatuation, and ambition. He also mentions other sources of joy that are all good in moderate degrees if they do not hamper and inhibit one another.

A second classification of joy is that derived from the contemplation of our own achievement, creativity, or—more broadly—activeness, and the joy derived from the contemplation of the causes of joy outside us. The first he calls satisfaction, or repose in ourselves (*acquiescentia in se ipso*); the other he calls *amor*. There can be too much of them, however, because they sometimes refer to parts, not to the whole.

According to Spinoza, what refers to the whole of the body also refers to the whole of the conscious mind and to the whole of the universe or, more generally, to the whole of Nature, insofar as we know it. This is understandable from Spinoza's so-called philosophy of identity, which proclaims the ultimate identity of thought and matter, and from his theory of knowledge, which relates all our knowledge of the world to interaction with the body—just as biologists tend to do today.

Lack of self-acceptance (*acquiescentia in se ipso*) accounts for much of the passivity displayed by an important sector of the public in environmental conflicts. Many people are on the right side, but few stand up in public meetings and declare how they, as private citizens, feel about the pollution in their neighborhoods. They do not have sufficient self-respect, respect for their own feelings, or faith in their own importance. But they themselves do not have to fight for the changes; it is only necessary that they state their feelings and positions in public. A small minority will then fight with joy—supported by that considerable sector of people.

The distinction between pervasive joy (covering all) and partial joy need not be considered an absolute dichotomy but rather one that exists in degrees. Joy may be more or less pervasive. Clearly, higher degrees of joy require high degrees of integration of the personality, and high degrees of such integration require intense cultivation of the personal aspect of interaction with the environment. It requires a firm grasp of what we call value priorities—which Spinoza would call reality priorities, because of his resolute location of value among "objective" realities. Spinoza distinguishes degrees of realness and perfection. That which is perfect is complete. Integration of personality presupposes that we never act as mere functionaries or specialists but always as whole personalities conscious of our value priorities, and of the need to manifest those priorities in social direct action.

The specific thing to be learned from Spinoza and certain modern psychologists is, however, to integrate the value priorities themselves in the world. We tend to say "the world of facts," but the separation of value from facts is, itself, mainly due to an overestimation of certain scientific traditions stemming from Galileo. These traditions confuse the *instrumental* excellence of the mechanistic worldview with its properties as a whole philosophy. Spinoza was heavily influenced by mechanical models of matter, but he did not extend them to cover "reality." His reality was neither mechanical, value-neutral, nor value-empty.

This cleavage into two worlds—the world of fact and the world of values—can theoretically be overcome by placing, as Spinoza does, joys and other so-called subjective phenomena into a unified total field of realities. This, however, is too much to go into here. I am more concerned with the place of joy among our total experiences. The objectivist conception of value is important, though, in any discussion in which technocrats tend to dismiss cheerfulness in the environment as something "merely subjective."

Spinoza makes use of the following short, crisp, and paradoxical definition of joy (*laetitia*): "Joy is man's transition from lesser to greater perfection." Somewhat less categorically, he sometimes says that joy is the affect by which, or through which, we make the transition to greater perfection. Instead of "perfection," we may say "integrity" or "wholeness."

Of central importance, in my view, is the difference between these formulations and subjectivist ones proclaiming that joy only *follows* or *accompanies* these transitions to greater perfection. For Spinoza, the relation between joy and an increase in perfection is an *intrinsic* one. That is, the two can be separated only conceptually, not in practice. Such a realistic view of joy suggests that joyfulness, like color, attaches to and forms part of objects, but, of course, changes with the medium and must be defined in terms of interaction with organisms. Joy is linked intrinsically to an increase in many things: perfection, power and virtue, freedom and rationality, activeness, the degree to which we are the cause of our own actions, and the degree to which our actions are understandable by reference to ourselves. Joy is thus a basic part of the conceptual structure of Spinoza's system.

An increase in power is an increase in the ability to carry out what we sincerely strive to do. Power does not presuppose that we coerce other people; a tyrant may be less powerful than some poor soul sitting in prison. This concept of power has a long tradition and should not be forgotten. What we strive to do is defined in relation to what actually happens; thus "to save the world from pollution" is not something anyone strives to do, but is rather a kind of limited effort to save the things around us.

Cheerfulness (*hilaritas*) requires action of the whole integrated personality and is linked to a great increase in power. In the absence of joy, there is no increase of power, freedom, or self-determination. Thus, lack of joy should be taken seriously, especially among so-called responsible people furthering a good cause. The joy of work, like any other partial joy, can dominate and subdue other sources of joy to such an extent that the overall result is stagnation or even a decrease in power. In Spinoza's terminology, this means a loss of perfection or integration and increased difficulty in reaching a state of cheerfulness.

"To be happy" is often equated with enjoying oneself, laughing, or relaxing in the sense of being passive. Enjoying oneself by becoming intoxicated, which decreases the higher integrations of the nervous system, results in resignation. It means giving up the possibility of joyfulness of the whole person. Cheerfulness, in the Spinozistic sense, may not always be expressed in laughter or smiling, but in concentration, presentness, activeness.

The example of Buddha may illustrate my point. Buddha was an active person, but had great repose in himself (*acquiescentia in se ipso*). Long before he died, he is said to have reached Nirvana, which, properly interpreted within Mahayana Buddhism, involves supreme integration and liberation of the personality, implying bliss or (in the terminology of Spinoza) *hilaritas*. Research by F. Th. Stcherbatsky (1974) and others concerning the term *dukkha* (conventionally translated as "pain") shows that so-called pessimistic Buddhism also has a doctrine of joy as a central aspect of reaching freedom in Nirvana.[12]

One may say, somewhat loosely, that what we now lack in our technological age is repose in oneself. The conditions of modern life prevent the full development of the self-respect and self-esteem that are required to reach a stable high degree of *acquiescentia in se ipso* (the term *alienation*, incidentally, is related to the opposite of *in se*, namely, *in alio*, wherein we repose in something else, something outside ourselves, such as achievement in the eyes of others—we are "other directed").

Humility, as defined by Spinoza, is sorrow resulting from the contemplation of one's own impotency, weakness, and helplessness. A feeling of sorrow always involves a decrease of perfection, virtue, or freedom. We can come to know adequately more potent things than ourselves. This gives us such joy because of our activeness in the very process of knowing them. The realization of our own potency, and our active relation to the more potent, result in joy. Thus, instead of humility (which is a kind of sorrow), we feel three kinds of joy: first, the joy resulting from the contemplation of our own power, however small, which gives us *acquiescentia in se ipso*, self-respect and contentedness; second, the joy resulting from increased personal, active knowledge of things greater than we are; and third, the joy resulting from active interaction, which, strictly speaking, defines us (as well as other objects or fragments) in the total field of reality (or in Nature, in Spinoza's terminology).

Adequate knowledge always has a joyful personal aspect because it reveals a power (never a weakness) in our personality. In Spinoza's words:

> Therefore, if man, when he contemplates himself, perceives some kind of impotency in himself, it does not come from his understanding himself, but from his power of action being reduced . . . To the extent that man knows himself with true rationality, to that extent it is assumed that he understands his essence, that is, his power.[13]

We say with some haughtiness that Spinoza belongs to the age of rationalism, to the pre-Freudian, pre-Hitler era. Nevertheless, Spinoza in many ways anticipated Freud, and his term *ratio* must not be translated into our term *rational* or *rationality* unless we immediately add that his *ratio* was more flexible and was internally related to emotion. Rational action for him is action involving absolutely maximal perspective—that is, where things are seen as fragments of total Nature—which is, of course, not what we tend to call rational today. Spinoza was not an intellectual in the sense of modern Anglo-American social science.

Pity and commiseration (*misericordia* and *commiseratio*) are not virtues for Spinoza, and even less so for Gandhi, although they may have some positive instrumental value. Spinoza says that "commiseration, like shame, although it is not a virtue, is nevertheless good in so far as it shows that a desire for living honestly is present in the man who is possessed with shame, just as pain is called good in so far as it shows that the injured part has not yet putrefied." A modest function, but nevertheless of instrumental value! Tersely, Spinoza adds that "a man who lives according to the dictates of reason strives as much as possible to prevent himself from being touched by commiseration." People who are crippled are among those who practically unanimously agree.

Commiseration is sorrow and therefore is, in itself, an evil. According to certain conventional morality, a duty should be carried out even if there is no joy. This suggests that we had better disregard our duties if we are not permeated with joy. I find this interpretation rather fanatical, however, except when one adds a kind of norm concerning the high priority of developing the *capacity* for joy. "Alas! I cannot do my duty today because it does not fill me with joy. Better to escalate my efforts to experience joy!" Spinoza does not stress the remedy to the above situation—greater integration—but he presupposes it. The case of humility shows how *ratio* changes sorrows to joys: Spinozistic psychoanalysis tries to loosen up the mental cramps that cause unnecessary pain.

Freud worked with the tripartition of id, ego, and superego. The superego, through its main application in explaining neuroses, has a rather ugly reputation: It coerces the poor individual to try the impossible and then lets the person experience shame and humility when there is no success. In Spinoza's analysis, the *ratio* also functions as a kind of overseer, but its main function is rather one of consolation. It directs our attention to what we can do rather than to what we cannot, and eliminates feelings of necessary separation from others; it stresses the harmony of rational wills and of well-understood self-interests.

A major virtue of a system like Spinoza's is the extreme consistency and tenacity with which consequences, even the most paradoxical, are drawn from intuitively reasonable principles. It meets the requirements of clarity and logic of modern natural science. The system says to us: "You do not like consequence number 101? But you admit it follows from a premise you had admitted. Then give up the premise. You do not want to give up the premise? Then you must give up the logic, the rules of inference you used to derive the consequence. You cannot give them up? But then you have to accept the consequence, the conclusion. You don't want to? Well, I suppose you don't want clarity and integration of your views and your personality." The rationality of a total view like Spinoza's is perhaps the only form of rationality capable of breaking down the pseudorational thinking of the conservative technocracy that currently obstructs efforts to think in terms of the total biosphere and its continued blossoming in the near and distant future.

THE PHILOSOPHICAL PREMISES OF ENVIRONMENTALISM

Personally, I favor the kind of powerful premises represented in Chinese, Indian, Islamic, and Hebrew philosophy, as well as in Western philosophy—namely, those having as a slogan the so-called ultimate unity of all life. They do not hide the fact that big fish eat small ones, but stress the profound interdependence, the functional unity, of such a biospheric magnitude that

nonviolence, mutual respect, and feelings of identification are always potentially there, even between the predator and its so-called victim. In many cultures, identification is not limited merely to other living things but also to
the mineral world, which helps us conceive of ourselves as genuine surface
fragments of our planet, fragments capable of somehow experiencing the
existence of all other fragments: a microcosm of the macrocosm.

Another idea, right at the basis of a system from which environmental norms are derivable, is that of self-realization. The mature human individual, with a broadened self, acknowledges a right to self-realization that
is universal. Consequently, he or she seeks a social order, or rather a biospheric order, that maximizes the potential for self-realization of all kinds
of beings.

Levelheaded, tough-minded environmentalists sometimes stress that it is
sheer hypocrisy to pretend that we try to protect nature for its own sake. In
reality, they say, we always have the needs of human beings in view. This is
false, I think. Thousands of supporters of unpolluted so-called wastelands
in northern Labrador wish simply that those lands should continue to exist
as they are, for their own sake. The wastelands are of intrinsic, and not only
instrumental, value. To invoke *specifically* human needs to describe this situation is misleading, just as it is misleading to say that it is egotistical to share
one's birthday cake with others because one *likes* to share with others.

Self-realization is not a maximal realization of the coercive powers of the
ego. The *self* in the kinds of philosophy I am alluding to is something expansive, and the environmental crisis may turn out to be of immense value for
the further expansion of human consciousness.

In modern education, the difference between a world picture—or better,
a world model—and a straightforward description of the world is glossed
over. Atoms, particles, and wave functions are presented as parts or fragments of nature or are even presented as *the* real, objective nature, as contrasted with human projections into nature—the "colorful" but subjective
nature.

So-called physical reality, in terms of modern science, is perhaps only a
piece of abstract mathematical reality—a reality we emphatically do not live
in. Our living environment is made up of all the colorful, odor-filled, ugly,
or beautiful details, and it is sheer folly to look for an existing thing without
color, odor, or some other homely quality. The significance of this subject
is a broad cultural one: the rehabilitation of the status of the immediately
experienced world, the colorful and joyful world. *Where* is joy in the world
of fact? Right at the center!

Beautiful Action:
Its Function in the Ecological Crisis[14]

Most of us have a stupid reluctance to learn from philosophers who belong to "trends" or "schools" that, we find, lead us astray. For me, the so-called critical philosophy of Kant and Kantians belongs to such a set of trends. I say *so-called* critical. Most trendsetting philosophers have been fiercely critical of other trends, but only Kant has been fortunate enough to influence twentieth-century historians to such an amazing degree that, in their surveys, they call Kant's philosophy critical and Spinoza's dogmatic. This is a rather arbitrary distinction. Already in the introduction to his *Critique of Pure Reason*, Kant makes assumptions with far-reaching consequences without any attempt to justify them.[15] They may well be called uncritical and dogmatic, at least for some plausible and important interpretations of these terms. Both Spinoza and Kant were firm believers in fundamental ideas that they did not justify in their writings. To compare their levels of criticalness in a timeless, absolute sense presupposes that one has a third system that must be accepted uncritically. Or perhaps we don't need that. Who knows?

In spite of Kant's—in my opinion, unfortunate—influence, his works somehow are, and will continue to be, a major source of inspiration. In what follows, I borrow his distinction between moral and beautiful actions. I foresee a bright future for this terminology. It offers a fairly new perspective on our actions within the realm of radical environmentalism or, more specifically, within the deep ecology movement.

The distinction was introduced by Kant in a work published in 1759, *Versuch einiger Betrachtungen über den Optimismus* ("An attempt at some reflections on optimism"), written in the period that uncritically is called his uncritical period. The distinction has been neglected by historians.

According to the terminology of 1759, an act deserves the name *moral act* if it is solely motivated by respect for the moral law: You do it simply because it is your duty; there is no other motive. Presumably, a factual mistake would not spoil the beauty of an action—if you have done your duty *trying* to find out the facts of the case.

Suppose you do your duty—you perform the action that the moral law prescribes—but not *just* because of respect for the moral law. You perform the act because you are inclined to act like that, or at least partly because you have the inclination. It "feels natural" to do it. In that case, Kant calls the act *beautiful*. It is a moral, not an immoral, act. An immoral act is one that conflicts with the moral law. The beautiful act is, in Kant's view, a morally complete act because it is benevolent. Benevolent action expands our love to embrace the whole of life. It completes us and perfects us.[16]

It is not Kant's habit in his main works to offer examples, but in his *Groundwork of the Metaphysics of Morals*, he offers an interesting one.[17] It is one's duty, he says, to strive to keep alive, and there is a spontaneous inclination to do that. If you act more or less from the inclination to stay alive, the actions are morally insignificant. Kant then paints a picture of a thoroughly unhappy human being who consistently desires to die but continues to try to stay alive, motivated solely by duty. This person acts in a morally right way, according to Kant. Today, many people do not think it is always a duty to try to stay alive. In special cases, yes, notably because of the unhappiness or destitution of one's own children and spouse. The temptation to follow inclination and make an end is resisted, solely because one conceives it a duty to continue. Here the term *beautiful act* seems appropriate. In a philosophical seminar, one may differ about the exact relationship among respect for the moral law, respect for a moral duty, and respect for a duty, but the conclusions and proposals in what follows do not seem to be gravely affected by this outcome.

Presumably, Kant would not deny that it may make people glad when they do their duty. The inclination may not be there, and they may find the duty painful or even cruel, as in a war, but they are glad *that* they resist the temptation *not* to do it. There is a conflict, a situation involving stress, we might say today. When we act beautifully, no conflict of feelings is involved. Above all, it is characteristic of beautiful acts "that they display facility and appear to be accomplished without painful toil." Incidentally, Kant entertained the opinion that women, more often than men, act beautifully, from compassion and good-heartedness. Men's morality has the form of nobility, not beauty, but nobility is "extremely rare."

So much for the Kantian distinction itself. I now turn to its application in countries manifesting an increase of ecological unsustainability and the large-scale destruction of the habitats of other living beings.

The individuals and institutions trying to influence ecologically highly relevant actions in the right direction manifest roughly three different strategies: appeal to the *usefulness* of ecologically positive actions, emphasize *moral obligations*, and encourage certain attitudes—*inclinations*, in Kantian terminology.

Recently, there has been in Norway and other countries an upsurge of interest in environmental ethics at the governmental level. It is accepted that environmentalism has a moral aspect, that both individuals and their governments have a *duty* or an *obligation* to act in ecologically responsible ways. The moral appeal is gaining ground among policy makers. Sums of a different order than before have been earmarked for ethical studies as a follow-up to the Brundtland Report.[18] No similar sums are available, or will in the near future be available, for the study of attitudes toward nature and the conditions favorable for changes in the direction of ecologically responsible actions on every level, including the governmental. These changes may, in Kantian terminology, be called changes in the direction of a greater inclination to act in ecologically responsible ways. An act to overcome the ecological crisis is a moral act if, and only if, it is motivated by the call to do one's duty. Then there are ecologically beneficial acts that "display facility and appear to be accomplished without painful toil"—they are *beautiful* acts within the realm of ethically and ecologically relevant contexts. Again incidentally, insofar as we rely on Kant's judgment, we should expect women to be the main driving force in fostering ecologically relevant beautiful acts.

A very common comment by people hearing a description of deep ecology for the first time is, "But I've always thought this. I just did not have words for it." They presumably had acted beautifully, without toil, and without words! It is unnecessary to add that the response "This means you have always acted beautifully!" might have made them proud and eager to continue.

Obviously, a beautiful act might not always have the intended short- or long-range consequences that were intended. According to Kant, this applies in principle to every action. When a policy is chosen on the basis of its usefulness or morality, there is also this fundamental uncertainty. During the first great green wave (the late 1960s and early 1970s), millions developed the habit of turning off the electric lights when the lighting served no immediate purpose. To leave lights burning was difficult, unnatural. Then came skeptics repeating that the useful life of a lightbulb would be severely shortened if turned off and on "too much," and to make a new bulb would consume much energy and resources. Many felt frustrated because they saw the uncertainty of both strategies: the calculation of the basis of utility versus the reliance on an acquired natural inclination.

Badly informed people *may* cause small ecological disasters, making false judgments of a factual character. Today more than ever, it is one of our duties to keep informed; the better informed we are, the better our basis for predicting consequences.

Acting from inclination is superior to acting from duty. This vague announcement needs comment. First, acting from duty requires a conscious analysis of the situation and does not exclude acting in spite of strong disinclination. The sense of duty is generally not very strong, and because conscious analysis is often required, the ways of avoiding unpleasantness through talk are considerable. "It *seems* it is now my duty to do such and such, but close analysis shows that I really do not need to do such and such."

If it is urgent to have people behave in a certain way in a particular situation, the question "Are there any ways we could make them *inclined* to act (energetically and nonviolently) in that way?" has priority. Noble heroes are scarce, and if people are influenced to act from inclination, a stable habit is formed, whereas the moral act, at least as it seems to be conceived by Kant, normally does not form a habit. If it forms a habit, it starts feeling natural, and an inclination occurs. In short, the moral act glides into a beautiful act. In the terminology of social science, norms are *internalized*. Perhaps Kant has underestimated this development. It increases the importance of appeals to moral capacity, but it does not reduce the importance of processes that tend to induce inclination directly, internalization with verbalized normative appeals: utterances like "See how nice this animal (or flower or landscape, etc.) is" or "I wish I could help these people who are forced to live in this polluted area; such work would make me happy!" There are appeals through body language that induce joy and a process of identification. Such processes are similar to the way children practice nonreflective imitation and adapt to society.

In his monumental *Kritik der praktischen Vernunft* (Critique of practical reason), Kant goes deeper, but I shall not bring this work into our discussion. We have such and such a special duty *in* such and such kinds of situations. The adequate reason in answer to the question "Why do we have that duty in that kind of situation?" is mostly in terms of higher-order moral norms combined with a relevant classification of the kind of situation at hand. Duties are *relational*, a term better suited than *relative*. Intense, protracted questioning more or less inevitably leads to codified systems of normative ethics. It has been done most thoroughly by the Catholic Church in the more stable Middle Ages. But here, it is only relevant to remind us of the moral *corrigibility* of any concrete announcement of a duty in a concrete situation and the analogous need for change in the direction of a beautiful action. Hypotheses about the "facts" of the situation are involved.

What are the main ways to promote more and more consistently beautiful actions in the fight for ecological sustainability? This battle has to be fought by individuals in their private capacity and by all sorts of institutions in the wide sense.

It is easiest to start with educational institutions in the materially rich countries—from kindergartens to postgraduate schools. In the kindergartens, the body language of the respected people taking care of the children is decisive. The care and respect manifested in every interaction with every living being have immediate and strong effect. One of the necessary conditions is the presence of such beings. In Tokyo and many other places, we find kindergartens (children gardens!) with practically no noticeable non-human life-forms, except some occasional flies, which are treated as intruders. Much of the space is occupied by various mechanical contraptions.

In elementary schools, knowledge is often considered as important as appreciation, insight, and feelings of nearness and wonder. (Children are conceived as beings who must be useful, successful, and well entertained.) Socialization is important, but unhappily, the "environment" children are mostly adapted to today is the extremely poor communities of human beings, dogs, cats, and perhaps some spectacular, big plants, roses, and so on. The teachers are not expected to manifest love and respect for life or to reveal the difference between life quality and standard of living in their interactions with the children.

At the other end of formal teaching are the postgraduate seminars. Even when life-forms are studied at this educational level, the style in which they are taught is from the viewpoint of an observer, not a participant. Field trips are rarely made in silence such that students can hear clearly what trees or tiny animals and plants are telling them. The focus on interaction with fellow students is permitted to go on as if they were alone and not living with a myriad of beings. Nor are students taught to express what they *really* experience and what gestalts they participate in, leaving subject-object relations out. They may obtain their doctorates without ever *sensing* what they are talking about, and if they have gained cognition (not only knowledge) of the third kind (according to Spinoza), they are not stimulated to consider how to *inspire* others, how to *lead* them with few words to acquire the third kind, the understanding love and loving understanding (*intellectualis* amor = *amor* intellectualis). '

When we proceed to the subject of institutions, the social and political framework of the individual, practically nothing is done to protect the insights a minority has gained and to stimulate further gains. The U.N. World Charter for Nature of 1982 is not taken seriously when it proclaims the intrinsic value of nature independent of narrow usefulness for human beings.

What about the sphere of policies for fisheries? Is the Kantian distinction relevant? The leaders of organized labor and the politicians of the labor party—for example, in Norway—know that previous policies have been disastrous for the richness and diversity of fish in vast areas. They know they have to propose exasperatingly small quotas. This perpetuates high unemployment. Their duty is clear, but the unemployed fishermen are furious. In this situation, the political life of the leaders is precarious. The temptation to propose somewhat bigger quotas is normally there, but for the few who have internalized ecological norms, there is no temptation whatsoever. To propose unpopular regulations based on ecological considerations is the only, and the completely natural, thing to do. Of course, they are risking their political life. But with joy? Certainly not. With inner satisfaction, yes. As a moral act in the Kantian sense? Perhaps.

Richness and diversity *must* be increased. This goal is so evident that to say it to oneself in words is superfluous. A Labor Party minister of fisheries resigned recently after having established strict quotas. She presumably had had enough unpleasantness from the furious fishermen who had lost their jobs. Had she acted beautifully? I think the Kantian distinction works better for people who do not have the kind of power and responsibility of leaders in Western democracies.

In short, there is little understanding that fostering *inclination* is essential in every aspect of socialization and acculturation and therefore also in the global ecological crisis. Moralizing is too narrow, too patronizing, and

too open to the question "Who are *you*? What is the relation of your preaching and your life?" An invitation to act beautifully, to show beautiful acts
rather than talk about them, to organize society with all this in mind, may
recognize and acclaim such acts and be a decisive factor that will at last
decrease the unsustainability. "Tell me about your beautiful acts today! Do
the authorities encourage such acts?"

What I have offered for reflection is a small variation in our perspective, looking at what goes on in terms of a Kantian distinction. Thank you,
Immanuel.

Lifestyle Trends
Within the Deep Ecology Movement

The following list offers ways that supporters of the deep ecology movement can joyfully adapt their lifestyle to the movement.

1. Use simple means; avoid unnecessary, complicated instruments and other sorts of means.
2. Choose activities most directly serving values in themselves and having intrinsic value. Avoid activities that are merely auxiliary, have no intrinsic value, or are many states away from fundamental goals.
3. Practice anticonsumerism. This negative attitude follows from trends 1 and 2.
4. Try to maintain and increase the sensitivity and appreciation of goods in sufficient supply for all to enjoy.
5. Eliminate or lessen neophilia—the love of what is new merely because it is new.
6. Try to dwell in situations of intrinsic value and to act rather than being busy.
7. Appreciate ethnic and cultural differences among people; do not view the differences as threats.
8. Maintain concern about the situation in developing nations, and attempt to avoid a standard of living too much higher than that of the needy (maintain a global solidarity of lifestyle).
9. Appreciate lifestyles that can be maintained universally—lifestyles that are not blatantly impossible to sustain without injustice toward fellow humans or other species.

10. Seek depth and richness of experience rather than intensity.
11. Appreciate and choose, when possible, meaningful work rather than just making a living.
12. Lead a complex, not complicated, life, trying to realize as many aspects of positive experiences as possible within each time interval.
13. Cultivate life in community (*Gemeinschaft*) rather than in society (*Gesellschaft*).
14. Appreciate, or participate in, primary production—small-scale agriculture, forestry, fishing.
15. Try to satisfy vital needs rather than desires.
16. Attempt to live in nature rather than just visiting beautiful places; avoid tourism (but occasionally make use of tourist facilities).
17. When in vulnerable nature, live "light and traceless."
18. Appreciate all life-forms rather than merely those considered beautiful, remarkable, or narrowly useful.
19. Never use life-forms merely as means. Remain conscious of their intrinsic value and dignity, even when using them as resources.
20. When there is a conflict between the interests of dogs and cats (and other pet animals) and wild species, try to protect the wild creatures.
21. Try to protect local ecosystems, not only individual life-forms, and think of one's own community as part of the ecosystems.
22. Besides deploring the excessive interference in nature as unnecessary, unreasonable, and disrespectful, condemn it as insolent, atrocious, outrageous, and criminal—without condemning the people responsible for the interference.
23. Try to act resolute and without cowardice in conflicts, but remain nonviolent in words and deeds.
24. Take part in or support nonviolent direct action when other ways of action fail.
25. Practice vegetarianism.

Section 3:

METHODOLOGY AND SYSTEMS

Reflections on Total Views[1]

This essay is written under the impression that broad philosophical systems (like Spinoza's) are of great value, insofar as they articulate the deepest insights humans are capable of. Such systems in the form of total views are therefore of great importance in philosophical thinking. But the essay does not seek to substantiate this position. Instead it points to the absurdity both of explicit total views themselves and of presuming to criticize such views without, at least implicitly, adopting one.

HOW FAR CAN I EXTEND THE AREA OF MY OWN IGNORANCE?

Most of us can become modest by changing in certain well-defined directions. There are limits, however, such that further steps in those directions no longer increase our modesty. If a person demands less and less attention from others, he or she soon gets into conflict with his environment. For example, if someone dramatically rescued a child from a fire, deliberate and systematic efforts to avoid subsequent favorable attention will tend to generate immodesty in the form of moral ambitiousness. The net result of his or her effort may thus ultimately be negative, because of both a lack of normal sensitivity and an uncritical persistence in assuming a certain kind of change to guarantee an increase of modesty, whatever the amount.

But it is not the ethics of modesty in claims about one's own ignorance that I am concerned with here. Rather, my concern is with the epistemological problem of how much—given a definite but gradually widening universe of discourse—one can explicitly claim not to know without making the mistake of underrating one's knowledge.

If I say with due humility that there is something most people know about but I know nothing about, this may be a genuine expression of modesty on my part. But if I say that I knew less than *any* other person or that I know nothing whatsoever, this involves not a further reduction, but a startling increase in the boldness of my claims to knowledge. Whether moral or cognitive, modesty seems to require abstention from any spectacular deviation from average behavior. Let me take an extreme instance of a claim to know very little—a claim that would seem to require vast knowledge to be justified. Suppose I confidently declare myself the most ignorant man in the world: I succumb to the gross immodesty of professing to know something very difficult indeed to know. (Socrates had to take the oracle's word for it; he did not find out for himself.) My claim concerns the world and all human beings, including Socrates and me. Thus, a vast conceptual framework is taken for granted. If the declaration is made as a serious statement in a dialogue, the author will find himself or herself in an awkward position. ("You know less than I do?" "Certainly." "I didn't know that; so you knew something that I didn't." "Socrates knew more than you?" "Yes." "Then you knew something Socrates did not." This kind of conversation might cover any subject.)

So much, then, for knowing about one's own ignorance!

But then there is another set of problems about increasing the area of one's ignorance. How complete can this ignorance become? How little can we knowingly or unknowingly assume to be true? Or, to put it in other words: Does what we assume to be true tally with the claims we make about our own ignorance? Now, it seems clear that even if we do not *affirm* our ignorance about something, we will nevertheless rather subtly reveal how we would classify and describe what we profess to be ignorant of. In much the way that ignoring something implies the possibility of eliciting from us a description or classification of whatever it is we are intent on not attending to, so a description or classification can be part of the "sense" of our actions in regard to what we claim to know nothing about.

Suppose I discover in a burning house some meteorologists who say they are studying typhoon tracks—a subject I have honestly claimed to know nothing about. I urge them to run out of the house before it is too late. I shall thereby implicitly claim to know that the study of typhoon tracks or the tracks themselves will not put out the fire. Then how is the claim to know or to presume absolutely *nothing* about typhoon tracks to be understood? And how could my ignorance of the phenomenon be increased beyond, say, my being able to give the sketchiest classification of it? Is the implicit claim about knowledge of typhoon tracks to be understood just as an isolated item in my knowledge of typhoon has no connection with what I really know, for instance, about burning houses? But I still *treat* the meteorologists as if their knowledge cannot reveal that my behavior (to get them out) rests on a set of mistakes. And if the meteorologists demand explanations for how I can presume their study to be irrelevant if I really know nothing about typhoon tracks, I may start arguing in support of my claim about the irrelevancy, and in that case I shall almost certainly show that I think I know a great deal about typhoons.

Tentatively I conclude, then, that any articulate *docta ignorantia,* or agnosticism, is embedded in Gnosticism or dogmatism. If this were not so, then my ignorance could hardly be experienced as ignorance *about* something. As soon as it is *about* something, a piece of ignorance is like a hole in a Swiss cheese—it is only there because of the cheese around it. If you want a colossal hole, then you must provide a colossal cheese.

An increase in claimed knowledge, a beautiful analogy tells us, is like the increasing light from a torch in the vast darkness. The larger the pool of light, the greater the periphery of the darkness surrounding it, that is, of admitted ignorance. But some "child of darkness and doubt" eagerly increasing the reign of gloom may conversely discover that the greater the sphere of darkness, that is, of known ignorance, the greater the expanse of enveloping light, that is, of knowledge.

On the articulate, neatly conceptual level, the level I am solely interested in here, the character of ignorance as ignorance *about* something reveals itself in the statement *within* a conceptual structure, a set of categories. And the responsible use of the conceptual structure presupposes or at least seems to presuppose extensive knowledge. Nor is the knowledge merely greater or lesser in extent; it is also systematic. A character of totality is implicit in most of our everyday reasoning and action, even if this does not show itself as an explicit total view about the world. Such an assumed unity seems to be a prerequisite if a person's particular arguments and acts are not to seem meaningless. There must be this connection with other mutually supporting arguments, beliefs, and attitudes, even if the person himself or herself may be unaware of the implicit unity and perhaps quite unable to verbalize the intricate web of mutually supporting elements. This emerges from the observation that withdrawals of claims to knowledge can only go so far. The attempt to extend and multiply disclaimers reveals and comes up against an underlying structure of unquestioned assumptions.

Dealing with limits of ignorance or a known lack of knowledge, we are tempted to introduce the terminology of *frames of reference*, saying something to the effect that the necessity of *an implicit frame of reference* makes it difficult, perhaps impossible, to justify or even formulate the claim that there is at least one thing about which a person knows nothing at all. Thus, in professing ignorance, Socrates placed himself and his ignorance within a total or comprehensive *framework,* which he implicitly presumed to be adequate. That which is not known is adequately classified as unknown only by virtue of what is assumed not to be unknown. Our search for truth or our belief or disbelief in finding it can only operate within a frame of reference, or at least within a succession of such frames. But then how do these frames stand with regard to knowledge, once they are discovered and made objects for inquiry?

EXPLICATION OF FUNDAMENTAL OR TOTAL FRAMES: HIGHER-ORDER SKEPTICISM

In the history of philosophy, the system builders have proposed solutions of *all* problems that are not considered questions of detail. The conventional classifications of the problems comprise logic, ontology, epistemology, methodology, ethics, and aesthetics.

Suppose our child of darkness and doubt now focuses on disclaiming knowledge within these higher-order categories. Applied to a set of fundamental ontological beliefs or basic premises, whether they are true or false, tenable or untenable, professed ignorance involves a claim to know something that is true of the whole world or of whatever is most fundamental within a certain area of it. The vastness of the pretension is of the same order, whether it is in the belief in knowing or in the belief in ignorance. If I maintain that I do not know, for instance, whether the ultimate source of knowledge is experience, I must regard myself as already acquiescing in the use of a conceptual framework that includes such terms as *knowledge*, *experience*, and *ultimate source*. If I know that I ignore the question of whether Aristotle's ontology is tenable, I must know what it is that I ignore. (And I must also be informed about what knowledge is.)

If I claim not to know whether a definite comprehensive ontology (Spinoza's, say) or set of basic principles (Aristotle's, say) is tenable, my explicit or implicit frame of reference is itself total, comprising all the world, whatever that is. My frame even encompasses the horizons of great philosophers.

The effect of assuming one framework rather than another makes itself felt, or is shown, over the whole area of reasoning or action covered by the categories in the framework. A conscious modification of a formerly implicit frame of reference may result in modifications not only of what we conceive to be true or false, but even of what we conceive to constitute a *search* for truth. This happens, for instance, when our attention is directed to research itself as an object of research and to forms of agnostic or skeptical conclusions as a particular instance of a possible result of research about research.

Suppose we develop a very strong form of epistemological skepticism, avoiding the classical inconsistency attributed to extreme skepticism by only a hair's breadth. Once having developed this skepticism, we might start to reflect upon our own developments and try to make explicit some of the implicit assumptions, rules, and premises used in it. Thus, we might grasp a fragment of the frame we were working inside as we developed our skeptical epistemology. Our explicit skepticism brings to light the "animal faith" we had in the conceptual structure and the fundamental assumptions underlying the arguments for our skepticism and the statements expressing it.

Thus, we may grow to doubt our skeptical methodology once its principles have come to light. To what extent, then, can we successively shun the enjoyment (or assumption) of truth with regard to total views that we come to get glimpses of? How far back can we consistently go toward "knowing nothing"?

It is usually assumed that a total viewpoint of something like "I know nothing" is at least in part due to the choice of an "I know" concept in the neighborhood of "I have incorrigibly true knowledge." This is due to a frame of reference that allows that once knowledge is corrigible, any belief backed by standard evidence in the field is automatically knowledge, that all we need is enough evidence. But at least some powerful skeptical attitudes are characterized not by a localized doubt concerning some mathematical or perceptual statements usually classed as absolutely certain, but by an all-pervading feeling of questionableness relating to all conceptualizations, to all positions whatsoever. Here the very act of saying or thinking that anything is such and such rather than anything else is not intimately accompanied by clear and articulate questioning, but is done in a mode of general questionableness. Reflections in this skeptical attitude may find expression, but not directly as assertions.

Here, of course, an important point arises: If the skeptic does not *assert* anything, if he or she fails even to pose an articulate question (based on the acceptance of a definite conceptual framework), then the skepticism hardly amounts to anything that philosophers can dispute. Perhaps they may be influenced by the skeptic's behavior, but only in the way their moods and tempers may be affected by the weather. This may be conceded, but it should be borne in mind that important parts of philosophical literature are writings that, taken as *wholes*, may not express any definite position. I think here of Plato's early dialogues and of Kierkegaard's *Concluding Unscientific Postscript*. Within such writings, we can recognize strings of reflections and limited conclusions. There are, however, trends of reflections obviously undermining the limited conclusions. Therefore, no position or conclusion seems consistent with all reflections. As conclusions, they are self-destructive. Nothing is left. The intention of the author may not have been to impart an opinion on any subject at all except within subordinate strings of reflections.

There are certainly many advantages in thinking of philosophy as an articulated search for something, giving rise, at its best, to the establishment of conclusions concerning some sorts of clearly formulated questions. On the other hand, it might be appropriate to view it, taken as a whole, as an essentially aimless activity, its reflections occurring in strings that occasionally condense into definite sets of opinions, but which mostly go beyond such products, releasing the thinker from his or her past work.

Naturally, if the published works of philosophers (of the Western tradition) are taken to reveal the essence of philosophy, one inevitably gets the impression that a philosophical achievement mostly consists of arriving at conclusions in an orderly fashion. But to look at it in this way involves ruling out those philosophers who are capable of *epoché* or abstention from commitment to any position in spite of being clearly aware of the arguments for and against.

But in conclusion of this note about a general *epoché*, I would say that the articulate skeptic need not (as A. J. Ayer seems to imply in his latest work) be thought of as choosing a set of *strong* requirements for "knowing," such as incorrigibility, but may choose any among a variety of requirements, including weak ones. But even then, "knowing" would be a kind of achievement, the end of a process of search. That knowledge has been achieved is something that must be believed before the unbeliever is to be refuted. And that is the important point.

DOES EXPLICATION OF A FRAME OF REFERENCE INVOLVE THE INTRODUCTION OF ANOTHER?

If we have an inclination to study the foundation rather than the superstructure—the presuppositions and assumptions rather than the conclusions of a system of beliefs—our interest is inevitably turned from the explicit to the implicit. If we study an argument and end up with a strongly skeptical conclusion in terms of its requirements, this indicates that our attention is turned toward the stringent requirements for "knowledge" that are implicitly assumed in arriving safely at the conclusion. Then our attention is apt to shift toward the question of how one is able to find out what concepts a skeptic implicitly uses. What are the methodological beliefs in this case? And once explicated, are we prepared to accept these formerly implicit assumptions? Quite possibly, a shift to a wider or deeper frame (n) will make us skeptically uneasy about any former skeptical uneasiness—or perhaps just no longer interested in what those $(n - 1)$ methodological beliefs led us to conclude.

The writers who in a few sentences prove that "skepticism" is incoherent usually presume a very weak concept of knowledge, a concept such that we practically cannot open our months without claiming to know something. Thus B. Lonegan writes: "Am I a knower? The answer, yes, is coherent, for if I am a knower, I can know that fact. But the answer, No, is incoherent, for if I am not a knower, how could the question be raised and answered by me? No less, the hedging answer, I do not know, is incoherent. For if I know that I do not know, then I am a knower; and if I do not know that I do not know, then I should not answer."[2] Here, the answer "no" is construed as equivalent to "I know that I am not a knower"—and the answer "I do not know" as equivalent to "I know that I do not know." Such equivalence would only hold, however, provided nothing or next to nothing is added in cognitive content by adding "I know that . . ." to a sentence. There is no good reason why a person inclined toward skepticism should be inclined toward an unusually weak concept of knowledge.

The shifting of attention from one frame, A, to another frame, B, in which A has been conceived, proceeds within a new implicit framework in which both A and B can be conceived and explicated. As we move back, we step immediately and inevitably from one frame in a regressive series to another. In this predicament, it is tempting to try to do without this talk of frames. Can we not dispense with it and thus also with the predicament? Do we really *use* or *have* an implicit frame of reference? How did we manage to get this idea involved in our reflections? What presuppositions did we use here? This kind of reflection about our frame-of-reference thinking is also a way of exceeding our own explicit assumptions. As an assumption, the frame of reference is itself a proper object for study. And since it is only an assumption about the nature of our methodological beliefs in general, it would seem to be dispensable even if they are not. Nevertheless, dropping this terminology does not seem to help us answer the questions that gave rise to it.

We feel caught in a trap, unable to free ourselves and make a fresh start; we can inspect all the beliefs we have had until the moment of critical inspection, but we never reach the critical inspection itself. It is tempting here to quote some acute reflections of Kierkegaard's concerning "the System," that is, in our context, any attempt to explicate a fundamental frame of reference: "The System begins with the immediate, and hence without any presuppositions, and hence absolutely; that is, the beginning of the System is the absolute beginning. This is quite correct, and has also been sufficiently admired. But before one started with the System, why is it that one did not raise the second, equally, aye, precisely equally important question: *How does the System begin with the immediate? That is to say, does it begin with it immediately?* The answer to this question must be an unconditional negative."[3]

We have referred above to the *intended* global character of a framework explicated as a set of fundamental beliefs or assumptions. The unavoidable slip into higher-order frames and the resulting infinite regressions suggest that it is in principle impossible to formulate a set that has the intended character. The character of wholeness refuses to reveal itself in what we grasp and formulate in discursive thinking. The impossibility of formulating a global set of fundamental principles, suggested by the inspection of beliefs itself involving uninspected methodological principles, is analogous to that of blowing up a balloon from the inside. To inspect the set, you must do something analogous to blowing new air in from outside. Then, to inspect that process, you have to regard the outside air as itself enveloped by another layer and so on. This illustrates the regressive character of explicating frames of reference.

This reasoning and the conclusion itself can, however, be made the object of critical inspection. Pieces of its frame of reference can be brought to light; tacit assumptions can be made explicit. This activity, however, even if highly successful, does not necessarily furnish a basis for rejection of that reasoning or its conclusion. It may be left "suspended in the air," because the rejection is itself only an example of the kind of thing rejected.

But there is another aspect of the impossibility of settling on a fundamental set of principles. This aspect emerges not in the question of attempts at increasing our ignorance but, in the closely related attempts to increase and multiply our doubts, with a view to establishing a platform, however small, of truths no sane person could dispute. As I will discuss, differences of procedures determine extreme differences in the resulting platforms, and differences in fundamental orientation or vision seem to determine the procedures.

Descartes *doubted*, using his *maix de omnibus dubitandum est*. But he conceived himself, René, born in 1496, to be inspecting beliefs he, René, had cherished. This egocentric frame of reference his doubt did not touch. There is nothing very strange in this situation as long as we take "all" (*omnibus*), as it is often used in everyday situations, as an expression of less-than-strict universality. If "all" is successively widened in scope, there will still be some frame of reference that is untouched by doubt. For Descartes, it was natural to persist in retaining himself, or his thinking, or his doubting, as something that breasts the waves of critical inspections. This fundamental orientation gave a frame inconsistent with a doubt that *he* was there all the time, *doubting*. Thus, as a consequence of his particular orientation, he grasped a first, indubitable truth.

What I should like to stress here is the intimate relation between the conscious, explicit conviction that he, René, was doubting and therefore, of course, existing, and the conception of the task that he, René, should doubt. As long as René's conception of his task is not challenged, the result follows. All the conceptualizations, points of view, and beliefs inherent in the *egocentrically* conceived task and its implementation are then left untouched by doubt. The consequences of the conceptualizations are experienced by René as absolute truths and therefore as a starting point for system building.

Let us now turn to Baruch de Spinoza, who as an admirer of Descartes in his youth presumably had the same idea of radical doubt and egocentric introspection. We will speak of Baruch rather than of Benedict in Wolff's terminology, stressing the Jewish religious core of his thinking rather than his relation to Descartes and the Renaissance. Baruch had a personality and background somewhat different from those of René. With Baruch, they lead to a critical inspection of concepts of the ego, especially in its relation to God. Baruch could not be Baruch and doubt without God, and critical inspection of the task of doubting was quite possible within the God-centered frame. Philosophical mysticism was so deeply seated in Baruch that everyday pursuits were strange except within a definite framework, but not one in which God was sought from somewhere outside God. Rather, the framework comprised God and contained the possibility of explaining Spinoza himself and his capacity to doubt. His starting point is deocentric, not egocentric like that of Descartes, and consequently such formulations as "I doubt; therefore, I exist" must have been foreign to him as a basic conceptualization or self-evident truth.

The highest kind of knowledge, the third kind, is conceptualized by Baruch in terms of "eternal things." Here, it would be rash to identify the relationship of the knowing subject to the known object with the relationship between a concrete person or an ego and an empirical or, more generally, a natural object of some sort.

In some sense, it is justifiable to say that the third kind of knowledge *can exist* without its *being held* by any person at all. Baruch cannot "have" the third kind of knowledge in any ordinary, naturalistic sense of having knowledge.

Thus, the task of doubting everything will have to undergo renewed conceptualization if it is to be understandable at all from the point of view of a philosophical mystic or a combined mystic and rationalist like Spinoza. Therefore, the assertion "I, Baruch, born in 1632, doubt," or, more generally, an assertion of the kind "I, so-and-so, doubt," is not found to be a constant, definite presupposition; rather, it is modified and changed with the renewed conceptualizations of the I, the ego, the self, the personality, and its relation to what is not I, not the self, and so forth. Thus, well within the framework of the third kind of knowledge, both the task to doubt all, and the result that it cannot be doubted that Baruch doubts, are absurd.

The easiest way into Spinozistic thinking may be through the epistemological section of *De intellectualis emendatione*. These sections are written within a less rigorous framework than that for the propositions, definitions, axioms, and proofs of the first part of his *Ethics*. Moving from the exoteric and didactic to the esoteric point of view, bridges or ladders are thrown away; retained is an exposition that is colored by the system itself, from the first section to the last. As an example, take the frequent parallel epistemological and ontological phrasings in the *Ethics* (*in se est et per se concipitur*, etc.). From the start of the exposition in the *Ethics*, Spinoza seems to take it for granted that if certain epistemological propositions are true, then certain ontological ones are also true, because their object is *ultimately* the same.

We have compared Descartes and Spinoza within the framework of a (roughly suggested) theory of ultimate orientations. I doubt the adequacy of this framework, however. When one goes deep into the philosophy of Descartes, one's acceptance of the theory of ultimate orientation seems itself to be affected. It acquires a Cartesian quality and is no longer suitable as a neutral frame within which both systems, Descartes' and Spinoza's, can be understood. On the other hand, if one goes deep into the philosophy of Spinoza, the same tends to happen, with Descartes gradually becoming absurd or incomprehensible. My conclusion, therefore, is that the framework accommodates both the views only at a very superficial level and that, in fact, the views are incomparable.

The experience of inspecting and judging the truth-claims of explicit basic views, and of going through a series of steps, from the inspection and judging of these basic views already enjoyed to an examination of the set of views implicit in our first-order inspection, and then from the explicated first-order views to an examination of the second-order ones, and so on, turns the notion of *fundamental* or *basic* into a relational concept. In other words, "B is fundamental or basic in relation to A," "C is fundamental in relation to B," and so on. The hunt for any natural resting point is as unrealistic as it is to reach out for the horizon. Maybe we have tried to make explicit what by its very nature cannot be made so, and perhaps all the explicit frames of reference, from the first to the *n*th-order frame, are on the same level in relation to a kind of personal, implicit total view. Maybe we have a kind of preconscious total view or frame—so total that all the higher-level reflections are in some way placed within it.

OUR PRECONSCIOUS TOTAL VIEW: A FICTION?
PARADOXES OF TOTAL VIEWS

If the preconscious view is a kind of matrix within which all attempts to unravel or bring to light the concepts and categories of any implicit frame of reference are to proceed, it cannot be identified with a philosophy like naturalism, naive realism, or any other intended systematizations of common sense. These are explicit and verbalized and are defenseless when attacked by means of frame-of-reference dialectics. But is it then "a view"? The term suggests something that can be grasped and therefore inspected. This in turn implies the possibility of making it explicit.

Conceptions of *explicit* total views as found in the history of philosophy are ridden with paradoxes. Either a total view is explicit but fragmentary or it is total but implicit. An analogous conclusion can be reached concerning the ordinary use of the term *view*. Views are of something from somewhere. This somewhere is not part of that something. So we cannot have a total view in this sense, comprising viewed and viewpoint. Admittedly, it would be misleading in ordinary situations to call a view fragmentary because it did not include its viewpoint, but then reflections on total views are themselves extraordinary.

It is perhaps only after studying attempts by philosophers and others to elaborate vast systems that we are led to ask, What makes systematizers with "totalitarian" aspirations believe in the possibility of reaching their goal? And only after considering what seems to be the unavoidable paradoxes, or contradictions, are we led to talk about and imagine a kind of view, or, rather, disposition, that we have *before* making philosophical inquiries—a "totalitarian" disposition that makes it appear reasonable and even important to elaborate an explicit total view. We may refer to such an initial view as *preconscious* in the sense that parts of it, perhaps any part whatever, can be made the object of our concentrated attention and will then appear to us as fresh, verbal expressions of something we had expressed already in indirect or nonverbal ways.

The study of the paradoxes inherent in conceptions of explicit total views makes it important to inquire whether any of the great philosophers really intended to elaborate such views. Aristotle's doctrine of absolute and final principles (for instance, the Principle of Contradiction) is an attempt to base all his thinking and the resulting all-embracing system upon an intuitively certain foundation. It testifies to his greatness that he knows he cannot *argue* in favor of his own first principles, because this would imply the existence of a still deeper layer of principles than the "first principles." That is, it would involve a contradiction, first principles being secondary, ultimates being penultimates. Recently, neo-Thomists have tried to elaborate a total view consistent with basic Aristotelian views and modern scientific knowledge. But perhaps the most famous undertaking since medieval times in the field of all-embracing, supreme synthesis is that of Spinoza in his *Ethics*. This book, together with his *Treatise on the Improvement of the Understanding*, in which some of the methodology of the *Ethics* is stated, represents a system that plainly intends to answer all *main* questions. And this includes questions of framework.

The supreme systematizers have always omitted details, relegating the work to the formal and empirical sciences working within a fixed, ultimate framework. In the conception of the International Encyclopaedia of Unified Science series (by O. Neurath and others), the vision of a scientific total view and that of an encyclopedia are merged into one. Adopting the so-called onion structure, that is, starting with two volumes of basic fields and adding sets of volumes, treating the same fields in greater and greater detail, the International Encyclopaedia of Unified Science was conceived as a total system.

The difference between a total view and a big encyclopedia, as here conceived, is that the encyclopedia must contain details, whereas no single detail is necessary to make a total view complete. In a total view, there is just enough said to cover the essentials or principles. How much this is we leave open.

Bentham tried to formulate all-embracing, general views and to elaborate some of them in the greatest detail. His total view would not have been less complete, however, if he had not prescribed definite color for ballot boxes. Whatever our views regarding the "depth" of particular philosophers, one may safely assume that most of the great philosophical systematizers intended to form explicit total views (discussed in an earlier essay). The question of their genesis is therefore a very real one.

THE GENESIS OF THE BELIEF
IN THE POSSIBILITY OF TOTAL VIEWS

From the point of view of psychology or social science how might we explain that we have started to talk—or started to believe we have been talking or can talk—intelligibly, even intelligently, about our total view—our logic, ontology, epistemology, value system—in general? How did we conceive of the possibility of regarding our own total view as one explicable view among others?

Perhaps the belief has developed in one specific way: It may strike us that a person always thinks and believes in some definite way, that is, in only one of the many possible ways we can envisage, the range of possibilities being implicitly determined by our own (the observer's) frame of reference. In order to articulate clearly and succinctly what distinguishes our own view from that of the other, we make explicit not only the other's view, but also our own. And we set about this latter job as if it were like the first, that is, like describing the other's view, something already accommodated well within our own framework. But because we ourselves are not accommodated within our own framework, the second job is totally different from the first. To carry it through seems as difficult as to eat not only part of oneself, but all of oneself. The analogy that generates the belief in the possibility of such an explication is spurious, a view that comprehends something else, the accommodating viewpoint. But this latter can be explicated in its own turn only by being accommodated in the same way, by being pinned down onto something else, and so on.

Since the views about the other person's views are conceptualized well within our own frame of reference, our own views as contrasted with the other's are also thus placed. Being primarily interested in contrasts, we take the part for the whole. That is, our own ultimate frame is overlooked.

The same goes for another possible way in which this belief is fostered, namely, when we look back to examine earlier phases of our own lives. "My particular education has equipped my mind with such elaborate shock-absorbing buffers and elastic defenses that everything seen and heard became automatically transformed to fit a preconceived pattern."[4] From the belief in an all-embracing knowledge of one's own mind as it was at a previous stage of development, only one small but errant step is required if one is to conceive oneself as having at the present moment, and knowing, a definite general outlook that can be made verbally explicit as one outlook among others.

In psychology as in other sciences of humans, concepts of total view have been introduced, and it has apparently been taken for granted that they can be used in research to make neutral, adequate classifications of individuals or groups. Let me quote some words from H. Walsby, a strong believer in total views: "Our revised, more dynamic and concrete conception of an ideology may now be defined as the complete system or cognitive assumptions and affective identifications which manifest themselves in, or underlie, the thought, speech, aims, interests, ideals, ethical standards, actions—in short, in the behavior—of an individual human being."[5] Walsby's belief in an underlying ideology has striking similarities to the belief in a god that manifests itself in all that happens in the world. It seems that there is a strong Hegelian trend in research about ideology, much influenced by the sweeping concepts of Karl Mannheim, who writes in *Ideology and Utopia:* "Here we refer to the ideology of an age or of a concrete historico-social group, e.g., of a class, when we are concerned with the characteristics and composition of the total structure of the mind of this epoch or of this group."[6]

The ideology of a person observed by Walsby would have to be described and classified in relation to a framework that has to be so comprehensive as to *completely* embrace that of the observed person. The ideology of an age or of a historico-social group observed by Mannheim must be transcended in every respect by that of the group or age of Mannheim. The "total structure of the mind" of Mannheim himself must, in the way of divine intellects, furnish a most-comprehensive or value-neutral frame of reference and conceptual structure.

Concepts such as these are potent factors in building up images of "the fascist," "the communist," and other creatures that cannot be reached by ordinary channels of communication, because of their fundamentally different total views from that of the observer.

Imre Hermann, Levy Bruehl, Karl Mannheim, Walsby, and many others seem to not doubt for a moment that the fundamental beliefs and attitudes of others, for instance their logic, can be described and compared with each other—irrespective of how different these beliefs are from those of the investigator.[7] In cases where the victims of a total description are so-called primitives, the observer is rarely confronted with a reversal of roles—the victim describing the total view of the scientist. But if the social scientist is faced with appreciative, ether critical or indignant, verbally nonprimitive proponents of the systems, he or she is apt to become acutely aware of at least *some* of the scientist's own assumptions and is led to talk—or believe it possible to talk—about his or her own general frame of reference. By rationalizing that he or she can discover and adequately describe the total views of others, the researcher thus may be led to believe that he or she has a total view (capable of being verbalized). What the scientist has more or less uncritically imputed to others must now be imputed to himself or herself: The person now insists on having a total view and is willing to verbalize it, using words like *the world, man, society, liberty, progress,* and so on.

It is not my aim here to detail hypotheses about the genesis of belief in the possibility of *explicit* total views. I merely suggest that such views have certain paradoxical characteristics, which makes their acceptance highly interesting.

The Limited Neutrality
of Typologies of Systems[8]

In reply to Ingemund Gullvåg's "Naess's Pluralistic Metaphilosophy," I concede that there are limitations to a pluralistic metaphilosophy.[9] The limits are not, however, specifiable. By increasing a philosophical system's comprehensiveness, one decreases its refutability, because the system then begins to incorporate its own rules of refutation and other concepts required for assessing validity, but there are no definite limits to comprehensiveness. By increasing a system's comprehensiveness, one also diminishes the possibility of comparing that system with others. There is a fairly neutral but vague and imprecise way of expressing oneself metaphysically, but such expressions can never attain absolute neutrality. Nevertheless, it might be useful to retain as a regulative idea the notion that all comprehensive systems try to embrace the same single reality.

INTRODUCTION

Gullvåg's "Naess Pluralistic Metaphilosophy" is a fine example of criticism that takes every care not to misrepresent the views under examination. Gullvåg offers some usefully succinct formulations of many aspects of these views and uses them to point to a number of weaknesses in the views. In what follows, I shall gratefully make some concessions and restate a way of thinking that I consider important in itself and also in its consequences for the policy of philosophy departments.

Typologies of systems have on the whole been *post factum*. They try to furnish a sufficiently broad frame of reference to accommodate existing specimens, not all possible future specimens. But even so, the typologies may not be broad enough. Indian surveys of *all* systems, the *sarvadarsanasmgraha*s, show a dependence upon specific Indian frames, while Karl Jasper's excellent typology manifests his psychological and existential leanings and can hardly be said to cover all Indian systems.[10] The Indian surveys reveal a certain narrowness of compass if we try to accommodate non-Indian systems, and Jasper illustrates how the inventor of a typology tends to make presuppositions that totally exclude them from the sphere of valid (consistent, true, tenable) systems.

A study of existing typologies suggests that wider and more neutral ones should be possible. More importantly, the higher the level of neutrality of the typology and the comprehensiveness of the system, the narrower the basis for establishing the invalidity of any of them. Propositions about philosophic systems in general presuppose an *understanding* of all systems. In my view, this understanding can only reach certain approximations, because any understanding that occurs can do so only on the basis of a definite set of presuppositions, which cannot be brought into and out of play without altering the personality of the person whose understanding it is. My view, indecently, presupposes that concepts of understanding involve that of some kind of a person.

REALLY EXISTING AND IDENTIFIABLE OBJECTS

Gullvåg writes:

> With respect to objects, Naess apparently takes a view that is strikingly similar to the ontological standpoint on particulars that C. S. Peirce accepted before he came, at a late stage in his philosophical development, to acknowledge them as existing and identifiable independently of conceptual frameworks ... My conclusion here is that if there is such a presupposition underlying Naess's semantics and doctrine of systems, he has already deviated quite radically from the programme of system-neutrality. (p. 406)

I hold that objects exist and are identifiable independently of concepts. With G. E. Moore, I say I have two hands—for certain. I hold it to be objectively true.

But all this I affirm, or rather admit, "on the T_0-level," that is, as point-of-departure formulations that allow extremely different philosophical interpretations.[11] Even philosophies that contain sentences such as "Nothing exists" seem to hold that, in certain senses, *something* exists. I say "seem to." It may well be that some concepts of *maya* are such that in no sense can I imagine that I really and objectively have two hands. This would mean that I cannot understand certain *maya* philosophies, and that they are not taken account of in my typology.

Earlier, Gullvåg says:

> But I am not at all sure that Naess would want to accept such a picture of the world as sets of *objects* of different kinds, which *are there* independently of our conceptual systems and descriptions. Possibly he would reject it as not a system-neutral account of the relationship between system and reality. Or perhaps he would accept alternative accounts incompatible with the one just mentioned. (p. 404)

This is *also correct:* When the T_0 version of the object-independency formulation is made more precise, most or all plausible interpretations form highly unneutral philosophical statements—and sometimes false ones, as far as I can understand. I will, as Gullvåg indicates, include views incompatible with some of those precizations in my typology. The typology includes systems I tend to regard as invalid or strange, but none that I consider utterly unintelligible. My hands may be unreal in many senses, but there is a (not easily described) limit to the degree of ontological unreality of my hands beyond which I would tend to say: "I do not follow; I cannot understand your position. Therefore, I cannot take it into consideration in my typology." I say this "undogmatically" (in Sextus Empiricus' sense). I do not preclude the possibility that I will come to understand your position, and *not* understand that I did not understand.

NEUTRAL SEMANTICS AS A TOOL IN SYSTEMS THEORY

Gullvåg thinks that "Naess's notion of a 'Kindergarten version' of his semantics is programmatic rather than actualized in any exposition" (p. 403).

The semantics of my *Communication and Argument* can be given an exposition that is highly system-neutral.[12] This is, as Gullvåg indicates, a programme and a hypothesis. But, I admit, the pluralistic metasystematic theory uses versions that are more precise. And the direction of precision is presumably philosophically not completely neutral. It is likely that metasystematic theory fails somewhat to fully reach the high level of neutrality intended. Readers can, with little effort, point out weaknesses. I can then try to reconstruct in order to avoid the specified weaknesses. But the weaknesses must be shown before they can be eliminated.

MODERATELY COMPREHENSIVE, MODERATELY PRECISE METATHEORY

Again, Gullvåg:

> Apparently, then, the pluralistic theory of systems cannot be a *theory* in any strict sense, that is, something that can in principle be evaluated with regard to truth, consistency, and entailments. Nor does Naess claim any such status for it. Some of his remarks suggest that his account of systems is a quasi-theoretical attempt to *show* or *indicate* something that cannot, *strictly speaking*, be stated. It cannot strictly speaking be correct to say anything about systems in general. (p. 402)

Gullvåg has a point, but there are less paradoxical levels of the metaphilosophy of systems. It must be borne in mind that there are *two* general dimensions—comprehensive systems and precise typological conceptual frameworks dealing with systems. Between the two, there is a complementary relationship—the more precise the conceptual framework, the less comprehensive the typology (see illustration).

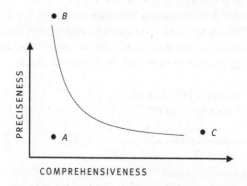

ILLUSTRATION 3: PRECISENESS VERSUS COMPREHENSIVENESS

The difficulties arise when we try to combine an extreme degree of comprehensiveness with even a modest degree of preciseness—like typology *C* in the diagram. Or where, as with *B*, a considerable degree of preciseness is combined with even a modest degree of comprehensiveness.

How precise must a theory be in order to be a theory in any strict sense? Gestalt theory and some other theories that have generated much insight never acquired any substantial level of interpersonal preciseness. The metaphilosophy of systems may also generate or promote insight despite its low interpersonal preciseness.

SYSTEMS: ABSOLUTELY OR RELATIVELY TRUE— OR SIMPLY TRUE?

Gullvåg quotes me as saying: "A system can legitimately claim truth and intersubjective validity, not merely expediency or subjective appropriateness" (p. 400).

What I try to convey is that metasystematic assertions of plurality do not invalidate or make assertions of the simple kind, such as "*p* is true," meaningless. This would invalidate or make meaningless the assertion *p*. In other words, the so-called absolute concept of truth remains. Only, strictly speaking, there is not just one such concept. A rich variety will occur if made precise in relation to different ontologies.

Furthermore, the substitution of "*p* is relatively true" or "*p* is true in relation to my system *S*" for "*p* is true" is of doubtful usefulness. If somebody calls a system "my system *S*," *S* is not his or her total system. The person administers typological concepts in such a way that he or she is able to place *S* within a class of different systems. Whatever the system, it is therefore wider than *S*. This implies that a metasystematic relativism of the kind I assert on the T_0 level cannot be stated within a definite total system, which is thereby relativized through assertions made by its own adherents.

REALITY AS A DIRECTIVE IDEA: THERE IS ONLY ONE REALITY

Gullvåg describes my views in this way:

> The rules for the use of the term "reality" make the notion of reality a kind of regulative or directive idea. "Reality" is not a term that stands for a definite structure or substructure. Here, however,

it is natural to ask: In what sense is the idea of reality a directive idea? Does it determine a direction? Apparently, it doesn't determine anything, since it does not exclude anything, for different, mutually incompatible systems are equally valid in the sense of agreeing equally well with reality. (p. 401)

The use of the term *real* is such that it determines a direction toward oneness. Reality is one. In advocating a definite view concerning reality and trying to refute opposing views, I do not permit the intrusion of the idea that the other views concern another reality, a second or third reality, *unrelated* to each other. If related, then they are mere parts of a greater whole.

A view may, of course, intend to cover a different part or aspect of reality from another view. If one philosopher says, "*This* is reality," and the other says, "No, *that* is," a decision must be made in favor of only one of the possibilities, provided they can be shown to be different. If among philosophers we assert agreement about reality, we assume inevitably and correctly that it is the *same* reality we speak about. This also holds true when we speak of extremely different aspects of reality.

THE VALIDITY OF COMPREHENSIVE SYSTEMS

Gullvåg makes this observation about the metaphilosophy of systems: "According to Naess's pluralistic metaphilosophy, different, mutually incompatible, all-encompassing systems are equally 'valid or true'" (p. 392).

He is correct, but the next step in the dialectical metaphilosophy of systems requires such utterances to be reformulated, as I do in the following points:

1. More accurately, I would say that there are no decisive arguments against an all-encompassing (consistent) system and that if *anything* is valid, such a system is valid. (*Consistency* must be thought of as being defined within the system.)
2. The formulation "different, mutually incompatible systems may agree equally well with reality" is of a moderate level of preciseness. The more comprehensive the system, the more difficult it is to make a systematic comparison, because more and more terms are defined *within* the system. This implies that hypotheses about incompatibility or compatibility have less and less basis for confirmation or disconfirmation. The degree of incomparability increases. Thus, it

is presumably more precise to say "different, mutually incompatible or incomparable systems may agree with reality." The term *equally well* suggests (wrongly) a kind of system-independent measure of agreement. Or we may use the following formulation: "There may be no adequate basis for a conclusion that one system agrees and another does not agree with reality, even if the systems are mutually incompatible."

3. A system cannot be all-encompassing without encountering grave logical problems. I would say, "To be strict or absolutely all-encompassing is impossible." On the other hand, metaphilosophy needs fruitful conceptions of "near-total" or "maximally encompassing systems." The term *total system* is only used on the T_0 level, as is the term *total view*.

4. "Anything is possible" must also be taken as a point-of-departure formulation. It serves to stress a trend toward a greater tolerance of assumptions that postulate states of affairs that generally tend to be called impossible.

If interpreted in an absolute way, the slogan "Anything is possible" implies "It is impossible that something is impossible." This goes against my epistemology. I will not exclude the possibility that something is impossible. Transcendental philosophy, especially from the time of Kant, has proffered valuable hypotheses about impossibilities.

Gullvåg's paper is a valuable contribution to the unending process of correction and elaboration, which metaphysical inquiry needs if it is to adapt to changing standards and contexts.

The Methodology of Normative Systems[13]

HARD AND SOFT METHODOLOGY

Historically, general methodological interest has concentrated on highly technical and prestigious science, like theoretical physics. One expects to hear about Einstein and quantum physics rather than the methodology of questionnaires. I am one of those who relish reading about the wonderful achievements in physics, cosmology, and related very "hard" fields of natural science. But beginning in the 1970s, an increasing number of methodological admirers of hard science have tried to do something meaningful in soft science, more particularly, in chaotic areas where science and politics meet—areas such as how to save some unpolluted nature and reserve some possibilities for a graceful and dignified life for our grandchildren. In these areas, such humble research instruments as questionnaires are important. Ordinary, decent *pro et contra dicere* becomes important. Here, methodology loses much of its scientific charm. There is, however, a vast number of important questions for the soft research methodologists to tackle.

The following essay is formed in close connection with a definite example of a research project involving the development of a system of norms and hypotheses.[14] It is also written with a commitment to social and political activity, the *deep ecology movement*.[15]

It is my contention that the tentative formulation of normative systems is highly desirable in many kinds of activity, both purely theoretical and mixed theoretical, and pedagogical, ethical, or political. These systems have so far received little attention.

"NORMS" AND "HYPOTHESES"

The sentences of normative systems are conveniently divided into two classes, those ending with an exclamation point, suggesting inducements to think or to act in certain ways, and those ending with a period, suggesting affirmations. The first I call norms, the second hypotheses. The term *hypothesis* is chosen primarily to suggest testability, not uncertainty. Secondarily, the name suggests a certain tentativeness or reversibility. These characteristics hold also for norms, as we shall see from the methodology suggested in what follows. Even basic norms are revisable. Some have objected that the term *norm* and the exclamation point make the norm-sentences seem absolutistic and rigid. Actually, their main function is that of proposing tentative guidelines. Little is gained by a more complicated, relativistic terminology. Decisions—the aim of normative thinking—are absolutistic in the sense of being either carried out or sabotaged.

DIAGRAM SHOWING TOP LEVELS OF A VERSION OF SYSTEMATIZATION 1 OF ECOSOPHY T

To avoid unnecessary abstractness, I shall permit myself to introduce and elaborate in some detail a definite example. As a first step, let us look at the accompanying diagram. Explanations will follow in successive steps, not all at once.

The diagram expresses a tentative synopsis, or condensed survey, of a philosophy inspired by the ecology movement. I call such a philosophy an *ecosophy*. My relation to this philosophy is complex: On the one hand, I am an adherent and a contributor to its development. On the other hand, I am a researcher interested in critical thinking about systems and interested in methodology as such.

Saying that the diagram "expresses" a synopsis must be understood elliptically: As the maker of the diagram, I *intend* to express the synopsis through certain sentences. But it is, of course, rather unlikely that the sentences convey the same thing to any reader. Certain approximations are all that can be expected.

Modern ecology has been an inspiration to many ecologists and philosophers, all of whom, of course, do not arrive at the same results. To stress the possibility and even desirability of a diversity of tentative philosophies inspired by ecology, I name the system outlined in the diagram *Ecosophy T*. Here again I use a shorthand expression: Strictly speaking, no absolutely

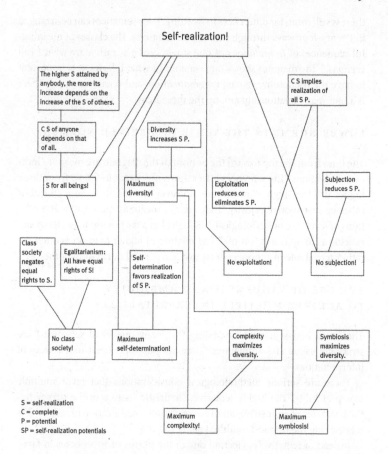

ILLUSTRATION 4: TENTATIVE SYNOPSIS OF AN ECOSOPHY

definite system is outlined. A set of sentences is offered. But plausible interpretations make up a class with more than one member. And my "definiteness of intention" is limited and constantly in flux.

A philosophy may be systematized in many ways. There is no one definite way of tracing lines of derivation. It is to some degree arbitrary which norms and hypotheses are chosen as ultimate in the sense of "not derivable." And even if the norms and hypotheses are arranged in a definite, authorized way, there is still room for differences in wording. Four sentences can be arranged in twenty-four ways through simple permutations. The classes of meaningful sequences of *formulations* of one single systematization are what I call *versions*.[16] The diagram shows one version. In what follows, it is important to have the trichotomy *system*, *systematization*, and *version* in mind. There is a one-many relationship among the three items.

LOWER NORMS IN THE SENSE OF DERIVED NORMS

The lines from the top toward the bottom of the diagram are meant to indicate derivations. The sentences lower down are meant to follow from those higher up. The "higher" norms are, however, not meant to have ethical or otherwise normative priority. They are not meant as more valid. The relations of levels are not axiological, but logical in a fairly wide sense, let us say, as wide as in Spinoza's "proofs." The relation of higher to lower is often the rather trivial one of a more general to a less general norm or hypothesis.

THE USE OF VAGUENESS AND AMBIGUITY
TO ACHIEVE MULTIPLE INTERPRETABILITY

The terms and sentences (including the many one-word sentences) are strikingly vague and ambiguous. They are *purposely* open to a variety of interpretations.

There are serious methodological considerations that favor multiple interpretability. The highly tentative, "heuristic" nature of the survey has the character of an instrument of research, not a codification of results. It is made along the way and modified along the way.

Instead of tentatively rejecting one of the norms or hypotheses in favor of a completely different one, it is often better to introduce alternative interpretations of the *initial* or *point-of-departure* wording. The initial vague and ambiguous sentence expressing the hypothesis or norm may tentatively be given more precise meanings, resulting in new formulations called *precizations*. The concept of precization is one of the central concepts of a semantical subsystem, often called *empirical semantics*.[17] Roughly, a sentence, s_1, is more precise than another, s_0, if and only if s_0 permits all the interpretations of the former, whereas s_1 does not permit all the interpretations of s_0, and does not permit any interpretation of the more precise sentence as a genuine subset of that of the less precise. The choice of a rather indefinite and ambiguous sentence in the most elementary survey makes it fairly short and easily understandable and opens a large variety of possibilities of more definite character. Instead of rather arbitrarily insisting that a sentence is to be interpreted, say, in the way expressed by No. 249, and in no other way, the options are kept open as long as this is heuristically convenient. Strictly speaking, the change of usage of words in No. 249 makes the sentence's meaning fluctuate in time and place. Openness is unavoidable.

FUNCTION OF ONE-WORD SENTENCES AND OTHER PRIMITIVE UTTERANCES: "NO EXPLOITATION!"

A striking feature of the survey are the many one-term sentences. One problem is, just who are the senders and who are the intended receivers of the survey considered a means of communication? If the survey is considered a kind of blueprint for a general utopia of self-realization, then the intended receiver is humankind at large. Humankind does not read, however. More concretely, the intended receivers may be conceived as the economically well-to-do in the industrial societies, and the sentences announce to them which norms should be followed and which goals (values) should be attempted and realized through changes in their society.

Thus conceived, the wording of one of the norms can be made more precise, as follows T_0: No exploitation! T_1: You (the economically well-to-do in the industrial societies) work toward, or support work toward, the elimination of economic and other kinds of exploitation. T_1 is more precise than T_0 in one direction of precization, namely, the receiver directed, but the ambiguous term *exploitation* is still employed.

What is exploitation? Evidently, there is room for further precization. But a highly precise sentence of the kind needed in a fairly abstract and general survey is apt to be very long and very complicated. Therefore, it cannot perform the special function of the less precise. The elaboration of the more definite, less vague, and less ambiguous survey of a system does not make the less definite, vaguer, and more ambiguous valueless. *We have to work continuously at various levels of preciseness. Various degrees of multiple interpretability are needed.*

The survey has six vertical levels, and at the top there is only one norm. With only one top norm, we eliminate the complication of rules of priority in case of norm collisions among any larger set of top norms. On the other hand, the choice of only one norm that is not derivable from other norms involves a fair amount of word magic or rather arbitrary rules of interpretation. The term *self-realization* carries an inordinately heavy burden!

If we put up, say, ten top norms, we would need to decide on numerous rules of priority. In general, the maximum realization of n_i is not compatible with maximum satisfaction of n_j, i and j taking the values 1, 2, 3, ..., 10. Or the maximum effort to realize n_i. To regulate the relations between n_i and n_j, we may need a vast number of rules.

SOME INTERPRETATIONS OF *SELF-REALIZATION*

Given different interpretations (in the sense of precization) of the term *self-realization*, the whole survey will get different meanings. Some derivations will not hold for some interpretations. In spite of this dependence on one single term, it will not be wise to assign to it a definite meaning. The choice must depend somewhat on which derivations are considered valid and important. Thus, the interpretation of the top norm sentences and the others of the version is a continuous process, where tentative modifications at one level interact with tentative semantical modifications at others.

The main semantical device used to adapt the term *self-realization* to Ecosophy T is to distinguish three concepts:

T_0: self-realization
T_1: ego-realization
T_2: self-realization (with lowercase *s*)
T_3: Self-realization (with capital *S*)

The last concept is known in the history of philosophy under various names, *the universal self*, *the absolute*, and *Atman*. Many Indo-European languages use terms corresponding to the English *self* in analogous ways. Thus, the Sanskrit *ātman* is used for all three concepts, but mostly as a simple reflexive pronoun.

In prevalent individualistic and utilitarian political thinking in Western modern industrial states, the terms *self-realization*, *self-expression*, and *self-interest* are used for what is above called *ego-realization* and *self-realization*. One stresses the ultimate and extensive incompatibility of the interests of different individuals. In opposition to this trend, there is another, which is based on the hypothesis of increased compatibility with increased maturity of the individuals. The compatibility is considered to have an ontological basis—compare the "illusion" of a separable ego. Ecosophy T leans heavily on such ideas, which were excellently developed in Spinoza's *Ethics*. Self-preservation, or in our terminology, self-realization, cannot develop far without sharing joys and sorrows with others or, more fundamentally, without the development of the narrow ego of the small child into the comprehensive structure of a Self that comprises all human beings. The ecological movement—like many earlier philosophical movements—goes a step further and asks for a deep identification of individuals with all life.

The development of life-forms, especially since the Cambrian period, shows an extreme degree of expansion of life space and a corresponding diversity of forms making use of different climatic and other conditions. There is no merely passive adaptation, no mere self-preservation in any narrow sense. Thus, the term *self-expression*, or *self-realization*, is better suited than *self-preservation*. If the term *self* is felt to be unfitting, we can use *life unfolding* or *life expansion*.

Whereas the top sentences, both the norms and the hypotheses in our survey, are somewhat metaphysical, the next levels introduce crucial ecological terms: diversity, complexity, and symbiosis. If a particular way of life is such that different species or different communities must compete and struggle with each other merely to survive, conditions are worse than if the different entities can somehow specialize, making use of each other's activities, and thus "live and let live"—that is, practice symbiosis. As conceived in modern ecology, symbiotic coexistence does not exclude killing—elk and wolf have lived in symbiosis, the wolves keeping the population of elk within a limit necessary to uphold good, not-too-competitive life conditions and healthy elk communities.

Other terms no doubt need elucidation. The main point, however, is that from the top norms and hypotheses, *general* ecological and ecopolitical principles are derived. Thanks to the normative aspect of the system, *it does not merely describe, but prescribes*. Thus, we are able to take care of the social and political views within the international ecology movement, of which the environmental concerns are only a part.

SUMMARIZING OBSERVATIONS ON SYSTEMATIZATION

In the preceding discussion, I have tried to render some of the hypotheses of the survey understandable. I am not trying to persuade anybody of the tenability of the hypotheses! But the discussion aims to point out the following general advantages of systematization:

1. Systematizations of norms and hypotheses are needed in research motivated by pedagogical, ethical, political, or other large-scale movements.

2. The systematizations visualize complicated logical or, more generally, cognitive relationships between important clusters of prescriptions and descriptions. The systemizations also bring to focus the basic premises and fundamental norms that guide concrete actions and minor research units having meaning only within, or mainly within, a major normative framework. They help unify and coordinate enterprises involving diverse groups and many persons.

3. As research instruments, systematizations must be flexible. They must be expressed at various levels of preciseness and in alternative terminologies. A multiplicity of versions are needed, each adapted to special functions.

4. Modifications can be carried out through the reinterpretation of terms and sentences as well as through negating or modifying propositions.

5. Whereas the simple, categorical way of announcement of norms and hypotheses makes survey and derivation the simplest, the assessment of degrees of uncertainty and qualifying phrases should be attached as notes and comments.

NORMATIVE SYSTEMS: THEIR ROLE IN SOCIAL AND POLITICAL CONTEXT

We now will look at the extrinsic or social use of a survey or synopsis—an instrument with pronounced multiple uses in social contexts. Again, we will use as a tool the survey from the deep ecology movement.

The destruction of ecosystems due to population explosion, heavy industry, and other factors has made it necessary to reform many laws and regulations. For example, until recently, laws specified exceptions to the general *permission* to kill wild animals. Today, laws are now specifying exceptions to a general *prohibition* against killing or injuring. A corresponding development is going on in relation to wild plants.

The reasons given for all these prohibitions mostly specify narrowly utilitarian aspects of the crisis. Or they stress in more general terms the interconnection of human life conditions with those of other forms. But the strongest motivation among the most prominent advocates of a new attitude toward nature and ecosystems has been more philosophical. The advocates have struggled for the recognition of the intrinsic value of the various life-forms and the right, in principle, of all of them to blossom. From the time of Rachel Carson's *Silent Spring*, the ecological movement in the West has been inspired by philosophy and still is so. The survey is a crude instrument by means of which the main, general outline of this philosophy can be codified. Not that all participants in the movement need to subscribe to the same hypotheses and norms, but they can *verbalize their own convictions in relation to the survey*. Very few of the active participants have any special training in systematic philosophical and scientific expositions. And the methodology of normative systems certainly does not belong to the curriculum of any traditional school. Thus, the survey facilitates *reasoning and argumentation from first principles* within the ecological movement—and of course, as a reaction within the groups who fight what they call the "prophets of doom."

THE ROLE OF ARGUING FROM FIRST PRINCIPLES IN TECHNOCRACIES

Why is it so important in some Western industrialized states to reason and argue from first principles? One reason depends on a value judgment concerning technical expertise. I wish, therefore, not to mention it as a universally valid reason for argument from the first principles.

The vast majority of experts with influence on the policy of Western industrial states avoid argumentation from fundamentals. They prefer to state which are the *preferences of the majority*, or are in harmony with *the stated goals of the government elected democratically* by the populace. The goals are in part vaguely formulated through slogans such as "welfare," or in a more specific way, defined as "continued economic growth," "less than 4 percent unemployment," and so forth. In any case, experience shows a marked unwillingness, perhaps sometimes combined with an inability, to argue from fundamentals.

Confronted with people from the deep ecology movement who argue from fundamentals, the experts are induced to do the same. This nearly always results in conclusions favorable to the movement. It lays bare that shortsighted, unecological policies have as a necessary condition the absence of argumentation from fundamentals. When such argumentation is introduced, there appear inconsistencies between basic norms and hypotheses and current policies. The experts often personally have the same basic value commitments as those in the ecology movement. But the experts' public function is primarily to help realize goals of some other authority and is backed by powerful special interests. Less powerful interests cannot afford to hire the experts.

Through argumentation from fundamentals, the experts are pushed into controversial issues and are led to criticize unecological policies and their own bosses. Thus, the clearer and more explicit the argumentation from fundamentals among supporters of responsible ecological policies, the greater the possibilities of introducing such argumentation among policy makers.

These *hypotheses* about the increase of possibilities do not imply any definite level of influence. It is easy to overestimate the influence of arguments in politics. The impact of ecological thinking upon policies has been slight, compared with what ecologists think is necessary to prevent catastrophic conditions less than a century from now. And if such argumentation is introduced, it generally favors the goals of responsible ecological policies. But this is perhaps too much talk about the ecology movement! And with the use of unclarified, value-laden expressions such as "responsible" ecological policies! Let us inspect the survey considered at a *point-of-departure formulation* (a T_0 formulation) of the uppermost levels of a normative system.

PREPONDERANCE OF NON-NORMATIVES IN A NORMATIVE SYSTEM

First, let us make some elementary observations about normative systems:

1. A normative system does not consist only of norms. Most codifications of normative views show a marked preponderance of non-normative sentences.
2. Norms are in general derived from other norms *and* hypotheses, not merely from norms.
3. The existence of at least one hypothesis as a premise for the inference of a norm establishes the *hypothetical character of derived norms*. Their *validity* depends on the validity of non-normative assumptions, postulates, theories, and observations.

Methodologically, the last point is of decisive importance in argumentation: When the intricate interconnections between norms and hypotheses are left unarticulated, each norm tends to be taken to be absolute or ultimate. This eliminates the possibility of rational discussion. In harmony with the methodology here proposed, when norms are opposed in debate, it is always appropriate to ask the opponent: "Which hypotheses do you think are relevant to the adoption of your norm?"

Today, if experts refer to public opinion in support of a norm, it is important to ask both for evidence in the form of published investigations of opinions and for norms justifying the *derivation* of a norm from descriptions of opinions, whether they are those of a majority or an authoritative minority. Opinions are, unfortunately, reported as if they can be isolated from (implicit) normative systems. A Norwegian survey concluded that three out of four think that the Norwegian standard of living is too high, 28 percent even "much too high," and only 1 percent too low. Supporters of economic growth contended that a different way of asking would show that a lesser majority are against the present average high standard of living. Subsequent surveys proved this. But it is plausible that a "deep interview" covering fundamental norms and hypotheses would indicate that more than three out of four think that the standard is too high. For methodological purposes, surveys need the use of a substantial number of different systemic contexts. As it is now, different political parties use only one questionnaire for each survey and form the questions in a way that is favorable to the party line.

ULTIMATE NORMS: THE EQUAL RIGHT TO LIVE AND BLOSSOM

The term *ultimate norm* is used mainly in two senses, "a norm not derived from any other norm" and "a norm of highest priority" (or "a norm of absolute, unconditioned priority"). In normative systems of the kind envisaged, only the first sense is used. In that case, there is a rational methodology for changing an ultimate norm. Any proposal for ultimateness will fundamentally have the character of a working hypothesis.

Given a consistent set of norms and hypotheses, there is in principle a plurality of possibilities of deriving them from a less numerous set. It primarily involves a process of generalizations. If the ultimate norm concerns adult humans, it may be generalized to concern all living beings with certain characters, determining the traits in a way that one can infer that all adult humans fall within the *range of intended validity*, but that others also *might* fall within that range. Whether we believe that such beings (e.g., angels and Martians) actually exist is not relevant to the previous question of derivation. We would get an ultimate norm, from which the previous ultimate norm concerning adult humans is derived.

The more frequent source of change of an ultimate norm is, however, the derivation of a (nonultimate) norm that we are certain we will *not* accept as valid. It must be remembered that a *systematization* is a methodological device made by certain persons for certain purposes. It has no independent authority.

If, for instance, "All living beings have equal rights of self-realization" is derivable from the ultimate norm "Complete self-realization," and "If your little daughter has an extreme hunger, and food can only be brought to her by killing the last tiger, but nevertheless do not kill it" can be derived from "All living beings have equal rights" (plus some hypotheses of unquestioned validity), then some of us would reject the ultimate norm. That is, we might say, "It is my duty to rescue my child, whatever the consequences for the tigers." (But not whatever the consequences for my human neighbor. That is, it is not my duty to kill my neighbor, even if the person were the only food available for my daughter.) The rejection of an ultimate norm has normally a kind of intuition as one of its presuppositions.

The principle of equal rights for all living beings to blossom is controversial today, but opinion seems to be rising in its favor. To avoid undesired consequences, especially in our world of increasing famine, the necessary injuring and killing of animals for food must be admitted through special hypotheses and norms. These have to do with mutual aid among beings of the same or similar kind. There are obvious advantages for a species whose parents take special care of their offspring, and whose kindred beings take special care about which groups are obnoxious to the "out-groups." Exactly where is the line to be drawn? Obviously, there cannot be general agreement here, and attempts to codify detailed norms covering all sorts of norm collisions are unrealistic and methodologically unjustified. There is, however, a movement toward establishing a norm against "inflicting unnecessary pain of injury to animals." What is here meant by "unnecessary"? It obviously depends on a complex structure of norms and hypotheses.

Clarification of the concept of *natural rights* has never been very successful. To clarify the egalitarian norm under consideration, I propose that a qualifying rule be added: "The right of A to live and blossom does not automatically exclude the justification of B to injure or kill A." To avoid confusion, I would not say B may have the right to kill; there are many kinds of justification other than through a so-called natural right.

DE PRINCIPIIS EST DISPUTANDUM

Now back to our consideration of norms placed as ultimate in a normative systematization. From the preceding discussion, it follows that the rule *de principiis non est disputandum* does not hold. Every proposal of ultimate norms is open to discussion. And the critical assessment can take many forms: nonacceptance of consequences, invoking norms from which the proposed ultimate norm can be derived, and other argumentative moves.

TEAMWORK AND ACTION RESEARCH

Hypotheses of central importance in an ecosophy exhibit an extremely wide range of subject matter, from quantum mechanics to political science and theory of communication. Teamwork is therefore essential in every ecosophical research, however modest. There are no specialists in ecophilosophy. The preceding research project that I used to illustrate systematization in this discussion comprises teamwork. The members are in constant touch with a very wide circle of researchers *and* participants in political and social struggles. This makes the research to some extent manifest the character of *action research*.

Action research has had a bad reputation among stern methodologists favoring the hard natural sciences. This is unfortunate because an increasing number of high-quality research problems have time limitations. The researchers get to know the dates, say, $d_1, d_2, \ldots, d_{10}$, as approximate dates of social and political decisions with grave ecological consequences. The researchers are asked to furnish evidence for or against certain crucial hypotheses before definite dates. Genuine questions of scientific methodology are specific to this unfortunate situation: The researcher has to solve the maximization problem of how to arrive at a maximum of evidence for or against a hypothesis, given limited resources, the severest limit being that of time available. Furthermore, the researchers have to accept modifying or reshaping the project after each political decision. Teamwork is essential because of the many shifts of relevance from one kind of subordinate problem to another.

The ecologically relevant researchers needed to assess atomic energy installations are typical: Safety investigations require atomic physicians, chemists, and engineers in the hard sciences; studies on the consequences for vegetation, fisheries, and so forth require "soft" natural science participants; the "human error" factor of social and psychological competence and the political implications (plutonium in the hands of an increasing number of governments, increased centralization, etc.) also require researchers in many social and humanistic fields. Therefore, all these researchers are subject to merciless requirements of priorities. Every relevant question may open interesting investigations that might take a hundred years and require the total material resources available.

The bad reputation of action research is mainly the result of two defects and one good thing: First, the uncertain character of certain hypotheses is not emphasized in research reports or popular forms of mass communication. Second, the researcher is pleading a cause in a way that hampers the utilization of the information by people of different opinions. And finally, action research sometimes hits narrow vested interests, which then hit back, trying to discredit action research as a whole.

Whereas military action research in established natural sciences has been going on for a long time (although the name *action research* was not used), action research in social science is new and must be expected to meet opposition. Action research must be led by researchers with some experience; otherwise, valuable contributions can be misused or neglected because of flaws in the way they are presented to the public. For example, a government institution involved in the efforts to protect forests hired scientists to report on different aspects of forest management, one of which was recreation. A young team investigated people's concept of a forest and what they expect from the forest. The public clearly expected and wished for diversity in the ecological sense. Those who have economic interests on the whole favor monocultures, broad highways for transportation, and other features that are ecologically undesirable. A hot public debate resulted, and the papers written by the young scientists were heavily criticized. Some of the criticism could have been avoided if they had *foreseen the clash* between opposite interests. In short, in action research, the participants should be generalists, with a field of study covering the question of how a scientific report is likely to be read and used or attacked by various power groups. Theory of communication and political science is relevant, whatever the special topic of an action research project.

I hope that this essay may inspire some friends in the field of "hard" methodology to shift toward the broad fields of "soft" methodology. Their general concern for "objectivity" may contribute to their being fair and unbiased, which is so important in the hot conflicts surrounding present-day social and political problems.

Pluralism in Cultural Anthropology[18]

What can I do except join Hans Skjervheim in his efforts to clarify and reject the absolutistic "scientism" of Claude Lévi-Strauss? But I can do it only with some trepidation because of the difference between the methodological jargon of Lévi-Strauss and that of myself. For example, Lévi-Strauss says that "the model should be so constituted as to make immediately intelligible all the observed facts."[19] Either Lévi-Strauss uses the word "model" so differently from myself that no "yes" or "no" is relevant in the discussion or I must say no with desperation. The function of a model is such that if it covers, and even makes intelligible, "all" pertinent observations, then it is not a *model*. Models are highly selective. And how can he use the word "facts" in this connection? An anthropologist notes that two members of such and such a culture play (or fight, make an axe, blame each other, etc.). The conceptual framework is his or her own, however talented the anthropologist is in putting "himself in the place of the people living there."[20] And however clever the theoretical models.

In my favorite terminology of the 1930s and later, the anthropologist *witnesses* things rather than observes. With the witness reports functioning as a sort of raw material, the anthropologist successively eliminates or changes the sentences that manifest the provinciality of his or her original concepts. Thus, if the report stated, "Then the friends shook hands," the anthropologist may be correct because of increasing evidence that "friendship" as "we" understand it is not *their* concept, and because the reaction sequence named "shaking hands" does not have that significance.

So, where are the "facts"?

Suppose anthropologists from cultures A, B, and C compare each other's reports as witnesses and their laboriously constructed accounts of the social relations of the Balinese. Why should we believe in a kind of *true* scientific account of those relations? In general, the greater the differences among A, B, and C, the greater the differences in their accounts. If the differences are very great, the classification of all three as anthropologists gets to be rather shaky. Which are the maximum methodological divergencies possible with the conceptualization *anthropologist*?

We may assume that through some sort of scientific methods, we are able to reduce the differences among the three accounts of the social relations of the Balinese. But even if, against all odds, the number of differences could be reduced to zero, the appearance of a fourth anthropologist, D, belonging to a young generation is likely to shatter the artificial joint account constructed by A, B, and C.

The problems faced are essentially the same as those facing us when we try to formulate a definition of a term, for example, *democracy*, on the basis of a set of use occurrences of the term. Or, the characterization of a *Verhaltensweise* (behavior) corresponding to the cognitive content of "the distance between the sun and earth is 149.5 million kilometers" based on a set of descriptions of behaviors (verbal and nonverbal) of scientists.

Pluralism is inescapable and nothing to lament. Reality is one, but if accounts of it are identical, this only reveals cultural poverty. Excessive belief in "science" favors acceptance of poverty as a sign of truth. According to Lévi-Strauss, good models will save us from pluralism because of their intimate relation to what he calls "reality," sometimes even "deep reality."

Strauss's references to Freud are important in this connection. The concepts Freud used to describe the function of the unconscious are socially understandable. "I intended to kill my father" may be unacceptable to the patient at a certain stage of the psychoanalysis, but patricide is part of a set of understandable social concepts. Physicists may introduce completely new concepts like quarks in fundamental explanations (i.e., explanations on the top level of hypodeductive systems). But social scientists must, I presume, narrow down the areas of basic concepts in their models to those of social acceptance, such as Richard Dawkins's assertion that we really are mere appendages of selfish genes.[21] But this conceptualization is useless in social science. The "realness" Dawkins asserts is only one in relation to certain *biological* models.

It is amusing to imagine that we are only appendages of certain kinds, just as it is entertaining to think of ourselves as swarms of atoms or multidimensional oceans of probability waves. If we live long enough, we can look forward to a series of new, wonderful models superbly popularized by eminent natural scientists.

In short, if Lévi-Strauss relies on models from the most modern natural science, logic, and mathematics, then pluralism is not only inescapable, but very clearly stated in modern general methodology. The models are mutually inconsistent; otherwise, the change of models would only be moderately interesting. If we think of reality as one, and I do not see how we can avoid that, the relation of the models to reality cannot be but indirect. They cannot put us in touch with deeper layers of reality in the way Freud tried to do. His conceptualizations served the aim to make our feelings and actions more understandable.

The astonishing success of physical models since Galileo justifies the belief that they *somehow* picture something real and independent of cultural differences among scientists. The equations themselves seem to be independent, but their use and interpretations are always dependent.

Despite what I have said so far, it may be argued that pluralism is absolutistic: The pluralist conclusion is asserted "monistically" at a higher metalevel. The pluralism is part of a total view that is not mentioned. If Lévi-Strauss has a different total view, my arguments for pluralism may be misconceived, irrelevant, or simply not understandable from his point of view.

I will not go into the problems of total views. Suffice it to say that some of my formulations are purposely made absolutist to remind the reader of those problems. This holds, for example, for the bombastic sentence "Pluralism is inescapable . . ." When I work toward a total view, pluralism becomes increasingly obvious, or gets to be derivable with increased rigor from fundamental norms and hypotheses.

Like Skjervheim, I agree that Lévi-Strauss seems to favor a kind of scientific absolutism. I would add "with an atomist flavor," considering his ideal of "reintegrating culture and nature and finally of life within the whole of its physico-chemical conditions."[22] Atomism I understand as the opposite of gestalt thinking, that is, thinking in terms of ever more comprehensive wholes and stressing the nonreducibility of higher-order wholes to lower-order wholes. Classical examples include melodies to sequences of noises or even tones, propositions or units of intended meaning to sentences or formulations, *Verhaltensweisen* or operations to reactions.

Mathematics, chemistry, sociobiology, and other branches of science are of heuristic help to social scientists as "auxiliary sciences." But they do not help dissolve the sciences of humans. They do not dissolve any *thing or process*. Reduction, as a part of the scientific enterprise, must be understood in a different way.[23]

Skjervheim's way of saying essentially the same or similar things that I have said so far in this essay is often not my way. The difference is instructive, but not easy to pin down in clear words. In what follows I shall try to clarify disagreements about how to interpret some points in my doctoral dissertation, *Erkenntnis und wissenschaftliches Verhalten* (Cognition and scientific behavior, University of Oslo, 1936, hereinafter cited as "*Erkenntnis*").

The biologist and philosopher Jakob von Üexküll worked out clearer than others that each species has a set of different reactions applied in different kinds of situations (defined by the biologists!). The world each species lives in has a number of discriminable features that manifest themselves in several kinds of reactions. This is all very inspiring, except that every reaction and situation is, of course, described in terms of the *human* observer, as features of *his or her* world.

Now, as Lévi-Strauss explains, if we as cultural anthropologists try to "study men as if they were ants," the reactions and situation we describe in our witness reports on culture B are in terms of our own particular culture A. The culture B cannot be described except as something *completely* within the cognitive framework of A. The world of B is either naively pictured as a part of the world of A or else said only to have an abstract structure corresponding (isomorphically) to a nonabstract structure within the world of A.

When it is said that a person N. N. within a culture B thinks he or she is actually *identical* with a particular animal, the terms *person, identical, animal*, and so on possess the connotations they have in A. We, members of A, get an exciting picture of B, but we should not pretend we can experience the world of B through the connotations of words belonging to A. If we do, we succumb to the mistake of *maze-epistemology*. (We describe the movement of an animal in a maze without clearly recognizing that the maze is a feature of our experienced world rather than that of the animal.)

The cultural provinciality of anthropologists can be reduced through successive (endless) modifications of their accounts. In the preceding example, the member of culture A will try to find out how people in B experience what *we* call animals, persons, and identities. Another example: How can Sherpas seem to say (in their language) that the mountain Tseringma *is* a mountain *and* a princess? How can we translate, *if at all*, their verbal utterances in such a way that we approximate *their* experience of Tseringma? The attempts to do so result in a plurality of versions.

Strangely enough, the successive approximations—if such are at all forthcoming—are reached by successive steps of methodological alienation: We *start* treating the members of B as colleagues: The Sherpas assert "mistakenly" that Tseringma also is a princess. Then we retreat from them, allowing for the possibility that their concept of a mountain is not the same as ours, nor that of a person, nor their use of language. We may even start looking for evidence that identification somehow is differently conceived.

If very successful, we may be able roughly to experience the world as a member of culture B, still retaining the ability somehow to describe the experience in the language of A. But with further approximations, this ability gradually vanishes: A basic feature of the experience within culture B is that it does *not* somehow contain the consciousness of being different from A. As long as the cultural anthropologist walks around *with a notebook in mind*, his or her experience is in one fundamental way different from that of B.

The eminent cultural anthropologist Fredrik Barth sometimes writes as if humans are capable of going in and out of many cultures, participating in each word they define.[24] I presume he does not pretend to grasp more than fragments. If he went in deep, I presume it would be next to impossible to get out.

Literally speaking, everything is affected by a culture—including the primary sense qualities like length and breadth. As perceived by members of the culture in which a coin is used, the size of the coin is perceived differently according to its value.[25] An axe is full of cultural traits, and in at least one culture, it is perceived as a status symbol in a way so complicated that it would take years to adjust one's behavior to its cultural ontology. The repugnance toward lack of intelligence is so pervasive in our competitive civilization that rats *classed* as dull are treated worse than those *classed* as bright—with the effect that the former perform even worse than necessary.[26] Cultural priorities determine behavior in ways completely unknown to the participants.

The terms *behavioral* and *behaviorism* are usually associated with the doctrines of J. B. Watson and other "molecular" behaviorists, not with the "molar" behaviorism of E. C. Tolman. The difference is philosophically essential because the molar view is an intentional view.[27] In *Erkenntnis*, I use the Tolmanian conception of behavior as action, not reaction. The term *Verhaltensweise*, "way of behavior," is *not* observable as a succession of movements or reactions.

Skjervheim suggests that in my earlier work (*Erkenntnis*), "behavior" did not yet have intentional import. I disagree. Perhaps I did not make it clear enough that the "stranger from another planet," which I introduce for certain purposes, is not a Tolmanian behaviorist. My *Verhaltensweise* was meant to offer a synthesis of *Erkenntnisinhal* (cognitive content) and *Erkenntnistätigkeit* (cognition as act). Only inherently purposeful ways of behavior could represent cognitions as acts and content—in the kind of science of science envisaged.

Operationists like Bridgman insisted that in the science of science, one should not listen to scientists but see what they do. I stressed that in that case, one should not even listen to how scientists define their various operations, but must take up the attitude of the anthropologists or even the rat psychologist in observing the scientist. An illustration:

A: What are those two scientists doing?

B: They each are performing an x-ray measurement.

A: But they move very differently. Look at their arms.

B: Nonsense: The one is left-handed, the other right-handed. You must understand that those differences in reactions are totally irrelevant.

A: But what are they doing now? They are behaving very differently.

B: Nonsense. They are still performing an x-ray measurement. One of them is smoking a cigarette, and the other is singing. You must understand that it is a completely irrelevant difference.

Insofar as "x-ray measurement" is a kind of *Verhaltensweise*, it is a complicated task to describe it in terms of relevant and *only* relevant traits. But if that could be done, the intentional aspect would be included, simply in terms of relevance. Intentionality does not manifest itself in pure consciousness, but in units of verbal and nonverbal behaviors.

This is the point of view of my *Erkenntnis*, and I accept it. But just as a cultural anthropologist starts out using the conceptual framework of his own culture uncritically, the science-of-science specialist starts out as a colleague of the scientists, that is, methodologically as a "witness." The kind of scientist of science envisaged in *Erkenntnis* tries step by step to get rid of the prejudices due to cultural affiliation. But where does this end? I agree with Skjervheim that there is a limit beyond which the scientist of the science B can no longer be said to *understand* B, or more precisely, does not produce an account of B that makes B *understandable*. I think the molar behavioral (*objektiv psychologische*) account envisioned in *Erkenntnis* is inside the limits, whereas that of the "researcher from a strange planet" is outside. He or she establishes a science of science of sorts, and according to the stated assumptions, one that in a strange but perfect way *explains* the difference in cognitive content between various human hypotheses about the distance of the sun. The researcher is completely inside (and perhaps very proud of this) in one way, but at the same time hopelessly outside in another way. Call it the hermeneutical way, if you insist.

The Principle of Intensity[28]

If you fill your bathtub half full with water at forty degrees Celsius and then after a moment's hesitation fill it completely, the temperature does not increase to eighty degrees. Forty plus forty is eighty, but because *temperature is an intensity*, more water of forty degrees does not increase the temperature. These are principles of great importance in theory, but perhaps less so in practice. One such principle has to do with intensities.

In Hiroshima on August 6, 1945, after 9:00 A.M., a great number of people and animals suffered intensely. We may therefore safely infer that some—we do not know who—suffered prolonged pain in the terrible realm of maximum intensity. The same day, thousands of miles away, other people presumably also experienced extreme suffering. With billions of people on our planet, there are presumably always people in a state of extreme felt suffering.

It is important to repeat the adjective *felt* because, in determining criteria of pain and suffering, we quite often use some "objective" situation rather than feeling. I add the term *suffering*, because pain is sometimes used for physical pain only. On the other hand, *suffering* is sometimes used without implied felt pain, as, for instance, in expressions like "suffering the lack of *x*."

People in Hiroshima wandered around with eyes intact but with the skin of their faces hanging down in a terrifying way. Some citizens seemed to be in a state of confusion rather than excruciating pain. When we compare pictures of one hundred people in hunger districts, our judgment about the relative intensities of pain tends to confuse the *awfulness* of what we see with the felt pain. Rescuers with limited supplies are in a difficult position. Who has priority?

Thinking of Hiroshima, we might say: "What a stupendous *amount* of pain!" But strictly speaking, the number of persons afflicted is irrelevant when speaking of *felt* pain. And what is pain that is *not* felt? Hiroshima was a catastrophe of staggering *dimension*. But the dimension is not an intensity. It may *cause* variation of intensities, but is in itself irrelevant.

During the Nazi regime, more than a hundred thousand people were severely tortured. Some torturers were "scientific," trying to use only a sufficient dose to get hold of all the information the victim could be *rationally* supposed to possess. Others started with extreme torture immediately and continued indefinitely, just trying to cause the most insufferable pain conceivable. Unfortunately, the situation was nearly always such that nobody could rescue the victims, even when the exact location of the torture chambers was known.

At a given moment, one may ask, What is the status of *felt* pain on the planet? With so many people in so many risky situations, the answer is plain: There is always a maximum felt pain and suffering.

The next question to be answered is, What can be done to reduce felt pain and suffering, given limited power and opportunity to do so? That is, what can be done by individuals and by institutions, what sort of collective action? This leads immediately to the question of priorities. If person A obviously is in extreme pain and B is only in moderate pain, and we have equal opportunity to significantly reduce or even eliminate the pain of one and only one of them, ethics tells us, or at least some of us, to act on behalf of A. But what about the situation when person A suffers extreme pain; hundreds of other people, group B, suffer moderate pain; and ten thousand, group C, suffer slight pain?

Here the maxim is relevant, but of little help: Reduce maximally the pain and suffering of a maximum number of people. Number comes in, and for good reason. It affects us more strongly to hear about a ship on which two hundred people were burned to death than to hear about one person facing the same death. Similarly the presumably moderate pain of two hundred people on the rescue boat, cold and miserable, affects us more than to hear about people suffering the same fate. If we as rescuers have to choose, we sometimes let sheer number be counted as relevant.

Suppose we have the opportunity to save either one person from extreme pain or one hundred from moderate pain. In order not to be led astray, suppose they do not interact with each other as they do in a boat.

From the kind of philosophy with which I feel most comfortable, my answer is this: Relieve the one person in extreme pain. But a feeling of absurdity enters me when I increase the numbers and decrease the difference of intensity of pain felt. Suppose that one person is in obviously more intense pain, or would get into a state of more intense pain, than a vast number of people who are suffering a *somewhat* lesser pain or who would get into this situation, if we decided on one action rather than another. I feel we should help the vast number and, talking more practically, explain the situation to the single person. I expect the person would say something like, "Yes, I see the point. I am glad you decided as you did!"

One thing that unavoidably crosses my mind is that we should also consider consequences more remote than the immediate decrease or elimination of pain. If we are able to help a vast number of people by a decision or an action, this may have better and longer-lasting effects, also in terms of expected new pain, than if one single person gets rid of a more severe pain. I expect that the situation is fluid and that decisive help of thousands could seriously decrease the possibility that many of them, or their children, would reach a high level of suffering because of vast numbers of sufferers. (I cannot avoid thinking of people interacting. But what we are asked to answer does not make remote consequences relevant, or interaction. Consequently, I would say: help the one who is suffering most!)

By now the reader may feel that *in practice*, it is often the most reasonable to let *quantity* of persons play a role. This is good, but the principle of intensity is not touched.

The conclusion I support so far may be formulated like this: Whatever the number within groups A and B, if A is clearly suffering more intense pain than B, other circumstances being equal, choose to relieve A rather than B, if there is an absolute either-or.

But such a norm is in practice not isolated. It is "in real life" part of a wide field of norms. Also the uncertainty of diagnosis enters the picture: Are you ever competent to decide whether a person is on such and such a level of intensity of pain? Furthermore, in practice, whether we like it or not, we mostly think about whether a person *deserves* to be helped. Another factor is age: The suffering of small children counts more than that of their parents. Here, "innocence" plays a role. Furthermore, dignity enters. Many people suffer indignities and desire more strongly to be relieved of them than of pain. One talks about "suffering with dignity," but not only in the form of only pain, but also in the form of indignation and anger (and perhaps more so with indignation and anger).

The norm to relieve fellow humans in a situation of intense pain is sometimes taken so seriously that people are rescued even though they have asked to be left alone. A well-known example is that of Mr. Fukai: After the explosion of the atomic bomb on Hiroshima, his head appeared above the rubble of his home. A warmhearted fellow human saw him and started to pull him out. But Mr. Fukai, polite that day as he was polite all other days, begged not to be removed from his home. He was carried away, anyway—he was a tiny man, it is said—away from areas threatened by fires. The warmhearted person eventually stumbled into deep water, and Mr. Fukai escaped. He was grabbed again, but escaped again. He ran away in the direction of his home, where he presumably died in the approaching fire. It is difficult for me to see the justification of grabbing Mr. Fukai, even if his behavior might be interpreted as expressions of insanity in a popular sense of that word.

The indirect political importance is great, or ought to be great. If in your own rich country or neighborhood, there is one person who *certainly* suffers great pain, and you reduce that pain, you do as much good as when you cause the same in a country or region where there certainly are thousands of people suffering great pain.

In 1945, I had the opportunity to locate a group with members likely to be in a situation of extreme mental pain. When the gate of the Nazi concentration camp near Oslo was supposed to be opened, parents streamed to the gate to meet their imprisoned sons. Some of the young men did not show up. For the parents, the realistic thought was that their sons had been tortured to death by the Gestapo, but the parents frantically hoped that their sons were alive somewhere. It was a meager, but not insignificant, help to investigate the cases and offer *certainty* to the parents that their sons were *not* alive somewhere in the world. The victims were rarely tortured to death, but had died of "exposure" or managed to use a poisonous pill to avoid torture. A group like this group of parents typically could not count on help from ordinary social institutions. More was done to inflict pain on the "Quislings," those who had directly or indirectly assisted the occupying Nazi power, than to reduce intense suffering.

Not enough is done to save people in intense pain and suffering. One forgets that there is in a sense no greater reduction in *felt* pain possible than saving a single person.

The false quantification of felt pain tends to reduce the efforts to reach the victims. In countries where torture is used regularly and ruthlessly, people who fight year after year against those in power face daily the prospect of being tortured themselves. Very little is done to organize secret routes out of those countries so that the fighters themselves can get out at short notice—and back again when they are tough enough. Such routes played an important role during the Nazi occupation of Norway from 1940 to 1945 and have a long history in the world of atrocities and terror. Today, people forget that opposition to systematic torture is going on now, and that it is an international task to support the activists in every way, including those ways intensely disliked by the torturers: pressure from the outside.

People tend to neglect quality of life in favor of quantity of objects and services *supposed* to secure quality. Suggestibility is a formidable force, and to some extent, a person can easily increase the quality of life by continuously noticing the great number of *means* available: "See what I *have* to secure happiness and avoid depression! I have everything!" Every *thing*, yes. But it is unrealistic to believe that a steady stream of socially acknowledged means, our affluence, and the resulting increase in the *standard* of living can ensure high *quality*.

At a deeper level, however, there is a tendency to help where we believe we *see* what is most needed. The "needy" are conceived to be those who *lack* something, and they themselves naturally express their wants in those terms. What *is* needed, more than anything else, is to relieve intense and prolonged felt suffering.

Creativity and Gestalt Thinking[29]

Long and intense training is required to express in words the major aspects of a spontaneous experience. We enter a room and "the room" makes an impression upon us which we express conventionally by terms like *light*, *dark*, *cozy*, *small*, *cold*, *conventional*, and *beautiful*. But the terms are (of course) class terms. We experience an *instance* of coziness, not coziness in general. By uttering "cozy," we have only started on a verbal report, namely, that of the particular content, different from any other, that makes us utter the general term "cozy." Perhaps it was the first time we entered the room that we thought, "cozy." The next ten times may also elicit a spontaneous experience, an aspect of which makes us utter, for instance, "cozy as usual," "cozier than usual," or which does not make us utter anything like that. We may for a moment think, "not *so* cozy," or there is at least a faint or weak feeling of disappointment that seems to relate to a less vivid or less convincing impression of coziness.

It is usual to look to poetry for vivid and beautiful verbal expressions of spontaneous experiences, such as this stanza from Oscar Wilde's "Impression du Matin":

> The yellow fog came creeping down
> The bridges, till the houses' walls
> Seemed changed to shadows, and St. Paul's
> Loomed like a bubble o'er the town.

Some expressions reveal distance from the spontaneous, for example, "Seemed changed to shadows." Others, however, do not. For instance, Wilde writes "The yellow fog came creeping down" instead of the reflective "The yellow fog seemed to be creeping down."

The poet makes us more or less adequately create spontaneous experiences, or better, elicit spontaneous experiences, some aspects of which are inspired by the poem. In a flash, we see yellow fog creeping down.

Accomplished poets, novelists, and a variety of artists brilliantly use words to express aspects of their spontaneous experiences, but, of course, we all verbalize, however crudely or conventionally. A spontaneous experience may be of burning intensity, but our words flat, dull, and conventional.

In artistic expressions, creativity is obvious, and the spontaneous experiences are the obvious, infinitely rich source. But what about creativity in mathematical physics? The physicist is not asked to express any spontaneous experience, but the need to use vernacular terms such as *waves* and *particles* for immensely abstract entities reveals a dependence on concrete contents of experience in order to create. What is called the function of imagination, whether it is in writing novels, inventing gadgets, or constructing physical theories, is to elicit a spontaneous experience where we "see" something. Instead of keeping only to the algebra involved, the equation is seen in the form of a "real" wave. However abstract an idea, the reasoning mind needs concrete contents. The world of metaphysics is polluted by creatures suggesting aspects of vivid spontaneous experiences.

Within contemporary literature loosely referred to as postmodern, we find interesting ways of speaking—ways that *seem to* tell us that we or our society "constructs" reality (as in "the social construction of reality"). Expressions like "the (dominant) conception of reality within a society" are avoided. It is sometimes suggested that we never reach reality as such but are limited to our texts and narratives about what is real.

Despite all this, it is pertinent to insist that the personal spontaneous experiences (of gestalt character) acquaint us with the real. The richness of those experiences is such that verbalization can only refer to aspects of them. The gestalt character obviously implies richness. When in a certain situation, a subordinate tonal gestalt within Beethoven's Fifth Symphony is experienced by a person who knows that symphony well, then aspects of the whole symphony and perhaps aspects of recent experiences of going to a concert will color the content of the *total* spontaneous experience. The complexity may be said to preclude the formation of a text adequately expressing the experience, that is, adequately describing the total spontaneous expressions (in their full richness). We are rarely motivated to engage in such an endeavor. And the need to act requires us to focus on definite aspects of the spontaneous experiences. The yellow fog creeping down a bridge over the Thames *instantly* elicits a decision to wear a coat or to do something else.

It has been suggested that the immense power of the new forms of mass communication narrows our conceptions of reality so decisively that our spontaneous experiences reflect what is mass communicated. The power of mass communication has also destroyed our capacity to experience anything that is squarely incompatible with the mass-communicated conceptions.

The importance of increasing the awareness of the influence of mass communication is obvious. But it should not diminish our trust that we can make full, creative use of our access to reality through our own spontaneous experience. The confidence of having a *source* of creativity that never disappears (until our mental capacity completely disappears) might be undermined by talking as if we are imprisoned in our conceptualizations, our socially accepted metaphors and texts. Spontaneous experience transcends personal, social, and cultural *specifications*. That is, any attempt to nail down the stream-and-process character of gestalt experience by specifying a person, a society, a culture, pretending that the gestalts belong to a definite kind, is in vain. The attempts by historiographers to characterize epochs (the Renaissance, Baroque, Enlightenment, Romantic periods) are frowned upon by historians who delight in complexity, not uniformity, in irregularities as much as in regularities. When we conceive an event as part of a whole, for instance, as part of a campaign or a war, the conception of the event is furnished with *emerging* properties. The event, defined in terms more or less *common* to the members of a group or society, becomes a social stereotype, but this does not totally inhibit the creation of nonstereotype gestalts. The range of creativity may be reduced, but not killed.

The formulation of communities and societies with a minimum of cohesion is said to depend on shared values, on consensus in vital matters of life. These have gestalt character, but even in traditional societies with stable, shared values, changes go on. They depend on creativity, and the main source is the richness of spontaneous experiences.

Gestalt Thinking and Buddhism[30]

IMPERMANENCE

In the oldest forms of Buddhism, monks were reluctant to answer metaphysical questions. If answers were offered, they were expressed undogmatically: Take it or leave it. Even if true, a philosophical opinion might be of little help, or even a hindrance on the Eightfold Path.

Permanence, even eternal being, is often asserted of substance (Descartes, Spinoza) and of some other types of metaphysical entities beyond or behind "appearance." Gestalt ontology considers these entities *entia rationis*, abstract constructions created (by reason) to facilitate rational analysis.

The concrete structure may have a lower or higher degree of permanence. The structure of an ecosystem may show notable change during a century or practically none at all. It may show a short or long *half-life*, in the sense that this term is used in the theory of radioactivity. Abstract structures are timeless, but reason employs them for a short or long time.

The concrete contents of reality are shifting. Discontinuity and universal impermanence characterize the world of gestalts, perhaps not quite in the sense of Buddhism, but in a closely related sense.[31]

ANATMAVADA AND SELF-REALIZATION

The doctrine of no (permanent) Self is essential to both Buddhism and gestalt thinking. In my personal outline of a deep ecology philosophy (Ecosophy T), "Self-realization!" is the logically (derivationally) supreme norm, but it is not an eternal or a permanent "self" that is postulated. When the formulation is made more precise, it is seen that the Self in question is a symbol of identification with an absolute maximum range of beings. Selves are frequently recurring entities, or "knots," in the structure of contents, but they do not have the concreteness of contents! Ego, self, and Self are *entia rationis*.[32] The same applies to a term such as *self-realization*. This status as instruments for thinking, however, does not exclude such terms from appearing in important statements. "Only through one's self-realization can one attain nirvana," says Masao Abe in his article concerning the special character (a bar over the *o*) in the name Dōgen.

EVERYTHING MAY BECOME BUDDHA

"Grass, tree, nations and lands, all without exception attain Buddhahood." This is taken to be a motto in the Japanese Tendai tradition.[33] Tentatively, I take "all without exception" to refer to gestalts, not to fragments or relata in abstract structures. Thus, it is not asserted that a tree defined solely by its primary or "objective" qualities may attain Buddhahood. Rather, I assert that attainment of Buddhahood is only permissible for gestalts, such as those that connect the tree with all qualities and attain semipermanence through recurring traits.

There are, of course, various interpretations of "becoming the Buddha," but some are closely related to the concepts of self-realization through identification. The Buddhist compassion extended to all beings implies "seeing oneself in all things," a process of identification. Without this, things appear foreign, *devoid of life*, and impossible as objects of compassion. If I have understood Abe correctly, Dōgen's concern for the elimination of the process of generation and extinction is central. The identification of human beings with animals, plants, and other natural objects rests on a common basic cosmic characteristic: generation and extinction.

There is a question of how wide a range of beings may be meaningfully said to realize themselves. Animals, yes; plants, yes; but including a wider range of things further dilutes the very concept of realization and Self. There is a limit here, but it is not definite, and the options regarding how to trace it are many.

The similarity to certain forms of *Mahayana* consists primarily of the tendency to widen the range of "becoming Buddha" or "realize the Self" beyond what common sense in our culture seems able to digest. The meaningfulness of everything's becoming Buddha is in part dependent on the disappearance of *distinct* things in (certain forms of) *Mahayana*. This leads us to the difficult problem of how to interpret the Buddhist *anatmavada*, the negation of the existence of selves.

SELVES AS PROCESSES

Personal pronouns and all other forms of language referring to individuals and groups of individuals are used freely and in a standard way in fundamental Buddhist texts. Consider the following examples:

> "Monks, do you not speak that which is known by yourselves, seen by yourselves, found by yourselves?"
>
> "Yes, sir!"
>
> "Good, monks! You, monks, have been instructed by me through this timeless doctrine which can be realized and verified, leads to the goal, and can be understood individually by the intelligent."[34]

> Engineers lead water,
> fletchers make arrows,
> carpenters form the wood,
> wise men master themselves.[35]

In the sentence "wise men master themselves," the word *atta* is used (Sanskrit *Atman*). In this passage and in others, there is no hesitation in proclaiming that wise men (*pandita*) have selves. The selves are tamed or mastered (*damayanti*), but not destroyed.

The famous sentences in the *Diamond Sutra* must, as I interpret the text, be understood in a way that does not make the use of personal pronouns and terms such as *self* questionable or even illegitimate. The individual selves are processes or aspects of processes, always changing, but always showing an important, limited continuity and permanence. The words of *Samyutta Nikaya* 1:135 are instructive:

> Why do you then harp on the word "person"? Mara, you are starting from wrong premises. This is nothing but a lot of processes; no "person" is found here. For just as the word "carriage" is used when the parts are combined, so the word "person" is commonly used when the factors are present.

One may, as in this translation (which is R. E. A. Johansson's), render the word *satta* with "person," but a more general term may also be used.[36] What appears to be said is that no entities exist that do not have the character of processes.

To "realize oneself," as I use the phrase, corresponds to some degree to the Buddhist expression "to follow the path." Each must follow his or her own path, because of different experiences (see the quotation from *Majjhima Nikaya*), but the different paths, if followed far enough, lead to states that have something in common.

The ultimate goal in Buddhism is indicated by the term *nirvana*. However interpreted, nirvana cannot be understood in terms of Hindu metaphysics. The idea of a universal, absolute *Atman* is foreign to Buddhism. As I use the expression "realizing the great Self," it does not correspond to a Hindu idea of realizing the absolute *Atman*. If I should choose a Sanskrit phrase for *self-realization*, I might select "realizing *svamarga*," or "realizing one's own way." The *great Self* corresponds to the maximum deepening and extending of the *sva* through deepening and extending the process of identification.[37] In any case, the great Self is an *entia rationis*, not a concrete content or the set of all concrete contents—but it is still unclear if such a concept can even be defined without paradoxes.

Once the status of egos and autonomous selves is downplayed, there is little left of the foundation for making sharp distinctions between anything. The warning not to take individuality too seriously or literally is forcefully expressed in the *Diamond Sutra*:

> Subhuti, what do you think? Let no one say the Tathagata cherishes the idea: I must liberate all living beings. Allow no such thought, Subhuti. Wherefore? Because in reality there are no living beings to be liberated by the Tathagata. If there were living beings for the Tathagata to liberate, he would partake in the idea of selfhood, personality entity, and separate individuality.

The special wording of this passage should also not be taken literally. The idea of liberation has validity, but one must not absolutize the distinctions and believe in substantial existence.[38]

TRANSCENDING SUBJECT-OBJECT DUALISM

The belief and acceptance that all whole beings can attain Buddhahood depend upon the rejection of subject-object dualism. That is, one must abandon the sentiment that there is always and always must be an ego involved in experience. An appeal to spontaneity, perhaps especially spontaneous experience in nature, is preferable to a detached view of subject-object relations.

The nondualism in Buddhism is sometimes expressed verbally by saying that all beings are one, or that each being is one with all other beings. Such a formula must not be taken in the counterintuitive sense that, for example, I cannot be cold and hungry and somebody else warm and satisfied. The formula does not imply rejection of personal pronouns or any psychology of the ego and self.

It is an interesting problem to formulate clearly the views that have rejection of subject-object dualism as a common characteristic. Whatever way we formulate the nondualism, adherents of deep ecology tend to feel sympathy with views such as the following, expressed by Yasuaki Nara:

> [I]n Dōgen, through the negation of the egocentric self, whole being, including man, animal, mountains, rivers, grasses, trees etc., is one with him, making both nature and himself encompassed within the world of the Buddha.[39]

Referring to a poem by the poet So-to-ba "in which the sound of the mountain river revealed reality and the poet had *satori* in listening to it," Dōgen emphasizes the oneness of So-to-ba and the sound of the river by asking whether it was So-to-ba who had *satori* or the river.[40]

As I see it, a happening refers to a whole constellation or gestalt of relations. "Satori!" might well be an expression of a kind of happening. In that case, it is not evident that one should be able to sort out a subject "having" satori, or an object eliciting satori and revealing reality to the subject. The satori as a content is one, and only an analysis of abstract structure leads to definite conceptions of parts of the whole.

The *words* of Buddhaghosa can be used in proclaiming the reality of gestalts rather than subjects and objects:

> For suffering is but no sufferer,
> not the doer but certainly the deed is found
> peace is but not the appeased one,
> the way is but the walker is not found.[41]

The term *suffering* (*dukkham*) may be a good name for a class of gestalts. Each member of the class has a structure comprising subject, object, and medium. The term *sufferer* (*dukkhita*) suggests a narrower connotation, pointing merely to a subject who suffers. Similar reflections may be made concerning the other pairs of opposites in the quoted text.

The indefiniteness and plurality of conceptual analysis are clearly indicated in what Yasuaki Nara says about another poem, one by Matsuo Basho:

> Old pond
> A frog jumps in
> The sound of water

Of the poem, Nara says: "Here Basho and surroundings are interfused; Basho, the frog, and the pond are one world and the one who jumps into the water may be a frog or Basho himself; the sound is of the water or of the frog or even of Basho."[42]

The poem is from the point of view of gestalt thinking a high-level expression of a concrete content. Conceptual analysis may split it up, but it has gestalt status, and the splitting will be more or less arbitrary. This applies even to the subject-object distinction. It may or may not apply as a significant abstract structure attributable to the gestalt.

Western historians of world literature tend to create conceptual analyses that stress the *internal* life of the mind. A Zen Buddhist poem "about" the branches of a tree might in this tradition be explained as follows: The poem tells about the sadness expressed by these branches, but in reality the poem expresses the sadness of the poet. The poetical style requires a projection of personal states of consciousness onto objects of the external world. This form of analysis makes Zen poetry and ontology into a subclass of Western poetry and ontology. Yasuaki Nara proposes a translation that is not essentially different and offers the following to the above analysis: "This poem is *not* a mere description of the scene communicating the quiet atmosphere but the expression of the poet himself, absorbed in the quietude."[43] In explaining the poem, Nara resorts to the distinction between the poet and the scene, a distinction similar to that between humans and environment in the shallow ecology movement.

What the both-answer can do in these matters is to delay, or hold back, the introduction of the subject-object distinction by admitting a diversity and richness of ontologically homogeneous traits (rather than "properties") of a constellation. Primary, secondary, and tertiary traits are completely on par.

The secondary and tertiary do not need a subject, a mind, a consciousness in the form of a container with subjective ponds, frogs, trees, and water inside it. The concept of things in themselves is held back because we do not find contradiction between dissimilar utterances about "the same thing." ("Things with properties" are described in terms of *fields*—comparable to what occurs in physics.)

The both-answer has, of course, a rather limited function; the same holds for the notion of concrete content, as contrasted with abstract structure. As starting points of reflection about "things," however, they liberate us from certain prejudices.

THINGS IN THEMSELVES AND VALUES IN THEMSELVES: "ALL THINGS HAVE VALUE"

There are some complications worth mentioning at this juncture. One must distinguish subject-object dualism from subject-object distinctions in general. The term *dualism* is used when the distinction is said to be fundamental, absolute, and pervasive. Dualism is accepted in the theory of duplication and in the theory that things in themselves do not have qualities. Everything we experience has such qualities. Rejecting them means establishing duplicate things inside the mind.

The outstanding dualist of Western philosophy is René Descartes. Many of the contemporary efforts to avoid the paradoxes and counterintuitive consequences of dualism are conceived in terms of anti-Cartesianism. It is not sheerly coincidental that Descartes is also the main proponent of the view that animals are insensitive machines and nature has value only as a resource for human beings. However, I shall not attempt to explore connections between dualism and these historically significant views.

The insistence that there is nothing, no substance, "behind" the concrete contents corresponds to the Buddhist conception of *sarvam tathatvam*, "all is such as it is." However, the conception of a world of concrete contents and fields rather than things in themselves may seem to undermine our concern for individual beings—animals and plants—and for abstract entities such as species. This need not be so. Spontaneous experience is not sense experience. It is experience of more or less stable things and processes of "the world we live in" (*Lebenswelt* in the terminology of philosophical phenomenology). When we see an orange, we see a thing, not a patch of yellow or orange or greenish color. When meeting an animal, we meet in our spontaneous experience something enduring and self-propelled. The essential aspect of the ontology of contents is not a negation of enduring beings, but of the omnipresence of the *we* or *I* and the duplication in external and internal worlds.

These words are meant to introduce my comments to Yasuaki Nara's interpretation of the Japanese notion *inochi* (life). He thinks the notion slowly came to refer to the intrinsic value of all beings: "Gradually, the Buddhist precept of *not-killing* has come to be understood not only as not taking life of animals, but also not taking *inochi* of all things. Sometimes it has further been said that *not-killing* is to let *inochi* live."[44]

The notion of intrinsic value as some form of life in a broad sense has important consequences. In some countries, the deep ecology movement is closely allied to lifestyles that are, in part, characterized by careful and respectful handling of things in general, not just sentient beings or living things in the sense of organisms. There is remorse for taking their *inochi*.

The Japanese custom of *kuyo* (memorial service) must be mentioned here.

> On a day sometime in Autumn, eel-dealers, restaurant managers and some ordinary people representing the general customers gather together to have a religious service. A small altar is constructed and one or more priests chant Buddhist sutras to the eels who were killed and eaten by us to nourish our lives. The Japanese do not exactly believe in the existence of a soul of an eel. The implication of the ceremony lies rather in the complex feelings of remorse for taking their lives and *inochi*, of thanks, and of soothing their souls, if any . . . In the Edo period, the housewife and daughters of each home were supposed to do *kuyo* for the used or broken needles with a sense of regret for their lost *inochi*, thanks, and also with prayers for the enhancement of their sewing talents. Since the Meiji period, the needle-*kuyo* has come to be observed by some temples or Shinto shrines collectively annually on February 18 . . .
>
> Some medical doctors and nurses sometimes join, bringing the needles used for injections. *Kuyo* is also done for old clocks, dolls, chopsticks, spectacles, tea-whisks, etc. To sum up, the traditional view of nature in Japan first of all does not make a clear distinction between man, animals, and things. Though the individuality of each exists, all are felt to be part of the one world of the Buddha, each revealing its value.[45]

This horizontal or antihierarchical way of feeling things is gained by using the notion of concrete contents as a starting point. Or, to be more precise, the kind of philosophy I think comes closest to truth and that I feel at home with supports this kind of horizontality, and the notion of concrete contents facilitates its formulation.

If we think of some of the cruelest parasites, inflicting slow, painful death on their victims, it is difficult to invest them with any sort of positive intrinsic value. That analysis applies even more strongly to chemical and other weapons—but they certainly are "things" and therefore seem to be eligible for *kuyo*.

In short, what about the "problem of evil" in relation to the concept of intrinsic value of all things? Clearly, this concept is as vulnerable as any other that tries to attach uniform positive value of some kind to all that is felt to be real (*sattva*). There is a need for clarification of the meaning of the intrinsic value conception, but I cannot go into the matter here.

The *inochi* and *kuyo* phenomena are primarily cultural in a general sense, not philosophical, but they furnish irreplaceable and invaluable raw material for philosophical reflection. In many Western countries, environmental struggle involves direct actions and violent confrontation. The norms of nonviolent group conflict as worked out by Gandhi and others exclude violence not only against the opponents, but also against their machinery and other equipment that, from a direct, causal point of view, destroy life and life conditions on a vast scale. The norms against so-called sabotage involving such equipment are based on deep attitudes that express themselves in cultural phenomena such as *inochi* and *kuyo*.[46]

Section 4:

NONVIOLENCE AND GANDHI, SPINOZA AND WHOLENESS

Nonmilitary Defense[1]

The traditional means of defending life and freedom have included a major emphasis on the military. Because of technical developments, the use of these traditional means may have the result that in ten or fifty years, few human beings may be left to enjoy freedom or to struggle against tyranny. But there also exist nonmilitary methods of struggle. It is the aim of this essay to explore to what extent these nonmilitary methods might be developed to serve more adequately the need to defend life and freedom, and along what general lines such a change might operate. I do not claim to offer a panacea, a detailed blueprint, a final answer to every single aspect of the problem, and certainly not an easy way without risks. No realistic response to the present crisis does not involve risks. I am seeking to establish here a reasonable case as to why there should be serious consideration of an alternative defense method that has, relatively speaking, been ignored. Having in mind the defense of the way of life of people with whom I identify—primarily Norwegians, but also many others in many countries—I shall attempt to broaden the traditional concept of defense and defense institutions. I believe that thinking in terms of the broader concept will strengthen the possibilities of peace and freedom.

THE INADEQUACY OF MILITARY DEFENSE

The need for defense is greater today [1962] than ever before. The decline in the importance of military defense does not reduce the importance of defense in general.

To defend Norway today means to defend our independence, our freedom to shape our lives within the framework of Norwegian social traditions and culture and to change our lives as we wish. It is to defend a way of life against all external forces that would alter our lives without our consent. From experience, we know that events in another country can endanger our freedom. Throughout the world, there exist under various labels dictatorships and other power concentrations that for ideological, economic, military, and other reasons may threaten the freedom of other countries. As this is being written, in 1962, the Soviet Union is one of them, and I share the view of those who are convinced that a continued advance in power and influence of the Eastern bloc sooner or later may reach the point at which Norway could be taken within that bloc's sphere of influence and possibly be occupied. This would clearly threaten our ability to form our own institutions and might even mean the deportation of our people to the expanses of northern Asia.

In the event of a nonnuclear war, Norway might hold out for hours or even weeks, but in any war between the major power blocs, we must expect occupation under a somewhat benevolent or malevolent military dictatorship. If the war should end with the (so-called) victorious states' introducing a way of life we despise and a totalitarian state machinery, conditions resembling those of the occupation during World War II would again exist. Even in the event of the establishment of a world state, the peoples of the world would need to develop means by which to check the possible abuses of power and dictatorial tendencies that could arise from such an extreme concentration of power in a few or a bloc of nations.

The most effective means of defense are relative to what is to be defended. In defending a way of life, the defenders must avoid the means that will undermine or destroy the way of life to be defended and the very people who cherish it.

For hundreds of years, the world was such that the defense of Norway could be identified with the defense of Norway's geographic borders. Defense of a territory against physical invasion was often to defend a way of life, a culture pattern, or an ideology. In this context, military forces strong enough to keep the invader out were conceivable and possibly effective. Today, however, we recognize that the relative independence that we enjoy is the result of many forces and conditions outside Norway. It is these forces and conditions that we must seek to influence in order to preserve our independence. Military preparations are inadequate to the task.

Against a powerfully armed totalitarian state, military defense of Norway's geographical boundaries by its 3.5 million people [4.5 million in 2007] alone might be heroic, but it would inevitably be futile and quixotic. Allied with NATO, our military resources are increased, but they are not more effective in the long run. Besides increasing the likelihood of occupation during a major war, alliance with nuclear powers exacerbates the danger of annihilation by nuclear weapons. Though not a single enemy soldier might cross our borders, our existence could be terminated. Moreover, strong alliances might force Norway to fight nuclear wars for aims that most of its inhabitants do not consider basic and of supreme value.

Hence the very notion of defense needs clarification. Simply *to call* something a defense measure does not make it capable of defending anything whatsoever. Let us therefore read *military defense* as "military preparation for the eventuality of war." Military preparation is the most thoroughly institutionalized means of defense, but there is no good reason for narrowing the concept of defense by identifying military defense with defense in general.

NONMILITARY DEFENSE

As wars have become increasingly more destructive, there has evolved a conviction that the use of modern weapons is justified only, if at all, in the service of fundamental values. But at present, foreign policies are generally shaped not to protect and extend fundamental values, but to uphold or change existing power relations in favor of this or that nation. Military means may still be somewhat effective for such customary aims. A foreign policy shaped mainly to protect and extend fundamental values could scarcely make use of modern weapons, and thus risk a nuclear war, because a war would violate some of those values that are to be defended.

However, immediate dissolution of military defense organizations is not likely to realize the aims of those who believe in substituting completely nonmilitary methods for military defense. If the present military organizations were to be greatly reduced unilaterally or even universally, many people would probably feel more insecure, threatened, and helpless than ever; the passive state of despair and fatalism would actually be reinforced. If one takes away the only means of defense a person *believes* to be truly effective, he or she certainly has every reason to feel frustrated. Thus, a reduction of reliance on the military must be preceded by *the development of increased confidence in, and the gradual adoption of, alternative means of defense.*

Let it be quite clear that I do not advocate what is usually called "pacifism" as an alternative to present policies. As an organized movement centering on individual conscientious objection to participation in war, pacifism must from the political scientist's standpoint be regarded mainly as nonpolitical.

It is also clear that although pacifists are not always without political influence, they have no common platform. I am interested in exploring a primarily nonmilitary defense policy determined by the political situation; such a policy cannot call for immediate disarmament.

COMMITMENT TO FREEDOM

Since a nonmilitary defense policy depends upon the active participation of the populace in times of emergency, it is vital that the citizens understand what they are trying to defend. The first stage of a nonmilitary defense policy is therefore the clarification of the principles that we value and the qualities of the way of life that we wish to pursue, so as to increase our commitment to these principles.

Various steps might further this understanding and commitment. The most apparent need is for a national self-examination by all parts of the population. We must as a nation examine what aspects of our way of life we cherish and wish to extend and preserve. Discussion groups, panels, debates, articles, books, essays, radio, and television [and today the Web], on both local and national levels, must be enlisted to facilitate this self-examination. Every scholar interested in the question should be provided with the opportunity to obtain funds for study and publication. Schools, universities, churches, and other educational institutions could serve as local centers for this national program.

This program might be called ideological, but the term must not be confused with ideologies, which are detailed systems seeking to force compliance and converts. What is needed is work on the ideas, ideals, and moral convictions associated with freedom, not with force. It is, of course possible and desirable that an effective program of this kind might influence other countries and contribute to their liberation from potentially aggressive dictatorial regimes. An influence like this would be one demonstration of the direct relation of this program to the problem of defense. On the home front, the program would strengthen the motivation for defense and assist in the mobilization of defense energy in times of crisis.

INTERNATIONAL SERVICE

The second general policy that would ultimately help fulfill society's ideals and contribute to human needs, including defense, is *international service.*

By this term, I mean service to friendly countries, "neutrals," and potential enemies alike.

Thanks to Henrik Wergeland, Fritjof Nansen, and others, Norway has a tradition stressing worldwide solidarity and responsibility. If the opposition to the programs advocated by Nansen had not found such strong backing in various powerful countries, there might have developed forms of international cooperation that would have reduced the likelihood of wars. Since 1945, Norway has organized help to countries in which physical disasters have occurred (floods in Italy and Holland, earthquake in Agadir, etc.). Fisheries in India have been supported in various ways with combined government aid and voluntary contribution, and a variety of other activities have been carried out, all of which might be said to exemplify international service. Other countries have made similar efforts, sometimes more comprehensive and better organized than those of Norway.

It is now time to show the close connection between such measures and defense, and to try to make such international service more effective on a larger scale. Such enterprises need to be integrated into the country's normal economic system, for instance, by lowering import duties on products from areas that we assist and encouraging an expansion of trade with them. In addition, it is important that there be some kind of reciprocal aid, such as cultural programs with the countries receiving assistance. Cooperation and *mutual* aid, not simply humanitarian help, will reduce tension in the long run.

International service should be undertaken for its own sake, to relieve suffering and meet human needs.[2] It is also important as a means of expressing and implementing our nation's way of life and principles, particularly the concern for human dignity and justice and freedom, upon which we like to think that our society is based. To undertake international service purely from the "ulterior" motive that it will assist our own defense effort will reduce or destroy many of its intrinsic values and its contributions to that effort. However, we must recognize the relationship between such efforts and the defense problem.

First, in relieving suffering and poverty, international service will contribute to the removal of the poverty, gross inequality, and suffering that lead to violent conflicts, hatred, and war. This contribution of international service is widely recognized and requires no detailed elaboration here.

Second, such programs increase "person-to-person" contacts and contribute to the development of personal loyalties between individuals of various countries. These "crisscross" loyalties can contribute to international solidarity and make it more difficult to obtain popular support for international conflicts with countries with which such contacts have been rich.

Third, international service can contribute to the creation of a more sympathetic attitude toward our country and our way of life, which would reduce the chances of aggressive action against us. The potential attacker would have clear evidence of our nonaggressive intention; and the fear of alienating "world opinion" would make it hesitate before invading. And in case of a crisis, our plight would receive more attention, publicity, sympathy, and concrete aid than might otherwise have been possible.

Fourth, carrying out an international service program will make our own country better prepared to meet crises. It will help create a positive sense of purpose and mission comparable to that which often accompanies military efforts, but without certain disadvantages of such measures. And in giving our citizens experience in working cooperatively in a common altruistic cause, the program will enhance their ability to practice this cooperation in other tasks in times of crisis.

Fifth, knowledge of international service conveyed to the troops and population of a potential enemy might reduce their motivation to take aggressive action against us, cause them to carry out repressive orders inefficiently, and increase the chances of their deserting and mutinying in support of freedom.

AREAS OF SERVICES

A wide program of international service would include a multitude of tasks. Emergency help in cases of natural catastrophes and famines and aid to refugees would be vital.[3] Technical help adapted to meet the needs and culture of the countries desiring it is an obvious means of international service. Another is various types of educational aid, particularly assistance to students who wish to study in other parts of the world.

A somewhat different service is to provide independent observers and investigators assistance in the study and resolution of specific international conflicts and perhaps of certain national political crises such as civil wars. This service would include operational research aimed at contributing to the solution of such conflicts and more general and fundamental research on conflict, war, and nonmilitary means of conducting and resolving conflicts, in short, on much the same nonmilitary defense program advocated here. The results of such research should be widely distributed. Other countries wishing to adopt a similar type of defense policy could be provided with special defense liaison officers, lecturers, and consultants to assist in the adoption of such a program.

This program of international service would, of course, require considerable resources, which I am convinced should be provided mainly through the government budget. There would also be a large demand for manpower, including both untrained workers and specialists. In addition to a highly trained long-term technical staff, there would be an important role to be played by persons serving for one or two years. Volunteers alone could not fill the demand. Manpower should therefore be supplied by conscription from the country's youth of both sexes. This form of service ought to be a full or partial alternative to the usual military conscription or alternative service for conscientious objectors. Essential training would include language skills as well as techniques and other knowledge required for particular jobs.

Ideally, such service corps would be organized on an international basis and made available to the United Nations or some other international body. The experience of several countries' corps working together—the Americans and Russians cooperating in building a steel plant in India—would contribute to closer understanding and develop cooperation in service projects. This might make resolution of other issues between such countries less difficult.

A considerable part of such a service program could be carried out through existing organizations that are already operating along the same general lines, such as the Red Cross, Save the Children, and War on Want. Some services could be conducted through national branches of international organizations, and other services through contributions of individuals and resources to such international organizations as UNESCO (U.N. Educational, Scientific and Cultural Organization), UNICEF (U.N. Children's Fund), WHO (World Health Organization), and FAO (Food and Agriculture Organization of the United Nations).

IMPROVING OUR OWN SOCIETY

Another aim of a nonmilitary defense program would be to make our own society more worthy of defense and more defendable by nonmilitary means. Frankly, our own society and that of others have numerous aspects that many people would not wish to defend and would certainly not make great sacrifices to defend. The victims of racial segregation and discrimination, for example, and those subjected to economic and political oppression would not be eager to defend their societies against foreign aggressors who may claim to be liberators. Neither would the more idealistic members of such societies, even though not victims of such policies, be eager to sacrifice heavily in the defense of such conditions.

At the time of Hitler's annexation of Austria, for example, Schuschnigg had already established a one-party system, had built concentration camps on the German model, had abolished individual liberties, and had carried out the principle of authoritarianism to its ultimate implication. There remained in Austria little basis for ideological resistance to Hitler. A similar though perhaps less severe situation existed in other European countries such as Poland and Yugoslavia; apart from the warnings of psychological warfare, there was often no basis for universal and determined resistance to Hitler. Societal house cleaning is a prerequisite of effective nonmilitary defense.

Another necessary improvement is the decentralization of decision-making power. Citizens must be more accustomed to making decisions individually and in small groups and less dependent upon the government or leaders of organizations. Admittedly, technical developments seem to have made inevitable a certain amount of centralization. But if the opportunity for local initiative and responsibility is destroyed rather than actively cultivated and nurtured, then the ability of citizens to resist encroachments on their freedom will be disastrously affected. We need a general strengthening of those institutions in times of crisis in the absence of the top governmental hierarchy and of all other major organizations. This would prevent demoralization if the state apparatus were seized by opponents of liberty and yes-men placed in key positions in all major organizations.

NONMILITARY RESISTANCE

All of the aforementioned components of a nonmilitary defense policy will contribute to the ability of the nation to cope with crises; at the same time, they will enrich and improve our own society. They will also reduce the chances of invasion and occupation. It is nevertheless necessary that we have an adequate program for dealing with the latter eventuality, for with modern weapons, it will always be possible to invade and occupy territories for shorter or longer intervals. Unhappily, the customary identification of military defeat with total defeat prevents governmental discussion of the problems of occupation and suppression, such discussion being considered defeatism or lack of "defense-mindedness." The opposite is actually nearer the truth; those who identify military defeat with total defeat neglect a vital sector of defense.

Perhaps the most positive way in which a small country like Norway could contribute to the prevention of a nuclear war would be to say "no thank you" to an offer from a friendly superstate to stop, through the use of nuclear weapons, an invasion of the smaller nation's territory. Such a policy is, however, irresponsible as long as the populace is no better trained to meet the problems of occupation than it was in 1940. As I have indicated previously, reliance on military methods of defense cannot be diminished until other means of defense are generally recognized as equally effective. It is therefore my proposal that, for the present, side by side with conventional military preparations, we institute a program of preparation for nonmilitary resistance. As the nonmilitary program gradually grew, it would be possible and desirable to reduce military preparations and to rely in a greater degree upon nonmilitary training.

In the event of invasion by an army possessing nuclear weapons, relatively little could be done militarily to prevent the invaders from disbanding major organizations and eliminating known leaders of opposition. Our citizens must understand that this military failure does not mean defeat; it does mean that the struggle is entering a new phase of more direct confrontation of human forces. The struggle ought not to be waged on a front where the opponent already has overwhelming superiority. Rather, it must be waged by nonmilitary weapons and by techniques that can continue to function, regardless of the invader's control of communications, ammunition, and supplies, and despite the aggressor's power of mass deportations. Also, there is likely to be an inverse relationship between the degrees of military and of nonmilitary preparedness for defense. The reason is that precisely those humanitarian values that give rise to spontaneous loyalty and affection for a way of life are likely to become undermined to the extent that military preparedness is maximized.

TECHNIQUES OF RESISTANCE

It must be kept in mind that our ultimate goal is to preserve our way of life. Hence, even under enemy occupation, *certain fundamental principles must be upheld*, regardless of what the opponent does and regardless of the cost. *No human being is to be sacrificed by others to achieve an end; each person must be something of a goal in himself or herself. No goal can justify destruction of respect for truth.*[4] *And under no circumstances may any human being be mistreated or tortured.*

It is important to distinguish this kind of a program from psychological warfare, which may resort to all types of threats and deception in verbal propaganda. It must also be distinguished from a program of general noncooperation, a program focused on the invaders. The weakness of a policy of general nonviolent resistance is that it cannot be upheld at all costs; if repression gradually stiffens, it is impossible to continue defending, for instance, the major organizations of a democratic government. For example, automatic refusal to cooperate with the invaders in food distribution may result in a famine. Self-inflicted hardships of this sort cannot easily be asked or expected of a populace except in very short, critical periods.

Techniques of resistance that would serve to defend the aforementioned principles could include many types of noncooperation: strikes, boycotts, civil disobedience, refusal to operate and participate in the existing governmental agencies and other major organizations once they have been taken over by the enemy, and refusal to provide the oppressor with labor, transportation, information, and so on.[5] Wherever the invader seeks to extend power by forcing the inhabitants to violate the basic principles, the invader should be met with those forms of nonviolent resistance best adapted to each case. Let there be no pretense that the enemy would not retaliate and inflict repression. But this is no argument against nonmilitary resistance, for it is at least as true of military means. The question is how to do the job, not whether it should be carried out.

At the same time, a large variety of efforts could be undertaken to encourage the occupying soldiers not to carry out measures that must be resisted by the inhabitants. These efforts would, of course, include no acts of terrorism against the soldiers themselves. Rather, by means of posters, underground newspapers, secret radios, acts of resistance and defiance, and personal contact where possible, the soldiers could be convinced of the pervasive and tenacious nature of the resistance offered. The history of recent occupations, for instance, that of Norway, shows that occupying soldiers and even high officials can be actively sympathetic to the occupied populace, can be lax or even negligent in carrying out orders, and can pass important information on to the underground. While maintaining the noncooperation and defiance, the resistance should be aimed at maximizing the amount and degree of this support from the occupying forces.

It is vital in such resistance movements for people to be willing and able to continue their customary ways of life in small units when the public life of a democracy is absent. During the occupation of Norway, for example, the teachers successfully prevented the schools from being used for spreading false information in the interest of the invaders. Further, by mass nonviolent noncooperation, the teachers openly refused to participate in the teachers' organization that Quisling was creating as a part of the foundation of his corporate state. When the schools were closed, the teachers taught in homes. The price was months in concentration camps for hundreds, but both the organization and the corporate state were stillborn and the schools remained free from control.

During the German occupation of Poland, the pressure on schoolteachers was in part so heavy that direct resistance at the schools and within the school-organizations was impossible. But teaching was conducted "privately" in tiny groups, a form of *microresistance*.[6] In Norway, repression and brutality did not reach such a high pitch that all large organizations, "legal" or "illegal," were destroyed. But with another five years of occupation and under steadily worsening conditions, the resistance might have disintegrated into microresistance. This would also happen in case of large-scale deportation. But if the citizenry was thoroughly prepared, even microresistance could be a weapon far more powerful than any military means to be used against it.

RESEARCH

Military defense methods have been carefully studied for centuries. Nonmilitary methods can be improved. In fact, we need study and clarification of nonmilitary methods and training and preparation in the use of such methods in concrete situations. And we need it now.

There has already been sufficient practical experience to indicate that, in the light of the obvious limitations of possible alternatives, such nonviolent resistance constitutes the best available means of combating an occupation. There has, on the other hand, been little academic study of nonmilitary techniques of war. Therefore, a first requirement is the initiation of a large-scale program of fundamental research, with specific attention to the application of nonmilitary methods against totalitarian opponents. This must include the study of totalitarian systems and the experiences of previously occupied countries under such regimes. Much of the research could be conducted through existing institutes for social research, defense academies, and universities, though it might also be desirable to establish a special institute or academy for the coordination of such projects. This program of study cannot wait until a nonmilitary defense program is adopted; it could begin immediately. We also need to train and develop a core of specialists in such methods. These specialists would be theoreticians and strategists from the military;

from a variety of academic disciplines, including sociology, political science, and psychology; and devotees of nonviolent philosophies.

CONCLUSION

The preceding discussion outlined certain aspects of a nonmilitary defense program whose primary purpose is to preserve and extend liberty and to prevent invasion and expansion of suppressive systems. The program is also capable of dealing with invasion and suppression.

It is, of course, important to recognize that such a program of nonmilitary resistance depends upon popular acceptance of the probability that the invader will inflict severe repression, torture, and executions, and that the nation will neither be in a position to retaliate in kind nor be willing to do so. Only such a program, however, could keep alive and active both the principles that furnish the ultimate basis of freedom and the willingness to fight for freedom.

Implementation of a nonmilitary defense policy could be cumbersome. Such a defense policy involves a reorganization of the existing defense department and a broadening of the tasks of the department of foreign affairs. The two departments might effectively be combined under one or the other auspices, or a new arrangement might be created. The cost of a nonmilitary program would be considerable and initially may have to be an addition to the present military budget.

This is admittedly not a program that will be adopted in a day. But whereas initial adoption of the policy may be difficult, once the program is worked out in fuller detail and put into practice, its adoption by many countries will be facilitated and accelerated. As more and more countries adopt such a program, the dangers of war will be further reduced as greater pressure is exerted for the abandonment of military aggression. In short, it may well be that the only direct means to achieve the fundamental social change required for the permanent prevention of war is the widespread and immediate implementation of the policies of nonmilitary defense.

Gandhian Nonviolent Verbal Communication: The Necessity of Training[7]

The combination of *humility* and *militancy* in emotionally charged social conflicts has always been rare. It is easy to succumb either to passivity or to verbal or nonverbal violence. Humility in confronting a human being, respect *for the status of being a human being*, whether the being is a torturer or a holy person, is essential.

People may be trained in nonviolent communication through sessions in which they confront others with different attitudes and opinions. In schools and universities, such sessions in the form of seminars or other discussions are easy to arrange. At the university level, proposals of norms or principles of nonviolent communication help students to master conflict situations. From 1941 to around 1993, the set of principles formulated in this essay has been used by about ninety thousand in small groups at the universities of Norway. An emotionally colored topic is often selected, and the students are asked to discuss it. Or they receive a written dialogue and are asked to analyze violations of the principles.

Gandhi, the man, his deeds, and his writings have made such a profound impact on millions of people that the influence is felt all their lives, even if it does not always show up in social conflict activism. People's veneration is serious and honest, but few have, or even try to get, training to face opponents and "antagonists" in a Gandhian way.

The way Gandhi at times described the views of people who opposed both him and his influence has made a lasting impression. One deed that struck me as glorious belongs to the area of practice of communication.

Instead of giving a broad historical account, I shall describe one series of communications.

Gandhi fought a state of injustice in South Africa, but a group misunderstood his intentions and saw him as a traitor. Consequently, two members of the group told him that if he continued his nonviolent activism the next day, they would kill him. When Gandhi ignored their threats the next day, they tried to kill him. But others intervened, and Gandhi was carried to the hospital. In spite of his serious condition, he used his energy to insist that the two people who attacked him were not to be prosecuted and imprisoned. The arguments and reasons were as follows: (1) It was understandable that the assassins viewed him as a traitor. (2) His own actions and his explanation of their motives had not been clear enough. (3) The group to which the attackers belonged wished as a whole that he should be killed, but only the two attackers were *brave enough* and tried to kill him. (4) The killing of traitors is a duty according to the culture and ethics of the attackers. (5) It could not be expected of the attackers that they should try to reform the ethics of their own culture. (6) Courage is a supreme virtue. The two were courageous.

As soon as Gandhi recovered, he continued to fight nonviolently the *views* of his opponents, *not the persons* opposing him—even if they used every trick to misrepresent what he was fighting for. He was militant, in a way that promoted contact. He converted thousands who started as violent antagonists.

The speech Gandhi gave at the hospital is a small part of the data available for a description of a Gandhian ethics of *verbal communication in conflicts*, social, political, and personal. The term *verbal communication* may be misunderstood. No communication is only by the contact of words. The interpretation of the text of a letter is influenced by the sort of envelope, the paper, the style of writing, and the recipient's relation to the sender. Young professors learn, sometimes to their dismay, that body language and a host of other externals are decisive in whether the students grasp what he or she is trying to convey. The *way* a quantum physicist, Harald Wergeland, looked at a famous equation on the blackboard and his melodious, slightly trembling voice when talking about it vitalized new energy and sheer joy in the students: "Yes, I'll go with *you* all the way, whatever the difficulties!" In the ecological crisis, every communication with people not seriously engaged or with fellow activists with different priorities and views depends on all aspects of communication. But this does not make the narrowly verbal aspect unimportant.

If we attempt to systematize the norms and the hypotheses implicit in

Gandhi's work for freedom, we must note that freedom in his sense of the word *svaraj* has to do with freeing oneself from the fetters of disruptive emotions and narrowness of scope. Political freedom is a necessary, but not a sufficient, condition of *svaraj*. Therefore, communication with the opponents (not enemies—they do not exist) is part of the content of *satyagraha*. A systematization, such as my attempt in *Gandhi and Group Conflict*, requires at least five norms and five hypotheses explicitly devoted to the topic of verbal communication.[8] For example, "Distorted description of your and your opponents' case reduces the chance to reach your goal." Perhaps it should be added "in the long run." In the short run, caricatures of the opponents' views may work.

One may not have the optimism about antagonists that is implicit and sometimes explicit in Gandhi's approach. A hypothesis such as this seems to be made by Gandhi: "There is a disposition in every opponent such that wholehearted, well informed, strong, and persistent appeal in favor of a good cause is able ultimately to convince him." If one does not believe in this, then there are less optimistic hypotheses of high relevance, namely, that the tendency to give up appeals to certain wide groups of opponents characterized as "hopeless" is unwarranted and counterproductive. Gandhi did not believe that he could convince everybody, but he did believe that massive manifestation of *satyagraha* in wide groups of the population would undermine and ultimately ruin the support for any tyrant, including Hitler. Nonviolent verbal communication constitutes one necessary component of the *satyagraha*. Vicious verbal attacks, including the distortion of one's position in the conflict, should never disturb one's equanimity, but should strengthen one's own nonviolent approach. Don't defend your own person, but your own views.

The highly emotional atmosphere in group conflicts may lead to wild accusations and irresponsible outbursts, which the "sender" regrets. Few are able to retract in public, but many try out some kind of excuse: "What I really wanted to say was such and such." Not very convincing! Better to retract and make a new start.

Conflicts often motivate clever manipulation, for instance, by the conscious exploitation of misunderstandings. In what follows, I offer rules that can serve as guidelines in serious discussions, whether they are emotionally loaded or not. I believe that these rules are derivable from the principles of Gandhian *satyagraha*.

This essay does not consider all kinds of verbal communication, but only those in which questions are posed in a serious way and where *plain, serious answers* are expected. I shall refer to this kind of communication simply as a *discussion*. It excludes pleasantries, witty stories, and other kinds of utterances that make up a considerable, indispensable part of the total verbal communication. Gandhi also made extensive use of such utterances, but in a way that facilitates rather than obstructs the serious exchange of views. Meeting his chief opponents in the morning, he often made a simple joke.

Exclamation marks are used in what follows to indicate the normative or rule-giving character of a sentence. The formulations are fairly short and need "precization" and comments so that they are clear enough to be applicable fairly consistently in practice. Such sets of more precise formulations, clarifications, and explanations will never be definitive.[9] We always have to return to the more vague and ambiguous, trying new avenues of clarification.

FIRST PRINCIPLE: AVOID EVASION!

Preliminary formulation: Keep to the point, even if it may sometimes harm one's own position and clever evasion would strengthen it!

As a primitive example, consider the following verbal exchange in a discussion about the pros and cons of competitive sports:

1. A: Competitive sports help to destroy a man's intelligence and spirit of cooperation.
2. B: A can only say that because he isn't a sportsman himself.
3. A: The last remark doesn't affect my argument; it only shows that I was right in saying sports help to destroy a man's intelligence.
4. B: You are a typical culture snob, carping at sports whenever you can.

At stage 2, B does not answer, but offers the hypothesis that A can only say what he says because of a personal trait he has. B does not answer or maintain that to answer is impossible. He *evades* the point.

At stage 3, assuming or knowing that B is engaged in competitive sport, A not only expresses a denial of the *relevance* of B's utterance, but seems to offer a hypothesis that to utter such an irrelevant thing supports his own view expressed at stage 1. This hypothesis is not, or is only marginally, relevant.[10]

Another form of irrelevant argument occurs when unnecessary emphasis is laid on some generally accepted viewpoint, which even one's opponent would agree to. It can reinforce one's own position to subscribe to some sentiment that no one will criticize, but which does not contribute materially to the discussion. Ignoring such banalities, an opponent, by his or her very silence on the point, may appear to others to be opposing them. In this way, the opponent loses credibility and the other gains it through cheating.

Accusations that the opponent violates norms of communication lead away from the core of the discussion. Such accusations demand answers, and cannot contribute to solutions. The nonviolent participant ignores the personal accusations and continues to focus on the most relevant and weighty arguments.

SECOND PRINCIPLE: AVOID TENDENTIOUS RENDERINGS OF OTHER PEOPLE'S VIEWS!

PRELIMINARY FORMULATION: In a discussion, an utterance that aims at *reporting* a point of view should be neutral in relation to all points of view represented in that discussion!

A common bad habit is to generalize an opponent's view, substituting "all *x* are *y*" for A's "this *x* is *y*" or "some *x* are *y*" or similar statement. Suppose participant A in a debate says, "Men are better suited than women to be bishops." If B reports this as "Every man is better than any woman to be a bishop," B makes a tendentious rendering of A's view, which sounds extremist, but need not be. The choice of the example may awaken suspicion of antifeminism.

PRECIZATION OF THE PRELIMINARY FORMULATION: In a serious discussion, an utterance that purports to give an account of A's viewpoint should be such that if we let the report stand in place of A's own formulation as an expression of the issue in a *pro-et-contra* survey, the force of A's view (tenability and relevance) is not lost.

Occasionally, a report has to be made substantially shorter than the original. In that case, it must inevitably diverge from the original in respect of some reasonable interpretations. The divergence, however, should not be biased. Distorting quotations is a familiar enough phenomenon. A sentence quoted without reference to context may make quite misleading and unfair sets of interpretations become "reasonable."

It is often helpful to introduce counterarguments through if-so sentences: If A means such and such (T_1), then I agree. But if A means this and that, (T_2), I disagree, because . . ."

THIRD PRINCIPLE: AVOID TENDENTIOUS AMBIGUITY!

PRELIMINARY FORMULATION: Resist the temptation to strengthen your case by the use of ambiguities that mislead the opponent!

A general proposes a truce to the enemy. They agree to a thirty-day truce. The same night, the general makes an attack and wins an easy victory. Afterward, he says they agreed only to a daytime truce. Their answer accepting thirty *days* was intentionally ambiguous.

This is a crude example, because the common convention that "thirty days" in the relevant kind of context includes nights. It is not a clear case of ambiguity.

A more elaborate formulation of the principle: An utterance in a serious discussion violates Principle 3 if and only if (1) the listener is likely to interpret it in a way that is incompatible with the way intended by the sender, (2) that way is apt to put the utterance in a more favorable light, and furthermore (3) the sender should be aware that such a misunderstanding is likely to occur.

Consider this example:

1. A: I have nothing against sports, but according to the view we Christians hold, I must say that . . .
2. B: "We Christians," who are they?
3. A: People like me, who actively subscribe to Christian beliefs.
4. B: But think of all the people who call themselves Christian. Do you speak for all of them?
5. A: Of course not, actually, I meant members of the Christian People's party.

We will now analyze this fragment of discussion in terms of relevance. Let us note the following interpretations:

a_0 We Christians
a_1 We who actively subscribe to Christian beliefs
$a_{1.1}$ We who actively subscribe to Christian fundamental beliefs
$a_{1.2}$ We who actively subscribe to Christian beliefs politically and otherwise
a_2 We members of the Christian People's party
a_3 We who adopt the Christian faith and morality

A uses a_0, $a_{1.1}$, and a_2 as if they were cognitively equivalent. Probably, $a_{1.2}$ and a_3 are reasonable interpretations, and A can be presumed to be aware of this. But A employs a special usage. If in this context, by a_0, the speaker means a_2, B will tend to confuse the reasonable interpretations. Thus, there is a quantitative and evaluative overrating of the group that A represents. Members of the Christian People's party make up only a small part of those normally referred to as Christians, in the sense understood by $a_{1.2}$ or a_3. If A did represent the whole spectrum, his or her standpoint would not be politically colored and would therefore acquire a greater authority. But then, A would succeed in arousing the opposition of Christians in senses other than $a_{1.2}$ and a_3. By adopting sense a_0, A might find it easy to influence others into accepting his or her own standpoint. A's use of a_0 is therefore a sign of small relevance.

In regard to the relevance of A's argument, it is also in A's favor that at stage 5, A recognizes his or her special usage instead of attempting to cover up with some irrelevant remark. If A had deliberately produced an irrelevant argument, there would be, psychologically, less likelihood of his or her uttering stage 5, since this utterance clearly confirms one's suspicion about irrelevance.

A tendency to irrelevant argument can perhaps be detected at stage 3. Quite likely, A understands what B hints at when B utters statement 2, but does not manage immediately to resist the temptation to offer the ambiguous expression a_1 instead of the more precise a_2.

Stage 2 is in the form of a question, but presumably B is aware that by a_0, A probably means a_2 and that A does not imagine that all persons subsumable under $a_{1.2}$ or a_3 are in favor of his or her own standpoint. Perhaps B thinks the rest of the hearers are aware of this. Under these assumptions, B *interprets* A with stage 2 and draws the attention of possible opponents to A within group $a_{1.2}$, and at the same time deals A a blow. According to the above assumptions, the interruption cannot be justified as a technique in discussion and is definitely misleading.

FOURTH PRINCIPLE: AVOID TENDENTIOUS ARGUMENT FROM ALLEGED IMPLICATION!

Suppose someone, B, argues as follows: "My opponent A says that he accepts T. But from T follows U, and U is untenable. Therefore, T is untenable." Here, it is important to know whether the opponent does in fact *accept that the clearly untenable U follows from T.* If the opponent does not and yet we proceed under the *assumption* that he or she does, then we have broken an elementary rule for relevant argument. And quite apart from this, of course, it can be quite tendentious for us to bring in U at all before we have discussed whether U does or does not follow from T.

A rather common way of proceeding is first to impute a consequence, U, of the acceptance of T—a consequence that the sender of T rejects *is* a consequence. Then, ignoring the arguments against U's being a consequence, the opponent imputes a new assertion, V, as a consequence. Both U and V express rather stupid or strange assertions, and the audience may start to feel that there is something wrong about T, even if it is open to doubt whether U and V are consequences.

When I say, "Every living being has intrinsic value" (T), it is sometimes said that from T follows that it is ethically unjustifiable to kill any living being (U). But if this were a consequence, how could I really accept T? It is impossible not to kill if we want to stay alive, and to stay alive must be justifiable. Therefore, T is untenable, if U follows. My view is that we are justified in trying to satisfy our vital needs, and this requires killing. But I also ask how U could follow from T. That is, one should ask what additional premises are used or whether the implication is considered completely self-evident. I do not find it at all irrelevant to discuss whether U follows from T. What is important here is that what is a consequence according to some people may not be a consequence according to others. If one is willing to *use a lot of time and effort* to clear up questions of implications, one is generally led into specifying *different sets* of premises. From some of them, U follows from T, but from others, not. We are led to consider *systems*, not isolated sentences.

No philosopher that I know of has offered "precizations" of "*x* has intrinsic value," "*x* has inherent value," or "it makes sense to do things strictly for *x*'s own sake." These statements (1) are fairly easy to understand and (2) are acceptable for most people who are interested in the use of the terms.

FIFTH PRINCIPLE: AVOID TENDENTIOUS FIRSTHAND REPORTS!

PRELIMINARY FORMULATION: An account violates Principle 5 if it leaves something out and lays emphasis on other things, otherwise conveys a distorted and unfavorable impression to the hearer, or gives a directly false impression that serves the interests of the speaker!

Consider this illustration:

A: Now we must go and catch the train, it's just 9 o'clock.
B: No, I'll change my clothes first, it's only a quarter to.

In fact, A's watch shows 8:55, and B's 8:50. A gives a false impression of what she has observed. So does B. A's tendentious report of what she sees supports her wish to be getting on her way, while B's account is designed to cater to B's inclination to linger a while.

An analysis of this kind will be less sure the closer A's and B's accounts come to that of some independent witness, and the less anything depends upon easy observations.

PRECIZATION OF THE PRELIMINARY FORMULATION: An utterance, T, in a serious discussion violates Principle 5 if and only if (1) T provides an incorrect or incomplete account of observations (or of the relation between observations), or T holds back information that must be considered relevant in judging the validity or relevance of an argument and (2) deviations that occur are intended to strengthen the speaker's position in the debate.

For example, suppose a correspondent of a foreign newspaper reports the result of a parliamentary election as "The Party A increased its vote." A more neutral and comprehensive account might show, however, that although Party A did indeed increase its vote, its proportion of the total votes decreased. The telegram presents Party A, which the correspondent favors, in a favorable light at the cost of the others. We conclude that the correspondent has violated Principle 5.

SIXTH PRINCIPLE: AVOID TENDENTIOUS USE OF CONTEXTS!

PRELIMINARY FORMULATION: A matter should be presented in a neutral way, in a neutral setting!

This principle concerns the context (or conditions) in which the matter is brought forward. In this category, we include in the context noncognitive as well as cognitive components in, or accessories to, the argument, that is, expressions of the following kind: "When a hypocrite like Mr. H. starts saying what he feels, one knows that . . ." Any use of terminology of a scornful, abusive, or otherwise nonargumentative nature can get into what we call the "context" of the discussion. In addition, there are properties of the broader context in which the discussion is presented, for example, the use of music, pageantry, the serving of expensive food and drink, and any other accessories of persuasion and suggestion. In the case of newspaper articles, for instance, it can be a question of the selection of typefaces, photographs, and so on.

PRECIZATION OF THE PRELIMINARY FORMULATION: An utterance in a serious discussion violates Principle 6 if and only if the context in both a wide sense and a narrow sense strengthens the position of the speaker without the influence of the utterance being attributable to the cognitive context of the matter. Evidently, there can be no clear border between acceptable and unacceptable contextual favors.

APPLICATIONS OF NONVIOLENT VERBAL COMMUNICATION WITHIN THE ECOLOGY MOVEMENT

Supporters of the ecology movement disagree on many issues related to the ecological crisis. It is important that the real agreements and disagreements are clarified and misunderstandings eliminated. Otherwise, common policies are more difficult to implement than necessary.

Mutual *accusations* of violating norms of public debate, whether Gandhian or otherwise, are generally ineffective. Substantial *clarification* can be brought about with few accusations and little publicity.

Suppose somebody says or writes: "We must take more care of the non-human environment." Call the formulation T_0. Among the interesting interpretations of T_0, there are two I wish to mention:

   T_1: We should distribute our present total care in such a way that non-humans get relatively more of it.
   T_2: We should enlarge our total care in such a way that there will be more care for nonhumans.

If person A, who is an author of articles or books, engages in humanitarian work in Africa and hears or reads T_0, it may be tempting to choose T_1 and not T_2. Let me make the unlikely assumption that A rejects T_0, insisting in articles that humans should *not* get less care than the little they get. The vital needs of people living in an area with protected animals must be given more care, *not less*. Those who accept T_0 are heartless and irresponsible. But why should T_0 imply *less* care of the animals? Why choose T_1 rather than T_2? If a person B tries to apply Gandhian guidelines in communication, B will try out T_2 before T_1. If there is no conclusive evidence that the user of T_0 means T_1 rather than T_2, why bother with T_1? If B accepts T_2 as an ethical norm, B will *join and support* A, because it is *important to encourage and support each other* in social conflicts.

Sentences are never unambiguous in a very strict sense. T_2 may be misunderstood. There are two interpretations of interest in present conflicts.

T_{21}: We should enlarge our total care only in such a way that there will be more for nonhumans.

T_{22}: We should enlarge our total care also in such a way that there will be more for nonhumans.

It may sometimes be important to use T_{22} because those engaged very actively in the care for nonhumans are often suspected of not esteeming people who are very active in promoting better care for destitute humans.

Perhaps most people do not need to study norms of nonviolent verbal communication in social conflicts. They may have "internalized" the norms, and formalities might only confuse them. Or they are firm adherents of confrontational styles. They may hold that sometimes violating all such norms in flagrant ways may awaken people and lead faster to desired ends. That may be so, but I am convinced that power obtained through violent means tends to corrupt more than power obtained without, and in the very long run, that is the only way to go.

Spinoza and the Deep Ecology Movement[11]

One of the strangest tasks a professor of philosophy can engage in—voluntarily or more or less involuntarily—is to write a history of philosophy. My own, about one thousand pages, is neither fish nor fowl, because I could never solve the question of how to combine "*history* of philosophy" and "*philosophy* of history."

The methodology of historical research is an entertaining subject. One learns, for instance, how a historian's account of a happening based on only one eyewitness is more detailed and written with more confidence than the account of a happening covered by two or more witnesses. What the witnesses have said or written normally differ so much that a highly responsible historian's account renounces some interesting details and is heavy reading because of the sprinkling of "if," "perhaps," "perhaps not," "unclear," "contradictory," "uncertain," and a host of more complicated reservations.

The *philosophy* of history is a discipline of another character. It has no definite methodology: There is abstract discussion on the essence of history, time, and change, but also discussion about the dependence of philosophy of history upon general philosophy. Good historians often repeat that they somehow must avoid being influenced by any definite philosophical system. That is impossible. In this century, the vast discussion on the relation of dialectical materialism to the philosophy of history and to actual historiography, the writings describing historical development, is at least as interesting and important as *historical* material on the metalevel persuasively manifesting general philosophical positions, say, those of Aristotle, Shankara, Thomas Aquinas, Spinoza, Hegel, or Marx.

Established historians tend to say something like the following: The historical works by the ablest historians, who are generally convinced dialectical materialists, do not reveal the doctrinal adherence to any definite general philosophical system. As historian Sverre Steen said to his colleagues in a great humanist faculty: "You are fortunate: you can use your different and complicated professional jargons, and you even improve your standing by sticking faithfully to them. We historians (*id est*, historiographers) must somehow renounce all that."

The historian of *philosophy*, focusing on general philosophy and not on the history of ideas as a part of the historiography of ideas, cannot or should not avoid asking himself or herself, When writing an account of the history of philosophy, from which viewpoint of general philosophy do I write? In particular, what kind of a philosophy of history, as a genuine part of general philosophy, do I subscribe to?

Obviously, my account of a philosophy, say, that of Spinoza, will depend upon my own philosophy, my own general philosophy of history, my view of historical causality, and so on. Because I am not a professional historian, I am not interested as a philosopher in hiding the dependence of my interpretation of the *Ethics* upon my general philosophy, including my philosophy of history.

If textbooks of history of *philosophy* ever tended toward agreement, not to speak of an asymptotic nearness of accounts, it would signify the disappearance of deep cultural differences, of deep differences in *Welt-und Lebensanschauungen*. (I cannot avoid the German words for this. The English translation is not serious, dramatic, or world-shaking enough. "Differences in worldview and life-outlook"? No, the translation is not good enough.)

Because of the plurality of the basic views about what history *is*, and because these views are part of philosophy, there can be no definite history of philosophy. We easily get into interesting paradoxes of logic if we proclaim that such and such is the only correct interpretation of Spinoza's texts, because you need a solution of the problems in the philosophy of history. There are different fundamental premises of what history is, and hermeneutics, or the philosophies of interpretation, are many. Only if you say that only *your* philosophy is correct, without reasons at all, can you offer the "correct" view of what Spinoza intended to say in the *Ethics*. A different way of saying this: Philosophy has no definite history.

Which philosophers of the past deserve to be called great? This question leads to another: Who is competent to judge? Which philosophy do we use as a frame when answering? I belong to those who do not feel competent to answer even what the question means, but let me use two possible indicators of greatness.

One indicator is the great philosophers' being rediscovered and highly appreciated by successive generations of philosophers in different cultures. Another indicator is the persistent richness and diversity of interpretations of their texts. Spinoza's texts are constantly reinterpreted by philosophers, poets, scientists, and others. Among the nineteenth century's well-known influential interpretations, we may mention those of Goethe and Hegel. Among the many distinguished interpreters of the twentieth century, I do not feel competent to pick out anybody in particular. But there is an encouraging variety. Encouraging in spite of a certain tendency to appreciate conformity. Of course, we would all like to avoid textual and purely factual, historical disagreement, but by interpretation, I mean philosophical agreement.

In what follows, I speak as a life philosopher, not as a historian. Study of the life and time of Spinoza is essential for any close study of the textual material, but for my purpose, it can only be a necessary instrument. Also, in the strict systematization of Spinoza's formulations in the *Ethics*, for instance, sentences such as "*x* means the same as *y*" can only be an instrument, a methodological technique, but my background is such that I find it natural to work systematically.

The history of interpretations of Spinoza's texts shows the intimate relations to changing traditions. The religious character of his philosophy makes the history comparable to what Albert Schweitzer tells us in his *Geschichte der Leben Jesu Forschung* (History of the research on the life of Jesus). Four periods are fairly clear, the time soon after Spinoza's death focusing on his atheism and his critique of the historicity of the Bible—the work of a pioneer in this field. Then we have the wonderful period when "everybody" declared themselves Spinozists—with Goethe as the greatest luminary. The period is in the history of ideas mostly called the Romantic period, but from an ecosophical point of view, it should be called the realistic period. The Kantian interpretation, heavily colored by its distinction between dogmatic and critical, should be mentioned. It was a useful distinction within professional philosophy at the time, but later it became clear that Kant introduced, as all great philosophers do, a new form of "dogmatism" in the sense of proceeding from sets of unquestioned assumptions—the presuppositions in the sense of R. G. Collingwood. Spinoza's metaphysics was interpreted by Kantians as based on illusions. I don't think it is proper to speak of a Kantian tradition in interpreting Spinoza. But a new period of interpretations, alive even today, started with Hegel and tended to find that, for Spinoza, the single, particular beings somehow drowned in the mighty substance. The long series of modern attacks on substance started with interpreting Spinoza as a substance-philosopher rather than a process-philosopher, like A. N. Whitehead. "The real is unchangeable, no dynamism, no time."

A fourth tradition made headway early in the twentieth century with "the *immanence* of God (and substance)" as a key expression.[12] This is the tradition to which I belong. The most radical version might be thus formulated: "Without modes (singular beings), no God nor Substance." Of course, a tradition of interpretation includes much more than the interpretation of the first part of the *Ethics,* but unfortunately, I think, that part has been by far the most thoroughly studied within professional philosophy.

What is the major lesson to be learned from history in this case? From the wealth of significantly different interpretations by intensely engaged, learned Spinoza researchers? For me, the lesson is primarily that new interpretations will occur in the future and that my own interpretation will only be one of a long series—forgotten in due time. What also seems to be learned from the history is that the interpretations ostensibly expressing "what Spinoza really meant," or at least suggesting this, can be viewed as interesting *reconstructions* of his philosophy—interesting because they make his texts meaningful for contemporaries of the authors of the interpretations. Reconstructions, as here understood, take the texts, sentence for sentence, as seriously as does the historian, and the reconstructor is supposed to use all historical materials, but he or she need not take seriously the question "If Spinoza could read the construction, what would he think of it?"

Many people who are engaged in the ecological crisis claim to have been inspired by Spinoza. They read some of Spinoza's texts or his comments on those texts. Some even read about Spinoza himself, but this does not mean that they try to find out exactly what Spinoza meant. Why should they? They make use of his image and his texts in their lives. What more could or should Spinoza expect of them?

Spinoza does not write about the beauty of wild nature. Perhaps he never talked about it. Not about the coastline of the Netherlands, the storms, the variety of light and darkness, the seabirds. There were people around him, Dutch landscape painters, who appreciated all this. Maybe he did also, but it scarcely influenced what he says in the *Ethics.* What he says about animals does not suggest that he had any wide or deep sense of identification with any of them. Nevertheless, his *kind of* philosophy of life, its structure, is such that he inspires many supporters of the deep ecology movement.

One of the most inspiring aspects of the *Ethics* is this: It outlines a total view—a set of ultimate premises in our thinking about ourselves and the greater reality we are part of, and Spinoza applies it to concrete situations. There are other great thinkers who try to do the same: Aristotle, St. Thomas Aquinas, Thomas Hobbes. Spinoza remains a unique source.

What is a total view? Here I speak of what might be called "a general orientation with concrete applications." The general orientation will include basic attitudes, and at the view's most important level, the applications are decisions to act in a certain way in concrete situations. A total view is *not* a philosophy in an academic sense. Any verbal articulation of a total view must inevitably be fragmentary, but must include praxis.

The term *premise* is important. The relation of premises to conclusion, in order to be valid, must be logical at least in a wide sense of that very ambiguous word. For reasons and through motivations historians do not quite agree about, Spinoza chose an exposition of his total view with great stress on the premise-conclusion relation—analogous but not very similar to Euclid's exposition of geometry.

In the *Elements* of Euclid, important and interesting theorems occur far from the axioms. These theorems can be modified—like ultimate premises in systems of formal logic. There are many options; one need not start with a principle of contradiction. The same applies to the *expositions* of the *Ethics*. If there seem to be inconsistencies between a sentence in part x and one in part y, a modification of the interpretation of the sentence in x is as relevant as that of the sentence in y, even if x has formal logical priority over y. That is, even if x may be part of the system of premises from which y is derived. In what I have to say, this way of looking at formal priority and relevance is often employed. We must not succumb to any irrational reverence for what is chosen as a premise. One metalogical theorem is generally underestimated: A given conclusion y can always be derived from different sets of premises, even rather odd ones. For example, the conclusion "All whales are warm-blooded" can be derived from the premises "All whales are fish" and "All fish are warm-blooded."

Academic philosophers are increasingly reflecting the ecological crisis in their writings. The sources of philosophic inspirations are many: the works of Aristotle, Spinoza, Bergson, Heidegger, Whitehead, to name a few. Personally, I have had a special relation to Spinoza's *Ethics* since I was seventeen, but this does not imply that I believe his work can help everybody articulate their basic attitudes. I believe there is a need for deeply different verbal articulations of a total view, including the poetic.

Several terms in the *Ethics* are to my mind extraordinarily helpful when we try to express the fundamental views that have motivated the environmental activism of some of us. In the next sections, I shall focus mainly on one of those terms, namely, *amor intellectualis Dei*, "the understanding love of God." The verb *intelligere* I translate as "understand." The adjective *intellectualis* should not be translated as "intellectual"—a too intellectual term today.

The term *amor intellectualis Dei* and closely related terms had for centuries been theological terms within the rich tradition Spinoza modified in his own particular direction. Among the wise historians who have studied Spinoza, I wish to point to Harry Austryn Wolfson. His account of the spiritual genesis of the famous fifth part of the *Ethics*, "on the power of the understanding or on human freedom," is so far unsurpassed, as far as I know. He mentions many authors studied by Spinoza and presumably influencing him. Among these influences is St. Thomas Aquinas and Leo Hebraeus:

> A model classification of love in which intellectual love is included is given by Thomas Aquinas. He distinguishes between (a) natural love (*amor naturalis*) exists even in inanimate objects, (b) sensitive or animal love (*amor sensitivus animalis*), and (c) intellectual, rational, or spiritual love (*amor intellectualis, rationalis, spiritualis*). It is this classification of Thomas Aquinas which seems to be the origin of Leo Hebraeus' three-fold classification to love into natural, sensitive, and rational and voluntary (*naturale, sensitivo, et rationale volontario*). The last kind of love is also called by him mental love (*l'amore mentale*), or, as in Thomas Aquinas, intellectual love (*l'amore intellettivo, intellettuale*).[13]

With love of God being the highest goal in the religious life of humans, Spinoza—carefully following the old tradition—furnishes this love with an appropriate place in Part Five of his *Ethics*.

But does the so-called rationalist system invented by Spinoza allow him to put so much "theology" into it? His supreme intention seems to have been both to stick firmly to reason and to nevertheless furnish his religious contemporaries with a strong faith as satisfactory, or more satisfactory, than theirs. As I see it, this was a project unlikely to succeed. The result? The use of the term *amor Dei*, which certainly admits various interpretations.[14] I shall stick to my consistently immanent interpretation of *Deus* and hold that *amor intellectualis* is directed toward "God, *not* as infinite" (*Deus non qua-tenus infinitus*, as in 5P36).[15] It is directed toward individual, finite beings. My minimum thesis here is that at least for one hermeneutically justifiable interpretation, the understanding of God, as part of the third and highest way of cognition, is directed toward individual, finite beings. This position requires discussion of the term *Deus*. I shall need to discuss the thesis of immanence before returning to the *amor intellectualis*.

The *Ethics* is full of occurrences of the term *Deus*. How is it that Spinoza was conceived as a diabolically clever atheist? It is very understandable. It was at his time inevitable.

God is said to be maximally perfect (*perfectissimus*). God is the cause of everything, even "himself." Nothing at all can be conceived except through God. This might be thought to be enough to calm the theologians. But they were not led astray by Spinoza's terminology. They knew, for instance, that Spinoza was using the adjective *perfect* (*perfectus*) in an old way, in which it basically means "complete" (from Latin *per*, "thoroughly," and *facere*, "to make or do"). Wolfson mentions "the original use of the term 'perfection' in the sense of 'completeness' and of not lacking anything required by one's own particular nature."[16] The nature or essence or power of the God of Spinoza is complete to the greatest possible extent—by sheer definition. (But Spinoza does not say anywhere that "He" is good, and there is nothing personal about "Him"!)

Perfection is not a term introduced in the *Ethics* by means of a separate definition. When not applied to nature, it admits of degrees. Joy is an emotion through which the mind is said to become "more perfect" (3P11Sch). "More whole" through more activeness and power. Whatever its connotation, "more perfect" cannot be separated in denotation from "more powerful." Compare proof of Proposition 61: "Joy . . . is the emotion through which the power of the body to act, increases or is furthered." The relation to activeness and understanding is not only intimate; it is internal. The more perfect, the more active and the less passive (5P40). In short, "more perfect than" cannot, in denotation, be completely separated from a number of other basic "in itself" relations. Among basic kinds of sentences, Spinoza used to express his system in the sense of interconnected sets of expressions such as "*x* is in itself," "*x* is conceived through itself," "*x* causes *y*, partially or totally," "*x* is more perfect than *y*." There is no place, as far as I can see, for a God that has completely different properties from those of the "in itself" family. On the other hand, the theorems 5P32 to 5P35 seem difficult to understand from the point of view of immanence. They are too close to transcendental religious views Spinoza entertained in his younger years. The *Ethics* is not a finished work, not a crystal.

More than any others, one expression has supported the concept of the immanent God: "God or Nature" (*Deus sive natura*). Some Spinoza students have supposed that Spinoza simply identified God with nature in a modern sense. This is clearly untenable, but the expression needs discussion, which will be offered in a later section. Suffice it here to mention a conclusion: The God of the *Ethics* may be identified essentially with Nature-as-creative (*natura naturans*)—the creative aspect of a supreme whole with two aspects, the creative and the created—*natura naturata*. The latter are the existing beings in their capacity of being there, temporarily. There is creativity but not a creator. The verb "to nature" (*naturare*) covers both aspects in its dynamic aspect. A comparable verb today would be "Gaia-ing," a term suitable for those who accept the most radical versions of the Gaia hypothesis: the planet Earth as a self-regulating, living being. Clearly, such ideas are inspiring for radical environmentalists.

Immanence of God was, of course, unacceptable to contemporary theologians. The term *atheist* referred to the denial of the God of the Old and New Testaments, not of every kind of God, and Spinoza was correctly classified in their terminology as an atheist, and a diabolical one insofar as his constant eulogy of God masked his basic terrifying aberrations.

When I contemplate the life of Spinoza, I suspect, like many others, that he never completely gave up his Jewish faith, the transcendent God he loved in his youth. As a result, he may not have managed to develop a system in which God clearly and consistently occurs as immanent in the particular beings we meet in our daily experience.

From God's essence follows his existence, but *only* "existence" as essence. "God's power is nothing except God's active essence" (2P3Sch). Its manifestations are the "modes," the individual beings. This is implied by his system, but sometimes Spinoza seems to feel that he needs more of God's power than mere essence, however eternal. The transcendent God of religion seems to appear from time to time in his texts and threatens the consistency of Spinoza's consistently philosophical thinking and articulation. The threat is most conspicuous in Part Five of the *Ethics*.

In accordance with the immanence theory, every actually existing being partakes in the infinite power of God. This power, the only power that exists, is distributed unequally among natural beings, humans being the most powerful. As we shall see, this inequality plus the theorem of equivalence between power and right implies inequality of right (or rights), humans having "more right" than other beings. Without careful delimitation of the terms *potentia* and *ius*, there is a source of incompatibility with certain radical environmental views.

The textual basis of the theory of immanence may be said already to start in Part One, with Propositions 25 and 26. According to Proposition 36, nothing exists from whose nature some effect does not follow. The proof of the proposition relates every single thing to God: "Whatever exists expresses in a definite and determined way (P25Cor) God's essence or nature, that is, (1P34), whatever exists expresses in a definite and determined way the power of God."

The texts of the *Ethics* furnish no basis for assuming that God expresses a nature, essence, or power, in any way other than through each existent being.[17] From this and from the previous discussion, I draw the following conclusion: *Amor intellectualis Dei* is a kind of love of the existent particular beings, that is, part of the total richness and diversity of life-forms on earth and in other parts of the universe.

In a sense, God as *natura naturans* is nothing else than a term expressing the unequally distributed, intimately interrelated creativity manifested by particular beings. The creativity of these beings, however modest, justifies calling them living beings. Spinoza's so-called panpsychism does not say much more, as I see it.

Would not the above interpretation render God finite, and would it not go directly against a way Spinoza would accept? No, because of the infinite creative aspect of the whole, which embraces *natura naturans* and *natura naturata*. Most students of Spinoza would presumably answer yes, but then they overlook a number of places in the text of the *Ethics*. In Part Two, Proposition 9, he talks about God "not as infinite" (*non quatenus infinitus*). But if finite, will God have an aspect of "modes"? Surely Spinoza talks of the modified God (*Deus modificatus*), of God being affected.[18] (See especially 2P9 and 2P11Cor.) God as *natura naturans* does not exist as something separate from *natura naturata*.

In short, the term *Deus* in the *Ethics* has two functions: one, to point toward an infinite whole with infinite dimensions of creativity, not *in* time, but making time possible, and another function, to point to the manifold of finite creative beings manifesting and expressing the parts of that whole. At least this is a way to interpret and feel what the text of the *Ethics* suggests. The finite, temporal beings are creative, *causa adequatae*, insofar as they are in themselves, *in se*.

By definition—or better, almost by definition—those who support the deep ecology movement are, like Spinoza, partly motivated by basic philosophical or religious premises and feel that all living beings have intrinsic value. It makes sense to care for these beings for their own sake, as creative beings. Clearly, they may appreciate something like the preceding verbal articulations of deep attitudes.

Acting with part of the power of the immanent God and knowing their own action, humans know God adequately: "The human mind has an adequate knowledge (*cognitio*) of the eternal and infinite essence of God." Interpreters have difficulty here. What is adequacy? If God is the creative power completely distributed among living beings, and humans know, or are conscious of, this creativity, one may say that their knowledge of God is adequate (Cp 1P34). Since the only things to be known as actual existing beings are the finite, particular things, "the more we understand (*intelligimus*) individual things, the more we understand God" (5P24).[19]

From the point of view of immanence, human understanding of the highest "third, intuitive kind" not only has a cognitive aspect but is also more specially a relation of love. It is a special kind of intuitive understanding of particular things that involve an internal love relation. The second kind of human understanding, culminating in scientific knowledge, does not have that relation to love, at least not as an internal relation, though there are external relations to love.

In his eagerness to convince his contemporaries that his philosophy furnishes all the satisfaction of Jewish and Christian faiths, Spinoza perhaps stretches too far. The reader easily gets the impression that a life centered on the love of God must be a life of unworldly contemplation, a life different from one centered on the loving understanding of particular things, say, like the life of Rachel Carson. *Amor intellectualis Dei* implies active loving concern for all living beings.

Spinoza certainly was a socially and philosophically active person. One need not, of course, be like Rachel Carson, interested in every living being along the shoreline. One may concentrate on humans, as Gandhi did, but the essential point is that the third kind of knowledge concerns particular beings, and that every one of them in a basically egalitarian way is an expression of the immanent God, part of *natura naturans*, Nature with a capital *N*, as well as of *natura naturata*.

One may say the understanding love of God, and the third (intuitive) way of cognition, concentrate on the content of reality, not its abstract structure.[20]

The abstract structure is investigated through the second way of cognition. Einstein and others obviously delight in God's thoughts in the form of abstract, but beautiful, laws of nature. Mathematicians delight in still more abstract structures. Spinoza, presumably, was delighted to study Euclid. In all this, reason operates, but it is also a form of reason that leads us inevitably to the third kind of cognition (5P28): The third way is rational in the sense that reason and reason alone leads us to this third way.

A supremely important rule that fits neatly in with the deep ecology slogan "rich life with simple means!" has to do with the function of reason as a servant of the third way: What is done that is not in harmony with ultimate goals of life cannot be reasonable. It is not enough to be reasonable and effective as means toward a subordinate goal. One must ask, Is this subordinate goal consistent with or, better, conducive to the realization of ultimate goals—situations with meaning in themselves?

Love of the immanent God is love of God's expressions, not of a separable God. A being expresses God's nature or essence; therefore, love of God cannot be different from love of such a being. But what is God's nature or essence? Part One, Proposition 34, answers: "God's power is God's essence itself"—as already said. In the proof, Spinoza says that through God's power, God and every being exist and act more or less freely. Because God is not separate from God's expressions, causality from God to God's expressions is immanent, not the causality of our natural science. When a human loves God "intellectually," the love can only be a love of one expression directed toward another expression as an expression of God and as such of intrinsic value.

There is basis for assuming that the particular beings that are understood the third way are understood in the light of a great, infinite whole, the creative aspect of that whole. The general structure of the *Ethics* is such that what is said about humans is basically an application of what is said about beings in general. Note the use of "consequently" (*consequenter*) in the proof of Part Four, Proposition 4:

> The power through which particular beings, and consequently humans, conserve their being, is God or Nature's power itself, not in so far / God or Nature / is infinite, but in so far / God or Nature / can be made explicit through human actual essence.

Supporters of the deep ecology movement like to say that they support ecocentrism, not anthropocentrism, and Spinoza certainly offers high-level premises for what has sometimes been labeled biocentric or ecocentric egalitarianism. I think these Latin or Greek terms are useless in serious discussions, but they may be helpful in offering some vague idea of a kind of basic attitude. Spinoza tried something immensely difficult, namely, to articulate with some preciseness certain basic attitudes.

Spinoza's holism, implied—vaguely implied?—all through the *Ethics*, is secured through his use of the term *God*, and by the generality of its theorems. His work *On the Improvement of the Understanding* contains a sentence that many people try to use as a key to understanding Spinoza's system: He says explicitly that he strives to attain a stable mental state characterized by the knowledge of the union that the mind has with the whole of nature. And he seeks to do this with others, not alone: "to strive that many acquire it with me." He envisages a society conducive "to the attainment of this character (state) by the greatest number with the least difficulty and danger." It necessitates a healing of the way we understand things. A way of caring understanding? Some movement toward "green communities"? Spinoza's words are at least not incompatible with such a movement. Of course, if supporters do find something inspiring here, it is not in the belief that Spinoza as a person would be supporting what they do, but that a philosophy like his could support what they do.

But is the foregoing the *most plausible* interpretation of the text of the *Ethics*? There can be no *most* plausible interpretation of the *Ethics*. Hermeneutics, as I understand it, precludes that. My job amounts to a reconstruction of parts of the system rather than to find out exactly what the complex person Spinoza in a certain period of his life intended to mean by his words and sentences. The development and structure of the text of the *Ethics* are very complicated, to say the least. We get a good impression of this through reading the excellent, but formidable, volume written by M. Gueroult on how to interpret Part One—one-fifth—of the *Ethics*.[21] It is difficult for the reader to "feel at home" with Spinoza at such a level of complication. The whole is lost. The level of complication of some of the fugues of Johann Sebastian Bach does not destroy the possibility of their being experienced as an integrated whole. He was a genius, as was Spinoza. The fugues are short; the *Ethics* is short. (If written in the style of M. Gueroult, the *Ethics* would be at least ten times as long.)

A question arises here: When do we write about Spinoza as a professor of academic philosophy, and when do we write as philosophers on our own—however modest in our pretensions of originality? The great philosophers we write about in our textbooks of the history of philosophy inspired each other often in a negative way: They felt a contrast and a need to articulate their own vision. Their freedom, or license, of interpretation of the others is astonishing from an academic point of view. The way leading Stoics interpreted Epicureans and vice versa, the way Hegel interpreted Hume, Marx and Kierkegaard interpreted Hegel, Kant interpreted Hume, Heidegger interpreted metaphyics—scarcely bear pedestrian academic scrutiny. Kant would probably have flunked any current university examination on Hume. He read very little and ignored *The Treatise on Human Nature*. Undergraduates could have corrected him.

I am not defending one-sidedness and wildly implausible interpretations, but I am insisting on the supreme value of working out things *under the inspiration of the texts*. As philosophers, we have an obligation to try out tentative answers to the questions we find urgent and inevitable. This ultimately means working out reconstructions rather than detailed interpretations of the great philosophers. Gueroult should be studied carefully, but he cannot function as a guru.

Philosophical and religious sources have played and will continue to play a role in environmental activism. The close relation to decision in concrete conflict situations precludes highly technical and complicated interpretations. One of the most characteristic, short answers to the question "Why is it so important to protect so-and-so from extinction here in your neighborhood?" runs like this: "It belongs here."

In the deep ecology movement, as in the two other great contemporary movements, the peace movement and the social justice movement, progress partly depends on the active participation of a few who are able to use part of their time and energy to serve a great cause. Reliable news about ecological crisis is nearly always bad. It is difficult not to get frustrated and join the many who passively deplore the destruction that is going on. Among the many sources of inspiration to enter and continue *activism*, we have at our disposal the teaching of Spinoza.

Activeness—a better term than *activity*—makes for joy, according to Spinoza. It expresses the nature of the active being, the being as far as it is in itself (*in se*), and the more directly it expresses its unique nature, the greater the joy. Sorrow is due to passivity, a *lack of* active expressions. There is an accident: You spontaneously engage all of yourself, wholeheartedly, and your own pain is not felt; there is a joy if the activeness is intense and comprehensive. The grave frustration and sorrow felt by millions in the present situation on earth can be overcome, and are being overcome, by jointly entering into active relations, each person taking part according to his or her own capacity and special interest. In the deep ecology movement, the activeness is supposed to be directly motivated by the *ultimate* attitudes toward life and meaningfulness ("level 1"). An activeness that follows *from our very nature as a whole*.

From a systematic point of view, the definition of activeness in Part Three of the *Ethics* is crucial:

> I say we act, when something in us or outside us happens, of which we are adequate cause, that is (according to the foregoing definition) when something follows in us or outside us from our nature, something that can only be understood clearly and distinctly from it alone.

The term *alone* is significant here. It is a supreme manifestation of freedom and creativeness. When we are active and free (*liber*) in this way, we are determined in our action by our (innermost) nature. We do something that is determined, completely determined, but we do it freely, because it is determined by our *own* particular, unique nature. We do it exercising part of the power of God or Nature. And we *cannot escape* being joyful, whatever the tragic circumstances. The whole Part Five centers on how this activeness or freedom can be expanded, increased, and deepened. No freedom without activism, no activism without freedom.

In the expression *Deus sive Natura*—Nature with a capital *N*—the connotation of the two words is not the same, but the denotation is. There are not two separate entities, two existent somethings, not even one. Sameness of denotation does not imply general substitutability of the two terms, but sometimes substitution offers new insights. Let us substitute "Nature" for "God" in Part Five, Proposition 15: "He who clearly and distinctly understands himself and his affects, loves Nature, and the more so the more he understands himself and his affects." It is the passive affects, hatred, jealousy, baseless hope, mindless anger, or sorrow (*tristitia*), that are the obstacles, the immaturity of humans.

The same substitution makes the introductory passage of the proof of Proposition 20 run as follows: "This love of Nature is the highest good we can strive for in harmony with the dictate of reason, and it is common to all humans, and we desire that all would enjoy it."

We cannot, of course, identify "Nature" with the set of particular physical and nonphysical things, including suffering humans and animals. Such an atomistic view forgets that *natura naturans* and *natura naturata* together make an integral whole: The creative and the created are internally (indissolubly) related. We are not invited to love the cruelty in nature.

Gestalt thinking and the concept of internal relations are useful in clarifying the interconnectedness of parts and whole. But I cannot go into this here.

Every single being deserves understanding love—this can be plausibly inferred from theorems in the *Ethics*. But like other great philosophers, Spinoza changed attitudes and terminology through the years. In the *Ethics*, there are still passages suggesting that the unchanging, permanent, and eternal is the supreme and most satisfactory as object of love and veneration. Thus, a sequence of theorems in Part Five, from Theorem 17 onward, seems to belong to a fairly early period of Spinoza's thinking. In the early period, love of God was probably seen in contrast to love of finite, "mortal" particulars. In some sections of Part Five, love of God is still somewhat similar to the love of a transcendent God, a God that has a power of "His" own, beyond and apart from the limited power of individual beings.

Let us substitute "God or Nature" for "God" in Part Five, the proof of Proposition 17: "The highest virtue (*virtus*) of the mind is to understand God or Nature, or to understand beings in the third way."

The translation of *virtus* as "virtue" is misleading today. There are not one-word translations available. The term has to do with capacity, like the Greek *arete*. Spinoza shuns moralizing.

Some might say that, like a green activist, Spinoza wishes to organize people and to contribute, using nonviolent means, to the establishment of a green society. The consciousness of the members will be characterized by awareness of their unity with nature, and they live according to that insight.

Such interpretations are going too far. But clearly the words of Spinoza do not diminish the feeling that a total view having important analogies to Spinoza's view is compatible with contemporary total views in part inspired by the ecological crisis, that is, analogous to an ecosophy.

What would Spinoza in heaven say to this? Perhaps he would make a scornful remark. But his personal applause is not *necessary* for us.

The very famous passage in his early work on human understanding, specifically the utterance about the union of the mind with nature as a whole, has led many to interpret Spinoza as an advocate of *unio mystica*, that is, as a "mystic." In the *Ethics*, however, there are no similar utterances. I find it plausible that in his later years, he experienced less mystical nearness to a supreme whole.

Nature, as conceived by many ecologists and expressed philosophically by James Lovelock and others, is not the passive, dead, value-neutral nature of mechanistic science, but is akin to the active, "naturing" nature of Spinoza. It is all-inclusive, creative (as *natura naturans*), infinitely diverse, and alive in the broad sense of Spinozistic so-called panpsychism. It manifests abstract structure, namely, the laws of nature, simulated by such models as Einstein's field equations. Goethe reaches deeper, perhaps, when he warns us: "*Die Natur hat weder Kern noch Schale, alles ist auf einem Male.*"

Because "everything affects every other thing," we cannot predict the long-range effects of our particular actions and policies. This is in harmony with Spinoza's warning that we should not think humans capable of ever fully understanding the "common order of nature." Very much less is needed to appreciate the overwhelming creativity of Nature. The *practical* importance of the intrinsic-value principle of deep ecology is mainly due to the imperfection and fragmentariness of our knowledge of the common order of nature. Calculations of "usefulness" are uncertain.

Nature (with a capital *N*) is intuitively conceived as perfect in the sense that Spinoza and ecologists hold more or less in common. It is not a narrowly moral, utilitarian, or aesthetic perfection. Nature is perfect "in itself" and not insofar as it serves specific human needs. Nor is it moral or immoral. It is amoral.

In Spinoza's medieval Latin, *perfection* means "completeness" of some sort. But suffering in nature? There is no reason to deny or underestimate it. Neither should its relation to perfection be overestimated. Stephan Lackner has published a highly stimulating book concerning this.[22] Some ecologists seem to ask us to completely refrain from intervention that is meant to help needlessly suffering animals. But as humans, we have obligations, primarily toward suffering humans, but also toward nonhuman beings. There are, of course, inevitable clashes of norms in this area, but some norms in the sense of general guidelines are fairly clear. We may refuse to passively witness what we consider unnecessary suffering. The predators kill, but we are free to intervene in some cases.[23] I don't know how the text of the *Ethics* may lend itself to this question of the deep ecology movement.

Spinoza uses all central philosophical terms of his time, but he defined them in his own way and he has the tendency to relate to each of them in a characteristic way. Without studying this very special way, one gets an inadequate picture of his *system*. To act, in the sense of expressing one's own nature, is to act freely, in a way that is determined only by one's own nature and not arbitrarily or by chance. But, of course, I do not mean determined in the sense of fatalism.

An act causes something adequately, and every being causes something this way. That is, every being shares, as we have pointed out earlier, in the creativity of God or Nature. Every being is not wholly in something other (*in alio*), in the terminology of Spinoza. Power is power to act, that is, cause adequately, and an increase of this cannot but increase the level of virtue. (Here Spinoza fundamentally differs from Hobbes.) Spinoza fixes the relation of *virtues* to other key terms through seventeen equivalences.[24]

In the contemporary philosophy of politics, a distinction is often made between "power over" (i.e., coercive power) and "power to." Spinoza's term clearly means "power to."

To be, and therefore to act, in oneself (*in suo esse*) is one of the basic notions in the *Ethics*, and it has a clear connection with self-preservation. But for important reasons, Spinoza prefers a different term, *perseverare in suo esse*. The relation of the ecosophically important notions of self-realization to the Spinozist *perseverare* justifies a closer inspection of the terminology and the significantly different concepts at hand.

The principle of self-preservation, as exemplified and as defined by philosophers and biologists at least since the Stoics, had a main component of defense against external threats. But it also covers behavior and structure adopted to maintain inner equilibrium under changing environmental conditions. Conceived in this way, the principle has acquired renewed importance through the deep ecology movement.

The notion of persevering in one's (particular) being is useful in arguments against the arbitrary manipulation of genes in animals and humans. The usual, more or less "instinctive" reluctance to interfere with the particular beings developed through millions of years may find philosophical justification at this point. Affinities between Stoic philosophy and deep ecology attitudes have been often noted, but the differences are clear: The latter implies social and political activism directed toward conditions significantly different from those in all or most countries. There is no quietism, and no lack of passion in the deep ecology movement. Insofar as it has affinities with Spinoza, it favors the strong positive emotions required for the advance in the level of freedom. But, of course, most supporters of the movement have never heard about Spinoza, and some might dislike what they hear.

The increased *level of* perseveration seems to be proportional to the increase in all eight or more *in-se* predicates: power, freedom, virtue, and so on. The expression *quantum in se est*, "insofar (the being is in itself)," is central not only in the *Ethics*, but also in Spinoza's *Theological-Political Treatise*: "It is a law of all nature (or: a highest law . . .) that every being endeavors (*conatur*) to persevere in its state, in so far as 'it is in itself'" (TTP, Cap.16).

The translation "to preserve" is misleading. H. C. K. Wyld formulates the dictionary meaning of the English term *persevere* as follows: "to persist doggedly and with determination, diligence and patience, with the object a) of completing a task; b) of overcoming difficulty or opposition; c) of attaining a purpose, securing an aim etc."[25]

C. T. Lewis translates the classic Latin term *perseverare* as "to abide, adhere strictly, continue steadfastly, persist, persevere."[26] For example, *navis perseveravit*, "the ship kept on its course." We choose the course and persevere.[27]

The term *perseverare* in the *Ethics* must, of course, be conceived in a more abstract and general way, but I think the English term furnishes an adequate basis. The dynamic character of Spinoza's thinking is, for instance, better served than by "preservation" or by "conservation."

Human power to act is proportional to the extent to which we are the adequate cause of something, which again, according to the definition of adequate causation, is proportional to the extent to which what is done follows from our nature or essence *alone*, and not from any *pressure* upon us. When we act (in the introduced sense of the word *act*), we persevere in our being or essence. A thing that perseveres in its being "insofar as it is in itself" perseveres in its essence.

"To persevere in one's being" is the same as "to persevere in one's essence" and not to persevere in someone else's essence, says Spinoza. Altruism, in the sense of caring for others or doing things for the sake of others, does not imply shedding one's essence and jumping into the essence of something else. A being is freer the more it acts out, or is caused by, *its own* nature *alone*. It is a question of maintaining identity, not of strengthening ego or egocentricity. The doctrine of Spinoza at this point, with its undermining of the standard conception of altruism, furnishes an excellent *kind of* basis for a deep ecology concept of identification with every living being. I say "kind of" because of the opportunity for a variety of conceptualizations.

The term *perseverare* acquires its function from its position within a structure that is unique to Spinoza's system and different from the function of related terms among other philosophers. But we would be led astray if we adopted *self-perseverance* as a fundamental term of Spinoza's system. No single term is fundamental in his system. There are at least a dozen, which are ultimates from a systematic point of view. Therefore, we cannot overemphasize the importance of keeping in mind the internal relations of a manifold of terms. If not, the system falls apart—a disorderly heap of postulates.

Taken at its crudest form—the endeavor to continue somehow to survive—the meaning of *perseverare in suo esse* is of little systematic interest. And taken to imply a resistance to change—a striving to keep on just as one always has done—the term is clearly un-Spinozistic. There is an urge for change. Humans and other beings are always "on the way"—without change of essence. The dynamic, interactionist view of the self makes it inevitable to interpret a basic principle of *conatus* as a striving for "self-causingness," activeness, power. We might connect it more specifically with the striving for perfection, wholeness, completeness, "self-madeness," as suggested by the special use of the term in the *Ethics*. The use of *conatus* in Part Five, Proposition 28, is instructive: "the conatus or desire to understand things in the third way of cognition." Love of particular beings, *amor intellectualis*, is not a luxury indulged by the few, but a bone-hard human reality.

The proof of Part Four, Proposition 20, offers an excellent occurrence of *grading* conatus, perseverance, conservation, power, and virtue:

> Virtue is the very power of man, and is defined solely by the essence of man, that is, which is defined through solely the striving by which man strives to preserve in his being. Therefore, the more each strives to conserve his being, and is able to do so, the more he is endowed with virtue. And as a consequence, to the extent a man neglects to conserve his own being, he is wanting in power.

And, of course, wanting in virtue. One is reminded of the Greek term *arete*, conventionally translated as "virtue," but the term lacks the specific moral atmosphere of "virtue." Spinoza's antimoralistic attitude may remind one of that of Hobbes, but not the general gentleness and ethical approach. In the ecosophy I feel at home with, a fundamental norm can be formulated in one word: "Self-realization!" The nearest term in the terminology of the *Ethics*, "to persevere in one's self," can be interpreted in the direction of *express oneself, self-fulfillment, realizing one's potentials—self-realization*.

The self can be said to comprise what one identifies with. The identification may be superficial or deep, the scope of identification narrow or broad. The person, I suggest, who is "all-round" mature cannot avoid identifying with every living being—seeing himself or herself in every being. If the two persons are Anne and Tom Taylor, evidently they do not see Anne and Tom in every being. But there is *something* they see in themselves *and* in any other being. What something? It is tempting to mention one particular metaphysical theory specifying the *x*. I refer to Bhagavadgita's announcement: "Those who are equipped with *yoga* look on all with an impartial eye, seeing *Atman* (the Self) in all beings and all beings in *Atman*" (chapter 6, verse 29, Gandhi's translation).

Nine out of ten times, the news about the ecological crisis is potentially discouraging. It is therefore understandable that some young supporters of the deep ecology movement despair, grow pessimistic, and become increasingly passive. This happens, in spite of their certainty that the goal of the deep ecology movement is in harmony with what they fundamentally and intuitively stand up for: They try to "persevere in their being, insofar as they are in themselves," that is, insofar as they are able to act as integrated, powerful people—in the Spinozistic sense of power.

People motivated by the positive (active) affects and not the negative (passive) ones have the same ultimate aim, taking part in the same highest virtue of the mind (5P25Proof), and are therefore capable of joining together in *peaceful communities*. The stronger these joyful affects are, the better. Spinoza is a rare bird among philosophers: He makes significant advance along the road to freedom on the basis of the strength of positive feelings! Reason points out the way to go, but only the strength of feelings can do the job, to travel along a long, difficult trail, each in a separate trail (*svamarga*), the way of one's own self.

There are—perhaps I should add "of course"—in the *Ethics* some sentences that are difficult to digest for supporters of the deep ecology movement. A passage in Part Four (4P37Sch) seems to rely on a curious theorem: The less similar the nature of people, the less easy it is to live together, and the less they are useful to each other. This theorem, I think, can be inferred from what he says about the nature of different living beings. From such a viewpoint, he talks about animals that have feelings, but have such a very different nature from ours that they cannot be our friends or members of our communities. He does not say that because they are inferior or lower, they cannot be our friends; he says their nature is too different.

Part of what Spinoza says in this connection is different from what supporters of the deep ecology movement tend to say. I refer to Spinoza's expression that animals have the *same* right in relation to humans as humans have in relation to animals, but that humans have *more* right than animals. Many supporters of the deep ecology movement say that animals have as much right as humans—that there is an equality of right.

I tend to disagree with any quantification here. Animals and humans may be said to have at least *one kind of right* in common, namely, the right to live and blossom. The concept I prefer if I use the term *right* in this connection is such that the term does not warrant quantification. If I intentionally kill a mosquito, I violate its right, but not because I, as a human, have more right. If Spinoza relates to another being with *amor intellectualis*, can he nevertheless deny doing things for *their own sake*? In modern terminology, *intellectual* love would not imply attributing intrinsic value, but that is irrelevant here. Spinoza does not use the term *right* in such a way, and he cannot avoid quantification.

Oddly, some people find it paradoxical that theorists of the deep ecology movement tend to cherish Spinoza: He talks about animals with so little respect. But the inspiration does not depend on reading texts as a holy scripture. We do not expect him to be influenced by at least some of the dominant opinions among his contemporaries. We have the right to treat animals "as is most convenient for us," he writes in one of his "notes," not as part of a theorem. But if some of us have advanced further than some others among us on the way toward the application of the third way of knowledge, *amor intellectualis*, the third way will have priority over conveniences. Animal factories that violate the dignity of animals cannot be operated in conformity with the active affect.

Among Spinoza's *terms*, none corresponds to the important term *(process of) identification*, by which humans attribute intrinsic or inherent value to every human being and to large sections of, or all, nonhuman beings. The structure of his system is such that all beings take part in the power of God. Because of the equivalences joining *power* with other terms, *the structure* is compatible with the intrinsic value and the self-realization views. The *content* of the note attached to Part Four, Proposition 37, is not. For my use of this note in Spinoza's text, it is enough to add to it: What partakes in the creative power of God has intrinsic value, and this applies to the total manifold of creatures. In this way, it is not difficult to move from the basic (level 1) announcements of Spinoza to my proposed eight (level 2) points of the deep ecology movement.[28]

Supporters of the deep ecology movement have been increasingly involved in social and political conflicts. Since the controversies on pesticides, the pervasive influence of social and political obstacles have made supporters more pessimistic about the near future. The question must here be raised: Can seventeenth-century Spinoza teach us anything about today's frustrating political situation? Not very much, I am afraid.

The understanding of Spinoza's political opinion clearly depends on what he says in the *Ethics* and other works and on the special social and political conditions in the Netherlands at that time. I shall here limit myself to some remarks on the relationship between the *Ethics* and his social philosophy insofar as they are fairly independent of the special conditions of his time. They concern primarily some of the central terms mentioned in the foregoing.

Adequate ideas are only available through the second (rational) and third (intuitive) kinds of cognition. These two kinds do not conflict, but the rational teaches us only what is required in our quest to understand in the third way, that is, ultimately what is necessary individually, socially, and politically, to reach a peaceful community.[29]

The social situation shows how far from reaching utopia we are: Most people are, according to Spinoza, led by passive rather than active affects, and they choose leaders who seem to help them reach goals derived from these passive affects. This means that even a democracy may fail to change policies.

Spinoza grew increasingly pessimistic. He changed opinions during the long time he was working on the manuscript of the *Ethics*. The last time was in 1674, two years after the politically catastrophic year of the assassination of Jan de Witt. Spinoza was politically active, and the depressing events of 1672 may have changed some of his ideas—he was led toward general pessimism about the future. But the pessimism did not influence the main structure of the *Ethics*, the propositions and their proofs. It is more likely that it affected some of the notes *(scholiae)* put in between the propositions.

It is not the personal opinions, but the main body (and the general structure) of the *Ethics* that has inspired, and will in the future inspire, those who, on the basis of their fundamental beliefs and attitudes, try to contribute, however modestly, to the solutions of the ecological crisis. It is clear to those who teach Spinoza at the universities that the appeal of Spinoza is close to universal. Not surprisingly, he is sometimes called *the* philosopher.

Spinoza had a vision, a small set of intimately connected, deep intuitions. He clearly saw that to convey the content of his vision, and of all main views dependent on it, he could not use a small number of words. The argumentation in the *Ethics* uses many words and many levels of the premise-conclusion relation. The intimacy of the relationship between the key terms enables the careful reader to get a feeling for the basic intuitions he tried to elicit in us.

Through Spinoza to Mahayana Buddhism, or Through Mahayana Buddhism to Spinoza?[30]

The increased interest in meditation and Mahayana Buddhism has resulted in a search for a philosophy that might be understandable in the West and reflect basic insights of the East. A philosophy inspired by Spinoza may be the answer—or one answer.

Jon Wetlesen has explored this possibility with great acumen.[31] There are, however, pitfalls of interpretation and construction: One may make Spinoza too much the Buddhist, or Buddhism too Spinozistic. This does not necessarily detract from the value of the resulting edifice. The comparison of Buddhist versions of Spinoza and Spinozistic versions of Buddhism may lead us nearer to truth.

The Buddhist conceptions of a temporal, instantaneous, or absolute freedom may well be valid, but they do not render the gradualist conceptions less important for life. Sudden enlightenment of great depth must be anchored in a mature, integrated personality, and this entity takes a long time and intensive action to develop. The distinction between external and internal action is fruitful, but a high level of activeness ("causedness" through oneself) is possible and is needed if one is to reach high levels of freedom (understanding, perfection).

The very concept of understanding in the *Ethics* points toward cognition-as-acts in a physical and social environment. Whatever the heuristic and cognitive value of meditation, insight for Spinoza is always insight expressed through an action, a "grasping" (the "*lambanological*" point of view).

SPINOZA BETWEEN EAST AND WEST

The practice of meditation has increased by leaps and bounds in the materially rich Western industrial states in recent years. Generally, the teachers are from the East and are exponents of Eastern metaphysical theories. The attitude toward theorizing of those interested in the practice of meditation is rather ambivalent—and for good reasons, as far as I can understand. The amount of woolly, talkative spirituality is staggering, and some excellent teachers of meditation may well be incompetent as exponents of classical Eastern metaphysics.

Persistent and serious practice of meditation, however, leads more or less inevitably to philosophical reflection. It is fortunate that in recent years, an increasing number of researchers have combined deep study of the East with a thorough training in Western analytical and other trends. This means that serious practice of meditation in the West can now be combined with, and integrated into, a mature philosophical outlook that uses both Eastern and Western sources.

Spinoza occupies a unique position in the Western academic textbook tradition. On the one hand, he is trustingly integrated into narrow Western traditions as one of the "great rationalists" of the seventeenth century. On the other hand, deep Jewish, mystical, Middle Eastern influence has always been acknowledged by most specialists on Spinoza's background. Part Five of the *Ethics* represents, as far as I can understand, Middle Eastern wisdom par excellence. Spinoza fits in with Eastern traditions in a way that makes it highly unlikely that he can be completely absorbed by any of the major Western trends.

Among the contributions to a comparative study of Spinoza *and* Eastern traditions, Wetlesen's works in 1978 and 1979 are in many ways outstanding. He combines a thorough knowledge of Spinoza's system with a not inappreciable acquaintance with meditation and Mahayana Buddhism. His work's greatest merit, however, is Wetlesen's careful, explicit, and testable use of textual sources.

The result of his work is an exposition of major parts of Spinoza's philosophy that broadly makes it a kind of Mahayana Buddhism. Or, if this is too crude a characterization, his work may be said to result in a Spinozistic system closely connected with certain central Mahayana texts. The *Heart Sutra* (*Prajñāpāramitā Hydaya Sūtra*) is one of them.[32]

Wetlesen's work is likely to be conceived as a transition from Spinoza to Mahayana. My comments argue for a dialectic turn back: Wetlesen furnishes a promising way of incorporating meditational practice and theory in a Spinozistic framework. Mahayana Buddhist texts are useful, perhaps indispensable, for this endeavor. In the end, though, the resulting *total view* will be closer to Spinoza's *Ethics* than to any Buddhist text.

Crucial for this turn back to Spinoza is my contention that Wetlesen underrates "*life* under the guidance of reason" and overrates the "tranquility of meditation." Instead of "tranquility," I propose the term *equanimity* as a more central one. Equanimity integrates internal and external balance and shows itself in contexts of vigorous action. The mode of human nature exposed by Spinoza, as I understand him, is maximally expressed in the supremely active life—internally *and externally*, insofar as internal and external can be distinguished at all. In other words, whereas Wetlesen's Spinoza is markedly otherworldly and tender-minded (in William James's sense of the words), as I see Spinoza, he combines marked "this-worldly" and tough-minded aspects with obvious tender-minded traits. The combination is highly precarious, but the system of Spinoza *is* highly precarious: Its pretension is extreme insofar as it tries to address everything of lasting value in every major tradition, East and West, even when the values seem mutually, utterly inconsistent.

FREEDOM₁, FREEDOM₂, ADEQUATE COGNITION, AND INTERNALITY

Wetlesen distinguishes two conceptions of freedom and two ways of freedom. Freedom₁ is absolute, and there is no "way" to it in the sense that it is "already there." It is the "highest" kind of freedom. Freedom₂ is relative and gradual. It takes time and effort to reach high levels of freedom₂. There is, according to Wetlesen, no continuity between these freedoms. Freedom₁ cannot develop from freedom₂. Some quotations will make his point clearer.

> I believe that we must distinguish between two fundamentally different ways to freedom in the philosophy of Spinoza. Borrowing from related conceptions in Indian and Chinese philosophy, especially from Mahayana Buddhism, I shall call these two ways the gradual and the instantaneous strategies of liberation. For the greater part, this distinction is not made explicit in Spinoza's own exposition . . . In some crucial contexts, however, he draws the distinction explicitly. If the former contexts are read in the light

of the latter, we shall have an interpretation of Spinoza's ethics of freedom along the lines that I attempt to reconstruct here.

Spinoza appears to imply a distinction between two kinds of internal freedom, one absolute, the other relative. Internal freedom of the absolute kind presupposes an intuition of oneself and other beings in nature from the viewpoint of eternity. This cognition cannot be approached through a gradual strategy, since approximation presupposes a process of time, while the viewpoint of eternity has no relation to time, but is incommensurable with it. Nor is there any need for such an approximation, as this intuition is already there, constituting the very essence of the mind. The act of becoming conscious of this can, in one perspective, be described as a sudden enlightenment. From another perspective, however, the notion of suddenness is also seen to be misleading. For the enlightened person sees that freedom, in the absolute sense, consists not in becoming something that he is not, but in being what one is from eternity. As Spinoza says in the passage above, the sage is conscious of himself, of God and of things by a certain eternal necessity. The difference between the sage and the ignorant is therefore above all a difference in self-awareness.[33]

One of the trends of argumentation supporting these conclusions is based on Spinoza's theory of affects:

> On applying the gradual strategies of liberation, a person may counteract those passions which are evil by means of other passions which are less evil, or which are good. Still, however, these antidotes are passions, and therefore the result will not be freedom in the absolute sense, since this requires that the strategies are based on actions. From this it seems to follow that freedom in the absolute sense cannot be achieved by means of a gradual strategy. This confirms once more what I said above concerning the relation between the gradual and the instantaneous strategies. Only the latter lead to freedom in the absolute sense, and are therefore more fundamental than the gradual strategies. (pp. 6–7)

Another trend takes account of the "internal" character of adequate cognition:

> If Spinoza's conception of adequate cognition is related to the viewpoint of eternity in the manner I suggest, then it seems reasonable to suppose that his conceptions of action and freedom must be primarily of an internal kind. The freedom of the sage consists in his power to conserve his being in this type of adequate cognition. His conation and cognition are adequately determined from within. (p. 24)

The concepts freedom$_1$ and freedom$_2$ are introduced using the preceding conceptions of actions and adequate cognition:

> When action is determined from within the way mentioned, it can be called free in an absolute sense. It is not contingent upon external conditions. It pertains to man as an eternal being. I shall call this freedom$_1$, and its contrary, which pertains to man as a temporal being, I shall call bondage$_1$.
>
> In addition to these conceptions Spinoza appears to have recognized a second kind of freedom and bondage, which may be called relative. They pertain to man as a temporal being, and relate to the degree of autonomy or heteronomy which a person may have in relation to his external environment. I shall designate these as freedom$_2$ and bondage$_2$. They are subspecies of bondage$_1$. (p. 24)

It is important to note that Wetlesen associates externality with external environment, which includes other people, society, political institutions, and so on.

> What the human condition really is, can only be understood from the viewpoint of eternity. To be ignorant of this viewpoint, is to be under bondage in the most fundamental sense, while to be aware of it, is to be internally free. This seems to be the foundation of his perennial wisdom. (p. 24)

It seems (anticipating some criticisms) that Wetlesen identifies the absolute freedom of Spinoza with an intuitive insight of a very special kind (*not* identical with the third kind of cognition, in Spinoza's terminology). The third kind involves interaction with the environment—for example, behavior toward friends, making a decent living, polishing lenses.

If a concrete person living in a particular society is to be characterized as being absolutely free, this should characterize his or her total life. If the cru-cial *insight* is an isolated mental act of a person who otherwise—that is, in regard to freedom₂—acts more or less as a slave, why should this person get the fabulous title of absolutely free? One of many basic questions is, Does Spinoza consider it possible to have freedom₁ without being on a high level of freedom₂? If so, why call freedom₁ a *higher* freedom? What is particularly high in a person living like a slave? On the other hand, if freedom is indis-pensable, it takes time and effort to reach freedom₁. Essential to Wetlesen's *definitions*, however, is that freedom₁ is there all the time, that is, even at a very low level of freedom₂.

Put crudely, I doubt that Spinoza would accept any ideal or model of a free human being that is consistent with a low degree of freedom₂. His descrip-tion of people on a low level of freedom, his "slaves of passion," tyrants, peo-ple reacting with hatred, without generosity, and so on, does not suggest that he would call them free in *any* sense. Or if he would do so, he would mean a potential, not actualized, freedom.

EQUANIMITY OR TRANQUILITY?

The equanimity characterizing the free human being may be conceived either in terms of meditative tranquility or as a basic steadiness in the face of the external strains and stresses of an active life. For example, a states-man like Johan de Witt, a leader of an expedition through the jungle like David Livingstone, or a *karmayogi* like Gandhi may have a high or a low degree of equanimity in "external action." Does Spinoza think of the sage as a meditative rather than a socially and otherwise active person? Wetlesen's interpretation goes in the first direction. I shall *argue* for the latter, but not dogmatically assert its greater historical accuracy or correctness. The inter-pretation of Spinoza is an endless task.

My main argument is, paradoxically enough, inspired by the same variety of Mahayana Buddhism as is Wetlesen's: the teaching that the farther along the path to supreme levels of freedom a human being proceeds, the greater the identification and compassion and therefore the greater the effort to help others along the same path. This implies activity of social and political rel-evance. Gandhi, considering Buddhism a reformed Hinduism, furnishes a good example. His mistakes were many, but he tried through meditation of sorts (combined with fasting) to improve the quality of his action, especially his consistency in maintaining a broad and lofty perspective. He deplored the followers in his ashrams who spurned outward action and concentrated on metaphysics, meditation, and fasting. He conceived this as a kind of spiritual egotism. He did not recognize yoga meditation and prayer as an *adequate* way to insight, perfection, and freedom. Advance toward the highest levels requires interaction with the terrifying complexities of social life.

It is not against anything in the *Ethics* to suppose that *understanding acts*, cognitions internally joined with active affects and constituting interactions between body and environment (under the attribute of extension), are complex and comprehensive, like gestalts of higher order. Examples are highly complex projects such as writing the *Ethics*, preserving and deepening friendships, acting as a mentor or guru, and administering a large monastery. As to the last gestalt, see the instructive *Born in Tibet*, by Chögyam Trungpa.[34]

If carried out in the spirit of eternity, the high level of "external" activity necessarily differs from that of a busybody. Retreats and meditation *may* be necessary in some cases, but this does not imply *tranquility*, only concentration and equanimity. Wetlesen writes in a slightly different vein, it seems:

> In the first place, it seems to be necessary for the person to be able to arrange his life in such a manner that he achieves certain periods of contemplative tranquility. This, I believe, is implied by 5P10:
>
> 5P10
> As long as we are not agitated by affects which are contrary to our nature do we have the power of ordering and connecting the affections of the body according to the order of the intellect.
>
> Actually, two conditions are involved here: The person must achieve tranquility in the sense of not being agitated by those affects which are contrary to his nature; and he must be able to understand things according to the order of the intellect. The first of these conditions requires, I suppose, that certain periods of seclusion must be set off for interior recollection, these being perhaps what we might call a sober type of mystical contemplation. At any rate, it will not do to be a busybody all the time. A certain detachment from temporal concerns is required now and again. (p. 377)

All this may be reasonable from a *pedagogical* point of view, like good advice from a guru. It will not do to be a busybody anytime. Activeness in the sense of Spinoza, however, requires integration and concentration, not tranquility. Gandhi prayed and meditated even during hectic political meetings.

Spinoza's theory of the second and third kinds of cognition does not rule out the person's ability to uphold the point of view of reason and of eternity when acting "externally" in a social environment. Ideally the "free person" may do this *without* retreats to meditation and social isolation. My point is one of principle, not at all meant to weaken the pedagogical importance of these interludes or what Wetlesen would call the strategy of retreats and meditation. These are means, however, not ultimate needs.

THE COMPLEXITY OF INTUITION

Freedom$_1$ is adequate intuition of oneself and other beings in nature from the viewpoint of eternity (see p. 138). More explicitly, "the highest freedom consists in an adequate cognition of man's own essence and existence through the essence and existence of God as his immanent cause."

Even if this insight is intuitive and in a sense eternal (which is difficult to grasp and convey in discursive, argumentative thought and articulation), I cannot see how it is something instantaneous. It is an extremely complex intuition, and we know from personal insights that such intuitions have a depth dimension.

Our first acquaintance with irrational numbers or Gödel's theorem makes us perhaps use correctly some definitions and makes us capable of solving certain problems, but our depth of intention improves only slowly over years of study. There is an abyss of depth in everything fundamental. Moreover, structure persists even if we have the feeling of touching something absolutely simple.

My conclusion is clear: I cannot believe in the instantaneousness of the intuition of freedom$_1$, nor in its lack of an improvable depth dimension.

INTERNALITY IMPLIED BY ABSOLUTENESS: TOTALITY AND PART

The requirement to act *in the strictest sense* from the laws of one's own nature, *only*, or to be *completely internally* caused seems to be satisfied only by God.[35] As Wetlesen points out, however, Spinoza certainly admits that some human beings are freer than others:

Should we conclude, then, that according to Spinoza, *freedom* is beyond the reach of man, and that it is the privilege of God alone? In a certain sense, this may well be what he means. Nevertheless, it must be interpreted in the light of other passages where Spinoza positively affirms that men may be *free*. I have already quoted 5P42Sch, where he contrasts the sage and the ignorant, and implies that the former enjoys freedom of mind. In 4P37Sch he draws a similar contrast between the truly virtuous and the impotent person, and in 4P66Sch between the free person and the slave. (p. 30)

Wetlesen adds a number of other quotations from the *Ethics*. I think one may safely assume that Spinoza thinks there are comparatively free human beings. Are there, however, *absolutely* free human beings? Yes, concludes Wetlesen. The argumentation is complex and precarious. It calls for extensive quotations.

God is absolutely infinite, and as a consequence is present in all his effects, and equally present in parts and wholes (cp. 2P45Dem, 46Dem).

For this reason the singular things in *natura naturata* cannot be separate substances. They are not really distinct from each other, but only modally; internally they are related to one another through their common immanent cause, God. In so far as a singular mode, such as a human being, cognizes himself and other modes in this manner, can he be absolutely free. (p. 31)

One of the decisive points in this difficult argumentation seems to be that God expresses himself (or herself or itself) *totally* in every part or mode. "Totality" is also decisive in the following elaboration:

And when a singular mode is cognized through God as its adequate cause in this way, it is adequately cognized. This cognition embraces in one single grasp, as it were, the totality of those causes which generate the thing. Through this cognition a person can be said to internalize the immanent causality of God, and thereby to participate in the absolute freedom of God . . .

Spinoza's philosophy should therefore be considered as panentheistic, rather than pantheistic. However, in so far as a human being cognizes himself and other modes through their first cause, and sees that this is an immanent and free cause, and that it is infinite, eternal, and indivisible, he feels and experiences that this cause is totally present in himself, and equally present in the parts and in the whole of himself, and consequently he participates in its freedom. (p. 32)

This freedom is absolute, but according to Spinoza, God does not share it with the modes—in spite of the immanence of God. We are therefore no closer to Wetlesen's freedom₁ in spite of his important interpretation of totality.

GRADUAL APPROACH NECESSARY IN LIFE

Wetlesen is, of course, aware of Part Four, Proposition 4:

It cannot happen that a man should not be a part of nature, and that he should be able to suffer no changes save those which can be understood through his nature alone, and of which he is the adequate cause. (p. 29)

If this is so, how can a human being be an absolutely *sole* cause of an action and a result of the action? Wetlesen uses his distinction between internal and external effects:

For even though it is impossible for a person to be an adequate cause of an external effect, he may be so of an internal effect. In that case the effect is internally determined by the nature of the agent, in so far as his nature is internally determined by God (cp. 5P30&Dem, 31&Dem). As Spinoza says in 4P68Sch, this may take place "in so far as we regard human nature alone or rather God, not in so far as he is infinite, but only in so far as he is the cause of man's existence." We should read this in the light of 2P45Sch: "For although each singular thing is determined by another singular thing to exist in a certain manner, yet the force by which each of them perseveres in its existence follows from the eternal necessity of the nature of God (see 1P24Cor)." (pp. 32–33)

It seems that according to Wetlesen, *a person* may remain in a state of absolute freedom, provided all the person's acts are internal:

> What kind of effects is it that such a free person can produce? I have already suggested that these effects must be purely internal, but what do they consist of? The answer, I believe, is to be found in this direction: If a person *cognizes* himself and all things adequately through God as the adequate and internal cause, then the person will have a power to determine his further cognitions in such a way that they maintain themselves on this adequate level (2P40, 5P41&Dem). This cognition, moreover, will engender active affects, such as the intellectual love towards God (5P20Dem, 32Cor, 33Sch, 36Sch), and these active affects will be sufficiently strong to counteract the passions, and thereby to liberate the person from his bondage (4P20Sch, 38, 40, 42). I quote:

> 5P20SCH
> From all this we easily conceive what is the power which clear and distinct cognition, and especially that third kind of cognition (2P47) whose foundation is the very cognition of God, can do with the affects, namely, that if it does not remove them entirely in so far as they are passions (5P3, 4Sch), at least it brings it about that they constitute the smallest part of the mind (5P14). Moreover, it begets a love towards an immutable and eternal thing (5P15) of which we are in truth partakers (2P45), and which therefore cannot be debased by the vices which are in common love, but which can always become greater and greater (5P15), and occupy the greatest part of the mind (5P16) and deeply affect it.

> (p. 33)

The quotation from Spinoza and the interpretation by Wetlesen apparently confirm that a person can *reach* a continuous level of absolute freedom only gradually, turning passive affects into active. There is an ambiguity here: Something is instantaneous, and the person "has" it all the time, even if not aware of it, but something is also gained gradually—I would say, gained through an increase in freedom$_2$.

Let us study the terminology in the following conclusion:

> From the interpretation set forth here we may conclude, then, that absolute freedom is possible for man, but only to the extent that his actions have internal causes as well as internal effects. This is a complete self-determination, and therefore a freedom of the type which I call freedom$_1$. (p. 34)

Seen from noneternal points of view, a person lives in time, and to say that a person is absolutely free would mean that he or she remains on a level of absolute freedom, whatever the cognitions required. But some actions certainly have external causes or effects. Therefore, a person cannot be absolutely free. On the other hand, a person may maximize purely internal actions, and thus we get a graded notion of absolute freedom. In the terminology of Wetlesen, we would add to the last quotation: "A person increases his or her level of attainment of freedom$_1$ if, and only if, the extent to which his or her actions have internal causes and effects, increases." Here freedom$_1$ *as a concept* is not subjected to grading, but a person's *attainment* of freedom$_1$. The latter is the more important if we wish to *gain* freedom.

The impossibility of the gradual approach as a *sufficient* strategy to reach absolute freedom should be distinguished from the possibility that such an approach is a hindrance to reaching freedom$_1$. Wetlesen seems to think that a person who strives to reach higher levels of freedom$_2$ ipso facto cannot reach freedom$_1$. The person must stop trying! This might be good Buddhism, but is it good Spinozism?

> [W]e may conclude that as long as a person strives to attain the ideals of his imagination, he will fail to attain freedom in the absolute sense. It makes no difference what kind of ideal he holds up for himself . . . However, as long as a person adopts such an exemplary model as an end to be achieved in the future, he will be bound to a process of time. He may be freedom-bound, perfection-bound, intellect-bound, love-bound, and so forth; but in any case he will be time-bound. Therefore he will not be free in the absolute sense defined in 1D7, since that requires emancipation from time-binding. (p. 388)

If previous comments are tenable, the likelihood that a person reaches conscious freedom$_1$ *increases* with increasing level of freedom$_2$. There are no purely internal actions—the mind is not a container of acts; all acts are explicitly or implicitly environmental. At least, I cannot see how Wetlesen has succeeded in establishing his concept of purely internal acts.

It seems that Wetlesen has not always distinguished conceptual problems from life problems where that needs to be done. Personal problems are always "in time," and therefore also *applications* of any concepts whatsoever to persons. The concept of eternity must be kept distinct from the criteria for determining whether a person *has* attained the viewpoint of eternity and *when*. It must also be distinguished from the criteria for determining to what extent this viewpoint has been attained. However, all this need not affect the *concept* of eternity. The concept can be retained in its nongraduated form.

Suppose a person has maximally attained the viewpoint of eternity. If the person is a *karmayogi* or a bodhisattva, he or she will nevertheless act, with increasing understanding, in the temporal environment and thus carry out cognitions in part based upon the activity of the imagination. Perhaps this is completely in agreement with Wetlesen's conceptions, but then the above quotation from his work is misleading.

ABSOLUTE FREEDOM THROUGH COGNITION ONLY OF OUR OWN MIND; CLOSENESS OF MIND TO GOD

From this closeness of mind to God, Wetlesen argues for freedom or even salvation through cognition of oneself alone:

> The highest freedom of man, which is nothing else than his salvation, consists in an adequate cognition of his own essence and existence through the essence and existence of God as his immanent cause (cp. 5P36Sch). (p. 75)

The evidence of the aforementioned scholium (5P36Sch) does not corroborate Wetlesen's thesis very strongly. Adequate cognition of one's own essence and existence is a time-consuming thing. We have to understand our passions and transform them into active emotions like generosity toward those who hate us.

It is no easy affair even to find out that an affect we have is not active, but passive. One of the ways is orthodox psychoanalysis. It is not possible, or only very rarely possible, to carry through such an analysis alone. There are other methods, but no shortcuts, it seems. God has *not* provided shortcuts. Wetlesen's strategy of attainment of freedom$_1$ is said to be instantaneous, but it seems to imply that we arrive gradually and painfully at a clearer and clearer understanding of more and more of our affects. It is not done in a general way, but with each affect taken separately. Wetlesen cites

Spinoza's ways of formulating the first two remedies against the passions, which he summarizes in 5P20Sch. The first step consists in this:

5P20SCH

It appears from this that the power of the mind over the affects consists:

1. In the cognition itself of the affects (5P4Sch).

That is to say, it consists in a reflection on the cognitive and affective acts, thereby forming a clear and distinct idea of them. The second step, moreover, is described in this way:

5P20SCH

2. In the separation by the mind of the affects from the thought of an external cause, which we imagine confusedly (5P2 and 4Sch).

When cognitive objects, as well as their affective coloring, are seen in this way, they are no longer hypostasized as external ontological realities, that is to say, they are not assumed to be transcendent things, but are seen to be projected by the consciousness itself. Furthermore, they may be understood through their immanent and adequate causes, and thereby cognized adequately. At this point, however, we move away from the phenomenological attitude of Husserl and into the ontological attitude of Spinoza. But this kind of ontology has nothing to do with the assumption of external objects. It consists in seeing all modes as the effects of the immanent causality of God. When a person has attained this degree of self-knowledge, his faculty of imagination is free, as Spinoza says in 2P17Sch. It then depends on his own nature alone. He lives entirely in this immanent field of his transcendental consciousness, as Husserl would say. He is mindful that his life-world is constituted through his own imaginations and affects, and through this awareness he neutralizes the binding effect of his own projections, thus remaining internally free. (pp. 361–362)

What is not convincing is that the "seeing *all modes* as the effects of the immanent causality of God" (my italics) can constitute one single set of seeing. What about our own passions, race prejudices, and ambition in understanding Spinoza? We certainly do not have the ability to understand instantaneously *each* of the passive affects so that we get a clear picture of their origins—and not just a *general notion* of their dependence on natural laws and God as their immanent cause. Spinoza scarcely recognizes *general* knowledge of passions as a liberating force. Passions as "confused ideas" are not turned into clear ones wholesale. This implies gradual, not instantaneous, freedom. The belief in sudden, definitive illumination of the life-world (*Lebenswelt*) goes against the realism of Spinoza and his critical attitude toward revelation in religion and otherwise.

ENLIGHTENMENT HAPPENS IN TIME, BUT DOES NOT DEVELOP OUT OF NONFREEDOM

The instantaneity of absolute freedom gets to be somewhat mystical in a bad sense if we cannot say that a person attained it or attained consciousness of it at a definite time or within a definite time interval, for example, "sometime between ages *x* and *y*":

> [W]e must beware of not construing the transition from bondage to freedom as a transition from inadequate cognition and passive affects to adequate cognition and active affects as if the latter emerged at a certain moment of time. For it is impossible that the latter could develop out of the former (cp. 2P41 and 5P28, together with 3P1 and 3). If adequate cognition and active affects can be actualized in a person at all, they must be potentially there from the beginning. (p. 389)

That something develops *out of* something else is a much stronger assertion than the assertion that the one was a necessary condition of the other. Beethoven's music was a kind of necessary condition for Schubert's music, but genuinely new things are present in the latter. One cannot say that what Schubert did developed *out of* what Beethoven did. Adequate cognition of something may emerge *after* degrees of inadequate cognition "of the same," and thus be fixed in the time order, without our assuming that the adequate *developed out of* the inadequate, like an adult from its imago.

A person undergoes development in time. There is a transition from one phase to another. New traits form; old ones vanish. One kind of transition is from a lower to a higher level of perfection; it is at the same time a transition to a higher level of freedom. This transition is also a transition to more adequate cognition and more active affects.[36]

We cannot understand the development of a person except by taking into account many parts of the body and many parts of the mind, and only when considering the person as a part or fragment of nature. Thus, I agree that adequate knowledge does not develop *out of* inadequate. The further inferences made by Wetlesen on the basis of this insight seem unwarranted, however.

Writing about the absolute freedom to an audience that has not attained, or is not conscious of, absolute freedom presupposes that the attainment of such (conscious) freedom *happens to a person*—that is, can be fixed in time. This does not exclude the possibility that the writer and the audience later agree that the time dimension is irrelevant or unreal. Having attained and retained this view, they are then clearer about the view of eternity. This state of affairs cannot be anticipated, however.

In the following passage, Wetlesen makes a concession, it seems, in the direction of the preceding remarks:

> So also may the viewpoint of eternity suddenly break forth to the conscious awareness of the mind, calm and clear, when the hindrances are removed.
>
> When this enlightenment has been attained, the person will know that in reality, and from eternity, he is free in the absolute sense. His freedom, in this sense, is an eternal truth and absolute necessity. However, if this be so, then it implies that he must reevaluate his former conceptions about himself and about the human condition in general with regard to bondage and freedom, as well as the transition from the one to the other . . . In so far as he cognizes the whole situation adequately from the viewpoint of eternity, he knows that his portrait of himself, as presented by the imagination and the memory, in a certain sense is an illusion. It does not tell what he really is, and is nothing but a mode of cognition, or an entity of the imagination. (pp. 390–391)

The viewpoint of eternity "may suddenly break forth," that is, it may emerge sometime *within* the time order. When this viewpoint becomes conscious, the biography of the enlightened person, understandably, looks quite different. The points of reference will be different—"all" will be different. It might be compared to what happens after a religious conversion, or when a person suddenly moves from communism to anticommunism (like Arthur Koestler and others). I think it is important to concede this and to stress *discontinuity*. There is a "jump," in the Kierkegaardian sense, or in a sense related to his.

All this may be conceded. Its relation, however, to Spinoza's conception of freedom remains unclear—unclear, to me, both in the use of the term *absolute freedom* and in its status as "higher" than any freedom attained gradually. The formulation "The person *P* is eternally, absolutely free and has never been otherwise" is an unhappy one outside Buddhism. The Spinoza quotations (5P31Sch) that Wetlesen uses to support such a formulation are compatible with the decision to leave it out. They are compatible with the theory of gradual enlightenment:

> The stronger every one is in this kind of cognition, the more he is conscious (*conscius*) of himself and of God, that is to say, the more perfect and blessed he is, which will appear still more clearly from the following. Here, however, it is to be observed that although we are now certain that the mind is eternal in so far as it conceives things from the viewpoint of eternity, yet, in order that what we wish to prove may be more easily explained and better understood, we shall consider the mind, as we have hitherto done, as if it had just begun to be (*tanquam jam inciperet esse*), and had just begun to understand things from the viewpoint of eternity. This we can do without any risk of error, provided only we are careful to conclude nothing except from clear premises. (p. 391)

The conclusion to all this discussion? The absolute freedom₁ is foreign to Spinoza's system.

WIDE AND NARROW CONCEPTS OF GRADING

The distinction between graded and ungraded entities calls for some clarification. A grading *need not be continuous*. Hardness of minerals is graded—for example, "scratchable with a fingernail," "scratchable with a steel knife," "scratchable with a diamond." A person may be said to gain in rationality when he or she behaves rationally in more kinds of life situations and is less rational in none. There is not, however, a continuous transition from one situation to another, from one behavior to another, or from an inadequate cognition to another inadequate one or to an adequate one. There may be abrupt changes, wild leaps. Nevertheless, a person may be said to develop and change gradually. The transition may be discontinuous, and there may be only two grades:

> Either a cognition is adequate, that is, complete, or it is inadequate, that is, incomplete or not complete. If absolute freedom is correlated with adequate cognition, and its contrary with inadequate cognition, it would seem to follow that the distinction between freedom and bondage must also be dichotomous. (p. 395)

Here it seems that Wetlesen does not distinguish between conceptual relations and life relations. A conceptual dichotomy does not itself permit grading—this is true by definition—but as soon as it is asked *to what extent* a person cognizes adequately or inadequately, a grading is possible. Spinoza uses grading, this in spite of a rigid, nongradual distinction between adequate and inadequate. There is also a place for grading the clarity, depth, and other characteristics of *an act of* adequate cognition. Grading is accepted here by Wetlesen himself:

> [I]t may be possible for a person to be more or less conscious of the adequate cognition which constitutes the essence of his mind from eternity.
> ... we may speak of degrees of freedom$_1$ after all, these degrees being in a one-to-one correspondence with the clarity of the conscious awareness which the mind *has* of the adequate cognition which it from eternity *is*. (pp. 395–396)

In his argumentation, however, Wetlesen sometimes tends to adopt or imply narrow conceptions of grading. For example, in the following quotation, grading seems to imply a quantitative element. Grading, though, is an ordering of qualities. Wetlesen himself says that freedom$_1$ is *higher than* freedom$_2$. The distinction between first, second, and third kinds of knowledge involves (among other things) a grading. About the third, Wetlesen says this:

> However, not all persons are conscious of it, and those who are, do not have an equally clear and distinct idea of it. This degree of conscious awareness and clarity brings in a quantitative element, which makes it possible to talk about degrees of freedom after all.

However, in this latter case we talk about degrees of freedom₂, and not about degrees of absolute freedom, which would sound rather queer in any case. (p. 396)

What Wetlesen says here about gradual strategies suits a rather narrow concept: A "quantitative element" makes it possible to talk about degrees. In part because of his tendency to associate degrees with quantification, he attributes negative characteristics to the "gradual strategy of liberation." Such strategies, however, require *wide* concepts of grading, concepts in which discontinuities are not excluded. Higher levels of understanding do not develop "out of" the lower. New qualities appear abruptly.[37]

SPINOZA'S WAY AND BUDDHIST MEDITATION

Wetlesen establishes some important parallels between Spinoza and Buddhism:

As mentioned earlier, it appears that Spinoza's chief remedy against the passions (cp. 5P4Sch quoted above) has a close affinity to Buddhist insight meditation (*vipassanā-bhāvanā*). Like insight meditation it starts with a certain kind of mindfulness or awareness; it goes on to a particular kind of insight concerning the ontological status of external things, and culminates in that kind of adequate cognition, or wisdom, which alone can liberate a person in the absolute sense.

I believe the first of these points is brought out quite clearly in 5P3&Dem&Cor and 5P4:

5P3&DEM&COR

An affect which is a passion ceases to be a passion as soon as we form a clear and distinct idea of it.

An affect which is a passion is a confused idea (3AffGenD). If, therefore, we form a clear and distinct idea of this affect, the idea will not be distinguished from this affect, except by reason, in so far as the affect is referred to the mind alone (2P2l&Sch), and therefore (3P3) the affect will cease to be a passion.

The better we are aware of an affect (*quo nobis est notior*), the more it is within our power, and the less the mind suffers from it.

5P4

There is no affection of the body of which we cannot form some clear and distinct conception.

The second point I think is brought out in 5P2, which I quoted at the beginning of this section (p. 198).

> If a person clearly and distinctly sees that his perceptions of things and egos in his life world are projections of his own imagination, he will develop what the Buddhists call insight, namely insight into the impermanence of things (*anicca*) and the unsubstantiality of egos (*anattā*). Thereby he overcomes the ignorance (*avijjā*) which was a necessary condition for his bondage under the passions (*dukkha*), and attains freedom instead. (pp. 198–199)

As far as I can see, Spinoza *can* plausibly be interpreted, as Wetlesen suggests. It is an important, worthwhile interpretation. It makes it possible to accommodate central parts of Buddhist theory and practice within a philosophical framework keenly studied in the West (cf. p. 200). In fairness to Buddhist traditions, we must keep in mind that they contain a rich variety of conceptions, and that we are here dealing with only one.

What I am now going to say is not an argument against Wetlesen's interpretation, but an alternative. The work required to get "a clear and distinct idea of a passion" may be, and has been, conceived as an analysis of the kind worked out by Freud and later "depth" psychologists. At least that much is established, that for a person to get a deep insight into an affective-cognitive complex acquired in infancy is extremely difficult and takes a long time. The trust in substantial egos and permanent things is acquired in infancy. The Buddhist theory of insubstantiality (as interpreted by Wetlesen) undermines or destroys conceptual frameworks acquired in infancy. So, it seems very strange, from the point of view of psychology, that any kind of *instantaneous* clarity could be brought about. More likely, there may be a gradual and partial elucidation of passions. This does not preclude that a high degree of clarity may all of a sudden break through the barriers necessary to invade consciousness. We know of such happenings from the study of religious conversion. (Deception is, however, more frequent than genuine sudden change of personality.)

What insight meditation might bring about is a sudden, fundamental change of *the general conscious, abstract conception of the world and the ego.*

The particular cognitive-conative complexes are largely left as they are, but they are somehow seen at a distance even in the personal interactions of the sage with his or her disciples and the community. Spinoza *may* be interpreted in harmony with this—but it strikes me as unlikely that any change in the abstract *conception* of the world and the ego can permanently change the person. We have to observe behavior and attitudes during work in the community. The new conception may be an inspiration and a source of strong motivation, but it would normally take years, I think, to change the structure of the interaction between person and environment. Human beings cannot, however, gain deep conceptions independently of such structures. We show our most genuine conceptions in action. The rest is likely to be dishonest or superficial.

The levels of freedom in the sense of Spinoza have to do with a multiplicity of like relations. Whatever the intensity and depth of an instantaneous experience, one's genuine conceptions change only gradually.

Absolute freedom is possible to the extent that one's actions have *internal* causes and *internal* effects, according to Wetlesen. Interaction with the environment, however, continues as before or with even more pervasive external causes and effects if the sage gets a worldwide following. Spinoza's idea of disconnecting passions from external objects does not entail a kind of life within the self. The status of self is precarious, anyhow, both for Spinoza and for Mahayana Buddhism.

CONCLUDING REMARKS

The many theses or hypotheses put forth by Wetlesen are supported explicitly through careful references to the works of Spinoza and others. A serious attempt to maintain opposite views ought to use the same excellent technique.

This essay has not consistently been such an attempt. It simply aimed to make some of the hypotheses better known and to suggest alternative interpretations.

According to Wetlesen's Spinoza, the supremely free human being is one of introvert tranquility. The foregoing comments favor an activist interpretation: The free human being is a wise human being permanently and with increasing momentum on the road to still higher levels of freedom. The supremely free shows perfect equanimity and forceful, rich, and deep affects and is active in a great variety of ways, corresponding to the many "parts of the body," and all of them bound up with increasing understanding—and certainly including social and political acts. Meditative tranquility may be one of the free human being's methods for getting freer, but not a stable characteristic of his or her life.

This image of the sage has in common with (a certain variety of) Mahayana Buddhism the idea that the higher the level of freedom reached by an individual, the more difficult it becomes to increase the level without increasing that of all other beings, human and nonhuman. The obstacle to individualistic freedom is deep-seated solidarity. It again rests on identification with all beings. The individual self develops into the universal self. (In general "relationism," the term *self* can, and ought to, be avoided.)

The trend of reasoning pursued by Wetlesen leads also toward Mahayana Buddhism in the sense that the highest freedom cannot be a lonely freedom, or rather, this freedom cannot be reached going alone and cannot be consummated alone. I am objecting to the conception of an absolute, instantaneous freedom that is supposed to be *higher* than the freedom of the wise human being supremely active through a development reached not without painful labor and danger.

What is more, various methods of meditation developed within Mahayana Buddhism might be accounted for within the framework of a Spinozistic philosophy. Considering the growing appreciation of serious meditational practices in the West, the possibility of conceiving them within the broad and deep framework of such a philosophy must be greeted with joy.

Freedom, Self, and Activeness, According to Spinoza[38]

A free thing is said in Part One, Definition 7, of the *Ethics* to be one that is determined to act or to be active solely through, from, or by itself (*a se sola ad agendum determinatur*). The phrase "be active" is crucial, because according to Spinoza, some emotions are forms of *agere* [to be active], but are scarcely actions in any standard use of the phrase "to act."

That is, we act when *we* cause and are not caused. The "we" here is identified with the self, "we our*selves*." The relation to "substance" is such that we cannot be absolutely active. We are intrinsically joined with other things, the *res particulares*. But even if we ourselves can never be the absolutely whole cause of an action, we can cause adequately for our own interests. To a finite extent, we are free and determine our actions. Considering what Spinoza says in Parts Four and Five, Definition 7 might have contained the qualification "absolute" or might have left out "*sola*." This would have made it easier to formulate consistent interpretations of his system.

Spinoza's account of self-preservation (3P6, 3P7, etc.) differs from that of Hobbes and others of his time. His account is highly suited to the use of *self-realization* or *preservation* as a basic term. Here are some important theorems derived from an interpretation of parts of the *Ethics* along those lines:

> All particular things strive to increase their level of being in themselves.
> All particular things strive to increase their power.
> All particular things strive to increase their level of freedom.
> To strive for self-perseveration mutually implies to strive for higher levels of being in oneself.

To strive for self-perseveration mutually implies to strive for higher
    levels of freedom.

To strive for self-perseveration mutually implies increase in power.

Increase in self-perseveration mutually implies increase in perfection.

Increase in self-perseveration mutually implies a state of joy.

There is no thing that has zero level of self-perseveration.

All in all, there is sufficient textual evidence that the term *self-realization* may be, but not must be, adopted in an interpretation of the *Ethics*. If
we adopt it, we get a number of theorems corresponding to those above.
For example, "An increase in self-realization is equivalent to an increase in
being in oneself."

Of particular importance for gestalt ontology is the intrinsic relation of
self-perseveration (or self-realization) and Spinoza's concept of *hilaritas*,
pervasive cheerfulness. According to Spinoza, "joy either affects all parts of
mind and body equally, increasing the total power, or unequally, increasing power, but unevenly." At least when intense, the unevenness directly
impedes the development of the neglected parts. In that case, there may be
no increase in total power, understanding, or perfection.

Because of the internal relationship between joy and activeness, we can
formulate theorems of the kind already quoted:

A state of (pervasive) cheerfulness is also a state in which we increase
    our level of being in ourselves.

A state of (pervasive) cheerfulness is also a state of a general increase
    in the understandability of oneself through oneself.

These internal relations are understandable when we accept that the content
of reality, as spontaneously experienced, has gestalt character. It is through
a kind of organic unity of perception, observation, apperception, and relation to a self with experience components of power, freedom, and joy that
Spinozistic equivalences obtain adequate meaningfulness.[39] Otherwise, they
may seem plainly false or paradoxical.

One is reminded of the Zen poet speaking about a sorrowful branch of
a tree. The Westerner says the sorrow is in the poet and projected out to
the branch. The gestalt ontological Spinozist rejects both statements. In one
grasp, there is a gestalt combining the poet's experience, the branch, and the
sorrowfulness. Discursive thinking is helped by an analytical breakup into
three items, but it need not affect our appreciation of the gestalt character
of our rich and deep spontaneous experience of reality.

Section 5:

PROBLEMS AND WAYS FORWARD

Industrial Society, Postmodernity, and Ecological Sustainability[1]

THE HUMAN CONDITION

It is a trait that belongs to human beings, and only human beings as far as we know, to try to make a kind of survey of their existence, to sort out what is of primary value and what they regard more or less with indifference; what they need and what are just whimsical wishes.

On their way to decreasing their own whimsicality and thoughtlessness, people in industrial societies like to learn about the problems that other people in other cultures have grappled with. This leads inevitably to rather broad and general talk, not just *small narratives*—a much-cherished term in deconstructive postmodernist literature. It leads to investigations that are immense in their breadth of perspective and to results that are always open to doubt and correction.

What follows reflects some thoughts by two sorts of human beings, those who for many years lived in a nonindustrial country and those who have spent many years together with tiny living creatures in grand mountains. Both sorts are, in a sense, products of modern Western industrial societies —but not mere products. Because the reflections cover a vast terrain, they lack the elaboration and concreteness that we need in our attempts to understand and modify our behavior in concrete situations.

Comparing nonindustrial with industrial societies, including the fate of local communities, one sees that many of the nonindustrialized societies have shown a continuity and strength that the industrialized societies cannot hope to achieve, because industrial societies are unsustainable ecologically. Industrialized societies also seem unable to stop ethical erosion and increased criminality, including those in the fifteen- to twenty-three-year-old age group.

Surveying the situation today, one sees also that the attraction of the industrial societies' *material* richness and technical acumen is overwhelming even the very young people in nonindustrial societies. This situation is tragic for at least two reasons. First, it would be ecologically catastrophic to have five billion people behaving as people in the industrial societies behave. Second, it is unrealistic to expect that substantial increases in material affluence can be reached in nonindustrial societies without unacceptable levels of criminality and the erosion of feelings of fellowship and mutual dependence.

Using the term *modern* to relate to the emergence of the culture of the industrial countries, one may still hope that today's nonindustrial societies will experience *a development from premodern to postmodern* cultures. The development of the industrial societies has brought humanity into a blind alley. The postmodern state of affairs implies the satisfaction of the vital economic needs of the total population, but not affluence. The key slogan would be "Enough is enough." When vital economic needs are satisfied, there is *enough* in terms of material richness. Of course, there are other forms of richness—in principle, limitless richness.

The near future of the industrial countries, let us say, the period until 2050, should emphasize a reduction in the use of energy and in material production, until the countries reach a level attainable by the total human population without the danger of gigantic catastrophes. The next step would be to reach *full* ecological sustainability.

In the years after World War II, a mighty slogan asked for a vast increase (mostly material) in production. When production and productivity in the richest countries soared as never before, a new powerful slogan appeared: "Consume! Consume!" because of overproduction. Today, this reason is replaced by an appeal to consume to overcome unemployment. The notorious appeal of the retail analyst Victor Lebow promoted consumption to relieve overproduction, but otherwise, the appeal provides an amusing picture of the strange sort of economy prevalent in the highly industrialized countries: "Our enormously productive economy ... demands that we make consumption our way of life, that we convert the buying and use of goods into rituals, that we seek our spiritual satisfaction, our ego satisfaction, in consumption ... we need things consumed, burnt up, worn out, replaced, and discarded at an ever increasing rate."[2]

The contribution to the ecological crisis by a minority of half a billion people has been such that an acceptable level of interference in the ecosystems by ten times as many people must be very much smaller per half billion. In the near future, "the total unecological product" created yearly by the industrial countries should be at such a level that, multiplied by ten, it would not point toward gigantic catastrophes. If we call the per-capita sum total of unecological consequences by production for a given community or country ΣP_u and that of consumption ΣC_u and the number of people in the community or country N, the total unecological consequences of policies ΣU may be put into a form looking like an equation:

$$\Sigma U = (\Sigma P_u + \Sigma C_u) \times N$$

The ΣU may represent a local community, a region, a country, or that of humanity in general.

For industrial societies, their ΣU_I should not be greater than 10 percent of the total ΣU_T. Without substantial progress toward that goal occurring each year in the industrial societies, this will be difficult to accomplish.[3]

As a firm supporter of the deep ecology movement, I hold that a decrease in consumption and a slow decrease in population will *not* necessarily result in a decrease in the quality of life. There will be a transition period, during which some people living according to the slogan "Enough is never enough" will have difficulties. But provided the downscaling is effectuated with a strong sense of justice, major uprisings may not occur.

It is an indication of a narrow time perspective when people reject the idea of a slow decrease in population because there will be too many old, unproductive people compared with younger, productive ones. The undesired ratio will make itself felt only for a short transition period, and the perspective we need covers hundreds of years.

DISRESPECT OF ONE'S OWN NONINDUSTRIAL CULTURES

Since World War II, the general *Western* disrespect for nonindustrial cultures has changed into a deep and serious respect among an increasing minority. In the same period, disrespect in the nonindustrial cultures of *their* own culture seems to have increased formidably, especially among the young. Among the factors contributing to this are an equally formidable increase in tourism and smart sales campaigns.

Depreciation is often expressed in front of representatives of the West. In Beding and other Sherpa communities of Garwal Himalaya, monks had libraries of old Tibetan scripts, for example, prayers directed to Tseringma ("the long good life's mother"), a formidable 7,146-meter-high peak directly above the village. In the 1950s and 1960s, the villagers showed reluctance to admit that they had such things. People hid such documents as shameful signs of backwardness. They were ashamed of their tradition of a cult of holy mountains going back many hundreds (or thousands?) of years. Their daily prayers to the mountain were beautifully written down and, until the twentieth century, regarded as treasures. How were scholars able to obtain such old documents? By buying them? No—by living among the families and showing *respect*. Then they could get the old scrolls as gifts. Otherwise, the scrolls might be destroyed.

Depreciation of one's own local or regional culture may be a worldwide phenomenon among young people, but nothing known in human history can be compared to what is happening in our time. Traditional cultures everywhere are under severe pressure—mostly with fatal results.

Disrespect of one's own culture includes disrespect of the land. In the Beding area and other Sherpa areas of Nepal, the forest was respected and no living trees were cut down for fuel. Each tree was looked upon as something that had its own life, it own interest, its own dignity. With the breakdown of customs, this deep ecology attitude vanished. The enormous mountaineering expeditions increased the mobility of the Sherpas, who were hired by the thousands to carry water—and often to heat it using wood—for daily hot showers for the sahibs. These practices generated completely different attitudes toward mountains and forests: disrespect of holiness, purely instrumental attitudes toward timber, wood, and fuel. Deforestation above 9,000 feet began in earnest. Without trees as cover, erosion started on a grand scale. Today, practically nothing is left. Nepal became an "export country," exporting hundreds of millions of tons of soil to India. The rivers brought much of the soil to the giant Indian dams, built largely through misguided efforts at "development," and became filled with silt.

With no cultural restraints and little Western scientific knowledge, the destruction of Nepal gradually reached gigantic proportions. Immigration from the countryside to the city of Kathmandu accelerated. The young were not willing to walk all day for fuel. They would rather live without dignity in Kathmandu.

A young, exceptionally gifted Sherpa who had been with many expeditions got the opportunity to start a sports shop in Canada, but he returned to his own country after a while. He expressed in a few words his reason for going back: "Here we enjoy peace with ourselves." So many of the people he met on expeditions and in Canada, evidently, had no peace within themselves. They wished to be different from what they were; they worked hard to develop, achieve, succeed, and be better. They could not let time flow. Unfortunately, very few young people have the necessary faculty of *independent* judgment, nor do they have the opportunity to compare the Western quality of life with their own in their "poor" countries. I am not referring here to the half billion people in nonindustrial countries who are desperately poor, who lack the most basic means to live a decent life.

WESTERN BELIEF THAT WE PROJECT PERSONAL TRAITS ONTO NATURAL OBJECTS

In traditional, nonindustrial societies, we find more and stronger "personification" of natural forces and nonhuman living beings. The tendency to personify is often said to be archaic, meaning that it precedes the great religions and cultures. The term *anthropomorphism* is often used in a pejorative sense for the erroneous attribution of specifically human traits to entities that are not human or not even capable of sense experience. Before starting to drink beer together, the Sherpas threw a little beer in the direction of Tseringma—beer for *her*.

If a big mountain precipice may be spontaneously experienced as dark and evil, it *is*, in an important sense, dark and evil. If this experience motivates us in the West to throw a stone at the mountain as a punishment for being evil, we have succumbed to a mistake. In a nonindustrial culture, throwing beer or a stone is meaningful—or was meaningful—but not within *our* conceptual framework.

Animals, plants, and some nonliving things may be experienced as evil or good. They may be experienced as arrogant, proud, insolent, and self-domineering or humble, sheepish, crestfallen, and so on. Education in industrial countries is strongly centered on a subject-object cleavage: Some traits of animals are real and objective attributes; others are said to be *projected* onto the animals. The latter traits are merely subjective.

In practical life, the distinction is a plus, but it downplays spontaneous experience with its richness, intensity, and depth. It favors thinking in terms of abstract relations and structures of reality, not in terms of content. When we depart and decide to meet again on a mountain, the mountain must be defined in terms of our society and culture, defined as an *object* we have *in common*. This, however, does not identify the mountain as an object "in itself."

Our vast abstractions are momentous cultural achievements specific to Western culture. Contemporary mathematical physics is an example. Here the link to spontaneous experience is extremely indirect and spotty, but strong because of the high level of mathematical deduction. Because of its severe limitation of modeling abstract structure, it expresses an intercultural type of knowledge, that is, intercultural if one does not rely on popularization but sticks to the severe mathematical form of what is asserted. In that case, the cultural background disappears! The equations are intercultural, but any *interpretations* in terms we are acquainted with in our daily life depend on specific cultures. Communication among experts is compatible with deep cultural differences among the participants.

There is no physical *world* with specifically physical *content*. There is a reality, the content of which we have direct contact with only through and in our spontaneous experiences. It is a reality of infinite richness.

No dichotomies of fundamental character seem adequate to describe it. Distinctions between physical and mental "worlds," or between subjective and objective worlds, are not adequate for describing reality. The philosophical reaction against taking the latter distinction as fundamental has increased in strength since the 1890s. Should we, mused A. N. Whitehead, stop admiring the beauty of a rose and instead admire the poet who admirably sings about it? Would not that be reasonable if the rose *in itself* is neither beautiful nor ugly? Is there "objectivity" only in electrons and similar colorless items? The beauty of the rose itself is spontaneously experienced and is as real as anything can be.

WESTERN SCHOOLS AND EUROPEAN UNITY

The school systems of the industrial states are all adapted to the common, very special way of life in those states. Unawareness of this limitation discourages reforms that would widen the perspective; consequently, the schools remain provincial.

A major concern in schools that attempt less one-sided perspectives is for the future of the children: How will they get jobs when their knowledge does not fit in with the established order? If the parents are economically rich, they can help the youngsters get along in the unique and strange world of the industrial-growth societies, in spite of their "far out" schooling—but otherwise, the young tend to get into trouble. Therefore, educators often give up the most radical sorts of reforms.

Let us look at some of the curricula children now have to learn, starting with mathematics. Mathematical instruction today is completely Western-ized and utilitarian, reflecting the typical Western emphasis on proof. There is no trace of Chinese or Indian old mathematical culture. Little is taught about bold mathematical conjectures such as those in number theory; little is taught about endless fractions and orders of the infinite. With more ade-quate education in mathematics, children are encouraged to love the subject and tend to continue to relish it after leaving school. Mathematics in itself is an ecologically very innocent hobby! Masses of excellent paper are wasted every day in schools, but some could be used to design geometrically inter-esting buildings.

Proper mathematics should, of course, not lack instruction about the existence of proofs and, in later years, of axiomatic or formal systems in gen-eral—but only basic notions, "axiomatic thinking," not complicated appli-cations. Perhaps three or four different proofs of the Pythagorean Theorem and a couple of other simple proofs would suffice to help students under-stand the miracle of proofs and—later—allow them grasp the *essentials* of deductive systems.

What about chemistry? Children love to play with (more or less) harmless chemicals. Let them see miracles, such as how two colorless liquids, brought together, may create fantastic colors! In organic chemistry, they may learn about the long series like CH_4, C_2H_5, and C_3H_8, . . . , and enjoy building molecules. Isomers of C_4H_{10}! Very inexpensive and elegant colored tools are available today. They may learn about colors used by Rembrandt and others. Children appreciate crystals, and with a magnifying glass, they may enjoy learning about some of the most beautiful forms. They can combine this with some mineralogy and petrology: the joy of finding stones, learning to enjoy natural things, of which there are enough for all. At the university level, there should be an opportunity to go deeply into modern, theoretical "hard" chemistry.

Let me now mention history. A major guideline is to focus on the local (bioregional) and the global, with less emphasis on the national. There should be more about interlocal movements, less about internationalism, more emphasis on cultural diversity and the Fourth World.

The distinction between global and international is important for many reasons. One of them is that few nations have much power, while the great global corporations have more than most nations, shaping economic life everywhere.

It has now been more than half a century since the school textbooks of the Scandinavian countries were "adjusted" to be compatible with one another.

Until then, a war between them was, as a matter of habit, described systematically, with each participant reporting and ethically judging what happened according to that participant's own extremely one-sided propaganda.

There is no hope of establishing peaceful, green societies as long as conflicts are described in a way that fosters prejudice and hatred. Equally pernicious is the underestimation of social and political calamities attributable to the destruction of one's own land. The tentative *history* of ecological calamities is now available, and the material should be integrated into school textbooks.[4]

Until recently, "world history" for children—at least in Europe—has been atrociously anthropocentric. The history of the planet and of life should be in focus as part of the global perspective. The history of bioregions takes care of the local perspective.

Social and cultural anthropology cannot be completely absorbed into textbooks of history, but there is room for some material on these subjects. The outlook of economic anthropology is relevant: Children should know that the economic system they are part of in the West is an extremely special kind. In the long view, general cultural and, especially, religious institutions have been stronger in comparison with the economic. In the industrial countries, the history of capitalism since the fifteenth century tells us a lot about our successes and our failures.

Here is not the place to go through the curriculum of schools and colleges. Wide differences of approach are needed, but the state of affairs today is deplorable: Pupils aged six to sixteen (what I call children herein) in the rich industrial societies are generally imbued with ways of thinking adapted to a kind of society that, hopefully, will disappear in their own lifetime. As has always been the case, though, schools mirror society, and the transition to green societies must occur simultaneously at many sections of the long frontier of change.

As they learn history in the schools of the future, our children and grandchildren may be confronted with sentences like the following: "The productivity of industry and agriculture increased exponentially in the richest industrial countries in the last half of the twentieth and early twenty-first centuries. A wild consumerism not only threatened the conditions of life on our planet, but also was accompanied by an impoverishment of relations between people, a degradation of fellowship, and an increase of asocial attitudes. (New phenomenon: criminal careers for children between eight and sixteen years of age.) The economy of a country was not expected to adapt to its culture, but the culture to the economy."

People in the developing countries do not seem to realize that the consumerism of the West is doomed. They have no chance to see that there is no future for the kind of life they observe the tourists living. Here is one of the great challenges in the years to come. What can be done to change the picture those people have of our common future? What can be done to assist a transition from the preindustrial to the postindustrial?

A combined focus on the local and the global is impossible under conditions of *economic* globalization, as the latter term is now used. *Economic globalization* is somewhat misleading. A better term might be *globalization of the four freedoms*, referring to the so-called four freedoms of the Treaty of Rome, which was the basis for the European Common Market and *is still* at the core of the present-day European Union (EU). The document's style of globalization implies successive expansion of its "four freedoms" until it also covers trade among the three giants, the European Union, the United States (and Canada), and Japan, and reluctantly over the rest of the globe. The term *four freedoms* refers to the free (duty-free) crossing of goods and materials through borders, the free flow of services, the freedom to compete for jobs anywhere (people), and the freedom of capital to flow across any borders. The four freedoms *imply four prohibitions*, the violation of which will be punished by the authorities. Namely, the freedoms involve strong, adequate *protection*—for social, medical, ecological, or other reasons of cultural relevance—against the import of certain goods or services, or against certain kinds of flow of foreign capital into a local, regional, or any other limited area, for example, the Arctic coast of Norway.

Representatives of the EU tempted politicians and the public in the four new countries that in 1994 had expressed a wish to join by emphasizing transition periods with less strict negative rules. In the long run, though, the overall tendency is to prepare for tighter and tighter economic unions—like that of the United States. The outlook is a world of *consumers* getting more products more cheaply than ever before through wider mobility. The only diversity of cultures here is one compatible with the supreme rules of a free world market!

Norway is the only Nordic country with family farms, and there is a definite agriculture, not just agribusiness. To protect this culture and to make it economically possible for its practitioners to survive, Norway "subsidizes" its agriculture. That is, there is a *transfer of income* so that the farmers can offer the public their products at low prices, prices that are not high enough to cover farm expenses. In an important sense, it is not the farmer, but the public, that is subsidized and protected against further increases of urbanized youth. The public has to pay more for milk, bread, and other agricultural commodities than it would on the *world market*. We are asked to destroy the farm culture in favor of city culture.

The Norwegian market today is not completely a part of the cheap world market. Nevertheless, what Norwegians pay for their food is absurdly little, usually about 15 percent of their average income. That is, expenses for transportation (private car, etc.) and other goods are much greater. We must expect that in future green societies, food calculated as a percentage of income will cost us substantially more than it does today. One may say that on average, today's cost to satisfy vital *needs* is only a small fraction of the cost of satisfying *wants*—or to be more exact, a small fraction of the cost of satisfying wants that are "normal" in the rich industrial countries. The economy of Norway is capitalist, but closer to a mixed economy than that of, say, the United States.

One may, very roughly, class as a mixed economy an economic system with a free market within a framework that permits fairly strong rules governing the operation of the market. Such rules make Norway, for example, capable of protecting certain activities—agricultural, industrial, and others—from foreign competition and, ultimately, from the world market. The government has recently said yes to a new round of the General Agreement on Tariffs and Trade (GATT), and this turns Norway into a more streamlined capitalist country, distancing itself from the ideals of a mixed economy. (Unhappily, the term *mixed economy* is sometimes used for any capitalist system having one or more rules protecting the environment. This makes the United States and every other industrial state mixed-economy countries. It is hoped that this erosion of the terminology will not continue.)

What is the current status of efforts to promote green economies in relation to all this? If a country can sell products more cheaply than certain others because it has a higher degree of irresponsible ecological policy, the four freedoms prevent the more responsible countries from keeping the products out. Consumers cannot be expected to keep track of the ecological atrocities in other countries. It is therefore unlikely that a green economy, at least in the near future, will suddenly be established in a single country. In the short run, countries with the most irresponsible policies will profit from export, but in the long run, other states will presumably introduce economic sanctions in favor of their own exports.

From the viewpoint of the Treaty of Rome, the individuality, or "personality," of local economic activity cannot be ideal, because of the lack of fierce competition and the failure to emphasize maximization of profits. The machinery of economic activity as conceived by supporters of the Treaty of Rome is taken to be universalizable, common to all possible cultures. That is, the introduction may always take place, and it will change the culture. This way of describing the treaty is, however, too simple for serious debate. Minor differences in an economic system may be tolerated, even supported—for example, because a difference favors tourism or because a difference belongs to the simple cultural traits of which the population is particularly proud.

At the moment, applicants for membership in the European Union will, as mentioned, be permitted to continue *for a time* particular activities inconsistent with the Treaty of Rome. The time is mostly longer than the interval between political elections. This makes it easier for particular governments to join the EU because many negative and controversial consequences of membership will not manifest themselves until after the government's time in power.

In concluding, I admit that centralization of power today is furthered by a greater number of benevolent people than ever before—people and institutions interested in fostering more trade, in letting people consume and travel more than ever. Until recently, it was widely held that capitalist competition leads to war. Today, it may lead instead to systems of tacit and explicit agreement between corporations in order to keep this system from failing. In Japan and the United States, the consensus is that wars of trade between the two giants are not, in the long run, in the interest of industry. The preferred situation, it is said, is for both to have a free market comprising Japan, the United States, and Europe, but with the leaders of the corporations forming mutual agreements aimed at avoiding undesirable kinds of competition. We might end up with a culture, including education, that is adapted to the world market rather than the other way around. Because of the central idea of "the more trade, the better," combined with a vastly increased mobility of people and goods, ecological problems can only increase.

OUR WAY IS BACK TO SUSTAINABILITY, NOT TO OLD FORMS OF SOCIETY

It is tempting to see "us"—members of the rich industrial countries—as "moderns," more or less disregarding nine-tenths of humanity. This major portion of humans also live today; they belong to the contemporary scene, but are considered relics of the past.

As to the exact delimitation of modernity in terms of age, one proposal is to think of the time from the European Renaissance to the present; another proposal is to include only the period from the start of the industrial revolution, covering about two centuries at least. Not without some arrogance, many of us now look forward to the creation of "postindustrial" societies.

The following reflections, colored by personal experiences, result from an urge to examine industrial society in the light of values established in nonindustrial, "traditional" societies and in light of lifeways that are ecologically fully sustainable. Such has been the life of human beings for long periods. Alaska was inhabited for thousands of years by people with ecologically sustainable, diverse cultures. In Norway, people followed the retreat of the ice eight thousand years ago. As soon as reindeer could prosper, human beings prospered.

Ecological sustainability was only one characteristic of traditional societies, and it did somewhat reflect the small numbers of people. Many of those societies we would class as ecologically unsustainable if they had had millions of members. The reindeer-based, very loose societies were dependent to some extent upon the ratio between the number of reindeer and the number of human beings.

Of course, there is "no way back" in general, but it is important to remember that global unsustainability is something very new and that for a wide variety of stable cultures, our planet was a tremendously big, rich, eminently hospitable, and benign world. Difficulties had to arise only when human beings pressed away other human beings from the areas where life was easiest, or at least not a greater challenge than desired.

It is to be hoped that an ever-increasing minority will view unsustainability as an undignified, stupid—if not plainly ridiculous—state of affairs. One also hopes that an increasing minority will express this attitude with increasing boldness—but without arrogance, since few activists can avoid making use of the facilities offered in the industrial societies.

In short, there is no way back to societies that belong to the past, but there is a way back to ecological sustainability. In fact, there is not just one way but many ways, so that widely different, sustainable cultures are possible. Valuable contributions to the study of these ways are not lacking, but they are mostly unknown to the public. Unavoidably, large segments of the public have the feeling that "environmentalists" want to turn back time. When some of these enthusiasts announce, "Back to the Pleistocene!" the suspicion is well-founded. The indication of ways to go does not, of course, amount to elaborate plans and blueprints. Such absence of detail has been the rule, not the exception, in all new major human undertakings. It has never stopped those who have the proper motivation to work for change.

There are not only rough plans of how to solve some of the most serious ecological problems, but also even tentative—very tentative—estimates of the costs in money and labor. A dollar estimate was published in *State of the World, 1988*.[5] An updated 1994 rough estimate could be—let us say—$250 billion annually. Here I shall only mention some theoretical aspects of such an estimate.

Owing to the current lack of institutional infrastructure necessary to use such a large sum rationally, the $250-billion-per-year expenditure may not be reached until ten years from now, that is, from 2005 onward. The sum, both in money *and in work*, would be paid almost entirely by the rich countries. The vast activity *within* the rich countries in preparation for the undertaking would demand workers in great numbers with a great variety of skills. Given present levels of unemployment, there is no doubt that the necessary number could be mobilized. Production, in the wide sense of theoretical economics, would increase. It would be registered as increased gross domestic product (GDP).

The undertaking, mostly done by the people in nonindustrial countries, but in close cooperation with people from the industrial countries, would be accomplished only through the substantial mobilization of people and capital. As an example, consider reforestation. Today, several hundred million people lack fuel for cooking their food or cleaning their drinking water—the distance to the nearest wood is simply too far. Under such circumstances, planted trees are normally used for fuel as soon as they reach the size of bushes. Therefore, the people must be offered other kinds of fuel for at least twenty years. Even then, a great number of honest people must act as protectors of the growing plants. In short, reforestation is a *socially* complex, labor-intensive undertaking, and the economies of both the industrial and the nonindustrial countries would be greatly stimulated by reforestation.

Inevitably, the consumption, not the production, of the rich countries would decrease. The increased consumption would come from the nonindustrial countries and would not interfere with the increased GDP in rich countries. GDP is *not* a measure of domestic consumption, as is often thought. If Norway produces a thousand tiny hydroelectric plants for use in poor countries, it decreases its unemployment and reduces poverty among others.

Global reforestation will not, of course, mean complete reforestation, but reforestation insofar as it both ensures ecological sustainability and meets the vital needs of the people. As already mentioned, however, the change would start out slowly, even if money and a workforce were available. It is not like mobilizing in times of war in a country whose military institutions have been prepared well in advance. Large-scale rational and ethically responsible reforestation is a new sort of undertaking that requires highly educated, corruption-resistant people. It will take a long time. One generation? Three generations? Nobody knows. There is, however, no point of no return. Compared with the investment of life, work, and money in a great war, the investment needed to overcome the ecological crisis is very small. Moreover, the work of a determined minority could get the work started in earnest.

Sustainability! The Integral Approach[6]

The Greek philosopher Diogenes of Sinope, or Diogenes in the Barrel, is well-known because of his meeting with Alexander the Great. When Alexander, standing in front of Diogenes' barrel, asked him to express a wish, he is said to have simply answered, "Please stop blocking my sun!" Alexander could have granted him much more. The philosopher could have had gifts produced through great expenditures of energy and natural resources. Although Diogenes was active in the rich cultural life of Athens, this did not require any gifts of that kind. Diogenes' solution to his housing problem was a nonverbal expression of a globally, regionally, and locally sustainable lifestyle, and his answer was a verbal suggestion of the same. Alexander was reminded of the ecological innocence of vital needs, and—let us not forget Diogenes' proverbial wit and joyful, spontaneous character—the king got a lesson in "rich life, simple means." It is said that most followers of Diogenes through the centuries have misunderstood him, taking him to be a proponent of a simple, not a rich, life.

I mention Diogenes of Sinope to point out that classical Greek philosophy as well as philosophy in the Middle and Far East combined the verbal and the nonverbal. You were not a philosopher if you did not. Today, we still say that so-and-so is a philosopher and use the word for such a combination, but the intended range of philosophies seems small. People mostly have in mind what the professionals call popular Stoicism, or, to give another example, popular Epicureanism. The very special form of Western academic philosophy does not ask for a philosopher. No combination of theory and practice is called for. If it were, some of us would perhaps be called sustainers, practicing a philosophy that combines theories of biodiversity and sustainable development with an appropriate, or at least intended appropriate, lifestyle. There is much talk about a "new" ethics of respect for life on earth, but it does not focus on the lifestyle of those who emphatically agree. One strong reason for the neglect is the plain fact that the complexity and structural density of modern society make it practically impossible to combine the consistent use of simple means with participation in social and political struggles.

Depressing? Yes, but we may allow ourselves to say that Diogenes in the Barrel went too far. Here I follow Aristotle in advocating "everything with (philosophical) moderation." A practicing Indian philosopher perhaps also carried the concern for citizens' self-sufficiency and equal-mindedness too far when he, old and satisfied with life ("enough is enough"), brought together some wood, started a fire, placed himself on top, and cremated himself (in conformity with a practice that caused deforestation in certain localities). Incidentally, yoga of some sort is part of most classical Indian philosophies. They integrated theory and practice.

Fortunately, there are possibilities for decreasing the unsustainability and "un-universalizability" of the "average" lifestyles in economically rich countries without decreasing life quality. To exemplify such a decrease is a great aim for some who wish to be taken seriously in the present struggles.

Discussing various interpretations of the term *sustainable development*, we may start with the following formulation: There is sustainable development if, and only if, it meets the vital needs of the present-day human population without compromising the ability of future generations to meet their own vital needs. This formulation resembles those of the Brundtland Report, but with a major difference: the substitution of *vital needs* for just *needs*.[7] Lists of needs made by decision makers in the rich countries include items that clearly are exorbitant and not universalizable. Even the *desire and demand* for more parking space is generally described as a satisfaction of a *need*. Parking lots are often placed in urban locations, where children have had their precious playgrounds, or where people have long lived but cannot afford a car, or among residents who are incapable of resisting the destruction of their habitat.

Rich countries often accept "needs" that, if met, exclude sustainable development in every acceptable sense. The term *vital*, although vague and ambiguous, is a good starting point for a critical approach to the term *need* in its relation to *demand* in the marketplace of the world's rich countries.

If we postulate that human beings have a special ethical obligation toward their fellows, then anything that serves the vital needs of humanity takes priority. This does not mean, however, that we have no serious obligations toward nonhuman beings, classes and systems of such beings, or the earth as a whole. These obligations, though, are mainly negative: obligations related to destructive consequences of our exponentially increasing interference in the ecosystems.

As to the satisfaction of human vital needs, at present a substantial number of human beings live in a desperate state of poverty or oppression, which clearly prevents a minimum satisfaction of those needs. They live mostly in countries one may call poor, using an economic measuring rod, and the term *sustainable development* should there imply *sustainable economic progress*.

The implied task is gigantic, considering that the number of people in poor countries may soon double, but the area of cultivable land will not. Under similar circumstances, Europeans who immigrated to North and South America introduced vast unsustainability, including a decrease of human cultural diversity.

In a major victory for the global ecology movement, the World Commission for Environment and Development announced clearly that sustainable development unconditionally requires ecological sustainability. The consequences of this admission are far-reaching because ecological sustainability requires significant economic, technological, social, political, and cultural changes in most or all countries. Here I shall first dwell on a terminological consequence: The term *developing country* automatically implies "ecologically developed country."

If we retain the *underdeveloped/developed* terminology, we must therefore class all ecologically unsustainable countries as *underdeveloped* without the need to add the adverb *ecologically*. It is implied by our terminology that these countries are underdeveloped. The richest industrial country is not a developed country if it is not in a process of ecologically sustainable development.

A revised terminology has already been introduced for Norway: When will it rise from being underdeveloped to being a developing country? That is, when will the rate of unsustainability (globally measured) decrease in a stable way? My guess is that by the year 2020 this may well happen. As it is now, Norway, like the United States, has not turned the tide of pollution, energy consumption, and other variables that must be taken into account. Those who think this guess is rather pessimistic are likely to neglect our wide perspective: It is the global situation that counts, and we must take into consideration that in the years 2010, 2020, and onward, with an even bigger population and with economic growth in terms of GNP in the poorer countries, the projected level of Norwegian pollution, growing energy consumption, and so on cannot be tolerated. Talking about 2020, I have assumed that the political ability to take ecological problems seriously will increase, but not in any revolutionary way. This would require a vast increase of active interest within the Norwegian population at large—many more sustainers!

One may hold that it is wiser to modify the old usage of *developed*. When we encounter an old use of the term in discussions, we can easily ask what the term means, and then strongly discourage any use that might support the old belief that the rich industrial nations are developed and somehow able to show the poor countries the way to development. This belief is still not uncommon within the power elites of the poorer nations, I am afraid.

In the 1980s, it was out of the question for a wide group of politicians to declare that life on earth, or life in the universe, has any value in itself apart from the rather narrow serving of human needs and interests. It was out of the question to declare that the richness and diversity of life are also worthy of care for its own sake, in the sense that we feel it obvious to care for children for their own sake. Such thoughts could not have been incorporated into a report such as the Brundtland Report. By now, only one country, New Zealand, can show a public document that affirms intrinsic value. If, within a few years, such an affirmation becomes commonplace, it will not make much difference in human practice, but it will *add to the force of argumentation* in favor of generous, wide sustainability. "You *said* it has intrinsic value! Why don't you act accordingly?"

The formidable capacity of our brains makes it easy for us to "see ourselves in others," not only in other human beings but in every living being. Sometimes, it is even easier to identify with certain animals than with certain human beings. Compassion, aided by the brain, encompasses everything capable of pain. The interest, in a broad, easily understandable sense, of a tiny plant to live and blossom is obvious, and under suitable circumstances, we act to serve this interest. The definition of sustainable development cannot ignore these facts. A wide and deep perspective is obviously needed. Human capacity to think and to feel, human dignity, requires it. Our contemplation of the development of life on earth through countless millions of years, the development of the richness and diversity of life-forms, almost inevitably makes mature, informed human beings adopt a wide perspective. In short, we demand that full ecological sustainability mean or include the conservation of the richness and diversity of life-forms. We cannot slavishly accept the narrow interpretations of the Brundtland Report, interpretations that, I suspect, some of the signatories, including Gro Harlem Brundtland herself, personally find too narrow.

Let us look closely at the term *sustainable development* as it occurs in the

Brundtland Report: "Humanity has the ability to make development sustainable—to ensure that it meets the needs for the present without compromising the ability of future generations to meet their own needs."[8] Plausibly, but narrowly interpreted, the report might consider satisfactorily sustainable any actions compatible with the maximal destruction of life conditions on earth, the maximal extinction of life-forms, the maximal destruction of the habitats of life-forms, and maximal gross human interference with landscapes and ecosystems—*as far as* these maxima supposedly allow the satisfaction of human needs as those needs are conceived at any definite time. In addition, we must ask, Conceived by whom? It is clear that by "reforestation," many decision makers do not refer to getting back real forests. The artificial tree plantations with fast-growing trees do not support the biodiversity of a forest. The number of species in them may be one-fourth, or less, of those of a decimated forest. In the objection that one must distinguish the forest *itself* from the animal and plant life in it, the ignorance of ecosystem thinking is clear. The way is open for a maximal destruction that will only too late be seen as incompatible with the satisfaction of the vital needs of additional billions of people born in the years to come.

In the present conflicts, the usual narrow interpretations of "sustainable development" are convenient for planners of gigantic destructive policies, because it is difficult to convince people that future generations will lack the ability to take care of themselves in the aftermath of whatever we find suitable to do. People read about technological inventions, even revolutions, that are likely to push the limits of responsible growth indefinitely. They do not read about the lack of economic and political will to make global use of the inventions made even long ago.

Rejecting the narrow concepts of ecological sustainability, which a plausible interpretation of the Brundtland Report admits, some of us are on the outlook for definite, wider interpretations. Preferably these should not be completely implausible interpretations of the document but should be in harmony with what at least one of the twenty-two people writing the document had in mind. The criterion I use in the following formulation does not explicitly refer to human beings, but they and the richness and diversity of their cultures are implied:

> There is ecological sustainability if, and only if, the richness and
> diversity of life-forms are sustained.

Ecology helps us understand and watch out for the destruction of ecosystems and habitats. The terms *ecosystems* and *habitats* are not used in the above formulation, because it should be widely understood and be emotionally attractive. By "richness," I do not refer to abundance of specimens of species but to their wide distribution locally and regionally, provided that wide distribution is realized today or was recently realized and it is practicable to restore the former situations.

The criterion is applicable to the earth as a whole and to regions, nations, and societies, but only to some extent to localities. It is perhaps of little use to talk about ecological unsustainability, for example, in small areas or localities of monoculture or city developments. A region may be called sustainable even if there are plenty of localities of that kind. Otherwise, sustainability is utopian. The term *development*, however ambiguous, must be used because of its importance in policy documents. A terminology proposal:

> A *development* is ecologically sustainable if and only if there is a long-term trend that ensures, or that may justifiably be considered to ensure, ecological sustainability.

The special obligations we have for our own species require us in the long run to ensure that a population has what is necessary to provide the conditions for reaching the ultimate goals of humankind and satisfying vital needs. Beyond that, our obligations to life in general and the earth as a whole acquire priority. These obligations will in the future scarcely determine policies with wide sustainability as a goal. If the most exciting threats, such as those involving climatic change and the ozone layer, seem to be overcome, and if spectacular animals and limited plant biodiversity are saved, certain regions may be classed as developing in an ecologically sustainable way. In a broad sense, crude ecological unsustainability may still be at hand. There is a long way to go.

If some poorer countries reach ecological sustainability in the next decades, which one will be the first? Costa Rica? In this country, the education level of women is high, the standard of living is increasing, the government is interested, and numerous "parataxonomists" (raised in the country) and others help map out the fauna and flora and do an important job of increasing the respect for and joy of life. Furthermore, much is done to develop sustainable uses of tropical biodiversity, thus integrating concern for ecological sustainability in society. The cooperation of researchers and local people is flourishing. The ecologist Daniel H. Janzen is the most well-known researcher working along "social ecological" lines and collecting millions of dollars in aid for Costa Rican projects. All this activity decreases the ecological unsustainability in some ways, but large-scale deforestations still go on. Some researchers guess that only about 10 percent of the habitats will be saved from complete human domination with extensive regions of monocultures and asphalt. It is, therefore, a wide-open question when sustainability will be reached, if at all.

One may wish that all other tropical countries would develop in the auspicious way of Costa Rica. The corresponding amount of money that would have to be collected in the rich countries would not be in the range of millions, but billions. Benevolent bureaucracies would have to be available, and an army of ecologists and their assistants working together with the local populations.

The great Danish philosopher Søren Kierkegaard, the father of existentialism as a philosophical movement, insisted that human beings are always in "deep water." Their decisions must be made on the basis of a total integrated view, but systems like Hegel's are mere fiction. This implies, in principle, going back to ultimate premises and to a conception of the main goal of human life, be it pleasure, happiness, or achievement of some sort. It implies also that if you consider a certain question of immediate relevance for actions in your life, your community, or life on earth, you must have an answer, whether it is expressed through deliberate words or through deeds. Moreover, we should remember that even if we do not answer deliberately, our actions or lack of actions express answers.

In life, one cannot say, "Leave me out!" Ignorance and incompetence furnish explanations, but not an excuse—not automatically. The question "Are we informed to an extent that should be expected of us?" is relevant.

Crudely expressed, if it is an important decision either to turn right or to turn left, then to do neither also has important consequences. One answer may be "I am too tired to reflect. I'll go left!" This or similar kinds of answers must, of course, sometimes be tolerated. The main thing is the awareness, with equanimity, that a choice is made, anyhow.

The practicing philosopher feels an obligation to answer but does not thereby pretend that it is worthwhile for others to listen. Perhaps all our answers are imperfect.

Those who are serious about somehow decreasing unsustainability locally, regionally, or globally may contribute to the effort in specialized jobs (e.g., as researchers) or as generalists, showing as much as explaining their choices in life. They are then to be classed as *practicing philosophers*, whatever their degree of ignorance of academic philosophy. Sometimes this ignorance may be an advantage.

In our very special kind of culture in the rich countries of the West, verbal articulations in the form of reasons are highly appreciated. Somebody may ask, "What is your reason for valuing priority A over B?" You may have a reason R_1, but then you are asked, "What is your reason for accepting R_1 as adequate?" Suppose you answer with an R_2, or you admit that you do not pretend to have a sort of reason R_2 such that if it were untenable, you would give up the priority of A over B. That is, you stop the chain $R_1, R_2, \ldots R_n$, after the first number of the series. Generally speaking, such behavior is wise, because it is likely that sooner or later, you will give misleading reasons, reasons that do not really fit your ultimate or complex motivation. Today, though, we must dig deeper—our global perspective makes it necessary.

One of the many great achievements of Aristotle was a clear denial that we can prove everything we assert. We cannot give good reasons for everything. We stop somewhere, normally outside science, and doing this, we may, if appropriate, quote Aristotle. We can say that belief in the possibility of proving everything shows a lack of education and that we like to be considered educated.

My advice is to stop giving reasons when you announce something you personally find *intuitively* obviously true or correct, or something that you cannot imagine yourself giving up except for reasons you have never heard of and cannot see how they could be convincing. This is not dogmatism. You are no less philosophical or deep or scientific for stopping at a certain point to repeat again and again certain announcements without giving reasons. You are no worse off than mathematicians and logicians who repeatedly use the basic rules of inference, which they, by definition, cannot prove or validate scientifically.

Intuitively based announcements are common today. Here are some examples:

Every life-form has a worth of its own, independent of its usefulness for human beings.
Animals have a right to exist, no less of a right than that of human beings.
Life diversity is a good thing, independent of human usefulness.
Life on earth is a value even without human beings to value it.

Some philosophers offer reasons for these pronouncements; other people accept them without offering reasons; still others do not accept them and give reasons for that. They also stop giving reasons somewhere.

All this would be pointless to say except that, again and again, we see people who *unreasonably* feel guilty for not giving reasons. Or scientists hide or never announce their basic norms or evaluations because the norms lack "scientific" reasons.

Human beings are never wholly functionaries; they never behave wholly as functionaries. As specimens of adult, sane *Homo sapiens*, they are always responsible as persons. The timid "As I see it . . ." and "In my personal opinion . . ." are misplaced if ultimate views are at stake. You try to step outside yourself, try to be a *mere* witness to your own intuitions.

What about conflicting intuitions—are they not a cause of violence and war? Yes, but they are also a partial cause of peace, progress, and nonviolence of the most superb kind.

In summary, full global and regional biodiversity is necessary for full ecological sustainability. Full ecological sustainability is necessary for sustainable development. Biodiversity is required to satisfy the vital needs of humanity. All this is now generally acknowledged. That the biodiversity of this planet should be protected also for its own sake was first internationally recognized through the U.N. World Charter for Nature. The initiative to get this established was taken by a group of economically poorer nations. The U.N. General Assembly adopted the charter in 1982 by a vote of 111 to 1, with the United States casting the sole dissenting vote. Only a *rich* nation dissented!

It serves the cause of biodiversity to maintain that it has a value in itself apart from narrowly conceived usefulness for human beings. It also helps when people who maintain this value testify to its profound implications through their lifestyle, at least in some kinds of life situations.

High-level humanitarian norms justify ecologically negative policies. The policies, however, should be short-range. And often, these short-range, ecologically harmful policies can be avoided through the cooperation of rich and poor nations on a greater scale than ever before.

Because of its touchy nature, I wish to end this essay with a remark on the size of the human population as seen from a cultural-philosophical perspective: A future long-range, gradual decrease of the human population would somewhat increase the chances of full biodiversity, sustainable development, deep cultural diversity, and the prospect of satisfying vital needs and reaching cultural and philosophical goals.

Population Reduction: An Ecosophical View[9]

The population issue raises such diverse and deep questions that we need a total view as a conceptual framework. When the articulation of such a view is largely inspired by ecology, I call it an ecosophy. We need various ecosophies; I call mine Ecosophy T. In what follows, I do not defend any controversial part of that view, but very briefly formulate certain views that are widespread today and try to support them ecosophically.

Taken together, two propositions form point 4 of the deep ecology movement:

1. The flourishing of human life and cultures is compatible with a substantial decrease of human population.
2. The flourishing of nonhuman life requires such a decrease.[10]

The acceptance of the first proposition is probably much more widespread now than it was only twenty years ago. The last part of formulation 1 is perhaps not the best phrasing. An alternative is "compatible with a substantially smaller human population." The critical period of decrease is then clearly left out of consideration. Its problems need separate treatment.

An occasional objection to proposition 2 is that if humanity adopted an entirely different way of life, the present large population would not necessarily encroach on the flourishing of nonhuman life, or at least not much more so than do other species. I agree. But if we try to imagine how this way of life would look, the result is likely to be that we despair of its early realization. At the very least, it is irresponsible to assume the realization of this way of life and today reject stabilization and subsequent reduction as a distant, albeit important, goal. In addition to the goals of a change in general behavior, we must have the long-range reduction in view. Every year, that goal increases in importance; every day it is relevant.

Propositions 1 and 2 concentrate on the flourishing of life. Even if "life" is taken broadly, it does not cover the full range of concerns of the deep ecology movement, which, of course, is concerned about the earth as a whole, including landscapes valued independently of the life-forms that sometimes live there. We are seriously concerned about the ecosphere in its widest sense, not only the biosphere (in its widest sense).

It is characteristic of the deep ecology movement that great efforts at conservation are argued *not only* as something good and profitable for human beings, but also as something valuable for what is intended to be conserved. It is worthy of conservation, independently of any narrow human interests. This is often called the nonanthropocentric or biocentric or ecocentric view. Nevertheless, in the current social and political milieu, success in conservation efforts depends heavily on arguments that *do* stress narrowly human interests, especially the requirements of human health. The supporters of the deep ecology movement combine such arguments with those that are independent of narrow human interests.[11] It is essential that "experts" and others who influence policies agree about this combination and that the public be made aware that basically there is agreement. Otherwise, the public is deceived.

Applying the preceding discussion to the question of human population, I shall tentatively defend a more radical proposition than proposition 1:

3. The flourishing of human life and cultures requires that the human population be substantially smaller than its present size.

With a global population of 6.6 billion in 2007 and possibly 10 billion within a couple of generations, the process of even a very slow reduction would be a formidable undertaking, perhaps a terrifying project for many. Should we, or even *can* we, contemplate such reduction over the centuries or millennia in realistic detail? Obviously not, but very long-range perspectives are necessary for the choice of wise policies *now*.

For the present discussion, it is perhaps best to discard the term *flourishing*. Instead I ask, What are the kinds of ultimate goals for humankind? Is one or more of them such that very great numbers of participants are required to maximize the prospect of realization?

The goals may be divided into individual, social (communal), and cultural. As one of the ultimate goals—that is, goals not having just instrumental character—I postulate a rich manifold of deeply different cultures. Looking back some thousand years, and imagining some distant futures, I reach a rather certain conclusion: On average, no very great population is required in each culture. On the contrary, huge numbers tend to reduce the manifold.

The goals of each individual are greatly dependent on the community, the larger social setting, the nation, or people. If, however, we try to go from subordinate to ultimate goals, we may tentatively simplify our reflections by subsuming individual ultimate goals under three headings: pleasure, happiness, and perfection.[12] By *pleasure*, I refer to what in the history of philosophy has often been called hedonism. Momentary, intense, positive feelings, especially sensual, are seen by the hedonist to be the only ultimate good and value. By the still more ambiguous term *happiness*, I refer to eudaimonism (harmoniously flourishing), which differs essentially from hedonism in taking time seriously—a happy *life*—and recognizing that happiness requires deep and complex positive feelings not reducible to sense experience. By *perfection*, I think of ultimate goals defined independently of pleasure or happiness, for example, "authenticity," "doing one's duty in life," "letting God lead," "self-realization." Usually, those proclaiming perfection (in my terminology) as an ultimate goal assume that attaining or seriously seeking the goal has a satisfactory degree of happiness as a consequence.[13] Others admit that no happiness is assured or that they expect unhappiness from seeking perfection.

The importance of focusing on ultimate goals stems in part from a *decrease of ecological destructiveness with decreasing distance from the ultimate*. An example may be useful.

In Benito Mussolini's years as *Il Duce*, most—perhaps more than 90 percent—of his proclamations about war suggested that he considered warfare an ultimate goal for humankind. Sometimes, though, he clearly classed wars started by Italy as instrumental: the best means to improve the Italian "race." He had contempt for what he considered the sloppy, pleasure-loving, and unwarlike qualities of Italians. As long as he lived, he said, he would see to it that Italy was always involved in at least one war. The ultimate goal, therefore, seemed to be a kind of perfection—to realize certain qualities of character—rather than an endless series of wars. Since he did not shun man's pleasure of "conquering" women, the ultimate goal seemed for him to be a sort of masculine character, including nonsloppy "masculine" pleasures. There are many ecologically innocent ways of realizing masculinity, short of war! Mussolini's destructive choice is not a necessary one.

Why not be content with one's own masculinity? Why spend time perfecting the masculinity of millions of others? Here, of course, we discern motives of ambition centering on coercive power. The many ways of satisfying ambition reveal perfection goals of various kinds. What this whole example is meant to illustrate is that few ultimate goals *inevitably* require ecologically destructive outlets.

Our first conclusion must be that the ultimate goals of humankind do not presuppose very large numbers of human beings on earth. A population significantly below the 6.6 billion of 2007 would be viable.

The next question must be, Given the geographical and other limitations of the earth, will the maximization of the prospect of realizing the ultimate goals be hindered rather than favored by a total population as large as 6.6 billion? For those who accept Self-realization as one goal, or the ultimate goal, and accept the tendency to identify with all life as an inevitable consequence of maturity, the answer is clear: It is vastly more difficult to reach the goal with a population of 6.6 billion than with a substantially smaller population—other conditions being held constant.

In line with the very limited aim of this essay, I shall now jump to a couple of conclusions, the first of which presents a softening of proposition 3:

4. The optimum conditions for the realization of the ultimate goals of humankind require a population that is substantially smaller than the present population.
5. There are no ultimate goals of humankind for which the realization requires a reduction in the richness and diversity of life on earth.

Given today's large population and given that a great part of it is, naturally, eager to reach a much higher standard of life, pollution and resource depletion will inevitably assume grave proportions. It is tempting to object, "But with soft and intermediate technology, with the stabilization of energy consumption, and with the realization of the major goals of green politics, ecological sustainability is ensured, even with 6.6 billion human beings!" Such a happy outcome may be possible, but I must repeat that it is irresponsible to neglect the population question in the *mere hope* that a radical green movement will be victorious.

Considering the immense pollution per capita in the rich industrialized countries, population reduction in those countries has at least as high a priority as in the poor countries. Our lopsided share of the reduction of life conditions on the planet should make us careful of trying to press the poor countries toward greater ecological responsibility. Furthermore, the large increase in the material standard of living in the rich countries since the 1950s may not have increased the level of attainment of the ultimate goals in life.

In Europe, only about 8 by 5 square kilometers (near the Polish–Russian border) are left of the old forest that covered Europe after the last ice age. As a philosopher, I may be permitted to say that we Europeans have made surprisingly little use of our brains to attend to our ultimate goals in life. We might have saved a lot of nature and added to our quality of life. Paying more attention to the ultimate is facilitated through thinking in terms of a total view rather than in fragments.

THE PERIOD OF TRANSITION IN RICH COUNTRIES: ECONOMIC CONSEQUENCES

A period of transition from higher to lower population will have a different character in different countries, and a different character in different parts of individual countries or regions.[14] Let me leave out the smaller units—parts of a small country—and concentrate on rich countries.

In rich countries with "mixed" economies—countries neither markedly socialist nor markedly capitalist—slight decreases of fertility have already been experienced and have elicited public discussion. The main reaction has been *alarm*, probably mostly of a rather instinctive character ("Are we dying out?"). Few conferences, if any, have been organized with the aim of discussing theories about various consequences of a slow decrease.

With regard to economic consequences, the main concern has been the increasing percentage of old, "unproductive" people. These individuals have to be given food and shelter; they "cost" a lot. If their numbers increase by 10 percent, productive people have to work more and produce more. On the other hand, economists (and here I think of people doing economic research without being hired by a public institution or a private firm) point out that children "cost" as much as or more than do their older counterparts. So if 10 percent fewer children are born, the percentage of productive people is affected at least as heavily the other way. Productive people might have to work less and produce less in the transition period. (By *work*, I mean salaried work. Much work of eminent social value is done today without salary, whereas much destructive production is paid for.)

Of great political importance is the difference between public and private budgets. With the disappearance of the extended family as an economic unit, old people are paid for largely out of public budgets. Children are paid for mostly out of private budgets. (In this discussion, I have in mind a mixed economy like that of Scandinavia.) Some of the alarm about a slow decrease is therefore alarm about higher taxes. On the other hand, the more than ten years' schooling, now paid for mainly by the public budget, will cost less during the transition period. Further, as it is now, people in economic charge of children pay lower taxes. A decrease of the number of children would increase public income. It is, therefore, an open question whether taxes would need to be increased or could be lowered.

Here is not the place to go into details. But in short, the economics of a slow population decrease is a fascinating theme for professional economists and population experts. Politicians have so far mainly asked for professional advice on how to *avoid* a decrease, not on how to think about its consequences, both good or bad, in relation to a value system. The advice of economists has largely ignored the economically important impact of population upon ecosystems—the forests, for example. Traditionally, there has been little cooperation between the social and the natural sciences; up-to-date literature employing both sciences is scarce.[15] Clearly, it is extremely difficult to predict the economic consequences of a slow decline in population, and numerous factors must be taken into consideration.

If your personal motivation for preaching long-range human population reduction is primarily concern for rapidly diminishing nonhuman life-forms, for continued evolution, and for the survival of the planet, is it not dishonest to concentrate on population reduction for the sake of human beings themselves? It is not dishonest, even if 90 percent of your argumentation is for the sake of human beings, provided you honestly believe what you say. Using argumentation in favor of a great long-range goal, we select (from among the many we believe in) those arguments that carry the most weight; such arguments must be used for what they are worth. Arguments in favor of human beings carry immeasurably more weight than those in favor of anything else.

Deep Ecology for the Twenty-Second Century[16]

This is not my title! Why did my friends insist on that title? Because of my many conversations of this kind:

NN: Are you an optimist or a pessimist?

AN: An optimist!

NN: (astonished) Really?

AN: Yes, a convinced optimist—when it comes to the twenty-second century.

NN: You mean, of course, the twenty-first?

AN: The twenty-second! The life of the grandchildren of our grandchildren. Are you not interested in the world of those children?

NN: You mean we can relax because we have a lot of time available to overcome the ecological crisis?

AN: No, every week counts. How terrible, shamefully bad conditions will be in the twenty-first century, or how far down we have to start on the way up, *depends on what you, you,* and others do today and tomorrow. There is not a single day to be lost. We need activism on a high level immediately.

The answer that I am an optimist is a reaction against the so-called doomsday prophets, people who talk *as if* nothing can be done to get things straight. They are very few, but they are heavily exploited by people in power who speak soothingly that the task ahead is not very great and that government policies *can* turn the tide toward the better. A telling example is the cover of the mighty *Newsweek* magazine, which, just before the Earth Summit of 1992 in Rio, used the headline "The End Is Not Near." In the article, there was no pep talk, not even an admission that we are in for a great task that will require new thinking. It was the very opposite of a slogan used when a big corporation is in the red: new thinking, greater efforts are called for, new leadership, and so forth. No slogan like those of Churchill in 1940: Of course we win, but there will be many tears and much sweat to be shed.

In short, there is no time for overly pessimistic utterances, which can be exploited by passivists and the dangerous pacifiers.

The realization of what we call *broad* ecological sustainability of the human enterprise on this unique planet may take a long time, and longer the more we *increase* unsustainability this year and in the years to come. The message is simple and well-known: The recovery from our illness will take time, and for every day that we neglect to try *seriously* to stop the illness from getting worse, the recovery will take more time. The healing policies today are not serious. The deep ecology movement is meant for today, but the definitive victories will scarcely be realized before the twenty-second century.

Roughly, I call ecological sustainability broad if and only if the change ("development") of life conditions on the planet is such that it ensures full richness ("abundance") and diversity of life-forms on earth (to the extent that *humans* can ensure it). Every key word of this criterion, of course, needs clarification, but it makes such sustainability obviously different from what is increasingly accepted politically, the "narrow" economic sustainability: the continuation of short- and long-range policies such that, most researchers agree, make ecological *catastrophes* affecting narrow, human interests less likely. This narrow view of sustainability is politically acceptable today as *a goal* for global development. But broad ecological sustainability centers on all ecological conditions, not only those of humanity, and the dangerous concept of development is avoided. In the narrow view, *development* still means something like an increase in GNP, rather than an improvement in the quality of life.

So, the big, open question is, How low are we going to sink before we start heading upward in the year 2101? How far down are we going to fall before there is a clear trend of *decreasing* regional and global ecological unsustainability? It may be useful to consider some scenarios for a moment:

1. *No major change in ecological policies or the extent of poverty.* An ecological catastrophe occurs because of the slowly accumulating effects of a century of ecological folly. The dramatic situation forces

new ecologically strict policies, perhaps through undemocratic, even brutal dictatorial military means used by the rich countries.

2. *The same development except for a major change in the poor countries: considerable economic growth of the Western kind.* Five times as many people live unsustainably. A breakdown follows very soon, and harsh measures are applied to fight chaos and to start a decrease of unsustainability.

3. *A couple of similar developments, ending in catastrophic and chaotic conditions and subsequent harsh, brutal policies implemented by the most powerful states.* There is a turn toward sustainability, but only after enormous devastation.

4. *Ecological enlightenment, a realistic appreciation of the drastic reduction in life quality, an increased influence of deep ecological attitude, a slow decrease of the sum total of unsustainability.* The planet follows a trend of decreasing unsustainability discernible in the year 2101.

Our hope, naturally, is for the rational scenario 4, the one that guarantees the least strenuous way toward sustainability by the year 2101.

Now a short note on three great contemporary worldwide movements that call for grassroots activism. First, the peace movement is the oldest and was remarkably dormant in the 1990s. But military expenditures between 1999 and 2007 and beyond are rapidly reviving it. Second are the many movements I put together under the name *social justice movement*. It includes the feminist movement and part of the social ecology movement. For the third movement, one might also use the more vague term *radical environmentalism*, because use of the specific terminology of deep ecology could eventually elicit boredom and aggression. But the word *environmentalism* smacks of the old metaphor suggesting humanity *surrounded* by something outside, the so-called environment of humans; it does not start with ecological concepts. And it will take a long time before radicalism loses its connection with the political *red–blue axis*. Broad ecological sustainability may be compatible with a variety of social and political structures, all pointing toward the green pole. Unfortunately, in 1993, there was a strong belief in Eastern Europe that policies must be blue—participation in the world market, and so on—*before* society could point toward the green pole.

It is not easy to be personally active in more than one of the three grassroots movements, but cooperation among the movements is essential. The ecological threat is not only of wars but also of the immense military opera-

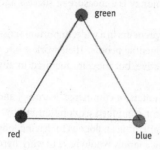

ILLUSTRATION 5:
POLITICAL TRIANGLE

tions and connected industrial activity in peacetime. For a long time, cooperation has been excellent. It has taken longer to establish close cooperation with all the social justice movements. But because the care of all living beings and capacity to identify with them are so prominent in the deep ecology movement, injustice is taken seriously.

The small minority of deep ecology supporters who write in periodicals, speak in public, and organize conferences will sometimes meet people who are skeptical about their ethical status: Are they not much more fond of animals than of humans? The answer is that whatever the intensity of their fight for animals or wilderness, deep ecology supporters recognize the very special obligations we have for our fellow humans. What we look for is not a shift of care from humans toward nonhumans, but an extension and a deepening of care. It is unwarranted to assume that the human potential for care is constant and finite and that any increase of care for some creatures necessarily reduces care for others. The twenty-first century will see a general increase of care if the ecofeminists are at least partially right.

I suspect that the societies developing in the twenty-second century, at the earliest, will not all look like the green societies envisioned since the 1960s. They will have more traits in common with what we have today. Conspicuous consumption? Of course! But what is conspicuous, what will secure prestige and wonder in that century, what will have required moderate physical energy? Several tremendously important things are different: There will be no political support of greed and unecological production. The tolerance of grave social injustice based on difference in levels of consumption will disappear.

To fight the *dominance* of something should be clearly distinguished from trying to *eliminate* something. We shall always need people who insist that their main goal in life has not been to amass money, but to create something useful in a world in which money is a measure of success and creative power.

In sociology, we often talk about entrepreneurs in a wide, important sense of socially highly energetic, creative, influential people. Their work is often controversial, sometimes clearly destructive, but they are required in any dynamic society.

I envisage big, but not dominating, centers of commerce, learning, and the arts: big buildings, vast machinery for continued exploration in physics and cosmology. But in order to do something analogous to driving long distances in a conspicuous, luxurious car, a family would have to work hard through long years and renounce many goods other people can afford. Most of the family's "Gaia gift" would be spent on traveling in their prestigious car.

Rich people who work in the world of business but are supporters of the deep ecology movement ask in all seriousness whether the green utopian societies *must* look so dreary. Why portray a society that seemingly needs no big entrepreneurs, only organic farmers, modest artists, and mild naturalists? A capitalist society is in a certain sense a rather *wild* society. We need some degree of wildness, but not exactly the capitalist sort. The usual utopian green societies seem so sober and tame. We shall need enthusiasts of the extravagant, the luxuriant, the big. But they must not dominate.

In short, I do not envisage the *necessity* of any dramatic, sudden turnaround in social and political variables, when I envisage things from the limited point of view of *overcoming the still increasing ecological crisis*. But as mature human beings—I imagine that some of us are mature or on the way to being mature—we are concerned also about nonviolence and social justice. Within the scope of this essay, I should not say anything more definite about these broad social and ethical issues. But I see the value of expressing vague ideas of how one's own ideal green societies may look. In my terminology, a green society is one that not only has to some extent solved the problem of reaching ecological sustainability, but has also ensured peace and a large measure of social justice. I don't see why so many people find reasons to despair. I am confident that humans have what is demanded.

Well, this is how I, a supporter of the deep ecology movement, feel today: impatient with the doomsday prophets and confident that we have a mission, however modest, in shaping a better future that is *not remote*. Just a couple of hundred years.

POSTSCRIPT

The expression *long-range movement* and my insistence that we have time to carefully choose priorities to make plans that will take a lifetime to carry out, sometimes left the impression that what I said was "Lean back, take it easy. We have plenty of time." To counteract this impression, I will clarify. When we talk in terms of centuries—for instance, when considering human population reduction—it is important to talk about what you—*you!*—do *today* and *tomorrow* is important for *how bad* conditions will be in the centuries to come.

Immediate action, yes, but the formidable size and vast diversity of things that must be done, "the length of the frontier," the very limited resources of people and funds today available for determined actions—all this points toward the importance of both a general long-range time perspective and, of course, a careful consideration of what should be done more or less immediately.

Notes

NOTES TO THE INTRODUCTION

1. Arne Naess and Per Ingvar Haukland, *Life's Philosophy: Reason and Feeling in a Deeper World* (Athens: University of Georgia Press, 2002). Much of my account of Arne Naess's life and philosophy is based on ongoing discussions I have had with him during the last twenty years and on the aforementioned book, *Life's Philosophy*.

2. Arne Naess, *The Selected Works of Arne Naess*, 10 vols. (Dordrecht: Springer, 2005), hereinafter cited as SWAN. The volume titles are as follows: 1, *Interpretation and Preciseness: A Contribution to a Theory of Communication*; 2, *Skepticism: Wonder and Joys of a Wandering Seeker*; 3, *Which World Is the Real One? An Inquiry into Inclusive Systems, Cultures and Philosophies*; 4, *The Pluralist and Possibilist Aspect of the Scientific Enterprise: Rich Descriptions, Abundant Choices and Open Futures*; 5, *Gandhi and Group Conflict: Explorations of Nonviolent Resistance, Satyagraha*; 6, *Freedom, Emotion, and Self-subsistence: Structure of a Central Part of Spinoza's Ethics*; 7, *Communication and Argument: Elements of Applied Semantics*; 8, *Common Sense, Knowledge and Truth: Open Inquiry in a Pluralistic World*; 9, *Reason, Democracy and Science: Understanding Among Conflicting Worldviews*; 10, *Deep Ecology of Wisdom: Exploration in Unities of Nature and Cultures*.

3. SWAN, vol. 10, 3.22.

4. SWAN, vols. 2 and 8.

5. Baruch Spinoza, *Ethics* and *On the Improvement of the Understanding* (New York: Hafner Press, 1995). See SWAN, vols. 6, 9, and 10.

6. Ludwig Wittgenstein, *Tractatus Logico-Philosophicus* (London: Routledge and Kegan Paul, 1958).

7. See especially SWAN, vols. 8, 9, and 10.

8. For examples of these studies, see especially SWAN, vols. 3 and 4.

9. See especially SWAN, vol. 9.

10. SWAN, vol. 6.

11. Wittgenstein, *Tractatus Logico-Philosophicus*.

12. See SWAN, vols. 1 and 7, for details.

13. For more on Naess's philosophy of education, see SWAN, vol. 8, 4.6; and vol. 9, 5.2.

14. See SWAN, vol. 10, 7.40–7.44, for an overview.

15. SWAN, vol. 9, 5.17.

16. For more on gestalt ontology, see especially SWAN, vols. 8 and 10.

17. SWAN, vol. 5.

18. SWAN, vol. 10, 5.33–5.36.

19. Arne Naess, "Self-Realization: An Ecological Approach to Being in the World," *Trumpeter: Journal of Ecosophy* 4, no. 3 (1987): 35–42, available in SWAN, vol. 10, 8.45.

20. SWAN, vols. 2 and 8.

21. SWAN, vol. 4.

22. Rachel Carson, *Silent Spring* (Boston: Houghton Mifflin, 1962).

23. Arne Naess, "The Shallow and the Long Range Deep Ecology Movement: A Summary," *Inquiry* 16 (1973): 95–100, available in SWAN, vol. 10, 1.2.

24. See SWAN, vol. 10, 1.1–1.12, for details.

25. Bill Devall and George Sessions, *Deep Ecology: Living as If Nature Mattered* (Salt Lake City: Gibbs Smith Publishers, 1985); and George Sessions, ed., *Deep Ecology for the 21st Century: Readings in the Philosophy and Practice of the New Environmentalism* (Boston and London: Shambhala, 1995).

26. Naess and Haukland, *Life's Philosophy*, 108–109. See SWAN, vol. 10, for detailed discussions of these principles.

27. Earth Charter Initiative, Earth Charter Web page, available at www.earthcharterin action.org/2000/10/the_earth_charter.html.

28. For examples of ecoforestry, see the anthology by Alan Drengson and Duncan Taylor, eds., *Ecoforestry: The Art and Science of Sustainable Forest Use* (Gabriola Island, British Columbia: New Society Publishers, 1997).

29. Naess, "The Shallow and the Long Range Deep Ecology Movement."

30. Arne Naess, *Ecology, Community, and Lifestyle* (Cambridge: Cambridge University Press, 1990), 36–37.

31. SWAN, vol. 10, 1.9. A version of this chart appears in Arne Naess, "The Basics of Deep Ecology," *Trumpeter: Journal of Ecosophy* 21, no. 1 (2005): 61–71.

32. For more on Naess and policy issues, see Harold Glasser, "Naess's Deep Ecology Approach and Environmental Policy," *Inquiry* 39 (1996): 157–187.

33. Naess, *Ecology, Community, and Lifestyle*.

34. Alan Drengson and Yuichi Inoue, eds., *The Deep Ecology Movement: An Introductory Anthology* (Berkeley, CA: North Atlantic Books, 1995), 10–12; and SWAN, vol. 10, 1.9.

35. Naess, *Ecology, Community, and Lifestyle*.

36. SWAN, vols. 1 and 7.

37. Naess, *Ecology, Community, and Lifestyle*, 197; see also SWAN, vol. 10.

38. SWAN, vols. 8 and 9.

39. SWAN, vol. 6.

40. See the article on Tvergastein in SWAN, vol. 10, 5.33.

41. Naess, "Self-Realization."

42. Warwick Fox, *Toward a Transpersonal Ecology: Developing New Foundations for Environmentalism* (Boston: Shambhala, 1990).

43. Matthew Fox, *Creative Spirituality: Liberating Gifts for the Peoples of the Earth* (San Francisco: HarperCollins, 1991).

44. Alan Drengson, *The Practice of Technology: Exploring Technology, Ecophilosophy, and Spiritual Disciplines for Vital Links* (Albany: SUNY Press, 1995).

NOTES TO SECTION 1

1. See, for instance, articles in Michael Tobias and H. Drasdo, eds., *Mountain Spirit* (Woodstock, NY: Overlook Press, 1979); and Dolores LaChapelle, *Earth Wisdom* (New York: Guild of Tutors Press, 1978).

2. A. Schilpp, *Albert Einstein: Philosopher-Scientist* (Evanston, IL: Library of Living Philosophers, 1949), 5.

3. For a *theory* of the world as concrete content, see Arne Naess, "The World of Concrete Contents," *Inquiry* 28 (1985): 417–428, available in Arne Naess, *Deep Ecology of Wisdom*, vol. 10 of Arne Naess, *The Selected Works of Arne Naess*, 10 vols. (Dordrecht: Springer, 2005) (hereinafter cited as SWAN).

4. Originally published in *The Mountain Spirit*, ed. Michael C. Tobias and Harold Drasdo (New York: Overlook Press, 1979), 13–16.

5. Originally published in *Environmental Ethics* 22 (2000): 333–336.

6. Mick Smith, "To Speak of Trees: Social Constructionism, Environmental Values, and the Future of Deep Ecology," *Environmental Ethics* 21, no. 4 (winter 1999): 360.

7. This essay is adapted from *Inquiry* 1985. I am grateful to the Research School of Social Sciences, the Australian National University, for giving me the opportunity to be a Visiting Fellow and to discuss and rewrite (in September 1984) what I have thought about the relationship of our *Lebenswelt* to objective reality.

8. Arne Naess, *The Pluralist and Possibilist Aspect of the Scientific Enterprise* (Oslo: Universitetsforlaget, and London: Allen and Unwin, 1972), available in SWAN, vol. 4.

9. I take Galileo as representative of the neither-nor answer because of his crucial position in the development of modern physics. There are, of course, a number of slightly or significantly different concepts of primary and secondary qualities. In the context of this essay, the essential aspect of primary qualities is their status as inherent in the objects themselves. Locke elaborates the "neither warm nor cold" answer in his *Essays Concerning Human Understanding*.

10. The full text of the crucial passage concerning Protagoras in Sextus' *Outline of Pyrrhonism* I, chapter 32, runs as follows: "Now, this man says that matter is a state of flux. As it flows, continuous additions may arise to take the place of the effluxions, and the senses undergo transformation and alternation in accordance with one's age and with other conditions of the body. He says also that the grounds of all appearances lie in the matter, so that in itself its power enables it to be all those things which appear to all beings capable of apprehension. And men apprehend different things at different times because the conditions they are in are different. The man who is in a natural state, he says, apprehends those material substances that can appear to those who are in a natural state, and a person who is in an unnatural state apprehends those things which can appear to those in an unnatural state. And the same reasoning applies as well to differences depending on one's age, one's sleeping or waking state, and every kind of condition."

11. J. J. C. Smart, "Colours," *Philosophy* 36, no. 137 (1961): 128–142, especially 128.

12. The nominalism I subscribe to is a consequence of the philosophy of hypothetical-deductive systems formulated in Naess, *Pluralist and Possibilist*, available in SWAN, vol. 4.

13. The term *ontology* is useful for naming the part of one's philosophy of science that tells "what there is." In physics and astronomy a hundred years ago, there were atoms, ether, planets, stars, forces acting upon these so-called objects. Today, the ontology proposed by astronomers and physicists is more complicated and is steadily being modified. It is mostly called classification of "objects," not ontology, but the function is clearly to classify what there is according to their sciences.

Ontology as part of a philosophy and not only a group of sciences is, of course, a much more controversial affair. And it must somehow accommodate the objects that the sciences talk about, or give reasons for their nonexistence. And which are the criteria of "existence"? Different views are open for discussion.

Until recently, the (basic) ontology of physics could be understood by people other than physicists. Now this is scarcely the case. The popularizations are wonderfully well written, but do not furnish adequate understanding. Some would lament this situation, but I think it is the most positive thing happening for a long time: It makes it clearer to all concerned that any account we offer about the world we live in (*Lebenswelt*) must be independent of the ontology of modern physics.

14. I. Baird Callicott, "Hume's Is/Ought Dichotomy and the Relation of Ecology to Leopold's Land Ethic," *Environmental Ethics* 4 (1982): 163–174.

15. This essay is adapted from a lecture delivered as the Fourth Keith Roby Memorial Lecture in Community Science, March 12, 1986, and published in Arne Naess, "Self-Realization: An Ecological Approach to Being in the World," *Trumpeter* 4, no. 3 (1987): 35–42, which was the print version of a lecture delivered as Fourth Keith Roby Memorial Lecture in Community Science, March 12, 1986.

16. Eric Fromm, "Selfishness, Self-Love, and Self-Interest," in *Self-Explorations in Personal Growth*, ed. Clark E. Mustakas (New York: Harper Colophon, 1956), 58.

17. Ibid., 59.

18. Ibid., 62.

19. Ibid., 63.

20. Ibid.

21. William James, *Principles of Psychology* (New York: Henry Holt and Co., 1890), l: 379.

22. This and other quotations from Gandhi are taken from my *Gandhi and Group Conflict*, Oslo, 1974, p. 35, available in SWAN 5, where the metaphysics of self-realization is treated more thoroughly.

NOTES TO SECTION 2

1. This essay was part of a lecture given at University of Victoria, Canada, 1989, and was published in Arne Naesas, "The Three Great Movements," *Trumpeter* 9, no. 2 (spring 1992).

2. The term *deep ecology* is said here to be used in a loose way to emphasize that my own efforts to formulate a platform of the deep ecology movement in eight points requiring about two hundred words should not be taken too seriously. Thousands of people might be unmoved by one or more of the points that I formulated, but they support the third movement as I conceive it. It would be arrogant and pretentious of me to compare the deep ecology movement with the historically tremendously important and strong movement against war, exploitation, and suppression *if* the term were to be closely associated with my modest effort in the way of terminology.

    As an example of characterizations other than the eight points, one might refer to Walter Schwarz and Dorothy Schwarz, "Deep Ecology," in *Breaking Through* (Devon, England: Green Books, 1987), which quotes Michael McCloskey, Donald Worster, Neil Evernden, Fritjof Capra, and others.

3. Michael Soulé, "A Vision for the Meantime," *Wild Earth*, Special Issue (1992–1993): 7–8.

4. This essay is adapted from a lecture presented at Australian National University, Canberra, 1986, and published in Arne Naess, "The Basics of Deep Ecology," *Trumpeter* 21, no. 1 (2005): 61–71.

5. Robin Attfield, *Ethics of Environmental Concern* (Oxford: Blackwell, 1983).

6. Patsy Hallen, "Making Peace with Nature: Why Ecology Needs Ecofeminism," *Trumpeter* 4, no. 3 (1987): 3–14.

7. Originally published in *The North American Review* (summer 1973).

8. There is an unfortunate confusion of terminology surrounding the term *cultural anthropology*. In Continental Europe, what in this article is called *cultural anthropology* is mostly called *ethnology*, and in Great Britain *social anthropology*. In Europe, the term *ethnography* is sometimes used about subject matters clearly falling under the American usage of *cultural anthropology*. Its antonym is *physical anthropology*. In Continental Europe, the term *philosophical anthropology* covers many subjects of

cultural anthropology and ecosophy in general, such as the debate about the essential differences between humans and animals. G. P. Gusdorf, "Anthropology," *Encyclopedia Britannica*, 15th ed. (Macropedia), vol. 1, furnishes an excellent survey of the terminological developments until about 1970.

9. The distinction of deep versus shallow cultural differences and the importance of articulated total views as expressions of the deep differences are elaborated in Arne Naess, *Hvilken verden er den virkelige?* (What world is the real?), 2nd ed. (Oslo: Universitetsforlaget, 1982), available in SWAN, vol. 3. Cultural anthropology should, I think, be distinguished from less comprehensive units of research: economic, technological, social, and (the central European) philosophical anthropology. In my terminology, a culture is the largest human unit and corresponds somewhat to the unit of species in biology. Before the 1960s, talks about cultures were considered unscientific within certain scientific communities. Expressions such as "the peoples of the world" were favored. But "the consumerism people" does not mean the same as "the consumerism culture." See R. W. Fox and T. H. Jackson Lears, *The Culture of Consumption* (New York: Pantheon Books, 1983).

10. Marshall Sahlins, *Stone Age Economics* (Piscataway, NJ: Aldine Transaction, 1972).

11. Karl Marx and Friedrich Engels, *The German Ideology* (London: Lawrence and Wishart, 1970).

12. F. Th. Stcherbatsky, *The Central Conception of Buddhism* (Delhi: Motical Banarsidas, 1974).

13. Benedict (Baruch) de Spinoza, *The Ethics* (New York: Hafner, 1955), 226–227. The passage was translated from Latin by Naess. All passages in this essay are from *The Ethics* and were translated by Arne Naess.

14. Originally published in *Environmental Values* 2 (1993): 67–71.

15. Immanuel Kant, *Critique of Pure Reason,* transl. Norman Kemp Smith (London: Macmillan, 1963).

16. Immanuel Kant, "An Attempt at Some Reflections on Optimism," in *Theoretical Philosophy, 1755–1770* (Cambridge: Cambridge University Press, 1992), 71–83.

17. Immanuel Kant, *Fundamental Principles of the Metaphysics of Morals* [also titled *Groundwork of the Metaphysics of Morals*], transl. Thomas K. Abbott (New York: Prentice Hall College Division, 1949).

18. U.N. World Commission on Environment and Development, *Our Common Future* (Oxford: Oxford University Press, 1987), also know as the Brundtland Report.

NOTES TO SECTION 3

1. Originally published in *Journal of Philosophy and Phenomenological Research* 25 (1964): 16–29.

2. B. Lonegan, *Insight: A Study of Human Understanding*, ed. F. E. Crowe and R. M. Doran (Toronto: University of Toronto Press, 1992), 329.

3. S. Kierkegaard, *Concluding Unscientific Postscript*, trans. D. F. Swenson and W. Lowrie (Princeton: Princeton University Press, 1941), 101. I have changed the translation at some points.

4. This quotation from Arthur Koestler in *The God That Failed*, ed. R. H. Crossman (New York: Arno Press, 1949), 68, is used by in a similar context in M. Polanyi, "The Stability of Beliefs," *British Journal for the Philosophy of Science* (1952): 218.

5. H. Walsby, *The Domain of Ideologies* (Glasgow: MacLellan, 1947).

6. Karl Mannheim, *Ideology and Utopia* (London: Routledge and Kegan Paul, 1952), 49.

7. For criticism of the doctrine that different logics can be described in the way attempted

by some social scientists, see A. Naess et al., *Democracy, Ideology, and Objectivity* (Oslo: University Press, and Oxford: Blackwell, 1956), 203ff. See also SWAN, vol. 9.

8. This essay is adapted from Arne Naess, "The Limited Neutrality of Typologies of Systems: A Reply to Gullvåg," *Inquiry* 20 (1977), 67–81, reprinted in *Trumpeter* 22, no. 1 (2006): 7–13.

9. Ingemund Gullvåg, "Naess's Pluralistic Metaphilosophy," *Inquiry* 18, no. 4 (1975): 391–408. All page numbers in parentheses in this essay refer to this paper.

10. Karl Jaspers, *Psychologie der Weltanschauungen* (Berlin, 1919).

11. See Gullvåg, "Naess's Pluralistic Metaphilosophy," 393ff.

12. Arne Naess, *Communication and Argument* (Oslo: Universitetsforlaget, and London: George Allen & Unwin, 1965), available in SWAN, vol. 7.

13. This essay is adapted from Arne Naess, "Notes on the Methodology of Normative Systems," *Methodology and Science* 10 (1977): 64–79, available in SWAN, vol. 10.

14. Norwegian National Research Council, project A79.24–15.

15. Some of the authors of central importance to the deep ecology movement include Gregory Bateson, Kenneth Boulding, Ottar Brox, Rachel Carson, Barry Commoner, Erik Dammann, René Dubos, Paul R. and Anne H. Ehrlich, Clarence J. Glacken, Edward Goldsmith, Ivan Illich, Sigmund Kvaløy, Ian McHarg, Joseph Meeker, E. J. Mishan, Ivar Mysterud, Marshall Sahlins, E. F. Schumacher, Harvig Sœtra, W. Zapffe.

16. What holds of theories in science holds of normative systems. For elaboration of the trichotomy theory, systematization, and versions as used in this essay, see Arne Naess, *Pluralist and Possibilist Aspect*, available in SWAN, vol. 4. For definiteness of intention, see Naess, *Communication and Argument*, 34ff, available in SWAN, vol. 7.

17. For a short exposition, see Naess, *Communication and Argument*, available in SWAN, vol. 7. For a more technical treatment, see Arne Naess, *Interpretation and Preciseness* (Oslo: I kommisjon hos J. Dybwad, 1953), available in SWAN, vol. 1.

18. Originally published in *Trumpeter*, Festschrift Section 22, no. 1 (2006): 80–87.

19. Claude Lévi-Strauss, quoted in Hans Skjervheim, "Ad Skjervheim," in *Regime under Kritikk: Om Hans Skjervheim I Norsk Filosofi Og Samfunnsdebatt*, ed. Hermund Slaattelid (Oslo: Aschehoug, 1997), 49–53 (in Norwegian only).

20. Ibid., 8.

21. Richard Dawkins, *The Selfish Gene* (New York and Oxford: Oxford University Press, 1976).

22. Lévi-Strauss, quoted in Skjervheim, "Ad Skjervheim," 13.

23. For culture in humans and other animals, see J. T. Bonner, *The Evolution of Culture in Animals* (Princeton, NJ: Princeton University Press, 1980).

24. F. Barth, *Andres Liv –og vårt eget* (Oslo: Gyldendal, 1980), 32.

25. Egon Brunswik, *Perception and the Representative Design of Psychological Experiments*, 2nd ed. (Berkeley: University of California Press, 1956).

26. R. Rosenthal and K. Frode, "Dull Rats and Bright Rats: The Effect of Experimenter Bias on the Performance of the Albino Rat," *Behavioral Science* 8 (1963): 183–189.

27. After the war, when E. Brunswik and I were going to write the psychology volume for the *International Encyclopedia of Unified Science*, even the mellow and sophisticated behaviorism of E. C. Tolman and Brunswik was too rigorous and antimentalist for me. Our ways parted. Brunswik wrote a highly competent volume alone.

28. This essay is adapted from "The Principle of Intensity," *Journal of Value Inquiry* 33 (1999): 5–9, available in SWAN, vol. 9. Since the first drafts in the 1940s, I have made some insertions, for instance, about life quality.

29. This essay is adapted from Arne Naess, "Creativity and Gestalt Thinking," *Structuralist* 33/34 (1994): 51–52, available in SWAN, vol. 9.

30. Original essay available in SWAN, vol. 8.

31. I follow here the gestalt terminology I used in "The World of Concrete Contents" essay in this book.

32. See, for example, what D. T. Suzuki, *Outlines of Mahayana Buddhism* (New York: Schocken, 1963), 140, calls the "ground-principles of the philosophy of Mahayana Buddhism, and, indeed of all the schools of Buddhism": (1) All is momentary, (2) all is empty, (3) all is self, and (4) all is such as it is. See also Masao Abe, *Zen and Western Thought*, ed. W. R. LaFleur (Honolulu: University of Hawaii Press, 1989), 30.

33. Nara Yasuaki, "The Practical Value of Dōgen's View of Nature," mimeograph, 1985: 1.

34. *Majjhima Nikaya* I: 265.

35. *Dhammapada*, verse 80.

36. See, for example, R. E. A. Johansson's excellent *Pali Buddhist Texts* (Lund, Sweden: Studentlitteratur, 1973), 35.

37. In the oblique cases, *sva* is used as a reflexive pronoun, synonymously with *atman*.

38. Therefore, I think the comment in D. G. Merzel, "No Mind, No Buddha; Gateless Gate: Case 33," in *The Ten Directions* (Los Angeles: Zen Center, 1980), 1, 3, might be misleading: "The teaching of the illusory nature of the ego is the core of Buddhism, and the *Diamond Sutra* is one of its most profound expressions. According to this sutra even the idea of liberating all beings must not be cherished because in reality there is not one to be saved. If we think, 'I must help this person,' we are seeing things dualistically. We are operating out of the idea that there is a self, an 'I,' that is doing the saving, and one that is going to be saved." In this quotation, Merzel freely uses the word *we*, "if we think . . . we are seeing . . . we are operating . . ." To me, this use of the personal pronoun is neither more nor less metaphysically relevant than the use of the word *I* in saying, "I must help this person."

39. Yasuaki Nara, "Dōgen's View of Nature."

40. Ibid., 4.

41. *Visuddhimagga* 16: 90.

42. Yasuaki Nara, "Dōgen's View of Nature," 5.

43. Ibid.

44. Ibid., 7.

45. Ibid., 9–10.

46. The Buddhist scholar Robert Aitken, who encouraged me to publish this article, made a couple of important comments (letter to author): "About the word *satori*: this usually refers to an experience, but sometimes it refers to a state or condition. It implies something complete, and in view of the ongoing process of realization after realization, Zen masters generally don't use it, preferring the word *kensho*, which means 'seeing into (true) nature,' and by usage implies a glimpse. D. T. Suzuki used *satori* a lot, so this practice is copied by others. I wonder if references to *inochi* and *kuyo* should include their ordinary translations, 'life' and 'memorial service.' I think that Professor Abe's statement 'Only through self-realization can one attain nirvana,' refers to a personal grasp of the fact that all things are empty, and also of the fact that nirvana and samsara are the same. I don't think that it reflects any concerns by Dōgen that the process of generation and extinction be eliminated. The Mahayana view that all beings are enlightened from the beginningless beginning makes process a matter of realizing what has always been true."

NOTES TO SECTION 4

1. Originally published in *Preventing World War III: Some Proposals*, ed. Q. Wright, W. M. Evan, and M. Deutsch (New York: Simon and Schuster, 1962), 123–135, available in SWAN, vol. 9.

2. It is probably true of most nonmilitary "methods" of defense that the actions recommended are more effective the more they are engaged in as ends in themselves—as parts of a way of life rather than as means for defense.

3. Examples of nonpolitical disasters include the earthquakes in Agadir and Chile, floods in India or England, and famine in China or India. Such help should be available on an adequate scale as soon as the need is known. Hence there must be reserve resources available on instant call. Refugee aid is equally important. Had adequate help been ready for the nine hundred thousand refugees from the Palestine conflict in 1945–1948, the present tensions in the Near East might have been of lesser intensity. The U.N. General Assembly appropriated the small sum of $5 million and requested all countries to contribute to a fund for a peaceful solution of the refugee problem. But few governments responded, and only $35 million was collected—about one-tenth the cost to Britain and France of the Suez invasion. Despite energetic efforts, the agencies involved could do relatively little. Now the problem is complicated by rigid official positions adopted by the Arab states and Israel and the constructive program is shoved into the background, while propaganda and fruitless discussions on the question of guilt occupy the foreground. This is only one of the many cases of refugee crisis throughout the world, from China to India, Africa, and Hungary.

4. This does not imply always providing the invader with all of the information requested.

5. For a classification with examples of sixty-five techniques of nonviolent resistance (in the sense of resistance without weapons), many of which would be applicable in such a situation, see G. Sharp, "The Methods of Non-violent Action," mimeographed paper, Oslo, Institute for Social Research, 1960.

6. *Microresistance* is defined as resistance by individuals or small, temporary groups carried out in such a way that exposure and annihilation of larger organizations and institutions do not affect it, at least not directly.

7. This essay was adapted from an article written in 1993 and first published as Arne Naess, "Gandhian Nonviolent Verbal Communication: The Necessity of Training," *Trumpeter* 22, no. 1 (2006): 100–111.

8. Arne Naess, *Gandhi and Group Conflict: Explorations of Nonviolent Resistance, Satyagraha* (Oslo: Universitetsforlaget, 1974), available in SWAN, vol. 5.

9. Revision will always be required in part because of the unending change of background, linguistic and otherwise, of the participants. This "revisability" has made some people with certain backgrounds propose that the term *norm*, which sounds "absolutistic," should be dropped and *guideline* be adopted. Due to my background in methodology and logic, I do not find *norm* absolutistic. Nor does the exclamation mark remind me too much of authoritarianism or giving orders. The formulations are in part translations from my book *Elements of Applied Semantics* (Oslo: University of Oslo Press, and London: Allan and Unwin Ltd., 1966), available in SWAN, vol. 7.

10. Perhaps we should write, "This hypothesis is hardly relevant"? "Hardly" might be inserted because, looking at the matter from an extremely formal point of view, a tendency to utter irrelevant things in a discussion might be seen as a sign of a person's lack of spirit of cooperation, a lack that might be seen in this situation to be a result of a too strong engagement in competitive sports. This is so far-fetched, however, that the insertion of "hardly" may properly be seen as an instance of sophistry.

11. This essay was written in 1982 and revised in 1991. It was originally published in *The Deep Ecology of Wisdom* (Dordrecht: Springer, 2005) (SWAN, vol. 10), 395–419.

12. Spinoza uses the term *causa immanens* only twice, in the *Ethics* 1P18 (Part One, Proposition 18) and Letter 73 when there is a positive reference to St. Paul.

13. Harry Austryn Wolfson, *The Philosophy of Spinoza* (New York: Ridian Books, 1958), 2:303–304.

14. Naess, "Limited Definiteness of 'God' in Spinoza's System: Answer to Heine Siebrand," *Neue Zeitschrift für systematische Theologie und Religionsphilosophie* 28 (1986): 275–283.

15. Throughout this essay, I use the standard citation method for references to Spinoza's *Ethics*. The first number in the citation refers to the part number of the *Ethics*. The letter *P* refers to "Proposition." The number after the *P* is the proposition number. For example, 5P36 means Part Five, Proposition 36, of the *Ethics*. If the abbreviation *Sch* is included in the citation (e.g., 3P11Sch), the citation is a scholium (annotation) to the proposition. Thus, 3P11Sch means a scholium to Proposition 11 of Part Three.

16. Wolfson, *The Philosophy of Spinoza*, 2:222–223.

17. One may speak of the finite God (*Deus modificatus*) of Spinoza as well as the infinite: Arne Naess, "Spinoza's Finite God," *Revue internationale de Philosophie* 35 (1981): 120–126. Researchers mostly take the first part of the *Ethics* more seriously than the last—the account of human freedom and power as genuine part of God's. Doing this, they seem not to be aware of the limitation of mere formal logical priority. They ignore *Deus modificatus* because it occurs only in the later parts. Deep ecology theorizing thrives neither on humans alone nor on God alone.

18. Cp. ibid.

19. It is important that Spinoza adds that 5P24 follows from 1P25Cor, that is, from the thesis of modes *expressing* God's attributes. It supports a radically immanent interpretation of *Deus*.

20. The distinction between content and abstract structure is worked out earlier in this book (see "The World of Concrete Contents").

21. M. Gueroult, *Spinoza I: Dieu* (Paris: Aubier, 1968).

22. Stephan Lackner, *Peaceable Nature* (San Francisco: Harper & Row, 1984).

23. For a little more on human intervention to decrease suffering, see Arne Naess, "Should We Try to Relieve Clear Cases of Extreme Suffering in Nature?" *Pan Ecology* 6, no. 1 (winter 1991), available in SWAN, vol. 10.

24. In Arne Naess, *Equivalent Terms and Notions in Spinoza's Ethics* (Oslo: Institute of Philosophy, University of Oslo, 1973), I have quoted 243 relations of equivalence among key terms.

25. H. C. K. Wyld, *The Universal Dictionary of the English Language* (New York: Dutton, 1932).

26. C. T. Lewis, *The Latin Dictionary for Schools* (London: Oxford University Press, 1951).

27. I have commented on *perseverare* and its relation to Hobbes in Arne Naess, "Environmental Ethics and Spinoza's *Ethics*," *Inquiry* 23 (1980): 313–325. In what follows, some formulations are borrowed from that article. In Part Four of the *Ethics*, the term *conservare* is sometimes used as a synonym for *perseverare*. (4P18Sch: "reason demands [*postulat*] that everyone endeavors to conserve its being [*esse*], in so far as it is in itself.") I think "conserve" is too passive; I shall, accordingly, write and talk as if *perseverare* were used consistently by Spinoza.

28. Bill Devall and G. Sessions, *Deep Ecology* (Salt Lake City: Gibbs M. Smith, 1985), 70. See also the discussion of the eight points in the introduction and in "The Basics of the Deep Ecology Movement" in this book.

29. Some central places in the *Ethics* show the way from Spinoza's *Ethics* to his political writings. On reason, he writes: "In so far as men live under the guidance of reason, to that extent only do they always agree in nature" (Part Two, Proposition 40, Scholium 2. From the terminology follows Proposition 35 of Part Four). This seems odd if one does not take into account Spinoza's somewhat special use of the term *ratio*. Concerning freedom, reason, mutual aid, peace, and friendship, he writes: "Only free men are truly advantageous (*invicem utilissimi*) to one another and united by a maximally close bond of friendship" (Part Four, Proposition 71, Proof). Here the term *freedom* must be interpreted in accordance with what is said about adequate causation and activeness (Part Three, Definition 2), and the resulting close relation between the terms *freedom* and *reason*: "A free human being, that is, a man who lives under the guidance of reason" (Part Four, Demonstration of Proposition 67). From these places, it is fairly clear that *a Spinozistic social utopia* is one that is conceived to furnish the best conditions for freedom for everybody—freedom being interpreted in his way. But what kind of practical politics is the best? The question is open. I don't think Spinoza's political work can offer much here.

30. This essay was adapted from Arne Naess, "Through Spinoza to Mahayana Buddhism or Through Mahayana Buddhism to Spinoza?" in *Spinoza's Philosophy of Man: Proceedings of the Scandinavian Spinoza Symposium 1977*, ed. J. Wetlesen (Oslo: Universitetsforlaget, 1978), 136–157.

31. J. Wetlesen, *The Sage and the Way: Spinoza's Ethics of Freedom* (Oslo: University of Oslo Press, 1979).

32. Edward Conze, ed. and transl., *Buddhist Wisdom Books* (New York: Harper and Row, 1958).

33. Wetlesen, *Spinoza's Philosophy of Man*, 3–4. All page numbers in parentheses in this essay refer to this book.

34. Chögyam Trungpa, *Born in Tibet* (New York: Penguin, 1971).

35. See IP17, 17Cor2, and 4P4, all quoted in Wetlesen, *Spinoza's Philosophy of Man*, 29.

36. Evidence referring to the text of the *Ethics* is given in Arne Naess, *Freedom, Emotion, and Self-Subsistence: The Structure of a Central Part of Spinoza's Ethics* (Oslo: Universitetsforlaget, 1975), available in SWAN, vol. 6. See especially part E, "The Road to Freedom Through Active Emotion," 82ff.

37. A rather wide concept is introduced and used in ibid., SWAN, vol. 6, 57. What Wetlesen says about grading does not automatically hold for the "gradual" approach of that work.

38. This essay was written in 1991 and is published here for the first time.

39. Connotation and denotation of Spinozist "equivalences" are discussed in Arne Naess, "Equivalent Terms and Notions in Spinoza's Ethics," *Inquiry* 5 (1962).

NOTES TO SECTION 5

1. This essay is adapted from Arne Naess, "Industrial Society, Postmodernity, and Ecological Sustainability," *Humboldt Journal of Social Relations* 21, no. 1 (1995): 131–146, also available in SWAN, vol. 10.

2. Victor Lebow, quoted in Alan Durning, *How Much Is Enough? The Consumer Society and the Future of the Earth* (New York: W. W. Norton & Company, 1992), 21–22.

3. See G. C. Daily and P. R. Ehrlich, "Population, Sustainability, and Earth's Carrying Capacity," *Bioscience* 42 (1992): 761–771.

4. Clive Ponting, *The Green History of the World* (New York: St. Martin's Press, 1992).

5. Lester R. Brown, *State of the World 1988: A Worldwatch Institute Report on Progress Toward a Sustainable Society* (New York: W. W. Norton and Co., 1988).

6. Originally published in *Conservation of Biodiversity for Sustainable Development*, ed. O. T. Sandlund, K. Hindar, and A. H. D. Brown (Oslo: University of Oslo Press, 1992), 303–310, available in SWAN, vol. 10.

7. U.N. World Commission on Environment and Development, *Our Common Future* (Oxford: Oxford University Press, 1987), also know as the Brundtland Report.

8. Ibid., 8.

9. This essay was written in 1987 and originally published in SWAN, vol. 10, 275–281.

10. See, for example, Arne Naess, "The Deep Ecology Movement: Some Philosophical Aspects," *Philosophical Inquiry* 8 (1986): 10–31, available in SWAN, vol. 10, 275–281.

11. The all-sided, mature human being has a need to "combine argumentation" regarding the richness and diversity of earth. That is the reason for adding the word narrow.

12. For more about this classification, see Arne Naess, *Ecology Community and Lifestyle* (Cambridge: Cambridge University Press, 1989), cha3.

13. Perfection (from Latin per-facere) does not necessarily imply something absolute in its perfection, but rather wholeness, a practicably attainable level of performance and state of being.

14. Tore Thonstad, "Perspectives of European Demographic Evolution: Expected Major Economic Consequences," in European Population Conference, 1982, Council of Europe, Strasbourg, EPC (82) 10-E, 21, weighs in on this issue: "In my opinion, the most serious aspect of a population decline is the regional one. Some production and consumption capital will be idle (at least temporarily) if the population decline is spread out too unevenly, or if it hits communities which are so small that the economic disadvantages of a further population decline can be disastrous. In other areas or cities, the economic gains by a reduced population could be considerable. This is a very important area for economic research and possibly for policy action."

15. I have profited most from Thonstad, "Perspectives of European Demographic Evolution."

16. This essay is adapted from a talk given to the Institute for Environmental Studies, University of California, Santa Cruz, April 28, 1992, and published as Arne Naess, "Deep Ecology for the 22nd Century" [title chose by the institute!], *Trumpeter* 9, no.2 (spring 1992), and slightly revised in July 1993 and available in SWAN, vol. 10.

Bibliography

This bibliography is based on one compiled by Harold Glasser from records kept in Oslo by Kit-Fai Naess. It is a fairly complete record of Naess's works available mostly in English, including some that were coauthored. For a more complete list of his published and unpublished work, see the Web site for the Center for the Study of Development and Environment (SUM) associated with the University of Oslo. A comprehensive bibliography of Naess's works published in English appears at the end of the *Selected Works of Arne Naess*, 10 vols. (Dordrecht, Netherlands: Springer, 2005) (SWAN), volume 10, where the original dates for each of Naess's major publications are noted. A complete list of the SWAN titles is provided in the front of each volume and is also included here, near the end of the first section of this bibliography.

ARNE NAESS WRITINGS (SOLE AUTHOR)

Erkenntnis und Wissenschaftliches Verhalten. [Science as behavior.] Oslo: Norwegian Academy of Sciences, Inaugural Dissertation, 1936.

"Common Sense and Truth." *Theoria* 4 (1938): 39–58.

"Truth" as Conceived by Those Who Are Not Professional Philosophers. Oslo: Norwegian Academy of Sciences and Jacob Dybwad, 1938.

"A Systematic Comparison of the Theoretical Approaches of Brunswik, Freud, and Others (Abstracts from Professor Hull's Informal Seminar, Yale)." Unpublished notes, May 1939.

"Citizenship as a Subject!" *Universitas* (Special Issue) 2 (1947): 1–2.

"Objectivity of Norms: Two Directions of Precization." In *Stencil: Filosofiske Problemer.* Vol. 9. Edited by Arne Naess. Oslo: Oslo University, 1948 (2nd ed., 1960).

"Notes on the Foundations of Psychology as a Science." In *Stencil: Filosofiske Problemer.* Vol. 9. Edited by Arne Naess. Oslo: Oslo University, 1948.

"Towards a Theory of Interpretation and Preciseness." *Theoria* 15 (1949): 220–241.

"The Function of Ideological Convictions." In *Tensions That Cause Wars* (Common statement and individual papers by a group of social scientists brought together by UNESCO). Edited by H. Cantril. Urbana: University of Illinois Press, 1950, 257–298. (Also in SWAN, vol. 9.)

"Norwegian Mountaineers in Chitral." *Pakistan Horizon* 3 (1950): 3, 5.

"Appendix I: The UNESCO Questionnaire on Ideological Conflicts Concerning Democracy." In *Democracy in a World of Tensions.* Edited by Richard McKeon with the assistance of Stein Rokkan. Chicago: University of Chicago Press, 1951, 513–521.

"The Norwegian Expedition to Tirich Mir, 1950." *Alpine Journal* (London) 58 (May 1951): 6–15.

"Towards a Theory of Interpretation and Preciseness." In *Semantics and the Philosophy of Language*. Edited by Leonard Linsky. Urbana: University of Illinois Press, 1952, 248–269.

Interpretation and Preciseness: A Contribution to the Theory of Communication. Oslo: Jacob Dybwad, 1953. (Also in SWAN, vol. 1.)

An Empirical Study of the Expressions "True," "Perfectly Certain," and "Extremely Probable." Oslo: Jacob Dybwad, 1953.

"Husserl on the Apodictic Evidence of Ideal Laws." *Theoria* 20 (1954): 53–63.

"Synonymity and Empirical Research." *Methodos* 8 (1956): 3–22.

"Synonymity as Revealed by Intuition (Discussion of B. Mates's *Synonymity*)." *Philosophical Review* 66 (1957): 87–93.

"What Does 'Testability' Mean? An Account of a Procedure Developed by Ludvig Løvestad." *Methodos* 9 (1957): 229–237.

"Systematization of Gandhian Ethics of Conflict Resolution." *Journal of Conflict Resolution* 2 (1958): 140–155.

"Logical Equivalence, Intentional Isomorphism and Synonymity as Studied by Questionnaires, Sacred to the Memory of Gerrit Mannoury." *Synthese* 10a (1956–1958): 471–479.

"Do We Know That Basic Norms Cannot Be True or False?" *Theoria* 25 (1959): 31–55. (Also in SWAN, vol. 8.)

"Typology of Questionnaires Adopted to the Study of Expressions with Closely Related Meanings." *Synthese* 12 (1960): 481–494. Reprinted in *Logic and Language: Studies Dedicated to Rudolf Carnap on the Occasion of His Seventieth Birthday*, edited by Yehoshua Bar-Hillel et al. (Dordrecht, Netherlands: Synthese Library, 1962), 206–219.

"The Inquiring Mind: Notes on the Relation Between Philosophy and Science." *Inquiry* 4 (1961): 162–189. Prepared in close cooperation with Eivind Storheim. Reprinted in *Philosophy Today* 5 (1961): 185–204.

"Can Knowledge Be Reached?" Lecture delivered at Oxford University, October 1960. *Inquiry* 4 (1961): 219–227. (Also in SWAN, vol. 8.)

"A Study of 'Or.'" *Synthese* 13 (1961): 49–60. (Also in SWAN, vol. 8.)

"Nonmilitary Defense." In *Preventing World War III*. Edited by Quincy Wright, William M. Evan, and Morton Deutsch. New York: Simon and Schuster, 1962, 123–135. (Also in SWAN, vol. 9.)

"We Still Do Not Know That Norms Cannot Be True or False: A Reply to Dag Österburg." *Theoria* 28 (1962): 205–209. (Also in SWAN, vol. 8.)

Equivalent Terms and Notions in Spinoza's Ethics. Oslo: Filosofisk Institutt, Universitet i Oslo, 1962.

"Knowledge and Definiteness of Intention." Unpublished manuscript, 1963. 10 pages.

"Reflections About Total Views." *Philosophy and Phenomenological Research* 25 (1964): 16–29. (Also in SWAN, vol. 10.)

"Pluralistic Theorizing in Physics and Philosophy." *Danish Yearbook of Philosophy* 1 (1964): 101–111.

"Nonmilitary Defense and Foreign Policy." In *Civilian Defense*. Edited by Adam Roberts. London: Peace News Pamphlet, 1964, 33–43.

"Definition and Hypothesis in Plato's Meno." *Inquiry* 7 (1964): 231–234.

"Was It All Worth While? Review of P. de Vomécourt: *Who Lived to See the Day: France in Arms: 1940–1945*." *Peace News*, March 6, 1964.

"Science as Behavior: Prospects and Limitations of a Behavioural Metascience." In *Scientific Psychology: Principles and Approaches*. Edited by B. Wolman and E. Nagel. New York: Basic Books, 1965, 50–67.

Gandhi and the Nuclear Age. Translated by Alastair Hannay. Totowa, NJ: Rowman, 1965.

"The South Wall of Tirich Mir East." *Himalayan Journal* 26 (1965): 97–106.

"Nature Ebbing Out." 1965. In SWAN, vol. 10.

"Psychological and Social Aspects of Scepticism." Paper presented at Samuel Rubin International Seminar on Mental Health at the Postgraduate Center for Mental Health, New York, March 18, 1965. *Inquiry* 9 (1966): 301–321.

Elements of Applied Semantics. Translated by Alastair Hannay. London: Allen and Unwin, 1966.

Sanskrit for Generalister. [Sanskrit for generalists.] Oslo: Institute for Philosophy, University of Oslo. Mimeograph, 1967.

"Physics and the Variety of World Pictures." In *Grundfragen der Wissenschaften, und ihre Wurzeln in der Metaphysik*. Edited by P. Weingartner. Salzburg: Pustet, 1967, 181–188.

"Civilian Defense and Foreign Policy." In *Civilian Defense: An Introduction*. Edited by T. K. Mahadevan et al. New Delhi: Gandhian Peace Foundation, 1967, 102–116.

"Notes on Some Similarities Between Spinoza on the One Hand and Kierkegaard, Heidegger, Sartre on the Other." Unpublished manuscript, 1967.

Scepticism. London and New York: Humanities Press, 1968. (Also in SWAN, vol. 2.)

Four Modern Philosophers: Carnap, Wittgenstein, Heidegger, Sartre. Translated by Alastair Hannay. Chicago: University of Chicago Press, 1968.

"Kierkegaard and the Values of Education." *Journal of Value Inquiry* 12 (1968): 196–200. (Also in SWAN, vol. 8.)

Hvilken Verden er den Virkelige? [Which world is the real one?] Vol. 37 of *Filosofiske Problemer*. Oslo: Universitetsforlaget, 1969. (Also in SWAN, vol. 3.)

"Freedom, Emotion, and Self-Subsistence: The Structure of a Small, Central Part of Spinoza's *Ethics*." *Inquiry* 12 (1969): 66–104. (Also in SWAN, vol. 6.)

"A Plea for Pluralism in Philosophy and Physics (and Discussions)." In *Physics, Logic, and History, Based on the First International Colloquium Held at the University of Denver, May 16–20, 1966*. Edited by Wolfgang Yourgrau and Allen D. Breck. Denver: Plenum Press, 1970, 129–146.

"Rudolf Carnap." *Inquiry* 13 (1970): 337–338.

"Can Violence Lead to Non-Violence: Gandhi's Point of View." In *Gandhi, India and the World: An International Symposium*. Edited by Sibnarayan Ray. Philadelphia: Temple University Press, 1970, 287–299. (Also in SWAN, vol. 9.)

"The Conquest of Mountains: A Contradiction." *Mountain* 14 (1970): 28–29. (Also in SWAN, vol. 10.)

"Language of Creative Research and Language of Science: A Contrast." In *Linguaggi nella societa e nella tecnica: Convegno promosso dalla Ing. C. Olivetti & C., S. p. a. per il centenario della nascita di Camillo Olivetti*. Milano: Edizioni di Comunita, 1970.

"Kierkegaard and the Educational Crisis." *Danish Yearbook of Philosophy* 8 (1971): 65–70.

"Letter to the King of Nepal." In *The Autobiography of a Shipping Man*. Edited and written by Erling D. Naess. Oslo: Seatrade Publications, 1971, 252–253. (Also in SWAN, vol. 10.)

"Notes on a Society in Approximate Ecological Equilibrium: The Sherpas." Unpublished manuscript, 1971.

"Language Under Stress." Lecture at New York University. Unpublished manuscript, 1971. 13 pages.

The Pluralist and Possibilist Aspect of the Scientific Enterprise. Oslo: Universitetsforlaget, 1972. (Also in SWAN, vol. 4.)

"Pyrrhonism Revisited." In *Contemporary Philosophy in Scandinavia.* Edited by Raymond E. Olsen and Anthony M. Paul. Baltimore and London: Johns Hopkins University Press, 1972, 393–403. (Also in SWAN, vol. 8.)

"The Place of Normative Ethics Within a Biological Framework." In *Biology, History, and Natural Philosophy.* Edited by Allen D. Breck and Wolfgang Yourgrau. New York: Plenum, 1972, 197–206.

"The Use of Normative Ethical and Political Models in Future Research." Unpublished manuscript, 1972. 7 pages.

"Green Socialism." Unpublished manuscript, 1972. 5 pages.

"Emotion and Value." Lecture at Edmonton, March 1972. Unpublished manuscript, 1972.

"The Shallow and the Deep, Long-Range Ecology Movement: A Summary." *Inquiry* 16 (1973): 95–100. (Also in SWAN, vol. 10.)

"A Place of Joy in a World of Fact." *North American Review* (summer 1973): 53–57. (Also in SWAN, vol. 10.)

"Attitudes Towards Nature and Interactions with Nature." Three lectures given at University of Hong Kong. Unpublished manuscript, 1973. 20 pages.

"Secondary Qualities in the Light of Sextus Empiricus' Interpretation of Protagoras." Unpublished manuscript, 1973. 19 pages.

"Introduction to Ecosophy." Lectures given at University of Hong Kong. Unpublished manuscript, 1973.

Gandhi and Group Conflict: An Exploration of Satyagraha. Oslo: Universitetsforlaget, 1974. (Also in SWAN, vol. 5.)

"The Ecopolitical Frontier: A Case Study." *Intercol. Bulletin* 5 (1974): 18–26.

"Is Freedom Consistent with Spinoza's Determinism?" In *Spinoza on Knowing, Being, and Freedom: Proceedings of the Spinoza Symposium Leusden, 1973.* Edited by J. G. van der Bend. Assen: Van Gorcum & Co. B.V., 1974, 6–23. Reprinted in *Spinoza,* edited by Martin Schewe and Achim Engstler (Frankfurt: Peter Lang, 1990) 227–247. (Also in SWAN, vol. 9.)

"Martin Heidegger." In *Encyclopedia Britannica.* 15th ed. 1974.

Equivalent Terms and Notions in Spinoza's Ethics. Oslo: Inquiry, Filosofisk Institutt, Universitet i Oslo, 1974.

Freedom, Emotion and Self-Subsistence: The Structure of a Central Part of Spinoza's Ethics. Oslo: Universitetsforlaget, 1975. (Also in SWAN, vol. 6.)

"The Case Against Science." In *Science Between Culture and Counter-culture.* Edited by C. I. Dessaur. Nijmegen, Netherlands: Dekker & Van de Vegt, 1975, 25–48. (Also in SWAN, vol. 9.)

"Why Not Science for Anarchists Too? (A Reply to Feyerabend)." *Inquiry* 18 (1975): 183–194. (Also in SWAN, vol. 9.)

"Possibilism." Unpublished manuscript, 1975. 16 pages.

"But the Sceptics Keep on Searching." Unpublished manuscript, 1975. 20 pages.

"Notes on the Methodology of Normative Systems." *Methodology and Science* 10 (1977): 64–79. (Also in SWAN, vol. 10.)

"Spinoza and Ecology." *Philosophia* 7, no. 1 (1977): 45–54.

"The Limited Neutrality of Typologies of Systems: A Reply to Gullvåg." *Inquiry* 20 (1977): 67–72. Also published in *Trumpeter* 22, 1 Feistschrift Section Winter 2006.

"Spinoza and Ecology." In *Specuum Spinozanum 1677–1977*. Edited by S. Hessing. London: Routledge, 1977, 418–425.

"Husserl on the Apodictic Evidence of Ideal Laws." In *Readings on Edmund Husserl's Logical Investigations*. Edited by J. N. Mohanty. The Hague: Martinus Nijhoff, 1977, 67–75. Reprinted in *Theoria* 20: 53–63. (Also in SWAN, vol. 8.)

"Friendship, Strength of Emotion, and Freedom." In *Spinoza Herdacht: 1677, 21 Februari 1977*. Amsterdam: Algemeen Nederlands Tijdschrift voor Wijsbegeerte, 1977, 11–19.

"Through Spinoza to Mahayana Buddhism, or Through Mahayana Buddhism to Spinoza?" In *Spinoza's Philosophy of Man: Proceedings of the Scandinavian Spinoza Symposium 1977*. Edited by J. Wetlesen. Oslo: Universitetsforlaget, 1978, 136–158. (Also in SWAN, vol. 9.)

"Ideology and Rationality." Lecture to the European University Institute, Florence, 1978. Revised and abbreviated in *Ideology and Politics*, ed. Maurice Cranston and Peter Mair (Alphen aan den Rijn: Sijthoff, 1980), 133–142. (Also in SWAN, vol. 9.)

"Self-Realization in Mixed Communities of Humans, Bears, Sheep, and Wolves." *Inquiry* 22 (1979): 231–241. (Also in SWAN, vol. 10.)

"Modesty and the Conquest of Mountains." In *The Mountain Spirit*. Edited by Michael C. Tobias and H. Drasdo. New York: Overlook Press, 1979, 13–16. (Also in SWAN, vol. 10.)

"Towards a Theory of Wide Cognitivism." In *Theory of Knowledge and Science Policy*. Edited by W. Callebaut et al. Ghent, Belgium: Communication and Cognition, 1979, 111–118.

"Environmental Ethics and Spinoza's Ethics: Comments on Genevieve Lloyd's Article." *Inquiry* 23 (1980): 313–325.

"Whole Philosophies as Data and as Constructs." In *Social Science for What? Festschrift for Johan Galtung*. Edited by H. H. Holm and E. Rudeng. Oslo: University Press, 1980, 182–188.

"Spinoza's Finite God." *Revue Internationale de Philosophie* 135 (1981): 120–126. (Also in SWAN, vol. 9.)

"The Empirical Semantics of Key Terms, Phrases and Sentences." In *Philosophy and Grammar: Papers on the Occasion of the Quincentennial of Uppsala University*. Edited by Stig Kanger and Sven Öhman. Dordrecht, Netherlands: D. Reidel, 1981, 135–154. (Also in SWAN, vol. 8.)

"The Primacy of the Whole." In *Holism and Ecology*. Edited by Arne Naess and Danilo Dolci. Tokyo: U.N. University (HSDRGPID-61/UNEP-326), 1981, 1–10.

"Spinoza and the Deep Ecology Movement." Unpublished manuscript, 1982. Revised in 1991 and published as *Spinoza and the Deep Ecology Movement*. Delft: Eburon, 1993. (Also in SWAN, vol. 10.)

"Simple in Means, Rich in Ends: A Conversation with Arne Naess." *Ten Directions* (summer/fall 1982): 7–12. Reprinted in *Voices for Deep Ecology* (Salt Lake City: Dream Garden Press, 1983).

"A Necessary Component of Logic: Empirical Argumentation and Analysis." In *Argumentation: Approaches to Theory Formation*. Edited by E. M. Barth and J. L. Martens. Amsterdam: John Benjamins, 1982, 9–22.

"An Application of Empirical Argumentation Analysis to Spinoza's 'Ethics.'" In *Argumentation: Approaches to Theory Formation*. Edited by E. M. Barth and J. L. Martens. Amsterdam: John Benjamins, 1982, 245–255.

"Spinoza and Attitudes Toward Nature." In *Spinoza: His Thought and Work*. Jerusalem: Israel Academy of Sciences and Humanities, 1983, 160–175. (Also in SWAN, vol. 10.)

"How My Philosophy Seemed to Develop." In *Philosophers on Their Own Work*. Edited by Andre Mercier and Maja Svilar. Bern: Peter Lang, 1983, 209–226. (Also in SWAN, vol. 9.)

"Einstein, Spinoza, and God." In *Old and New Questions in Physics, Cosmology, Philosophy, and Theoretical Biology: Essays in Honor of Wolfgang Yourgrau*. Edited by A. van der Merwe. New York: Plenum Press, 1983, 683–687. (Also in SWAN, vol. 9.)

"A Defense of the Deep Ecology Movement." *Environmental Ethics* 6 (1984): 265–270.

"Identification as a Source of Deep Ecological Attitudes." In *Deep Ecology*. Edited by Michael Tobias. San Marcos, CA: Avant Books, 1984, 256–270.

"Intuition, Intrinsic Value and Deep Ecology: Arne Naess Replies." *The Ecologist* 14 (5–6 1984): 201–203.

"The Arrogance of Anti-Humanism?" *Ecophilosophy* 6 (May 1984): 8–9. (Also in SWAN, vol. 10.)

"Deep Ecology and Lifestyle." In *The Paradox of Environmentalism: Symposium Proceedings in Downsview, Ontario*. Edited by Neil Everndon. Toronto: Faculty of Environmental Studies, York University, 57–60, 1984. (Also in SWAN, vol. 10.)

A Sceptical Dialogue on Induction. Assen, Netherlands: Van Gorcum, 1984.

"Cultural Anthropology: A New Approach to the Study of How to Conceive of Our Own Future." 15 lectures given in Vienna. Unpublished manuscript, 1984.

"The Green Utopia of 2084." Paper presented at the University of Minnesota. Unpublished manuscript, 1984. 9 pages.

"The Politics of the Deep Ecology Movement." 1984. In SWAN, vol. 10.

"The World of Concrete Contents." *Inquiry* 28 (1985): 417–428. (Also in SWAN, vol. 10.)

"Ecosophy T." In *Deep Ecology: Living as If Nature Mattered*. Edited by Bill Devall and George Sessions. Salt Lake City: Gibbs Smith, 1985, 225–228.

"Gestalt Thinking and Buddhism." 1985. 9 pages. In SWAN, vol. 10.

"Deep Ecology in Good Conceptual Health." *Trumpeter* 3 (1986): 18–22.

"Intrinsic Nature: Will the Defenders of Nature Please Rise?" In *Conservation Biology: The Science and Scarcity of Diversity*. Edited by Michael E. Soulé. Sunderland, MA: Sinauer Associates, 1986, 504–515.

"The Deep Ecology Movement: Some Philosophical Aspects." *Philosophical Inquiry* 8 (1986): 10–31. (Also in SWAN, vol. 10.)

"Consequences of an Absolute *No* to Nuclear War." In *Nuclear Weapons and the Future of Humanity: The Fundamental Questions*. Edited by Avner Cohen and Steven Lee. Totowa, NJ: Rowman and Allanheld, 1986, 425–436. (Also in SWAN, vol. 9.)

"Self-Realization: An Ecological Approach to Being in the World." Keith Roby Memorial Lecture in Community Science, Murdoch University, Australia, March 12, 1986. (Also in SWAN, vol. 10.)

"The Connection of 'Self-Realization!' with Diversity, Complexity, and Symbiosis." Unpublished manuscript, 1986. 4 pages.

"From Ecology to Ecosophy, From Science to Wisdom." Unpublished manuscript, 1987. 7 pages.

"Solidarity, Money, and the Well-to-Do." *Pan Ecology: An Irregular Journal of Nature and Human Nature* 1, no. 3 (1987): 1–4.

"For Its Own Sake." *Trumpeter* 4, no. 2 (1987): 28–29.

"Notes on the Politics of the Deep Ecology Movement." In *Sustaining Gaia: Contributions to Another World View*. Edited by Frank Fisher. Glen Waverly, Victoria, Australia: Aristoc Offset, 1987, 178–198.

"Scientific and Technological Biomedical Progress as Cultural Concepts (Colloque de l'Académie Internationale de Philosophie des Sciences, organisé à Bruxelles, April

23–28, 1984)." In *La Responsabilité Ethique dans le Dévelopement Biomedical*, Louvain-la-Neuve, France: CIACO éditeur, 1987, 199–203.

"Self-Realization: An Ecological Approach to Being in the World." *Trumpeter* 4, no. 3 (1987). (Also in SWAN, vol. 10.)

"Environmental Ethics and International Justice." 1987. Revised and abbreviated in *Ecospirit* 4, no. 1 (1988).

"Population Reduction: An Ecosophical View." 1987. 8 pages. In SWAN, vol. 10.

"The Period of Transition in Rich Countries: Economic Consequences." 1987.

"Ecosophy, Population, and Free Nature." Unpublished manuscript, 1987. Revised in *Trumpeter* 5, no. 3 (1988): 113–119.

"Green Society and Deep Ecology." Schumacher lecture. Unpublished manuscript, 1987. 14 pages.

Ekspertenes Syn På Naturens Egenverdi. [Expert views on the intrinsic value of nature.] Trondheim: Tapir Forlag, 1987. (Also in SWAN, vol. 10.)

"The Basics of Deep Ecology." *Resurgence* 126 (1988): 4–7. Reprinted in *The Green Fuse*. Edited by John Button (London: Quartet Books, 1990), 130–137. (Also in SWAN, vol. 10.)

"Self-Realization: An Ecological Approach to Being in the World." Excerpted from the Keith Roby Memorial Lecture, March 12, 1986. In *Thinking Like a Mountain: Towards a Council of All Beings*. Edited by John Seed et al. Philadelphia: New Society Publishers, 1988.

"Deep Ecology and Ultimate Premises." *Ecologist* 18 (1988): 128–131.

"Sustainable Development and the Deep Long-Range Ecology Movement." *Trumpeter* 5 (1988): 138–142.

"Norway: A Developing Country with Good Prospects." In *One Earth—One World*. Oslo: Ministry of Environment, 1988. (Also in SWAN, vol. 10.)

"On the Structure and Function of Paradigms in Science." In *Theories of Carcinogenesis*. Edited by Olav Hilmar Iversen. Washington, DC: Hemisphere Publishing Corporation, 1988, 1–9. (Also in SWAN, vol. 9.)

"A European Looks at the North American Branches of the Deep Ecology Movement." *Trumpeter* 5, no. 2 (1988): 75–76.

"What Is Gestalt Thinking? A Note." 1988. In SWAN, vol. 8.

"Should We Try to Relieve Cases of Extreme Suffering in Nature?" 1988. In SWAN, vol. 10.

"Cultural Diversity and the Deep Ecology Movement." Unpublished manuscript, 1988. 10 pages.

Ecology, Community, and Lifestyle: Outline of an Ecosophy. Translated and revised by D. Rothenberg. Cambridge: Cambridge University Press, 1989.

"Ecosophy, Population, and Sustainable Development." Unpublished manuscript, 1989. 15 pages.

"The Deepness of Deep Ecology." *Earth First!* (December 1989): 32.

"Quality of Life Research." Unpublished manuscript, 1989.

"Sustainable Development and the Deep Ecology Movement." 1989. Reprinted as "Sustainable Development and Deep Ecology," in *Ethics of Environment and Development: Global Challenge, International Response*, edited by R. J. Engel and J. G. Engel (Tucson: University of Arizona Press, 1990), 87–96. (Also in SWAN, vol. 10.)

"A Note on Definition, Criteria, and Characterizations." Unpublished manuscript, 1989. 3 pages.

"Ecosophy and Gestalt Ontology." *Trumpeter* 6, no. 4 (1989): 134–137.

"Metaphysics of the Treeline." *Edge* 2 (1989): 25–26.

"Finding Common Ground." *Green Synthesis* (March 1989): 9–10.

"Metaphysics of the Treeline." *Appalachia* (June 15, 1989): 56–59. (Also in SWAN, vol. 10.)

"The Basics of Deep Ecology." *Actual English* (All English General Information Society, Kyoto, Japan), 1989.

"Arne Naess Gives His Support to Edward Goldsmith's 'The Way.'" *Ecologist* 19, no. 5 (1989): 196–197.

"Ecosophy: Beyond East and West (an interview with Richard Evanoff)." *Kyoto Journal* 11 (summer 1989): 40–44.

"The 18 Points, 1972 Version of The 'Deep Ecology Movement: An Outline.'" Unpublished manuscript, 1989.

"The Norwegian Green Party: Some Theoretical Reflections." Unpublished manuscript, 1989. 5 pages.

"Gestalt Ontology and Gestalt Thinking." 1989. In SWAN, vol. 10.

"Docta Ignorantia and the Application of General Guidelines." Unpublished manuscript, 1989. 4 pages. In SWAN, vol. 10.

"Deep Ecology, Wilderness, and the Third World." 1989. In SWAN, vol. 10.

"Japan's Second and Last Mistake." *Japan Environment Monitor* 3, no. 2 (1990): 6–7.

"Deepness of Questions and the Deep Ecology Movement." Unpublished manuscript, 1990.

"'Man Apart' and Deep Ecology: A Reply to Reed." *Environmental Ethics* 12 (summer 1990): 185–192.

"Spinoza and Attitudes Towards Nature." 1990. In SWAN, vol. 10.

"An Intramural Note on Transpersonal Ecosophy." Unpublished manuscript, 1990.

"Deep Ecology and Conservation Biology." *Earth First!* (March 20, 1990): 29. (Also in SWAN, vol. 10.)

"Pushing for a Deep Change." (Interview.) *English Journal* 4 (April 1990).

"The Deep Ecology Movement and Ecologism." *Anarchy* (summer 1990): 33.

"Politics and the Ecological Crisis: An Introductory Note." *ReVISION* 13, no. 1 (1991): 142–146. (Also in SWAN, vol. 10.)

"The Connection of 'Self-Realization!' with Diversity, Complexity and Symbiosis." Unpublished manuscript, 1991. 7 pages.

"Should We Try to Relieve Cases of Extreme Suffering in Nature?" *PanEcology* 6, no. 1 (1991): 1–5. (Also in SWAN, vol. 10.)

"Paul Feyerabend: A Green Hero?" In *Beyond Reason*. Edited by Munénar. Dordrecht, Netherlands: Kluwer Academic Publishers, 1991, 403–416. (Also in SWAN, vol. 10.)

"A Memorial Tribute to Peter Wessel Zapffe." *Norwegian Literature 1991* (1991).

"A Note on the Prehistory and History of the Deep Ecology Movement." 1991. In SWAN, vol. 10.

"Freedom, Self, and Activeness According to Spinoza." Unpublished manuscript, 1991.

"To Understand Without Translations." Unpublished manuscript, 1991.

"Sustainability! The Integral Approach." In *Conservation of Biodiversity for Sustainable Development*. Edited by O. T. Sandlund, K. Hindar, and A. H. D. Brown. Oslo: Scandinavian University Press, 1992, 303–310. (Also in SWAN, vol. 10.)

"The Encouraging Richness and Diversity of Ultimate Premises in Environmental Philosophy." *Trumpeter* 9, no. 2 (1992): 53–60. (Also in SWAN, vol. 10.)

"The Principle of Intensity." Originally written in the 1940s. 1992. In SWAN, vol. 8.

"To Grow Up or to Get to Be More Mature?" *Trumpeter* 9, no. 2 (1992): 80–81.

"What About Science in Ecologically Sustainable Societies? Unpublished manuscript, 1992.

"The Three Great Movements." *Trumpeter* 9, no. 2 (1992): 85–86. (Also in SWAN, vol. 10.)

"Deep Ecology for the 22nd Century." *Trumpeter* 9, no. 2 (1992): 86–88. (Also in SWAN, vol. 10.)

"Tvergastein: An Example of Place." 1992. In SWAN, vol. 10.

"The Deep Ecology Platform Revisited." Unpublished manuscript, 1992.

"Ayer on Metaphysics: A Critical Commentary by a Kind of Metaphysician." Vol. 25 of *The Philosophy of A. J. Ayer.* Edited by Lewis Edwin Hahn. La Salles, IL: Open Court, 1992, 329–340.

"How Can the Empirical Movement Be Promoted Today? A Discussion of the Empiricism of Otto Neurath and Rudolph Carnap." (The original German version, "Wie fördert man heute die empirische Bewegung? Eine Auseinandersetzung mit dem Empirismus von Otto Neurath und Rudolph Carnap," was written during 1937–1939. It appeared in Oslo University's *Filosofiske Problemer* 19, 1956.) In *From an Empirical Point of View: The Empirical Turn in Logic.* Edited by E. M. Barth, J. Vandormael, and F. Vandamme. Gent, Belgium: Communication and Cognition, 1992, 107–155. (Also in SWAN, vol. 8.)

"Introductory Biology and 'Life Appreciation' Courses." *Trumpeter* 9 (1992): 126.

"Third World, Deep Ecology, Socialism, and Hitlerism: An Open Letter." *Deep Ecologist* 43 (1992): 4–5.

"Deep Ecology and Potters in Our Planet." *Studio Potter* 20 (1992): 38–39. Reprinted in *Trumpeter* 21, no. 2 (2005): 24–28.

"Beautiful Action: Its Function in the Ecological Crisis." *Environmental Values* 2, no. 1 (1993): 67–71. (Also in SWAN, vol. 10.)

"Simple in Means, Rich in Ends: An Interview with Arne Naess by Stephan Bodian." In *Environmental Philosophy: From Animal Rights to Radical Ecology.* Edited by Michael E. Zimmerman et al. Englewood Cliffs, NJ: Prentice-Hall, 1993, 437.

Deep Ecology and Politics. Working Paper 1993. Oslo: Centre for Development and Environment, University of Oslo, 1993. 7 pages. (A revision of three articles "The Three Great Movements," "Comments on the Planned Official Norwegian Presentation in Rio, April 1992," and "Politics and the Ecological Crisis: An Introductory Note.")

"The Politics of the Deep Ecology Movement." In *Wisdom and the Open Air: The Norwegian Roots of Deep Ecology.* Edited by Peter Reed and David Rothenberg. Minneapolis: University of Minnesota Press, 1993, 82–99. (Also in SWAN, vol. 10.)

"Everything Really Important Is Dangerous: An Interview with Arne Naess by David Rothenberg." In *Wisdom and the Open Air: The Norwegian Roots of Deep Ecology.* Edited by Peter Reed and David Rothenberg. Minneapolis: University of Minnesota Press, 1993, 99–111.

"'You Assert This?' An Empirical Study of Weight-Expressions." In *Empirical Logic and Public Debate: Essays in Honour of Else M. Barth.* Edited by Erik C. W. Krabbe, Reneé José Dalitz, and Pier A. Smit. Amsterdam and Atlanta: Rudopi, 1993, 121–132. (Also in SWAN, vol. 8.)

"Logical Empiricism and the Uniqueness of the Schlick Seminar: A Personal Experience with Consequences." In *Scientific Philosophy.* Edited by Friedrich Stadler. Dordrecht, Netherlands: Kluwer Academic Publishers, 1993, 11–25.

"The Tragedy of Norwegian Whaling: A Response to Norwegian Environment Group Support for Whaling." *North Sea Monitor* (December 1993): 10–12. (Also in SWAN, vol. 10.)

"How Should Supporters of the Deep Ecology Movement Behave in Order to Affect Society and Culture?" *Trumpeter* 10 (1993): 98–100.

"The Breadth and the Limits of the Deep Ecology Movement." *Wild Earth* 3 (1993): 74–75.

"The Deep Ecological Movement: Some Philosophical Aspects." In *Environmental Ethics: Divergence and Convergence*. Edited by Susan J. Armstrong and Richard G. Botzler. New York: McGraw-Hill, 1993, 411–421. (Also in SWAN, vol. 10.)

"Culture and Environment." In *Culture and Environment: Interdisciplinary Approaches*. Edited by Nina Witoszek and Elizabeth Gulbrandsen. Oslo: Centre for Development and Environment, University of Oslo, 1993, 201–209. Reprinted in *International Journal of Ecoforestry* 10 (1994) and *Trumpeter* 21, no. 1 (2005): 53–58.

"Mountains and Mythology." Unpublished manuscript, 1993. 2 pages.

"In Praise of Books of the Big Outside." *Wild Earth* 3 (1993): 88–89. Reprinted in *Trumpeter* 21, no. 2 (2005): 61–64.

"Climbing and the Deep Ecology Movement." Unpublished manuscript, 1994. 3 pages.

"The Heart of the Forest." *International Journal of Ecoforestry* 10 (1994): 40–41. Reprinted in *Ecoforestry: Art and Science of Sustainable Forest Use*, edited by Alan Drengson and D. M. Taylor (Gabriola Island, British Columbia: New Society Publishers, 1997), 358–360.

"The Norwegian Roots of Deep Ecology." In *Nature: The True Home of Culture*. Edited by Børge Dahle. Oslo: Norges Idrettshøgskole, 1994, 15–18. Reprinted in *Trumpeter* 21, no. 2 (2005): 38–41.

"History, Postmodernism, and Deep Ecology." Unpublished manuscript, 1994.

"The Arctic Dimension Outside and Inside Us." Paper presented at Ecophilosophy Symposium, Svalbard, Norway, August 28–September 2, 1994. Unpublished manuscript, 1994.

"A Green History of the World." Lecture at Schumacher College, Totnes, England, July 1994. Unpublished manuscript, 1994.

"Apron Diagram: An Example." Unpublished manuscript, 1994. 3 pages.

"How My Philosophy Seemed to Have Developed: 1983–1994." 1994. In SWAN, vol. 9.

"Creativity and Gestalt Thinking." *Structuralist* 33/34 (1994): 51–52. (Also in SWAN, vol. 8.)

"The Apron Diagram." In *The Deep Ecology Movement: An Introductory Anthology*. Edited by Alan Drengson and Yuichi Inoue. Berkeley, CA: North Atlantic Books, 1995, 10–12. (Also in SWAN, vol. 10.)

"The 'Eight Points' Revisited." In *Deep Ecology for the 21st Century*. Edited by George Sessions. Boston and London: Shambhala, 1995, 213–221. (Also in SWAN, vol. 10.)

"Deepness of Questions and the Deep Ecology Movement." In *Deep Ecology for the 21st Century: Readings on the Philosophy and Practice of the New Environmentalism*. Edited by George Sessions. Boston and London: Shambhala, 1995, 204–212. (Also in SWAN, vol. 10.)

"Deep Ecology in the Line of Fire." *Trumpeter* 12, no. 3 (1995): 146–149.

"Industrial Society, Postmodernity, and Ecological Sustainability." *Humboldt Journal of Social Relations* 21 (1995): 131–146. (Also in SWAN, vol. 10.)

"Deep Ecology for the Twenty-Second Century." In *Deep Ecology for the Twenty-First Century*. Edited by George Sessions. Boston and London: Shambhala, 1995, 463–467. (Also in SWAN, vol. 10.)

"The Third World, Wilderness, and Deep Ecology." In *Deep Ecology for the Twenty-First Century*. Edited by George Sessions. Boston and London: Shambhala, 1995, 397–407. (Also in SWAN, vol. 10.)

Foreword to *The Interconnected Universe*, by Irvin Laszlo. Singapore: World Scientific, 1995, v–vii. Reprinted in *Trumpeter* 22, no. 1 (2006): 4–6.

"Mountains and Mythology." *Trumpeter* 12, no. 4 (1995): 165.

"Heidegger, Postmodernism Theory, and Deep Ecology." Unpublished manuscript, 1996. 4 pages.

"Living a Life That Reflects Evolutionary Insight." *Conservation Biology* 10, no. 6 (1996): 1557–1559.

"Comments on Harold Glasser's 'Deep Ecology Approach' (DEA)." In *Philosophical Dialogues: Arne Naess and the Progress of Ecophilosophy*. Edited by Nina Witoszek and Andrew Brennan. Oslo: Center for Development and the Environment, 1996, 399–401.

"Ecosophy, Community, and Lifestyle." In *Humanism Toward the Third Millennium*. Vol. 2. Edited by Fons Elders. Amsterdam: VUB Press, 1996, 83–93.

"Vagueness and Ambiguity." In *Philosophy of Language*. New York: Walter de Gruyter, 1996, 1407–1417. Reprinted in *Trumpeter* 22, no. 2, Festschrift Section (2006): 56–74.

"A Response to Rowe's 'From Shallow to Deep Ecological Philosophy.'" *Trumpeter* 13, no. 1 (1996): 32.

"Deep Ecology in the Line of Fire." In *Rethinking Deep Ecology: Proceedings from a Seminar at SUM, University of Oslo, 5 September 1995*. Edited by Nina Witoszek. Oslo: Center for Development and the Environment, University of Oslo, 1996, 107–115. Reprinted from *Trumpeter* 12, no. 3: 146–149.

"The Arctic Dimension Outside and Inside Us." In *Deep Ecology in the High Arctic: Proceedings of the 1994 International Ecophilosophical Symposium, Svalbard, Norway, 29th August–2nd September*. Edited by Elisabeth Stoltz Larsen and Robin Buzza. Longyearbyen: Norwegian Polar Institute, 1996, 13–16. Reprinted in *Trumpeter* 21, no. 2 (2005): 42–47.

"Living a Life That Reflects Evolutionary Insight." *Conservation Biology* 10 (1996): 1557–1559.

"Does Humanity Have a Cosmic Role? Protecting and Restoring the Planet." *Environment Network News* (May/June 1996). Reprinted in *Trumpeter* 21, no. 1 (2005): 49–52.

"An Outline of Problems Ahead." Talk given at Environmental Justice Conference, Melbourne, October 1997. 1997. In SWAN, vol. 10.

"Conquest of Mountains." *Resurgence* 183 (July/August 1997): 24–25. Reprinted in *Trumpeter* 21, no. 2 (2005): 55–56.

"'Free Nature': An Interview with Ian Angus." *Alternatives Journal* 23, no. 3 (1997): 18–21.

"Insulin Shock Method and the Economic Crisis in Vienna in 1934." In *Some Notes on Madness*. Edited by Tarja Heiskanen. Helsinki: Finnish Association for Mental Health, SMS Publishers, 1997.

"Heidegger, Postmodern Theory, and Deep Ecology." *Trumpeter* 14, no. 4 (1997): 181–183.

"All Together Now: A Review of E. O. Wilson's *Consilience*." *New Scientist* (August 22, 1998): 42–43.

"The Spirit of the Vienna Circle Devoted to Questions of *Lebens- und Weltauffassung*." In *Game Theory, Experience, Rationality*. Edited by W. Leinfellner and E. Köhler. Dordrecht, Netherlands: Kluwer Academic, 1998, 359–367. (Also in SWAN, vol. 8.)

"The Term 'Development' Today." *Development Today* 8, no. 1 (1998): 10–11.

"Interview of Arne Naess by Casey Walker." *Wild Duck Review* 4, no. 1 (1998): 18–20.

"Arne Naess Speaks About Ecophilosophy and Solidarity." *Ragtime* 5 (1998): 16–17.

"The Principle of Intensity." *Journal of Value Inquiry* 33 (1999): 5–9. (Also in SWAN, vol. 8.)

"Ecoforestry and the Deep Ecology Movement." In *Proceedings of the Fourth Biannual Conference of the Taiga Rescue Network, October 5–10, 1999*. Edited by Rein Ahas et al. Tartu, Estonia, 1999, 72–73.

"An Outline of the Problems Ahead." In *Global Ethics and the Environment*. Edited by Nicholas Low. London and New York: Routledge, 1999. (Also in SWAN, vol. 10.)

"Avalanches as Social Constructions." *Environmental Ethics* 22 (fall 2000): 335–336. (Also in SWAN, vol. 10.)

"Ranking, Yes, but the Inherent Value Is the Same: An Answer to William C. French." 2005. In SWAN, vol. 10.

"Notes on Gestalt Ontology." *Trumpeter* 21, no. 1 (2005): 119–128.

"The Basics of Deep Ecology." *Trumpeter* 21, no. 1 (2005): 61–71.

"Articulation of Normative Interrelation: An Information Theoretical Approach." *Trumpeter* 21, no. 1 (2005): 103–109.

"Architecture and the Deep Ecology Movement." *Trumpeter* 21, no. 2 (2005): 29–34.

"Mountains." *Trumpeter* 21, no. 2 (2005): 51–54.

"Trust and Confidence: An Answer to Rescher's Reappraisal of Scepticism." 2005. In SWAN, vol. 8.

"Creativity and Gestalt Thinking." 2005. In SWAN, vol. 8.

"The Deep Ecology '8 Points' Revisited." 2005. In SWAN, vol. 10.

"What Do We as Supporters of the D.E.M. Stand for and Believe In?" 2005. In SWAN, vol. 10.

The Selected Works of Arne Naess, 10 Volumes, Dordrecht, Netherlands: Springer, 2005. The volume titles are as follows: 1, *Interpretation and Preciseness: A Contribution to a Theory of Communication*; 2, *Skepticism: Wonder and Joys of a Wandering Seeker*; 3, *Which World Is the Real One? An Inquiry into Inclusive Systems, Cultures and Philosophies*; 4, *The Pluralist and Possibilist Aspect of the Scientific Enterprise: Rich Descriptions, Abundant Choices and Open Futures*; 5, *Gandhi and Group Conflict: Explorations of Nonviolent Resistance, Satyagraha*; 6, *Freedom, Emotion, and Self-subsistence: Structure of a Central Part of Spinoza's Ethics*; 7, *Communication and Argument: Elements of Applied Semantics*; 8, *Common Sense, Knowledge and Truth: Open Inquiry in a Pluralistic World*; 9, *Reason, Democracy and Science: Understanding Among Conflicting Worldviews*; 10, *Deep Ecology of Wisdom: Exploration in Unities of Nature and Cultures*.

"A Note on the Methodology of Normative Systems." *Trumpeter* 22, no. 1 (2006): 14–28.

"Gandhian Nonviolent Verbal Communication: The Necessity of Training." *Trumpeter* 22, no. 2, Festschrift Section (2006): 100–111.

ARNE NAESS WRITINGS (WITH COAUTHORS)

Austin, John L., and Arne Naess. "On Herman Tennessen's 'What Should We Say.'" In *Eighteen Papers on Language Analysis and Empirical Semantics*. Edited by Herman Tennessen. University of Alberta, Edmonton: 1964, 143–149.

Galtung, Johan, and Arne Naess. *Gandhis Politiske Etikk*. [Gandhi's political ethics.] Oslo: Johan Grundt Tanum, 1955; 2nd ed. 1968.

Grøn, Øyvind, and Arne Naess. *Introduction to General Relativity and Its Mathematics*. Oslo: Høgskolen in Oslo report, 1998, 14.

Gullvåg, Ingemund, and Arne Naess. "Vagueness and Ambiguity." In *Philosophy of Language*. Vol. 2. Edited by Marcelo Dascal et al. Berlin and New York: Walter de Gruyter, 1996, 1407–1417. Also published in *Trumpeter* 22, 1 Festschrift Section, Winter 2006.

Mysterud, Ivar, and Arne Naess. "Philosophy of Wolf Policies II: Supernational Strategy and Emergency Interim Management." Unpublished manuscript, 1990. 14 pages.

Naess, Arne, and A. J. Ayer. "The Glass Is on the Table: An Empiricist Versus a Total

View (A Debate Between Ayer and Naess)." In *Reflexive Water: The Basic Concerns of Mankind*. Edited by Fons Elders. London: Souvenir Press, 1974, 11–68. (Also in SWAN, vol. 8.)

Naess, Arne, and Johan (Bilder) Brun. *Det Gode Lange Livs Far: Hallingskarvet sett fra Tvergastein*. Oslo: N. W. Damm and Son, 1995.

Naess, Arne, Jens Christophersen, and Kjell Kvalø. *Democracy, Ideology, and Objectivity: Studies in the Semantics and Cognitive Analysis of Ideological Controversy*. Oslo: Universitetsforlaget, 1956.

Naess, Arne, and Johan Galtung. *Metodelaere*. [Methodology.] Oslo: Universitetsforlagets Trykningssentral, 1969.

Naess, Arne, and Alastair Hannay. "An Appeal to the Cramped Scholar by Way of a Foreword." In *An Invitation to Chinese Philosophy: Eight Studies*. Edited by Arne Naess and Alastair Hannay. Oslo: Universitetsforlaget, 1972, vii–xv.

Naess, Arne, and Alastair Hannay, eds. *An Invitation to Chinese Philosophy: Eight Studies*. Oslo: Universitetsforlaget, 1972.

Naess, Arne, and Per Ingvar Haukeland. *Livsfilosofi: Et personlig bidrag om følelser og fornuft*. Oslo: Universitetsforlaget, 1998.

Naess, Arne, with Per Ingvar Haukeland. *Life's Philosophy: Reason and Feeling in a Deeper World*. Foreword by Bill McKibben and introduction by Harold Glasser. Translated by Roland Huntford. Athens and London: University of Georgia Press, 2002.

Naess, Arne, and Jon Hellesnes. "Norway." In *Handbook of World Philosophy Since 1945*. Edited by John Burr. Westport, CT: Greenwood Press, 1980, 159–171.

Naess, Arne, and Sigmund Kvaløy (translator). "Some Ethical Considerations with a View to Mountaineering in Norway." *Alpine Journal* (American Alpine Club) (1969): 230–233.

Naess, Arne, and Ivar Mysterud. "Philosophy of Wolf Policies I: General Principles and Preliminary Exploration of Selected Norms." *Conservation Biology* 1 (1987): 22–34.

Naess, Arne, and Helena Norberg-Hodge. "Self-Realization and Society." *Resurgence* 180 (1997).

Naess, Arne, and Stein Rokkan. "Analytical Survey of Agreements and Disagreements." In *Democracy in a World of Tensions*. Edited by Richard McKeon and with the assistance of Stein Rokkan. Chicago: University of Chicago Press, 1951, 447–512.

Naess, Arne, and George Sessions. "Basic Principles of Deep Ecology." *Ecophilosophy* 4 (May 1984): 3–7.

Naess, Arne, Liu Shiao-Ru, and Nicholas Gould. "Deep Ecology (A Conversation on 'Deep Ecology' and Taiwan's Environmental Problems)." *Issues and Options* 44, no. 1 (1989): 1–6.

Naess, Arne, and Jon Wetlesen. *Conation and Cognition in Spinoza's Theory of Affects: A Reconstruction*. Oslo: University of Oslo, 1967.

Naess, Erling D. "The Autobiography of a Shipping Man." Oslo: Seatrade Publications, 1971.

Naess, Siri, Torbjørn Moum, and Tom Sørensen, with the cooperation of Arne Mastekaasa. *Quality of Life Research: Concepts, Methods, and Applications*. Oslo: Institute of Applied Social Research, 1987.

Naess, Siri, and Arne Naess. "Psychological Research and Human Problems." *Philosophy of Science* 27 (1960): 134–146.

Seed, John, Joanna Macy, Pat Fleming, and Arne Naess, eds. *Thinking Like a Mountain: Towards a Council of All Beings*. Philadelphia: New Society Publishers, 1988.

SELECT FESTSCHRIFTS, BOOKS, AND JOURNAL ISSUES DEVOTED TO ARNE NAESS

Drengson, Alan, ed. "The Long-Range Deep Ecology Movement and Arne Naess." Special edition of *Trumpeter* 9, no. 2 (1992).

Drengson, Alan, and Bill Devall, eds. Special Arne Naess Series. *Trumpeter* 21, nos. 1 and 2 (2005), and 22, nos. 1 (Festschrift Section) and 2 (2006).

Gullvåg, Ingemund, and Jon Wetlesen, eds. *In Sceptical Wonder: Inquiries into the Philosophy of Arne Naess on the Occasion of His Seventieth Birthday*. Oslo: University of Oslo Press, 1982.

Light, Andrew, and David Rothenberg, eds. *Arne Naess's Environmental Thought*. Special edition of *Inquiry* 39 (1996).

Rothenberg, David. *Is It Painful to Think? Conversations with Arne Naess*. Minneapolis: University of Minnesota Press, 1993.

Singh, Rana P. B., ed. *Environmental Ethics and the Power of Place: Festschrift to Arne Naess*. Varanasi, India: National Geographic Journal of India, 1994.

Witoszek, Nina, and Andrew Brennan, eds. *Philosophical Dialogues: Arne Naess and the Progress of Ecophilosophy*. Oslo: Centre for Development and the Environment. Lanham, MD: Rowman and Littlefield, 1998.

GENERAL REFERENCES

Carson, Rachel. *Silent Spring*. Boston: Houghton Mifflin, 1962.

Devall, Bill, and George Sessions. *Deep Ecology: Living as If Nature Mattered*. Salt Lake City: Gibbs Smith Publishers, 1985.

Drengson, Alan. *The Practice of Technology: Exploring Technology, Ecophilosophy, and Spiritual Disciplines for Vital Links*. Albany: SUNY Press, 1995.

Drengson, Alan, and Yuichi Inoue, eds. *The Deep Ecology Movement: An Introductory Anthology*. Berkeley, CA: North Atlantic Books, 1995.

Drengson, Alan, and Duncan Taylor, eds. *Ecoforestry: The Art and Science of Sustainable Forest Use*. Gabriola Island, British Columbia: New Society Publishers, 1997.

Fox, Matthew. *Creative Spirituality: Liberating Gifts for the Peoples of the Earth*. San Francisco: HarperCollins, 1991.

Fox, Warwick. *Toward a Transpersonal Ecology: Developing New Foundations for Environmentalism*. Boston: Shambhala, 1990.

Glasser, Harold. "Naess's Deep Ecology Approach and Environmental Policy." *Inquiry* 39 (1996): 157–187.

Sessions, George, ed. *Deep Ecology for the 21st Century: Readings in the Philosophy and Practice of the New Environmentalism*. Boston and London: Shambhala, 1995.

Spinoza, Baruch. *Ethics* and *On the Improvement of the Understanding*. New York: Hafner Press, 1995.

Wittgenstein, Ludwig. *Tractatus Logico-Philosophicus*. London: Routledge and Kegan Paul, 1958.